Moons of the Solar System

Also by John Stewart and from McFarland

Italian Film: A Who's Who (1994; paperback 2012)

The Acrobat: Arthur Barnes and the Victorian Circus (2012)

Antarctica: An Encyclopedia, 2d ed. (2 vols., 2011)

Byron and the Websters: The Letters and Entangled Lives of the Poet, Sir James Webster and Lady Frances Webster (2008)

Confederate Spies at Large: The Lives of Lincoln Assassination Conspirator Tom Harbin and Charlie Russell (2007)

African States and Rulers, 3d ed. (2006)

Broadway Musicals, 1943–2004 (2006)

The British Empire: An Encyclopedia of the Crown's Holdings, 1493 through 1995 (1996)

MOONS OF THE SOLAR SYSTEM

An Illustrated Encyclopedia

John Stewart

McFarland & Company, Inc., Publishers
Jefferson, North Carolina, and London

The present work is a reprint of the library bound edition of Moons of the Solar System: An Illustrated Encyclopedia, *first published in 1991 by McFarland.*

LIBRARY OF CONGRESS CATALOGUING-IN-PUBLICATION DATA

Stewart, John, 1952–
Moons of the solar system : an illustrated encyclopedia / John Stewart.
p. cm.
Includes bibliographical references.

ISBN 978-0-7864-7390-8
softcover : acid free paper ∞

1. Satellites—Handbooks, manuals, etc. 2. Moon—Handbooks, manuals, etc. I. Title.
QB401.S74 2012
523.9'8—dc20 91-52641

BRITISH LIBRARY CATALOGUING DATA ARE AVAILABLE

Cover images: iStockphoto/Thinkstock

Manufactured in the United States of America

McFarland & Company, Inc., Publishers
Box 611, Jefferson, North Carolina 28640
www.mcfarlandpub.com

For
Gayle Winston
who shines
so brightly

Contents

Preface

A moon (with a small "m") is the natural satellite of a planet. It is a body in constant orbit around a larger, primary body. Not all of the nine planets in the solar system have moons, and some have more than others. A number of the moons have interesting functions, some became moons in unusual ways, and some are doomed. There is a great deal of individuality among the satellites of the solar system.

Venus and Mercury have no natural satellites. Earth has one, the Moon (with a capital "M"), although in the past some people have thought there may have been more than one. In fact there may be, but such a satellite would be so small that it would hardly qualify for the term "moon." (See ***Toro,*** page 220.) It would best be described as a piece of debris, a rock, probably less than 15 feet across. This leads us to the main criterion when talking about a moon—its size.

The smallest moon in the solar system is probably Leda, one of Jupiter's satellites; it may be as little as 2 km across. That is far too big to be called space debris, whereas an object of only 100 meters diameter, say, would fail to qualify as a moon. There is no scientifically agreed-upon minimum diameter, but the moons discussed in this book are all moons (except those that *may* be moons, and this is discussed in the relevant entries), and any new objects discovered in the future will be deemed moons or otherwise largely on the basis of their size and whether or not they orbit a primary body. Ring particles, for instance, are not moons, although collectively they may have been at one time.

There has been some speculation that some of the larger asteroids have moons. So far a couple may have come up, but even so these would be outside the orbit of this book, as we are discussing only planetary satellites. Ever since Clyde Tombaugh discovered the planet Pluto in 1930, certain dissenting astronomers have claimed that it is too small to be a planet, and that it is in fact an asteroid (or minor planet, as the terminology sometimes is). The discovery in 1978 of a moon orbiting Pluto quieted some of these voices, but others formulated the theory of asteroidal moons. The mainstream of astronomy, however, regards Pluto as a planet, and tends to be cautious about the theory of asteroidal moons.

Mars has 2 moons, Jupiter has at least 16, Saturn has between 18 and 25, Uranus has 15 known ones and probably many more small ones, while Neptune has 8 so far discovered. Some of the moons, like Pandora and Cordelia, serve the purpose of keeping the planetary rings from dispersing and are called shepherd moons. Most moons seem to have been created as part of the natural process of planetary formation billions of years ago, while others, especially those which orbit their primary body in a retrograde fashion, were probably asteroids captured by the gravitational pull of the planet. Still others, notably those nearer to their planet, moons like Phobos, are doomed eventually to fall within the Roche limit of three planetary radii (Phobos has already fallen within this limit). When this happens a moon is then bound for disintegration. When that occurs the broken-up moon may well form a planetary ring, a ring of small particles which then begins a never-ending circuit around the planet.

Discovery of the moons was largely dependent on the invention of the telescope in 1609. Before that only Earth's Moon, and possibly Ganymede, had been seen with the naked eye. In 1610 Galileo looked at Jupiter through his telescope and discovered the four big moons of the Jovian system—the Galileans as we know them today. In 1655 Huygens observed Saturn's major moon, Titan, and later that century Cassini found the next four satellites of Saturn. Over a hundred years later Herschel found two moons of Uranus, and another two for Saturn. Neptune's big one, Triton, was observed in 1846, another Saturnian in 1848, and two more Uranians in 1851. In 1877 Asaph Hall confirmed what Jonathan Swift had described in *Gulliver's Travels* 150 years earlier, that Mars has two satellites. Other moons (and a planet, Pluto) in the solar system were discovered periodically over the course of the next hundred years (see Appendix 2), and then came Voyager.

The two Voyager probes, especially Voyager 2, went where no machine had gone before, and discovered and photographed new moons all over the solar system. The two metal adventurers then headed toward the edge of the solar system, to vanish forever in deep space.

It is probable that for the next few generations no Voyager equivalents will go out in search of new moons. The cost factor alone is prohibitive in an age when Earth has more than its share of domestic problems to be sorted out. Yet, there is always the hope...

There were many ways in which a book on moons of the solar system could have been presented. This is the way I chose to do it. Really, this is two small books joined together to make one larger whole. The first is about our moon, Luna, Earth's Moon. The second is about all the other moons in the solar system. In between is a section of photographs. There are appendices at the back of the book.

How to present Part I, especially, was a question that could only be answered arbitrarily. There has been so much, yet strangely so little, written about Earth's Moon. There is a great deal of material written about the Moon, but comparatively little in book form. Our satellite has been in and out of vogue, mostly out, as an astronomical topic, for centuries, and astronomical books for the public have tended to concentrate on the stars, or other planets of the solar system. So while this book is another book about the Moon, it is still one of few, and is presented, I hope, in a way that has never been done before—as a lunar encyclopedia, an A–Z direct reference, including such subjects as features, eclipses, spacecraft, lunar landings, phenomena, and map making. Preceding the A–Z is a table of scientific data, and following the A–Z is a bibliography.

Part II of the book then follows, consisting of 62 black-and-white and color photos (with an initial checklist of the moons that are depicted).

Part III, essentially the second half of this book, is about the 70-odd other moons of the solar system. They are arranged alphabetically by the names in use at the time of writing (February 1991). The most up-to-date, complete information is given on each, without becoming a scientific treatise confusing to the nonscientist. This book is intended for all people interested in moons, not just the physicist. This is the first book ever written for the general reader on the subject of moons of the solar system.

A note on maps: It proved impossible to reproduce adequate maps of the moons in a 6×9 book. Maps of our moon, however, are available from NASA, while the U.S. Geological Survey has maps of Callisto, Europa, Ganymede, Io, Dione, Enceladus, Iapetus, Mimas, Rhea, Tethys, Ariel, Miranda, Oberon, Titania and Umbriel.

Large thanks to Jurrie Vanderwoude of the Public Information Office, Jet Propulsion Laboratory, Pasadena, California. He sent me a mass of photos taken by the Voyagers and Galileo. Thomas Jaqua of NASA's photographic and motion picture department in Washington, D.C., also came through with photos. Thanks to him, and to Joyce Stipe of NASA's library for putting me in touch with Mr. Jaqua, and for being so helpful herself.

I used the facilities of the Forsyth County library system in North Carolina, run with a cool but exciting efficiency by Bill Roberts. Cindy Jones is the head of the periodical and government documents section, which proved utterly equal to the task of providing me with research material. Thanks to Cindy and her staff for putting up with me, and for guiding me. My thanks also to Bill Sugg, Bob Shar, and Ann Hendrix, for their continued help in getting interlibrary loan material for me, and for their support of my projects. I also used Wake Forest University Library in Winston-Salem. I would like to thank the staff there for their constant encouragement.

Thanks, in an offbeat way, to Cheryl Roberts for being the original inspiration for this work. Cheryl and her husband, Robbie Franklin, my publisher, began a similar project many moons ago, and I only regret not having access to her original notes.

There were people who in one way or another supported me on this project, and I thank them. Senator Anne Bagnal, Senator Harry Bagnal, Kathy Burns, Don Burns, Leroy Snodgrass, Morris Bernstein, Julian Crockett, Scott Crockett, Carlos Wight, Luigi Bozzo, Dewey Wilkerson, J. W. Tatum, Mary Lyons Rearden, Ian Darke, Debbie Darke, John Bushby (Johnny B), Buzz Aldrin, John Gates, Brad Schang, Megan Schang, Steve Brown, Gary Sluder, Keith Monroe, Debbie Monroe, Jeff Green, Judith Sutherin, J. A. C. Dunn, Jerry Beauchamp, Marc Lehmann, Neil Armstrong, Nathan Hobbs, Zetta Hamby, Yuriy Gagarin, Virginia Ring, Miranda Hope Henning, Louise Barton, Tim May, Anne May, Berk Ingram, Nancy Ingram, and Dr. Billy Ray Craig.

Special thanks to Patrick Moore, who, by virtue of his vast knowledge and personality, has inspired a passion for astronomy in so many people over the years, and without whose many pioneering works this book could never have been written.

Special thanks to Joe Gleason who, as much as any of my good friends, makes me feel as if I should continue writing.

Special thanks to Rick Blakeley and the Forsyth County Astronomical Society, for making me feel more important than I might be.

Special thanks to Susan. This is a tough one for me. Susan was in on the beginning of this book, and will always get special thanks. There is a star in Sagittarius named Susan Surman Stewart.

Special thanks to Gayle Winston, to whom this book is dedicated. Without Gayle this book could not have been finished so expeditiously, if at all.

Special thanks, for discoveries and rediscoveries, to my brother Pete, my sister-in-law Marion, my nephew George, and my other brother, Dave.

My hope for the future is given fresh fire by my sister, Mary Stewart Young, who, aside from her own credits, was inspired to marry that excellent Scotsman William Young, and to produce another excellent Scotsman, William Young, Jr.

John Stewart (1991)

A Note on the Naming of Lunar Features

It might be interesting to speculate on the reason why the lunar feature Baco was thus named when it honors Roger Bacon. Did the I.A.U. and its historical predecessors just leave the "n" off (as they left off the "i" in Reiner, *q.v.*)? The researcher looks in vain for a Baco who might have achieved astronomical eminence.

The authorities tell us that the scientist Priestley gave his name to the feature Priestly. It should, one suspects, have been Priestley (with the "e"). Several individuals spell their name without the "e" but none fits the bill. Priestley, however, does, but he spells his with an "e."

There are a small number of individuals, long dead, who gave their names to lunar features, and I have been unable to tie them to Earth. My publisher and I would welcome authoritative input from readers that might accord an identity to these individuals. A few of my findings in the naming area may be subject to dispute or correction. Cyril? Ansgarius? Naonobu? Ariadaeus? a few others: these presented major research challenges. The conclusions I have drawn are based on the preponderance of evidence, and a feel for the general practice of naming lunar features over the centuries. The vast majority of the features were named for astronomers.

"'Leibnitz'?" my editor asked, with vigor. "Surely you mean Leibniz." No, I mean Leibnitz. That's the name of the feature. I do care what the name of the philosopher from Leipzig was, but even more I care about the correct name of the lunar feature. I care as much about the constantly seen misspellings of features like Bergstrand (instead of the correct Bergstand), Scalinger (instead of Scaliger), and Poynting (instead of Poyning).

In this reference work, it is the internationally agreed upon name of the feature that is given, not the form of the name as spelled by its bearer. One cannot really complain about Leibnitz any more than one can about Magellan, Purbach and Joffe. We honor the broad approach of those medievals who conferred an honorary Christian status on such "Arabs" as Alfraganus and Albategnius, to name but two. They did not do so for Averroes (ibn-Rushd to his compatriots), however. There are many nomenclatural curiosities on the Moon.

Originally the astronomers named objects as they saw them. Now, it is official organs like the International Astronomical Union that take the burden. The results are mixed. Da Vinci instead of Leonardo, Regiomontanus for Johann Muller, Longomontanus for Christian Severin, Rabbi Levi (for some reason alphabetized under his honorific rather than his name), and Shuckburgh (to give Sir George Shuckburgh-Evelyn only half his name).

Most names are only last names, but some like Marco Polo, Julius Caesar, Jules Verne, Omar Khayyam and Tycho Brahe have both and are (properly) alphabetized herein under M, J, J, O and T respectively. Others, like Spencer Jones (under S), Vening[-]Meinesz (under V), and Piazzi Smyth (under P once and under S once) are compound last names (the last, not to be confused with his Italian predecessor and likely namesake, Giuseppe Piazzi). Some persons had two features named after them—Piazzi Smyth, Banachiewicz, Sven Hedin and Spiru Haret, to name but eight (and Mr. Haret's entries are under H and under S; Spiru is his first name).

As in many orthographical and alphabetization ventures, there are peculiarities with the von and de entries. Lemonnier became Le Monnier, Lavoisier became La Voisier, but Le Verrier stayed Le Verrier, although the reader will see variants of all these. There is a feature named La Paz. Named for the Bolivian city? Unlikely. The best I could do was a mathematician named Lapaz, but that's all one word.

With initials it's a lot easier. G. P. Bond and W. C. Bond became Bond, G. P. and Bond, W. C., and a similar thing happened to the Mayers, C. & T., whereas H. G. Wells stayed as H. G. Wells (under H), although researchers in selenology will see it as Wells, H. G., and as just Wells. One may also see it misspelled as Welles (confusing the British writer of science fiction with Orson Welles). More witting, perhaps, is the fact that Herschel, J. and J. Herschel (which were the same feature) both became Herschel, John—and the same thing happened to Caroline Herschel (latterly Herschel, Caroline)—all this to avoid confusion with the feature named simply Herschel (for Sir William).

The one who consults this reference work and has doubts or suspicions about a spelling is probably right—but so is the book.

Part I

Luna, Earth's Moon

Lunar Data

Names: The **Moon, Luna** (in most European languages), **Cynthia** (in Roman mythology), **Selene** (in Greek mythology)

Distance from Earth: Its mean distance from the center of Earth is 384,400 km. The closest (perigee) is 356,410 km, and the furthest (apogee) is 406,967 km. The mean distance from the surface of Earth to the surface of the Moon is 376,284 km. The closest (perigee) is 348,294 km, and the furthest (apogee) is 398,581 km

Synodic period: 29 days 12 hours 44 mins 2.9 sec

Sidereal period: 27.321661 days (or 27 days 7 hours 43 mins 11.5 secs), which is exactly equal to its axial rotation period

Orbital velocity: A mean of 3680 km per hour

Orbital eccentricity: 0.0549

Orbital inclination: A mean of 5°08'43"

Escape velocity: 2.38 km/sec

Axial inclination of equator, referred to ecliptic: 1°32'

Visible magnitude: A mean of −12.7 (when full). When full, the Moon is about 250,000 times as bright as a first magnitude star, but 470,000 times fainter than the Sun

Albedo: 0.07

Diameter: 3475.6 km

Apparent diameter as seen from Earth: (mean): 31'05", (max.): 33'31", (min.): 29'22"

Mass: 8.1×10^{19} tons (0.123 that of Earth)

Density: 3.33 times that of water

Temperature: Surface temperature when sunlit is about 100° Centigrade. When in shadow, the temperature is lower than −100° Centigrade

Surface (near side): Early Moon watchers thought that the Moon had oceans and seas, but the telescope soon revealed that the lunar surface was rough and mountainous. It didn't take long before lunar cartography began (see "Mapping the Moon," in the A–Z) and later photography and space probes revealed the surface for what it really is. The best time to observe the Moon from Earth through a telescope is near half moon. The boundary between the near and far sides is known as the terminator, and near half moon the terminator shows a very rugged appearance, and the Sun's light catches several mountains at the right angle. The most dominant lunar features are the craters, or ringed formations, whose origin is uncertain. Other notable features are ray systems radiating from craters often for miles, the maria (or "seas"), and rills, or cracks in the lunar surface. There is no air or water on the Moon, and the temperature range is vast. Of the Moon's total surface, 0.410 percent is always visible from Earth

Surface (far side): Until 6:30 a.m. (Moscow time) on October 7, 1959, only 59 percent of the Moon had ever been seen. On that date Luna 3 took the first photos of the far side of the Moon, from a range of 70,400 km. Two cameras whirred for 40 minutes, and on October 18 of that year Earthlings saw the dark side of the Moon for the first time when the photos were received on Earth. On October 24, 1959, the USSR gave these photos to the world. We are familiar with the near side of the Moon. The far side is distinctly different. The major difference is that it has no large maria, or "seas," Mare Moscoviense being the largest, with a diameter of 420 km, and that is not big at all when compared to the giant maria on the near side. Mare Ingenii is even smaller. However, various maria (plural of "mare") do straddle the limb of the Moon from the near side to the far side—Orientale, Humboldtianum, Marginis, Symthii, and Australe. Everywhere on the far side are craters. There are also basins, but light-floored rather than filled with dark-colored mare material. The chief features of the far side, aside from the craters and maria, are Vallis Schrödinger and Vallis Planck, both radiating from the crater Schrödinger. The differences between the near and far sides must be due to the fact that the Moon has always presented the same face toward Earth, and thus this near side has been much more "protected" from outside bombardment. Alphonsus Fresa drew up the first map of the far side, in 1959. The only people ever in person to see the far side of the Moon have been the Apollo astronauts

Features: There are thousands of features on the Moon, both on the near and far sides. The principal ones are covered in the following pages. The brightest spot on the Moon is Aristarchus. The greatest ray crater is Tycho (second is Copernicus). The deepest crater is Newton. The most famous plateau is Wargentin. The largest regular mare is Mare Imbrium, and the largest irregular mare is the Oceanus Procellarum

Luna A–Z

Abbe. Far side. 58°S, 175°E. 67 km. To the east of Poincaré, and just SW of Boyle. Named for Cleveland Abbe (1838–1916), American astronomer.

Abbot. Near side. 6°N, 55°E. 10 km. Formerly called Apollonius K. Just outside the NE edge of Mare Fecunditatis, south of Mare Crisium. Named for Charles G. Abbott (1872–1973), American astronomer.

Abel. Near side. 35°S, 86°E. 114 km. SE of Humboldt, and south of Barnard. Named for Niels Abel (1802–1829), Norwegian mathematician.

Abenezra. Near side. 21°S, 12°E. 42 km. West of Mare Nectaris. Well-formed. Forms a pair with Azophi, which breaks in on its SE rim. Under morning illumination it seems to be cut in two by a curved ridge. Named for Abraham ibn Ezra (Abenezra) (c.1090–c.1167), Spanish astronomer.

Abetti. Near side. 20°N, 28°E. 7 km. NW of Vitruvius, on the extreme SE edge of Mare Serenitatis. Named for Antonio Abetti (1846–1928), Italian astronomer.

Able Spacecraft. A series of U.S. moon efforts. Only four are relevant. *Thor-Able 1.* Launched August 17, 1958. This was the first attempted lunar probe. It failed after 77 seconds, at 20 km from Earth. *Atlas-Able 4.* Launched November 26, 1958. Failed just after takeoff. *Atlas-Able 5A.* Launched October 25, 1960. A complete failure. *Atlas-Able 5B.* Launched December 15, 1960. Exploded 70 seconds after lift-off.

Abulfeda. Near side. 14°S, 14°E. 64 km. Larger than Almanon, with which it forms a pair in the area of Abenezra. It has terraced walls. Named for Abulfeda (1273–1331), Syrian geographer.

Abul Wafa. Far side. 2°N, 117°E. 55 km. Between Mare Smythii and Mendeleev. Named for Abul Wafa (940–998), Persian astronomer.

Acherusia, Cape. Near side. 17°N, 22°E. 10 km. Also known as Promontorium Acherusia, Cape Archerusia. At the east end of the Haemus Mountains, in the Mare Serenitatis. Named for the Bog of Acherusia in Greek mythology.

Acosta. Near side. 6°S, 60°E. 13 km. Formerly called Langrenus C. Immediately NW of Langrenus, on the extreme eastern edge of Mare Fecunditatis. Named for José de Acosta (1539–1600), Spanish geographer.

Adams. Near side. 32°S, 68°E. 66 km. East of Vendelinus. Has irregular walls, a central crater, and hills on its floor. Named for John Couch Adams (1819–1892), British astronomer.

Aenarium, Cape. Near side. 19°S, 7°W. 70 km. Also known as Promontorium Aenarium, and originally called Cape Taenarium. NW of Thebit, in the area of the Straight Wall, in Mare Nubium. Named for Taenarum, the southernmost cape in Greece.

Aestatis, Lacus. Near side. 15°S, 69°W. 90 km. Means "Lake of Summer" in Latin.

Aestuum, Sinus. Near side. 12°N, 8°W. 230 km. Also known as the Bay of Heats, its English translation. A conspicuous dark plain east of Copernicus. Bordered by the southernmost extension of the Apennines. Has very few important craters on its floor.

Agarum, Cape. Near side. 14°N, 66°E. 70 km. Also known as Promontorium Agarum. Near Condorcet, in the eastern part of Mare Crisium. Named for William Agar (1894–1972), American geologist.

Agassiz, Cape. Near side. 42°N, 2°E. 20 km. Also known as Promontorium Agassiz. Named for Louis Agassiz (1807–1873), American scientist.

Agatharchides. Near side. 20°S, 31° W. 49 km. In the area of Mare Humorum. It has irregular walls, and the south wall is cut through by parallel valleys trending toward Hippalus. On the floor is a low central mound, and it has the remnant of a central peak in it. Named for Agatharchides of Cnidos (fl. 2nd quarter of the 2nd century B.C.), Greek geographer.

Agatharchides, Rima. Near side. 20°S, 28°W. 50 km. Named in association with nearby Agatharchides.

Agricola Mountains. Near side. 29°N, 54°W. 160 km. Also known as Montes Agricola. Named for Georgius Agricola (1494–1555), German chemist.

Agrippa. Near side. 4°N, 11°E. 44 km. A regular arc-shaped crater, it forms a pair with Godin, in the area of Mare Vaporum. It has a straight north wall, and has a large central peak in it. Named for Agrippa (fl. 1st century A.D.), Greek astronomer.

Airy. Near Side. 18°S, 6°E. 37 km. Forms a pair with Argelander, in the area of Albategnius. Has irregular walls. Named for Sir George Airy (1801–1892), British astronomer.

Aitken. Far side. 17°S, 173°E. 131 km. Crater SE of Heaviside. Named for Robert G. Aitken (1864–1951), American astronomer.

Al-Bakri. Near side. 14°N, 20°E. 12 km. Formerly called Taquet A. SW of Plinius, in the area south of Mare Serenitatis. Named for al-Bakri (d. 1094), Arab geographer.

Albategnius. Near side. 11°S, 4°E. 136 km. Companion to Hipparchus, west of Alphonsus and Ptolemaeus. A large walled plain, it has terraced irregular walls and a central peak over 400 feet. Named for al-Battani (Albategnius) (c.858–929), Mesopotamian astronomer.

Al-Biruni. Far side. 18°N, 93°E. 78 km. NE of Goddard, on the NE side of Mare Marginis. Named for al-Biruni (973–1048), Persian astronomer.

Alden. Far side. 24°S, 111°E. 105 km. To the SE of Hilbert, and SW of Tsiolkovskiy. Named for Harold L. Alden (1890–1964), American astronomer.

Alder. Far side. 49°S, 177°W. 77 km. SE of Von Kármán, and SW of Nishina. Named for Kurt Alder (1902–1958), German organic chemist.

Aldrin. Near side. 1°N, 22°E. 3 km. In the extreme western portion of Mare Tranquillitatis. Named for Buzz Aldrin (b. 1930), American astronaut.

Alekhin. Far side. 68°S, 130°W. 71 km. Just south of Zeeman. Named for Nikolay Alekhin (1913–1963), Russian rocket designer.

Alexander. Near side. 40°N, 14°E. 82 km. At the north end of the Caucasus Mountains. It has a darkish floor, and low walls. Named for Stephen Alexander (1806–1883), American astronomer.

Alfraganus. Near side. 5°S, 19°E. 21 km. It is the center of a minor ray system, NW of Theophilus. It is very bright, and has a central hill. Named for al-Farghani (Alfraganus) (d. c.865), Egyptian astronomer.

Alhazen. Near side. 16°N, 72°E. 33 km. On the west border of Mare Crisium. It was named by Schröter, but could not be found by Beer and Mädler, so they transferred the name to this crater further south. Today's Alhazen is not the original. Named for Alhazen (c.965–c.1038), Iraqi astronomer.

Aliacensis. Near side. 31°S, 5°E. 80 km. Forms a pair with Werner, in the area of Walter. It has high terraced walls, rising on the east to 16,500 feet. The inner west slope has much complex detail, an excellent sight under the right illumination. Has a central peak. Named for Pierre d'Ailly (Aliacensis) (1350–1420), French theologian.

Al-Khwarizmi. Far side. 7°N, 106°E. 65 km. SE of Moiseev, in the area to the NE of Mare Smythii. Named for al-Khwarizmi (c.1795–c.1849), Iraqi astronomer.

Almanon. Near side. 17°S, 15°E. 49 km. A crater chain runs from its north wall into Abulfeda, with which it forms a pair. It has an irregular polygonal outline. Named for al-Mamun (Almanon) (786–833) Arab astronomer.

Al-Marrakushi. Near side. 10°S, 56°E. 8 km. Formerly called Langrenus D. SW of Langrenus, in the southern portion of Mare Fecunditatis. Named for al-Marrakushi (1185–c.1224). Arab historiographer.

Alpes, Vallis. Near side. 49°N, 2°E. Also known as Alpine Valley, it is a 180 km long valley cutting right through the mountains (*see* **Alps**). A delicate rill runs down it. The valley looks astonishing, even in a small telescope, and is one of the Moon's great attractions. Named in association with the mountains.

Alpetragius. Near side. 16°S, 4°W. 43 km. Outside Alphonsus. It has high terraced walls and a vast domed central peak with a summit pit. Named for al-Bitrugi (Alpetragius) (fl. c.1190), Spanish astronomer.

Alphonsus. Near side. 13°S, 3°W. 129 km. In the Ptolemaeus group. This walled plain has broad, complex walls, over 50 craterlets on the interior, rills on the floor, and dark marial spots on the floor, three of which are large and prominent. It has a low central peak. It has activity of some sort within it. Ranger 9 landed inside Alphonsus. Named for Alfonso X of Leon and Castile (1221–1284), Spanish astronomer.

Alphonsus, Rimae. 80 km. The rills in the walled plain of Alphonsus (see above). Named in association with that feature.

Alpine Valley *see* **Alpes, Vallis**

Alps. Near side. 49°N, 2°E. 250 km long. Also known as Alpes. A bright mountain range between Plato and the Caucasus Mountains, on the northern border of the Mare Imbrium, in fact it forms part of the circular wall of Imbrium. Trouvelot, Mont Blanc, and the Alpine Valley are here. Named after the Alps in Europe.

Altai Scarp. Near side. 24°S, 22°E. 480 km. Also known as Rupes Altai. Formerly called the Altai Range (renamed by Spurr, because it is not really a chain of mountains). SW of Piccolomini, it forms part of the ring system of the Mare Nectaris, but is really SW of that mare also. Rises to an average of 6000 feet above the general level to the east, but only very slightly above the level to the west. Named after the Altai Mountains in Russia.

Alter. Far side. 19°N, 108°W. 64 km. Just SW of Robertson. Named for Dinsmore Alter (1888–1968), American astronomer.

Ameghino. Near side. 3°N, 57°E. 9 km. Formerly called Apollonius C. Just south of Mare Crisium, on the NE edge of Mare Fecunditatis. Named for Fiorino Ameghino (1854–1911), Argentine paleontologist.

Amici. Far side. 10°S, 172°W. 54 km. Between Icarus and McKeller, to the SW of Korolev. Named for Giovanni Battista Amici (1786–1863), Italian astronomer.

Ammonius. Near side. 8°S, 1°W. 9 km. Formerly called Ptolemaeus A. In the area of Ptolemaeus, between Mare Nubium and Mare Tranquillitatis. Named for Ammonius (c.175–242), Alexandrian philosopher.

Amontons. Near side. 5°S, 47°E. 3 km. SW of the Messier twins, on the Mare Fecunditatis. Named for Guillaume Amontons (1663–1705), French physicist.

Amoris, Sinus. Near side. 19°N, 38°E. 250 km. Also known as the Bay of Love, its English translation.

Ampère, Mount. Near side. 20°N, 4°W. About 11,000 feet. Also known as Mons Ampère. Between Huygens and Wolff, in the Apennines. Named for André Marie Ampère (1775–1836), French physicist.

Amundsen. Mostly on the near side. 84°S, 83°E. 105 km. NE of Scott, it is the nearest feature to the South Pole. Named for Roald Amundsen (1872–1928), Norwegian polar explorer, the first man to reach Earth's South Pole.

Anaxagoras. Near side. 73°N, 10°W. 51 km. Distorts Goldschmidt, in the area of the North Pole. Has a major ray center and a central peak. Named for Anaxagoras (c.500–c.428 B.C.), Greek philosopher.

Anaximander. Near side. 67°N, 51°W. 68 km. Forms a pair with Carpenter, in the area of Pythagoras. Has no central peak. Is excellent to look at. Named for Anaximander (c.611–c.547 B.C.), Greek mathematician-astronomer.

Anaximenes. Near side. 73°N, 45°W. 72 km. A ring near Philolaus. It has rather low walls which rise to 8000 feet. It has four craters on the west part of the floor and one on the SE. Named for Anaximenes of Miletus (fl. 6th century B.C.), Greek philosopher.

Anděl. Near side. 10°S, 12°E. 35 km. To the west of Theophilus, in the highlands. Has low, irregular walls. Named for Karel Anděl (1884–1947), Czech astronomer.

Anders. Far side. 42°S, 144°W. 41 km. Breaks into the SE rim of Apollo. Named for William Anders (b. 1933), American astronaut.

Anderson. Far side. 16°N, 171°E. 105 km. Between Zernike and Sharonov, between Korolev and Mare Moscoviense. Named for John A. Anderson (1876–1959), American astronomer.

Andronov. Far side. 23°S, 146°E. 16 km. Breaks in on the SW rim of Gagarin. Named for Aleksandr Andronov (1901–1952), Russian physicist.

Ångström. Near side. 30°N, 42°W. 11 km. North of the Harbinger Mountains, in the Mare Imbrium. Named for Anders Ångström (1814–1874), Swedish physicist.

Anguis, Mare. Near side. 22°N, 68°E. 130 km. Also known as the Sea of Serpents, its English translation. A patch of dark lava, NE of Mare Crisium.

Ansgarius. Near side. 13°S, 80°E. 94 km. Forms a pair with La Peyrouse, east of Mare Fecunditatis. Distinct, it has a few hills on its otherwise smooth floor. Named for Ansgarius (801–864), German theologian.

Antoniadi. Far side. 69°S, 173°W. 135 km. NW of Zeeman, and NE of Schrödinger. One of the larger fresh craters. Named for Eugène Antoniadi (1870–1944), French astronomer.

Anuchin. Far side. 49°S, 101°E. 58 km. South of Lamb, in the area SW of Mare Australe. Named for Dmitri Anuchin (1843–1923), Russian geographer.

Anville. Near side. 2°N, 49°E. 11 km. Formerly called Taruntius G. North of the Messier twins, in the Mare Fecunditatis. Named for Jean Baptiste Anville (1697–1782), French geographer.

Apennines. Near side. 20°N, 2°W. Over 600 miles long. Also known as Montes Apenninus. The most spectacular mountains on the Moon, the range borders Mare Imbrium and separates it from Mare Vaporum. It stretches from Mount Hadley to Eratosthenes (actually at Cape Fresnel). Their peaks cast long, dark shadows across Imbrium. The Apennines can be seen best and most magnificently at the time of the half moon. Mount Huygens is the highest peak (18,000 feet). Other peaks in the range include Mount Bradley, Mount Hadley, Mount Wolff, Mount Ampère. Also here are Serao, Conon, Marco Polo. Apollo 15 astronauts landed here. Named after the Apennines in Italy.

Apianus. Near side. 27°S, 8°E. 63 km. In the area of Aliacensis. It has high walls and a dark gray floor. Named for Peter Bienewitz (Apianus), (1501–1552), German mathematician-astronomer.

Apollo Basin. Far side. 36°S, 150°W. 503 km. A ringed formation SE of Mare Moscoviense, and SW of Hertzsprung, it is one of the largest features on the far side of the Moon. Dryden, Chappell and Lovell are in it, and it shows sign of flooding by lava flows. Named after the Apollo space program.

Apollo Spacecraft. A series of U.S. spacecraft, mostly manned. On September 30, 1977, all recording Apollo stations on the Moon were closed down. Only the following Apollos are relevant. *Apollo 6:* Launched April 4, 1968. Failed to reach the Moon. *Apollo 7:* Launched October 11, 1968. Carried Schirra, Eisele, and Cunningham. Orbited Earth. Was up for 10 days 20 hours. *Apollo 8:* Launched December 21, 1968. This was the first manned flight to the Moon, with Borman, Lovell, and Anders. They approached within 70 miles of the Moon, and made 10 lunar orbits in the command module, but did not land. Views of the lunar surface were televised to Earth. The mission lasted 147 hours 42 secs, and ended on December 27, 1968. *Apollo 9:* Launched March 3, 1969. It carried McDivett, Scott and Schweickart. It tested the lunar module in Earth's orbit. The mission lasted 10 days 2 hours. *Apollo 10:* Launched May 18, 1969. Carried Stafford, Cernan and Young to the Moon, and tested the lunar module in lunar orbit. Did not land, but got to within 14.9 km of the Moon's surface. The mission lasted 8 days exactly. *Apollo 11:* Launched July 16, 1969. This was the "big one," the first manned Moon landing, the first time Man had been on a body other than Earth. It carried Armstrong, Aldrin and Collins. The lunar module landed on July 20, 1969, at 00°67'N, 23°49'E, in the Mare Tranquillitatis. Neil Armstrong and Buzz Aldrin stepped out onto the Moon's surface, and stayed there for 2.2 hours. *Apollo 12:* Launched November 14, 1969. It carried Conrad, Bean and Gordon to the Moon, where Conrad and Bean landed on November 19, at 3°12'S, 23° 23'W, in Oceanus Procellarum. The two men were on the surface for 7.6 hours. It was the first manned landing near an unmanned craft (Surveyor 3). *Apollo 13:* Launched April 11, 1970. It was to have carried Lovell, Haise and Swigert to the Moon for the landing, but failed on the outward trip. It splashed down on Earth on April 17. *Apollo 14:* Launched January 31, 1971. It carried Shepherd, Mitchell and Roosa to the Moon, where Shepherd and Mitchell landed on February 5, at 3°40'S, 17°28'E, at Fra Mauro. This was the first manned landing in the highland region. The two astronauts were on the surface for 9.2 hours. *Apollo 15:* Launched July 26, 1971. It carried Scott, Irwin and Worden to the Moon, and Scott and Irwin landed at 26°06'N, 3°39'E, on July 30. The two astronauts were on the surface for 18.3 hours, and used the first LRV (lunar roving vehicle) to drive around the Hadley Rille in the area of the Apennines. *Apollo 16:* Launched April 16, 1972. It carried Young, Duke and Mattingley to the Moon, where Young and Duke landed on April 21, at 8°36'S, 15°30'E. The two astronauts were on the surface for 20.1 hours, used an LRV, and reached the highest lunar elevation reached by Man, 25,688 feet (7830 m), in the Descartes highlands. *Apollo 17:* Launched December 7, 1972. It carried Cernan, Schmitt and Evans to the Moon, where Cernan and Schmitt landed on December 11, at 20°10'N, 30°46'E, in the Taurus-Littrow section of the Moon. The mission was similar to that of Apollo 16, but it sampled highland and adjacent valley material. The two astronauts stayed on the surface for 22 hours.

Apollonius. Near side. 5°N, 61°E. 53 km. In the uplands south of Mare Crisium. Well-formed. Named for Apollonius of Perga (fl. 247–205 B.C.), Greek mathematician.

Apollonius, Rimae. Near side. 5°N, 53°E. 230 km. Rills in the area of Apollonius (q.v.), in association with which they were named.

Appleton. Far side. 37°N, 158°E. NE of Mare Moscoviense. Named for Sir Edward V. Appleton (1892–1965), British physicist.

Arago. Near side. 6°N, 21°E. 26 km. On Mare Tranquillitatis. There are domes nearby. Named for François Arago (1786–1853), French astronomer.

Aratus. Near side. 24°N, 5°E. 11 km. In the Apennines. Bright, and irregular. Named for Aratus of Soli (c.315–c.240 B.C.), Greek astronomer-poet.

Archerusia, Cape *see* **Acherusia, Cape**

Archimedes. Near side. 28°N, 4°W. 83 km. A very regular walled plain, the largest of its kind on the Mare Imbrium. It has broad, complex walls, a very smooth interior, craterlets on the floor, and no central peak. It is seen best at sunrise. Named for Archimedes (c.287–212 B.C.), Greek mathematician.

Archimedes, Rimae. Near side. 27° N, 4°W. 150 km. Rills in the area of Archimedes (q.v.), in association with which they were named.

Archimedes Mountains *see* **Stag's Horn Mountains**

Archytas. Near side. 59°N, 5°E. 32 km. On Mare Frigoris. Bright, and distinct, it has a central peak. Named for Archytas of Tarentum (fl. c.400–350 B.C.), Greek mathematician.

Archytas, Rima. Near side. 53°N, 3°E. 90 km. A rill in the area of Archytas (q.v.), in association with which it was named.

Argaeus, Cape. Near side. 19°N, 29° E. A high promontory near Littrow, it guards the strait between Mare Tranquillitatis and Mare Serenitatis. Named for the ancient volcano in Asia Minor.

Argaeus, Mons. Near side. 19°N, 29°E. A mountain in the area of Cape

Argaeus (q.v.), in association with which it was named.

Argelander. Near side. 17°S, 6°E. 34 km. Forms a pair with Airy, in the area of Albategnius. Has a central peak. Named for Friedrich Argelander (1799–1875), German astronomer.

Ariadaeus. Near side. 5°N, 17°E. 11 km. Just north of Dionysius, in the area of Mare Vaporum. The Ariadaeus cleft starts near here (see following entry). Named for Ariadaeus (d. 317 B.C.), Macedonian king.

Ariadaeus Rille. Near side. 7°N, 13° E. 220 km long. Also known as Ariadaeus cleft and Rima Ariadaeus. Near the crater Ariadaeus. Through a telescope it looks like a crack in the Moon. It is visible with a very small telescope. Named in association with Ariadaeus (see above).

Aristarchus. Near side. 24°N, 47°W. 37 km. On Oceanus Procellarum. This is the brightest crater on the Moon, so bright that Herschel thought it was an active volcano. Polygonal in shape, it has a rough floor, and a central peak, and dark interior radial bands run from the floor up the inner walls. The walls are terraced and complex. Named for Aristarchus of Samos (fl. c.280–264 B.C.), Greek astronomer.

Aristarchus, Rimae. Near side. 28° N, 47°W. 120 km. Rills in the region of Aristarchus (q.v.), in association with which they were named.

Aristillus. Near side. 34°N, 1°E. 56 km. The center of a bright ray system in the Archimedes group. It has an excellent three-peaked central mountain, and terraced inner walls. A dark band runs up the NW inner slope and extends over the rim. Named for Aristillus (fl. c.300 B.C.), Greek astronomer.

Aristoteles. Near side. 50°N, 17°E. 87 km. An excellent walled formation, it forms a pair with Eudoxus. It is hexagonal in shape and rows of little hills radiate outward from its walls. It has high terraced walls with peaks rising to 11,000 feet. There are many hills on the floor, and the remains of an old crater ring. Named for Aristotle (384–322 B.C.), Greek philosopher.

Arminski. Far side. 16°S, 154°E. 27 km. Immediately NE of Gagarin.

Armstrong. Near side. 1°N, 25°E. 5 km. West of Maskelyne, in the Mare Tranquillitatis. Named for Neil Armstrong (b. 1930), American astronaut.

Arnold. Near side. 67°N, 36°E. 95 km. NW of Democritus, in the area north of Mare Frigoris. Has low walls. Named for Christoph Arnold (1650–1695), German astronomer.

Arrhenius. Far side. 55°S, 91°W. Just on the dark side, south of Hausen. Named for Svante Arrhenius (1859–1927), Swedish physical chemist.

Artamonov. Far side. 26°N, 104°E. Between Lomonosov and Deutsch, east of Joliot, in the NE region of the far side of the Moon. Named for Nikolay Artamonov (1905–1965), Russian rocket engineer.

Artamonov, Catena. Far side. 26°N, 106°E. 150 km. In the area of Artamonov (q.v.), in association with which it was named. To the east of Joliot.

Artem'ev. Far side. 10°N, 145°W. To the NW of Hertzsprung. Named for Vladimir Artem'ev (1885–1962), Russian rocket designer.

Artsimovich. Near side. 28°N, 37°W. 9 km. Formerly called Diophantus A. West of Diophantus, and South of Ångström, in Mare Imbrium. Named for Lev Artsimovich (1909–1973), Russian physicist.

Aryabhata. Near side. 6°N, 35°E. 22 km. Formerly called Maskelyne E. NE of Maskelyne, in Mare Tranquillitatis.

Named for Aryabhata I (b. A.D. 476), Indian astronomer.

Arzachel. Near side. 18°S, 2°W. 97 km. A walled plain, south of Alphonsus, in the Ptolemaeus group. It has high, complex, terraced walls and a central peak of 4900 feet high. A deep crater is on the west part of the floor. There are over 25 hills and craterlets on its floor as well. Named for al-Zarqali (Arzachel) (d. 1100), Arab astronomer.

Arzachel, Rimae. Near side. 50 km. Rills in Arzachel (q.v.), in association with which they were named.

Asada. Near side. 7°N, 50°E. 12 km. Formerly called Taruntius A. NE of Taruntius, in the northern portion of Mare Fecunditatis. Named for Asada Goryu (1734–1799), Japanese astronomer.

Asclepi. Near side. 55°S, 25°E. 43 km. West of Hommel, in the southern uplands. Distinct. Named for Giuseppe Asclepi (1706–1776), Italian astronomer.

Asperitatis, Sinus. Near side. 6°S, 25°E. 180 km. Also called the Bay of Bitterness, its English translation.

Aston. Near side. 33°N, 88°W. 43 km. East of Röntgen, and west of Ulugh Beigh, in the area to the west of Oceanus Procellarum. Named for Francis W. Aston (1877–1945), British physicist.

Atlas. Near side. 47°N, 44°E. 87 km. Forms a pair with Hercules, north of Lacus Somniorum. Polygonal, it has high walls and much interior detail. It has a small central peak and several clefts and two dark patches on its floor. Named for the Greek mythological character, and for the spacecraft.

Atlas, Rimae. Near side. 60 km. Rills in Atlas (q.v.), in association with which they were named.

Atwood. Near side. 6°S, 58°E. 29 km. Formerly called Langrenus K. To the NW of Langrenus, on the east rim of Mare Fecunditatis. Named for George Atwood (1745–1807), British physicist.

Australe, Mare. On the near and far sides, but mostly on the far side. 46°S, 90°E. 900 km. Also known as the Southern Sea, which is its English translation. A former basin, it contains lava-flooded craters and is irregular in shape. It lies close to the eastern limb of the Moon, as seen from the Earth, and is best seen just after full moon, when it is on the terminator.

Autolycus. Near side. 31°N, 1°E. 39 km. In the Archimedes group. Regular and distinct, it has wide, terraced walls, and a chain of three craters on its floor. Named for Autolycus (fl. late 4th century B.C.), Greek astronomer.

Autumni, Lacus. Near side. 14°S, 82°W. 240 km. Means "Lake of Autumn" in Latin.

Auwers. Near side. 15°N, 17°E. 16 km. In the foothills of the Haemus Mountains. Not very bright. Named for Arthur von Auwers (1838–1915), German astronomer.

Auzout. Near side. 10°N, 64°E. 33 km. Outside Mare Crisium. Has a low central peak. Named for Adrien Auzout (1622–1691), French astronomer.

Avery. Near side. 1°S, 81°E. 9 km. Formerly called Gilbert U. In the western part of Mare Smythii. Named for Oswald Avery (1877–1955), American biologist.

Avicenna. Far side. 40°N, 97°W. NW of Nernst. Named for Avicenna (980–1037), Arab philosopher.

Avogadro. Far side. 64°N, 165°E. 124 km. Between D'Alembert and the North Pole, and between Birkhoff and Schwarzschild. Named for Amedeo

Avogadro (1776–1856), Italian chemist.

Azophi. Near side. 22°S, 13°E. 48 km. Forms a pair with Abenezra, west of Mare Nectaris. Well-formed, it has a dark interior with some light spots. Named for Azophi (903–986), Persian astronomer.

Baade. Near side. 45°S, 82°W. 55 km. Named for Wilhelm Baade (1893–1960), German astronomer.

Baade, Vallis. Near side. 46°S, 76° W. 160 km. A valley in the area of Baade (q.v.), in association with which it was named.

Babakin. Far side. 21°S, 123°E. 20 km. West of Tsiolkovskiy, and south of Fermi. Named for Georgi Babakin (1914–1971), Russian space engineer.

Babbage. Near side. 58°N, 52°W. 144 km. An irregular enclosure which forms a companion to South crater, near Pythagoras. Not really a crater, it was formed by the fusion of two large rings. Named for Charles Babbage (1792–1871), British astronomer.

Babcock. Far side. 4°N, 94°E. 100 km. On the NE rim of Mare Smythii. Named for Harold D. Babcock (1882–1968), American physicist.

Back. Near side. 1°N, 81°E. 35 km. Formerly called Schubert B. Named for Ernst Back (1881–1959), German physicist.

Backlund. Far side. 16°S, 103°E. 75 km. On the southern rim of Pasteur, to the SE of Mare Smythii. Named for Johann Backlund (1846–1916), Swedish astronomer.

Baco. Near side. 51°S, 19°E. 70 km. In the area of Licetus. Has high walls, and a low central peak. Named for Roger Bacon (c.1220–1292), English philosopher.

Baillaud. Near side. 75°N, 40°E. 90 km. In the uplands NE of Meton. Has quite low walls. Named for Édouard-Benjamin Baillaud (1848–1934), French astronomer.

Bailly. Near side. 66°S, 65°E. 303 km. The largest of the walled plains, it is to be found on the limb of the Moon. Hare crater is in it. Ruined now, it has a huge floor on which are ridges and some craters, as well as curved valleys. The peaks on its walls rise to 14,000 feet on the east and 13,000 feet on the west. The east wall is magnificently terraced. Named for Jean Bailly (1736–1793), French astronomer.

Baily. Near side. 50°N, 31°E. 27 km. North of Bürg, in the area of Mare Frigoris. Named for Francis Baily (1774–1844), British astronomer.

Balandin. Far side. 19°S, 153°E. 12 km. Between Gagarin and Cyrano. Named for Aleksey Balandin (1898–1967), Russian chemist.

Balboa. Near side. 19°N, 83°W. 70 km. Named for Italo Balboa (1896–1940), Italian aeronautics pioneer.

Baldet. Far side. 54°S, 151°W. 55 km. Between Bellingshausen and White, to the SW of Chebyshev. Named for François Baldet (1885–1967), French astronomer.

Ball. Near side. 36°S, 8°W. 41 km. On the edge of Deslandres. Has high walls and a broad, deep groove running from the crest and down the inner south slope to a crater on its floor lying to the south of the central peak. Named for Sir Robert Ball (1840–1913), Irish astronomer.

Balmer. Near side. 20°S, 71°E. 112 km. Named for Johann Balmer (1825–1898), Swiss mathematician.

[1]**Banachiewicz.** Near side. 5°N, 80°E. 92 km. Named for Thaddeus Banachiewicz (1882–1954), Polish astronomer.

[2]**Banachiewicz.** Far side. 51°N, 135°W. To the east of Carnot, and to

the NW of Landau. One of the few repeat names on the Moon. Named for Thaddeus Banachiewicz (1882–1954), Polish astronomer.

Banat. Near side. 17°N, 26°W. A cape, near T. Mayer, in the Carpathian Mountains. Named after the range in the Southern Carpathians in Europe.

Bancroft. Near side. 28°N, 6°W. 13 km. Formerly called Archimedes A. Named for Wilder Bancroft (1867–1953), American chemist.

Banting. Near side. 27°N, 16°E. 5 km. Formerly called Linné E. Named for Sir Frederick Banting (1891–1941), Canadian physiologist.

Barbier. Far side. 24°S, 158°E. 67 km. Between Gagarin and Mare Ingenii. Named for Joseph-Émile Barbier (1839–1889), French astronomer.

Barkla. Near side. 11°S, 67°E. 43 km. Formerly called Langrenus A. Named for Charles G. Barkla (1877–1944), British physicist.

Barnard. Near side. 30°S, 86°E. 100 km. Named for Edward Barnard (1857–1923), American astronomer.

Barocius. Near side. 45°S, 17°E. 82 km. Outside Maurolycus. Has high, broken, terraced walls and a nearly central crater on its floor. Named for Francesco Barozzi (1537–1604), Italian astronomer.

Barringer. Far side. 29°S, 151°W. 69 km. Breaks into the northern rim of Apollo. Named for Daniel M. Barringer (1860–1929), American geologist.

Barrow. Near side. 73°N, 10°E. 93 km. North of Bond, W.C., in the northern polar uplands. Has low, broken walls. It is easily visible in a telescope. Named for Isaac Barrow (1630–1677), English mathematician.

Bartels. Mostly on the near side, but just spreads over onto the far side. 24°N, 90°W. 55 km. NW of Einstein, and NE of Ball. Named for Julius Bartels (1899–1964), German geophysicist.

Bayer. Near side. 51°S, 35°W. 47 km. Outside Schiller. Has high, terraced walls. Named for Johann Bayer (c.1572–1625), German astronomer.

Beaumont. Near side. 18°S, 29°E. 53 km. On Mare Nectaris. A ridge runs from it to Theophilus. Named for Élie de Beaumont (1798–1874), French geologist.

Becquerel. Far side. 41°N, 129°E. 65 km. East of H. G. Wells and NW of Mare Moscoviense. Named for Antoine H. Becquerel (1852–1908), French physicist.

Bĕcvár. Far side. 2°S, 125°E. 67 km. SW of Mendeleev, between Prager and Abul Wafa. Named for Antonin Bĕcvár (1901–1965), Czech astronomer.

Beer. Near side. 27°N, 9°W. 11 km. Forms a pair with Feuillé, on the Mare Imbrium. Named for Wilhelm Beer (1797–1850), German astronomer.

Behaim. Near side. 16°S, 71°E. 56 km. East of Vendelinus. Has high walls and central craters. Named for Martin Behaim (d. 1506), German cosmographer.

Beijerinck. Far side. 13°S, 152°E. 71 km. Between Marconi and Geiger, to the SE of Mendeleev and to the NW of Mare Ingenii. Named for Martinus Beijerinck (1851–1931), Dutch microbiologist.

Beketov. Near side. 16°N, 29°E. 8 km. Formerly called Jansen C. Named for Nikolai Beketov (1827–1911), Russian chemist.

Bel'kovich. Just on the far side, it also crosses over onto the near side. 60°N, 92°E. 198 km. One of the main features on the Moon. NE of Mare Humboldtianum. Named for Igor Bel'kovich (1904–1949), Russian astronomer.

Bell. Far side. 22°N, 96°W. 86 km. NW of Einstein, between Mees and Laue. Named for Alexander Graham Bell (1847–1922), Scottish physicist.

Bellingshausen. Far side. 61°S, 164° W. 63 km. Between Berlage and Bhabha. Named for Fabian von Bellingshausen (1778–1852), Russian polar navigator.

Bellot. Near side. 12°S, 48°E. 17 km. On the edge of the Mare Fecunditatis. It has a bright floor. Named for Joseph Bellot (1826–1853), French arctic explorer.

Belopol'skiy. Far side. 18°S. 128°W. 60 km. Just south of Joffe, south of Hertzsprung. Named for Aristarch Belopol'skiy (1854–1934), Russian astrophysicist.

Belyayev. Far side. 23°N, 143°E. 55 km. Also spelled Belyaev. Breaks in on the SW rim of Mare Moscoviense. Named for Pavel Belyayev (1925–1970), USSR cosmonaut.

Benedict. Far side. 4°S, 141°E. 14 km. Between Pannekoek and Vil'ev, in the area between Mendeleev and Gagarin. Named for Francis Benedict (1870–1957), American chemist.

Bergman. Far side. 7°N, 137°E. 21 km. In the NW portion of Mendeleev. Named for Torbern Bergman (1735–1784), Swedish chemist.

Bergstand. Far side. 19°S, 176°E. 44 km. Between Korolev and Mare Ingenii. Named for Carl Bergstand (1873–1948), Swedish astronomer.

Berkner. Far side. 25°N, 105°W. 86 km. Just to the north of Robertson, and just to the east of Parenago, to the NE of Hertzsprung. Named for Lloyd V. Berkner (1905–1967), American physicist.

Berlage. Far side. 64°S, 164°W. 92 km. Just to the SE of Bellingshausen, and to the NE of Antoniadi. Named for Hendrik Berlage (1896–1968), Dutch geophysicist.

Bernouilli. Near side. 34°N, 60°E. 47 km. East of Geminus. Fairly regular. Named for Jacques Bernouilli (1654–1705), Swiss mathematician.

Berosus. Near side. 33°N, 70°E. 74 km. Forms a pair with Hahn, east of Cleomedes. Has terraced walls. Named for Berosus (fl. c. 3rd century B.C.), Chaldean natural philosopher.

Berzelius. Near side. 37°N, 51°E. 51 km. In the area of Taurus. Has a darkish floor and a central peak. Named for Jöns Berzelius (1779–1848), Swedish chemist.

Bessarion. Near side. 15°N, 37°W. 10 km. A banded crater. Named for Bessarion (c.1400–1472), Greek scholar.

Bessel. Near side. 22°N, 18°E. 16 km. The largest crater on the surface of the Mare Serenitatis. Named for Friedrich Bessel (1784–1846), German astronomer.

Bettinus. Near side. 63°S, 45°W. 71 km. In the area of Bailly. Has high walls and the inner walls are terraced. Some peaks are 13,000 feet, and it has a central peak. Named for Mario Bettini (1582–1657), Italian optician.

Bhabha. Far side. 56°S, 165°W. 65 km. Between Stoney and Bose, to the SE of Von Kármán. Named for Homi Bhabha (1909–1966), Indian physicist.

Bianchini. Near side. 49°N, 34°W. 38 km. In the Jura Mountains, almost on the edge of Sinus Iridum. Polygonal and irregular, it has a central peak. Named for Francesco Bianchini (1662–1729), Italian astronomer.

Biela. Near side. 55°S, 52°E. 76 km. In the area of Vlacq. Has high walls and a central peak. Named for Wilhelm von Biela (1782–1856), Austrian astronomer.

Bilharz. Near side. 6°S, 56°E. 43 km. Formerly called Langrenus C. Named for Theodor Bilharz (1825–1862), German anatomist.

Billy. Near side. 14°S, 50°W. 46 km. Forms a pair with Hansteen, on the southern edge of the Oceanus Procellarum. It has a flat, very dark floor with two light spots on the northern part and two small craters on the southern part. Named for Jacques de Billy (1602–1679), French astronomer.

Billy, Rima. Near side. 15°S, 48°W. 70 km long. A rill in the area of Billy (q.v.), after which it was named.

Bingham. Far side. 8°N, 115°E. 34 km. SE of Lobachevsky, and south of the western rim of Guyot, to the west of Mendeleev. Named for Hiram Bingham (1875–1956), American explorer and aeronautics pioneer.

Biot. Near side. 23°S, 51°E. 13 km. On Mare Fecunditatis. Very bright. Named for Jean Baptiste Biot (1774–1862), French physicist-astronomer.

Birkeland. Far side. 30°S, 174°E. 82 km. Breaks into the SE rim of Van de Graaff, to the NE of Mare Ingenii. Named for Olaf K. Birkeland (1867–1917), Norwegian physicist.

Birkhoff. Far side. 59°N, 148°W. 326 km. A basin between D'Alembert and Rowland. Named for George D. Birkhoff (1884–1944), American mathematician.

Birmingham. Near side. 64°N, 10°W. 92 km. A huge, irregular rhomboidal plain north of Mare Frigoris. It has low walls, a central crater, and is bordered by ridges. Named for John Birmingham (c.1816–1884), Irish astronomer.

Birt. Near side. 22°S, 9°W. 17 km. A banded crater west of the Straight Wall, on Mare Nubium. It has an irregular profile, and a rill to its west. Two darks bands run up the east wall. Named for William Birt (1804–1881), British astronomer.

Birt, Rima. Near side. 21°S, 9°W. 50 km long. The rill associated with Birt (q.v.), after which it was named.

Bjerknes. Far side. 38°S, 113°E. 48 km. To the east of Mare Australe, and to the west of Clark. Named for Vilhelm Bjerknes (1862–1951), Norwegian physicist.

Black. Near side. 9°S, 80°E. 18 km. Formerly called Kästner F. Named for Joseph Black (1728–1799), Scottish chemist.

Blackett. Far side. 37°S, 116°W. 137 km. East of Apollo, SW of Mare Orientale, and NW of Mendel. Named for Patrick Blackett (1897–1974), British physicist.

Blagg. Near side. 1°N, 2°E. 5 km. In Sinus Medii. Distinct. Named for Mary A. Blagg (1858–1944), British astronomer.

Blanc, Mont. Near side. 45°N, 1°E. 11,800 feet high. Near Vallis Alpes, in the Alps. Named for the European mountain of that name.

Blancanus. Near side. 64°S, 21°W. 105 km. A large walled plain forming a pair with Scheiner, near Clavius. Has broad, light gray walls, not very high, and bright inner walls. Has 3 central peaks and 3 prominent craters in it (actually the peaks may be craters, or vice versa). Named for Giuseppe Bianchini (1566–1624), Italian astronomer.

Blanchinus. Near side. 25°S, 3°E. 61 km. North of Werner. Has a rough floor and uneven walls. Named for Giovanni Bianchini (fl. c.1548), Italian astronomer.

Blazhko. Far side. 31°N, 148°W. 54 km. To the NW of Joule, and to the NE of Mach. Named for Sergei Blazhko (1870–1956), Russian astronomer.

Blue Moon. When two full moons occur in any one month, the second is a blue moon. December 31, 1990, was one. The next will be in September 1993. They occur about one year out of three.

Bobillier. Near side. 20°N, 15°E. 7 km. Formerly called Bessel E. Named for Étienne Bobillier (1797–1832), French mathematician.

Bobone. Far side. 29°N, 131°W. 31 km. Coterminous with the SW rim of Kovalevskaya, north of Hertzsprung. Named for Jorge Bobone (1901–1958), Argentine astronomer.

Bode. Near side. 7°N, 2°W. 19 km. Outside Sinus Aestuum. It is bright and is the center of a minor ray system. Named for Johann Bode (1747–1826), German astronomer.

Bode, Rimae. Near side. 10°N, 4°W. A system of unrelated, scattered rills in the area of Bode (q.v.), in association with which they were named.

Boethius. Near side. 6°N, 72°E. 10 km. Formerly called Dubiago U. Named for Boethius (c.480–525), medieval philosopher.

Boguslawsky. Near side. 75°S, 45°E. 97 km. Also spelled Boguslowsky. A large ringed formation in the southern uplands. Has high terraced walls and a large crater on its floor. Named for Palm von Boguslawsky (1789–1851), Prussian astronomer.

Bohnenberger. Near side. 16°S, 40°E. 33 km. On the edge of the Mare Nectaris. Has low walls. Named for Johann G. von Bohnenberger (1765–1831), German physicist.

Bohr. Near side. 13°N, 86°W. 71 km. Named for Niels Bohr (1885–1962), Danish physicist.

Bohr, Vallis. Near side. 10°N, 89°W. 100 km long. A valley in the area of Bohr (q.v.), in association with which it was named.

Bok. Far side. 21°S, 172°W. 45 km. North of Sniadecki, and NE of Orlov, in the area NW of Apollo. Named for Bart Jan Bok (1906–1983), American astronomer.

Boltzmann. Far side. 55°S, 115°W. The name Boltzmann was originally given to a 77 km crater just to the north of Drygalski, in the area east of Zeeman, but the name was later transferred to another crater between Mendel and Watson, where it remains today. This crater used to be called Lippmann (q.v.). Named for Ludwig Boltzmann (1844–1906), Austrian physicist.

Bolyai. Far side. 34°S, 125°E. 100 km. Between Pizzetti and Lampland, to the NE of Mare Australe. Named for János Bolyai (1802–1860), Hungarian mathematician.

Bombelli. Near side. 5°N, 56°E. 10 km. Formerly called Apollonius T. Named for Rafael Bombelli (1526–1572), Italian algebraist.

Bond, G. P. Near side. 32°N, 36°E. 23 km. East of Posidonius. Quite regular. Named for George P. Bond (1825–1865), American astronomer.

Bond, W. C. Near side. 64°N, 3°E. 158 km. A very large formation in the upland terrain north of Mare Frigoris. It is an old, broken plain bordered by ridges, and has a vast floor crossed by rows of hills running NW–SE. Named for William Cranch Bond (1789–1859), American astronomer.

Bonitatis, Lacus. Near side. 23°N, 44°E. 130 km. A patch of dark lava NW of Mare Crisium. Name means "Lake of Goodness" in Latin.

Bonpland. Near side. 8°S, 17°W. 58 km. A ring plain in the Fra Mauro group in the Mare Nubium area, it forms the group with Fra Mauro and Parry. It is quite regular, but looks ruined. It has craterlets and hillocks in the interior. The interior is crossed by three clefts. Named for Aimé Bonpland (1773–1858), French naturalist.

Boole. Near side. 64°N, 87°W. 63 km. Named for George Boole (1815–1864), British mathematician.

Borda. Near side. 25°S, 47°E. 44 km. West of Petavius. Has low walls. Named for Jean Charles Borda (1733–1799), French mathematician-astronomer.

Borel. Near side. 22°N, 67°E. 15 km. Formerly called Le Monnier C. Named for Émile Borel (1871–1956), French mathematician.

Borman. Far side. 37°S, 142°W. 50 km. To the east of Apollo. Named for Frank Borman (b. 1928), American astronaut.

Born. Near side. 6°S, 67°E. 15 km. Formerly called Maclaurin Y. Named for Max Born (1882–1970), German physicist.

Boscovich. Near side. 10°N, 11°E. 46 km. Also spelled Boscovitch. On the edge of the Mare Vaporum. It is one of the darkest patches on the lunar surface, with a very dark floor. It varies in tint. This feature has low walls. Named for Ruggiero Boscovich (1711–1787), Italian mathematician-astronomer.

Boscovich, Rimae. Near side. 40 km. Rills in the crater Boscovich (q.v.), in association with which they were named.

Bose. Far side. 54°S, 170°W. 91 km. A crater NW of Bhabha and SE of Von Kármán. Named for Sir Jagadis Chandra Bose (1858–1937), Indian physicist.

Boss. Probably mostly on the near side, but listed as on the far side. It is just on the border. 46°N, 90°E. 47 km. NW of Fabry. Named for Lewis Boss (1846–1912), American astronomer.

Bouguer. Near side. 52°N, 36°W. 23 km. In the Jura uplands. Distinct. Named for Pierre Bouguer (1698–1758), French mathematician.

Boussingault. Near side. 131 km. A large ring formation consisting of 3 almost concentric rings. Named for Jean Baptiste Boussingault (1802–1887), French chemist.

Bouvard. Near side. 37°S, 87°W. 129 km. In the area of Schickard. Has a central ridge rising to a peak. Named for Alexis Bouvard (1767–1843), French astronomer.

Bouvard, Vallis. Near side. 39°S, 83°W. 280 km long. A valley in the area of Bouvard (q.v.), in association with which it was named.

Bowditch. Far side. 25°S, 103°E. 40 km. East of Perel'man, with which it forms a pair, in the area west of the southern rim of Tsiolkovskiy. Named for Nathaniel Bowditch (1773–1838), American astronomer.

Bowen. Near side. 18°N, 9°E. 9 km. Formerly called Manilius A. Named for Ira S. Bowen (1898–1973), American astronomer.

Boyle. Far side. 54°S, 178°E. 57 km. Just to the NE of Hess, south of Von Kármán. Named for Robert Boyle (1627–1691), British chemist.

Brackett. Near side. 18°N, 24°E. 9 km. Named for Frank P. Brackett (b. 1865), American astronomer.

Bradley, Mount. Near side. 22°N, 1°E. 16,000 feet. Also called Mons Bradley. Near Conon, in the Apennines. Named for James Bradley (1693–1762), British astronomer.

Bradley, Rima. Near side. 23°N, 2° W. 130 km long. A rill in the area of Mount Bradley (q.v.), in association with which it was named.

Bragg. Far side. 42°N, 103°W. 84 km. To the south of Stefan, to the east of Landau, and to the NE of Lacchini. Named for Sir William H. Bragg (1862–1942), British physicist.

Brashear. Far side. 74°S, 172°W. 55 km. To the SW of Zeeman and to the SE of Schrödinger. Named for John Brashear (1840–1920), American astronomical lens maker.

Brayley. Near side. 21°N, 37°W. 16 km. A banded crater on Oceanus Procellarum. Has a low central peak. Named for Edward W. Brayley (1802–1870), British science writer.

Bredikhin. Far side. 17°N, 158°W. 59 km. To the NE of Raimond, and to the west of Mach. Named for Fyodor A. Bredikhin (1830–1904), Russian astronomer.

Breislak. Near side. 48°S, 18°E. 50 km. SE of Maurolycus. Quite regular, and has no central peak. Named for Scipione Breislak (1748–1826), Italian geologist.

Brenner. Near side. 39°S, 39°E. 97 km. Adjoins Janssen in the southern uplands. It is broken. Named for Leo Brenner (1855–1928), Austrian selenographer.

Brewster. Near side. 23°N, 35°E. 11 km. Formerly called Rømer L. Named for Sir David Brewster (1781–1868), Scottish physicist.

Brianchon. Near and far side. 75°N, 86°W. 145 km. NE of Birkhoff, SW of the North Pole. Named for Charles-Julien Brianchon (1783–1864), French mathematician.

Bridgman. Far side. 44°N, 137°E. 80 km. NE of Becquerel and SW of Campbell, in the area NW of Mare Moscoviense. Named for Percy W. Bridgman (1882–1961), American physicist.

Briggs. Near side. 26°N, 69°W. 37 km. In the area of Struve, Otto (q.v.), in the Oceanus Procellarum. Similar to Seleucus, it has a level floor, on which is a long ridge running in a north-south direction. Named for Henry Briggs (1561–1630), English mathematician.

Brisbane. Near side. 50°S, 65°E. 47 km. In the area of Mare Australe. Quite regular. Named for Sir Thomas Brisbane (1773–1860), Scottish astronomer.

Bronk. Far side. 26°N, 134°W. 64 km. SW of Bobone, and east of the southern rim of Joule. Named for Detlev Bronk (1897–1975), American physiologist.

Brouwer. Far side. 36°S, 125°W. 116 km. Just to the east of Langmuir, east of Apollo. Named for Dirk Brouwer (1902–1966), Dutch astronomer.

Brown. Near side. 46°S, 18°W. 34 km. In the area of Longomontanus. Irregular. Named for Ernest W. Brown (1866–1938), British celestial mechanician.

Bruce. Near side. 1°N, 0°. 7 km. In Sinus Medii. Distinct. Named for Catherine W. Bruce (1816–1900), American art and science patron.

Bruggencate, ten *see* **ten Bruggencate**

Brunner. Far side. 10°S, 91°E. 53 km. Breaks onto the extreme SE rim of Mare Smythii, just on the far side of the Moon. Named for William O. Brunner (1878–1958), Swiss astronomer.

Buch. Near side. 39°S, 18°E. 54 km. Forms a pair with Büsching, in the area of Maurolycus. Regular. Named for Christian von Buch (1774–1853). German geologist.

Buffon. Far side. 41°S, 134°W. 101 km. South of Chebyshev and east of the southern limits of Apollo. Named for Georges Buffon (1707–1788), French naturalist.

Buisson. Far side. 1°S, 113°E. 57 km. NW of Vesalius, to the east of Mare Smythii. Named for Henri Buisson (1873–1944), French astronomer.

Bullialdus. Near side. 21°S, 22°W. 61 km. One of the best examples of a ringed plain, this is the most notable object in the Mare Nubium. Ridges radiate in all directions on the outside, and on the inside it has magnificently terraced inner slopes. The central mountain has four peaks. Named for Ismaël Boulliaud (Bullialdus) (1605–1694), French astronomer.

Bunsen. Near side. 41°N, 85°W. 52 km. Named for Robert Bunsen (1811–1899), German chemist.

Burckhardt. Near side. 31°N, 57°E. 57 km. North of Cleomedes. Named for Johann K. Burckhardt (1773–1825), German astronomer.

Bürg. Near side. 45°N, 28°E. 40 km. North of Lacus Mortis. Has a large central peak with a pit. It is associated with a rill system (*see* **Bürg, Rimae**). Named for Johann Bürg (1766–1834), Austrian astronomer.

Bürg, Rimae. Near side. 45°N, 26°E. 100 km long. A rill system in the area of Bürg (q.v.), in association with which it was named.

Burnham. Near side. 14°S, 7°E. 25 km. In the area of Albategnius. Has low walls. Named for Sherburne W. Burnham (1838–1921), American astronomer.

Büsching. Near side. 38°S, 20°E. 52 km. Forms a pair with Buch. Irregular. Named for Anton Büsching (1724–1793), German geographer.

Butlerov. Far side. 9°N, 109°W. 40 km. Between Kolhörster and Elvey, to the NE of Hertzsprung. Named for Aleksandr Butlerov (1828–1866), Russian chemist.

Buys-Ballot. Far side. 21°N, 175°E. 55 km. A crater between Freundlich and Hayford, in the area between Mare Moscoviense and Korolev. Named for Christoph Buys-Ballot (1817–1890), Dutch meteorologist.

Byrd. Near side. 85°N, 10°E. 94 km. In the area of the North Pole. Named for Richard E. Byrd (1888–1957), American polar explorer.

Byrgius. Near side. 25°S, 65°W. 87 km. West of Mare Humorum. Has walls rising to 7000 feet. Byrgius A, a crater on its eastern crest, is a ray center. Named for Justus Byrgius (1552–1632), Swiss mathematician.

C. Herschel *see* **Herschel, Caroline**

C. Mayer *see* **Mayer, C.**

Cabaeus. Near side. 85°S, 20°W. 98 km. Also spelled Cabeus. In the South Polar uplands. Has quite high walls. Named for Niccolò Cabeo (1586–1650), Italian meteorologist.

Cabannes. Far side. 61°S, 171°W. 81 km. To the NW of Berlage, and SE of Poincaré. Named for Jean Cabannes (1885–1959), French physicist.

Cajal. Near side. 13°N, 31°E. 9 km. Formerly called Jansen F. Named for Santiago Ramón y Cajal (1852–1934), Spanish histologist.

Cajori. Far side. 48°S, 168°E. 70 km. SW of Von Kármán, and east of Garavito. Named for Florian Cajori (1859–1930), American historian of science.

Calippus. Near side. 39°N, 11°E. 33 km. At the north end of the Caucasus Mountains. Irregular. Named for Calippus (fl. 4th century B.C.), Greek astronomer.

Calippus, Rima. Near side. 37°N, 13°E. 40 km long. A rill in the area of Calippus (q.v.), in association with which it was named.

Cameron. Near side. 6°N, 46°E. 11 km. Formerly called Taruntius C. Named for Donald Cameron (b. 1912), American astronomer.

Campanus. Near side. 28°S, 28°W. 48 km. Forms a pair with Mercator, on the west edge of the Mare Nubium. Has a central hill on its dark floor. A mountain arm projects from the north wall. Named for Johannes Campanus of Novara (d. 1296), Italian astronomer.

Campbell. Far side. 45°N, 152°E. 225 km. SW of D'Alembert. Named for William Wallace Campbell (1862–1938), American astronomer.

Cannizzaro. Far side. 55°N, 100°W. 56 km. Between Chapman and Smoluchowski. Named for Stanislao Cannizzaro (1826–1910), Italian chemist.

Cannon. Near side. 20°N, 81°E. 57 km. Named for Annie Jump Cannon (1863–1941), American astronomer.

Cantor. Far side. 38°N, 118°E. 81 km. SW of H. G. Wells, and SE of Fabry. Named for Georg Cantor (1845–1918), German mathematician.

Capella. Near side. 8°S, 36°E. 49 km. Companion of Isidorus, which it slightly overlaps, in the uplands north of Mare Nectaris. Has terraced walls cut through by rill valleys on the SE, and has an excellent central peak. Named for Martianus Capella (fl. 5th century A.D.), Latin writer.

Capes. Promontories jutting out from maria. (*See* **Acherusia, Aenarium, Agarum, Agassiz, Argaeus, Banat, Deville, Fresnel, Heraclides, Kelvin, Laplace.**)

Capuanus. Near side. 34°S, 26°W. 60 km. On the south edge of Palus Epidemiarum. Its floor is higher than the surrounding terrain, and it has large, low domes on its dark floor. Named for Francesco Capuano (fl. 15th century), Italian astronomer.

Caramuel *see* **Einstein**

Cardanus. Near side. 13°N, 73°W. 50 km. A prominent ring which forms a pair with Krafft, on the Oceanus Procellarum. Has a light gray floor, a central peak and several craterlets in the interior. It has bright, terraced walls 4000 feet high. A deep valley of note is on the outer west slope. Named for Girolamo Cardano (1501–1576), Italian physicist.

Cardanus, Rima. Near side. 11°N, 72°W. 200 km long. A rill in the area of Cardanus (q.v.), in association with which it was named.

Carlini. Near side. 34°N, 24°W. 11 km. On the Mare Imbrium. Quite bright. Named for Francesco Carlini (1783–1862), Italian astronomer.

Carmichael. Near side. 20°N, 40°E. 20 km. Formerly called Macrobius A. Named for Hugh Carmichael (b. 1906), Scottish physicist.

Carnot. Far side. 52°N, 144°W. 117 km. Immediately south of Birkhoff. Named for Nicolas Carnot (1796–1832), French physicist.

Carpathian Mountains. Near side. 15°N, 24°W. 400 km long and no higher than 7000 feet. Also called Montes Carpatus. A discontinuous chain of mountains, in the area of Copernicus, forming part of the circular wall of the Mare Imbrium, bordering that mare on the south. Named by Mädler after the Carpathians in Europe.

Carpatus, Montes *see* **Carpathian Mountains**

Carpenter. Near side. 70°N, 50°W. 60 km. An excellent regular ring, next to Anaximander, north of Mare Frigoris. Has a central peak. Named for James Carpenter (1826–1875), British astronomer.

Carrel. Near side. 11°N, 27°E. 16 km. Formerly called Jansen B. Named for Alexis Carrel (1873–1944), French research biologist.

Carrillo. Near side. 2°S, 81°E. 16 km. Named for Edward Carrillo (1876–1964), American civil engineer.

Carrington. Near side. 44°N, 62°E. 30 km. In the Messala group. Named for Richard C. Carrington (1826–1875), British astronomer.

Cartan. Near side. 4°N, 59°E. 16 km. Formerly called Apollonius D. Named for Élie Cartan (1869–1951), French mathematician.

Carver. Far side. 43°S, 127°E. 60 km. East of Van der Waals, and SW of Roche, to the east of Mare Australe. Named for George Washington Carver (c.1864–1943), American chemist.

Casatus. Near side. 75°S, 35°W. 111 km. An excellent ring plain which breaks into the SE wall of Klaproth, south of Clavius. It has walls rising to 18,000 feet on the west and a peak rising to 22,000 feet above the floor on the east. Named for Paolo Casati (1617–1707), Italian mathematician.

Cassegrain. Far side. 52°S, 113°E. 55 km. Between Lebedev and Kimura, north of Schrödinger. Named for Giovanni D. Cassegrain (1625–1712), French astronomer.

Cassini. Near side. 40°N, 5°E. 57 km. On the Mare Imbrium. Polygonal, it has low, broad walls and a narrow crest. The floor is only just below the level of the surrounding terrain. First shown on Cassini's map of 1692, it was named for him. It is conspicuous under low lighting only. Named for Giovanni Domenico (Jean Dominique) Cassini (1625–1712), Italian-French astronomer.

Cassini, J. J. Near side. 68°N, 16°W. Large plain bounded by ridges, near Philolaus, in the northern uplands. Named for G. D. Cassini's son, Jacques Cassini (1677–1756), French astronomer.

Catalán. Near side. 46°S, 87°W. 25 km. Named for Miguel Catalán (1894–1957), Spanish spectroscopist.

Catenae. A catena is a chain of craters. (*See* **Artamonov, Dziewulski, Gregory, Kurchatov, Leuschner, Lucretius, Mendeleev, Sumner**.)

Catharina. Near side. 18°S, 24°E. 100 km. In the Theophilus group. It has a curved ridge on the rough floor and no central peak. Named for Catherine I (c.1684–1727), empress who founded the Russian Academy of Sciences.

Caucasus Mountains. Near side. 36°N, 8°E. 520 km long. Up to 12,000 feet. Also called Montes Caucasus. An important range, it separates Mare Serenitatis and Palus Nebularum. Named by Mädler after the Caucasus in Russia.

Cauchy. Near side. 10°N, 39°E. 12 km. On Mare Tranquillitatis. Bright. Named for Augustin Cauchy (1789–1857), French mathematician.

Cauchy, Rima. Near side. 10°N, 39° E. 210 km long. A rill in the area of Cauchy (q.v.), in association with which it was named.

Cauchy, Rupes. Near side. 9°N, 37° E. 120 km. A line of rocks in the area of Cauchy (q.v.), in association with which it was named.

Cavalerius. Near side. 5°N, 67°W. 58 km. In the Hevel group. Has terraced walls rising to 10,000 feet above the floor, and has an elongated central mountain with three peaks. Named for Bonaventura Cavalieri (Cavalerius) (1598–1647), Italian mathematician.

Cavendish. Near side. 25°S, 54°W. 56 km. West of Mare Humorum. Has broad, quite high, terraced walls, and some low rings on its floor. Named for Henry Cavendish (1731–1810), British chemist.

Caventou. Near side. 30°N, 29°W. 3 km. Formerly called La Hire D (*see* **La Hire, Mons**). Named for Joseph Caventou (1795–1877), French chemist.

Cayley. Near side. 4°N, 15°E. 14 km. In the uplands west of Mare Tranquillitatis. Very bright. Named for Arthur

Cayley (1821–1895), British mathematician.

Celsius. Near side. 34°S, 20°E. 36 km. In the Rabbi Levi group. Elliptical. Named by J. Schmidt for Anders Celsius (1701–1744), Swedish astronomer.

Censorinus. Near side. 0°, 32°E. 4 km. In the uplands SE of Mare Tranquillitatis. Extremely bright. Named for Censorinus (fl. c. A.D. 238), Roman astronomer.

Cepheus. Near side. 41°N, 46°E. 40 km. Forms a pair with Franklin, in the area of the Lacus Somniorum. Named for the Ethiopian mythological king.

Ceraski. Far side. 49°S, 141°E. 56 km. To the SE of Pauli, and to the NE of the Rima Planck, north of Schrödinger. Named for Vitold Tserasky (Ceraski) (1849–1925), Russian astronomer.

Chacornac. Near side. 30°N, 32°E. 51 km. Near Posidonius, on the edge of the Mare Serenitatis. Irregular in outline. Named for Jean Chacornac (1823–1873), French astronomer.

Chacornac, Rimae. Near side. 29° N, 32°E. 120 km. A series of rills in the area of Chacornac (q.v.), in association with which it was named.

Chaffee. Far side. 39°S, 155°W. 50 km. One of a curved line of formations lying on the inner ring of Apollo. Named for Roger B. Chaffee (1935–1967), American astronaut.

Challis. Near side. 78°N, 9°E. 56 km. Forms a pair with Main, in the area of the North Pole. Named for James Challis (1803–1882), British astronomer.

Chamberlin. Far side. 59°S, 96°E. 58 km. At the northern end of the Rima Schrödinger, NW of Schrödinger crater. Named for Thomas C. Chamberlin (1843–1928), American geologist.

Champollion. Far side. 37°N, 175°E. 58 km. Between Moore and Hutton, NE of Mare Moscoviense. Named for Jean-François Champollion (1790–1832), French egyptologist.

Chandler. Far side. 44°N, 171°E. 85 km. SE of D'Alembert. Named for Seth Chandler (1846–1913), American astronomer.

Chang Heng. Far side. 19°N, 112°E. 43 km. NE of Fleming and SW of Olcott. Named for Chang Heng (fl. mid-2nd century A.D.), Chinese seismologist.

Chant. Far side. 41°S, 110°W. 34 km. North of Mendel, NW of Fenyi, and east of Stetson. Named for Clarence Chant (1865–1956), Canadian astronomer.

Chaplygin. Far side. 6°S, 150°E. 124 km. North of Gagarin, and SE of Mendeleev. Named for Sergei Chaplygin (1869–1942), Russian mechanician.

Chapman. Far side. 50°N, 101°W. 71 km. NE of Stefan. Named for Sydney Chapman (1888–1970), British geophysicist.

Chappell. Far side. 62°N, 150°W. 80 km. NW of Birkhoff, and SE of Stebbins. Named for James F. Chappell (1891–1964), American astronomer.

Charlier. Far side. 36°N, 132°W. 100 km. NW of Kovalevskaya, and SE of Fowler. Named for Carl L. W. Charlier (1862–1934), Swedish astronomer.

Chaucer. Far side. 3°N, 140°W. 45 km. Just to the west of the western rim of Hertzsprung, NW of Vavilov, and east of Kibaltchich. Named for Geoffrey Chaucer (c.1344–1400), English writer.

Chauvenet. Far side. 11°S, 137°E. 82 km. South of Mendeleev, and NW of Gagarin. Named for William Chauvenet (1820–1870), American mathematician-astronomer.

Chebyshev. Far side. 34°S, 133°W. 183 km. Between Apollo and Mare Orientale. Named for Pafnuti Chebyshev (1821–1894), Russian mathematician.

Chernyshev. Far side. 47°N, 174°E. 58 km. NE of Chandler and NW of Dunér, in the area SE of D'Alembert. Named for Nikolay Chernyshev (1906–1963), Russian rocket engineer.

Chevallier. Near side. 45°N, 52°E. 52 km. In the Atlas area. Has low walls. Named for Temple Chevallier (c.1794–1873), British astronomer.

Chladni. Near side. 4°N, 1°E. 14 km. Joins to Murchison, in the area of the Sinus Medii. Bright. Named for Ernst Chladni (1756–1827), German physicist.

Chrétien. Far side. 33°S, 113°E. 89 km. South of Milne, to the NE of the Mare Australe. Named for Henri Chrétien (1879–1956), French optician.

Cichus. Near side. 33°S, 21°W. 41 km. On the west edge of the Palus Epidemiarum. Well-formed, a crater is on its east rim, and there are two low hills near the center of its floor. Named for Cichus (Cecco) (1257–1327), Italian astronomer-astrologer.

Clairaut. Near side. 48°S, 14°E. 75 km. A walled plain in the Maurolycus area. Has broken walls. Named for Alexis Clairaut (1713–1765), French mathematician.

Clark. Far side. 38°S, 119°E. 50 km. East of Bjerknes, and north of Van der Waals, to the east of Mare Australe. Named for Alvan G. Clark (1832–1897), American astronomer.

Clausius. Near side. 37°S, 44°W. 25 km. In the Schickard area. Bright and distinct. Named for Rudolf Clausius (1822–1888), German physicist.

Clavius. Near side. 56°S, 14°W. 225 km. A huge, great walled depression in the southern uplands. Its irregular wall is broken on the south by Rutherfurd. A major arc of craters is on its light-colored floor, and many craterlets. It has no central peak. It is one of the Moon's most interesting attractions. Named for Christopher Clavius (1538–1612), German astronomer.

Cleomedes. Near side. 27°N, 55°E. 126 km. In the area of Mare Crisium. It is distorted by Tralles. Named for Cleomedes (fl. c.200 B.C.), Greek astronomer.

Cleomedes, Rima. Near side. 30 km long. In Cleomedes (q.v.), in association with which it was named.

Cleostratus. Near side. 60°N, 74°W. 63 km. In the Pythagoras area. Distinct. Named for Cleostratus (fl. between 538 and 432 B.C.), Greek astronomer.

Clerke. Near side. 22°N, 30°E. 7 km. Formerly called Littrow B. Named for Agnes Clerke (1842–1907), British astronomer.

Cloos, Dorsum. Far side. 1°N, 91°E. 100 km long. A ridge in the Mare Smythii. Named for Hans Cloos (1885–1951), German geologist.

Coblentz. Far side. 38°S, 126°E. 34 km. SW of Eötvös, south of Bolyai, and NW of Roche, to the east of the Mare Australe. Named for William Coblentz (1873–1962), British astronomer.

Cockcroft. Far side. 30°N, 164°W. 94 km. Between Evershed and Fitzgerald. Named for John D. Cockcroft (1897–1967), British nuclear physicist.

Cognitum, Mare *see* **Nubium, Mare**

Collins. Near side. 1°N, 24°E. 2 km. Named for Michael Collins (b. 1930), American astronaut.

Colombo. Near side. 15°S, 46°E. 76 km. In the Mare Fecunditatis. Irregular. Named for Realdo Colombo (c. 1510–1559), Italian astronomer.

Compton. Far side. 55°N, 104°E. 162 km. A fresh crater, one of the larger ones of its type on the Moon, between Fabry and Schwarzschild. It has the very rare combination of a central elevation and an inner ring of peaks. Named for Arthur Compton (1892–1962), American physicist.

Comrie. Far side. 23°N, 113°W. 60 km. NE of Sternberg, and NW of Robertson, to the NE of Hertzsprung. Named for Leslie J. Comrie (1893–1950), British astronomer.

Comstock. Far side. 21°N, 122°W. 73 km. NE of Fersman and NW of Sternberg, to the NE of Hertzsprung. Named for George Comstock (1855–1934), American astronomer.

Concordiae, Sinus. Near side. 11°N, 43°E. 160 km. Name means "Bay of Harmony" in Latin.

Condamine. Near side. 53°N, 28°W. 37 km. Also known as La Condamine. On the southern edge of the Mare Frigoris. Rhomboidal. Named for Charles M. de la Condamine (1701–1774), French scientist.

Condon. Near side. 2°N, 60°E. 35 km. Formerly called Webb R. Named for Edward Condon (1902–1974), American physicist.

Condorcet. Near side. 12°N, 70°E. 74 km. Outside Mare Crisium. Regular, it has no central peak. Named for the Marquis de Condorcet (1743–1794), French mathematician.

Congreve. Far side. 0°, 168°W. 58 km. To the NE of Icarus, and west of the north rim of Korolev. Named for Sir William Congreve (1772–1828), British engineer.

Conon. Near side. 22°N, 2°E. 22 km. In the uplands of the Apennines, it is quite distinct and several of its details seem to change position. If there are clouds on the Moon, they're here. Named for Conon (fl. 3rd century B.C.), Greek astronomer.

Conon, Rima. Near side. 18°N, 2°E. 30 km long. A rill in the area of Conon (q.v.), in association with which it was named.

Cook. Near side. 18°S, 49°E. 47 km. On the edge of Mare Fecunditatis. Has a dark floor. Named for Captain James Cook (1728–1779), Scottish navigator.

Cooper. Far side. 53°N, 176°E. 36 km. To the east of D'Alembert and to the NW of Debye. Named for Gordon Cooper (b. 1927), American astronaut.

Copernicus. Near side. 10°N, 20°W. 93 km. In the Oceanus Procellarum. It is the Moon's finest crater and is the center of the second most extensive ray system on the lunar surface. It is isolated. Ridges radiate from it. It has a circular floor and five bright peaks rising from the floor. Its massive complex walls rise to a sharp thin crest 12,000 feet above the floor. Named for Nicolaus Copernicus (1473–1543), Polish astronomer.

Cordillera Mountains. Near side. 27°S, 85°W. 1500 km long. Also called Montes Cordillera. A limb range in the Grimaldi/Darwin area, it makes up part of the ring boundaries of the Mare Orientale, forming the inner wall of that sea. Named after the Cordilleras in the Andes in South America.

Cori. Far side. 51°S, 152°W. 65 km. SW of White, and north of Baldet, in the area south of Apollo. Named for Gerty Cori (1896–1957), American biochemist.

Coriolis. Far side. 0°, 172°E. 79 km. NE of Heaviside, and NW of Daedalus, to the east of the southern extremity of Mendeleev. Named for Gaspard de Coriolis (1792–1843), French mechanician.

Cosmos Spacecraft. A series of USSR Moon probes: *Cosmos 60:* Launched March 12, 1965. A failure. *Cosmos 111:* Launched March 1, 1966. A failure.

Coulomb. Far side. 54°N, 115°W. 89 km. North of Landau, and east of Birkhoff, in the NW region of the Moon's far side. Named for Charles Augustin de Coulomb (1736–1806), French physicist.

Craters. There are about 1500 major craters, or crater-like features, on the Moon. They all have entries of their own in this book. An entry with no description, i.e. just a name, is a crater, or a walled plain, or a ringed plain, or some such depression, and the description will follow in the text. A letter after a crater name—e.g., Proclus F (*see* **Crile** below)—designates an auxiliary crater within a larger crater or ring plain. This designation is usually temporary, until the crater gets a name of its own. Newton is the Moon's deepest crater, Aristarchus is the brightest spot on the Moon, and Tycho is the center of the greatest ray system.

Cremona. Far side. 68°N, 93°E. 85 km. North of Belkovich, and west of the southern rim of Schwarzschild. Named for Luigi Cremona (1830–1903), Italian mathematician.

Crile. Near side. 14°N, 46°E. 9 km. Formerly called Proclus F. Named for George Washington Crile (1864–1943), American surgeon.

Crisium, Mare. Near side. 18°N, 58°E. A very conspicuous "sea," almost at the eastern limb, but separated from the main system of maria. Its dimensions range in estimate, but 590× 460 km seems reasonable, and it is elongated in an east-west direction. It is regular in shape and is just over 4 billion years old. It contains 3 major craters—Picard, Peirce, and Peirce A (formerly Graham). Name means the "Sea of Crises" in Latin.

Crocco. Far side. 47°S, 150°E. 76 km. South of Koch, and SW of Mare Ingenii. Named for Gaetano Crocco (1877–1968), Italian rocket engineer.

Crommelin. Far side. 68°S, 147°W. 94 km. SW of Eijkman, and NW of Zeeman. Named for Andrew Crommelin (1865–1939), British astronomer.

Crookes. Far side. 11°S, 165°W. 49 km. A smaller fresh crater on the SW rim of Korolev. Named for Sir William Crookes (1832–1919), British chemist.

Crozier. Near side. 14°S, 51°E. 22 km. SE of Colombo, in the area of the Mare Fecunditatis. It has a central peak. Named for Francis Crozier (c.1796–1848), British navigator.

Crüger. Near side. 17°S, 67°W. 46 km. SW of Oceanus Procellarum. Has a very dark floor. Named for Peter Crüger (1580–1639), German mathematician.

Ctesibius. Far side. 1°N, 119°E. 37 km. Immediately east of Abul Wafa, in the area between Mare Smythii and Mendeleev. Named for Ctesibius (fl. c.250 B.C.), Alexandrian physicist.

Curie. Far side. 23°S, 92°E. 139 km. SW of Sklodowska, and south of Mare Smythii. Named for Pierre Curie (1859–1906), French physicist.

Curtis. Near side. 15°N, 57°E. 3 km. Formerly called Picard Z. Named for Heber D. Curtis (1872–1942), American astronomer.

Curtius. Near side. 77°S, 5°E. 95 km. In the Moretus area. Has massive terraced walls and a large dome on its high eastern rampart. Named for Albert Curtz (Curtius) (1600–1671), German astronomer.

Cusanus. Near side. 72°N, 71°E. 63 km. Named for Nicolaus Cusa (c.1401–1464), German mathematician.

Cuvier. Near side. 50°S, 10°E. 75 km. Forms a pair with Jacobi, in the Licetus group. Has high, terraced walls, a central peak, and craterlets on its floor and lower inner slopes. Named for Georges Cuvier (1769–1832), French naturalist.

Cyrano. Far side. 20°S, 157°E. 81 km. East of Gagarin, and SW of Keeler. Named for Cyrano de Bergerac (c.1620–1655), French writer.

Cyrillus. Near side. 13°S, 24°E. 98 km. In the Theophilus group. Square, it has complex walls, and a low, triple-peaked mountain near the center of the floor. Within the east wall is the brilliant crater Cyrillus A. Named for Saint Cyril (827–869), Greek pioneer of Cyrillic alphabet.

Cysatus. Near side. 66°S, 7°W. 49 km. Forms a pair with Gruemberger, in the Moretus area. Has a small floor and on it is a central peak. Has high walls. Named for Johann Baptist Cysat (1586–1657), Swiss astronomer.

Daedalus. Far side. 6°S, 180°. 93 km. West of Icarus, between Korolev and Mendeleev. Named after the Greek mythological character.

Daguerre. Near side. 12°S, 34°E. 46 km. In the Mare Nectaris. Has very low walls. Named for Louis Daguerre (1789–1851), French inventor.

Dale. Near side. 10°S, 83°E. 22 km. Named for Sir Henry Dale (1875–1968), British physiologist.

D'Alembert. Far side. 52°N, 164°E. 225 km. SW of Birkhoff. Named for Jean le Rond d'Alembert (1717–1783), French physicist.

D'Alembert Mountains. Near side. Like the Leibnitz Mountains, the D'Alemberts were found not to be a range at all, so the name was given to a feature on the far side of the Moon.

Dalton. Near side. 17°N, 84°W. 61 km. Named for John Dalton (1766–1844), British chemist.

Daly. Near side. 6°N, 60°E. 17 km. Formerly called Apollonius P. Named for Reginald Daly (1871–1857), American geologist.

Damoiseau. Near side. 5°S, 61°W. 37 km. East of Grimaldi. Very irregular. Named for Marie-Charles-Theodore Damoiseau (1768–1846), French astronomer.

Dana, Dorsa. Far side. 3°N, 90°E. 70 km long. A system of ridges in the Mare Smythii, just over on the dark side of the Moon. Named for James D. Dana (1813–1895), American geologist.

Daniell. Near side. 35°N, 31°E. 29 km. Adjoins Posidonius. Has no central peak. Named for John F. Daniell (1790–1845), British physicist.

Daniell, Rimae. Near side. 37°N, 26°E. 200 km long. A rill system in the area of Daniell (q.v.), in association with which it was named.

Danjon. Far side. 11°S, 123°E. 72 km. To the SE of Langemak, and to the SW of Perepel'kin, in the area SW of Mendeleev. Named for André Danjon (1890–1967), French astronomer.

Dante. Far side. 25°N, 180°. 55 km. SW of Fitzgerald, and east of Freundlich, in the area east of Mare Moscoviense. Named for Dante Alighieri (1265–1321), Italian poet.

Darney. Near side. 15°S, 24°W. 15 km. In the Fra Mauro area in the Mare Nubium. Bright. Named for Maurice Darney (1882–1958), French astronomer.

D'Arrest. Near side. 2°N, 15°E. 30 km. West of Sabine and Ritter. Has low walls. Named for Heinrich d'Arrest (1822–1875), German astronomer.

D'Arsonval. Far side. 10°S, 125°E. 29 km. Breaks in on the NE rim of Danjon, to the east of Langemak and west of Perepel'kin. Named for Arsène d'Arsonval (1851–1940), French biophysicist.

Darwin. Near side. 20°S, 69°W. 130 km. In the area of Grimaldi. Is very irregular, has low walls, and contains a large dome. Named for Sir George Darwin (1845–1912), British astronomer.

Darwin, Rimae. Near side. 20°S, 67°W. 280 km long. A rill system in the area of Darwin (q.v.), in association with which it was named.

Das. Far side. 14°S, 152°W. 39 km. Immediately to the NE of Galois, and SE of Korolev. Named for Amil Das (1902–1961), Indian astronomer.

Daubrée. Near side. 16°N, 15°E. 14 km. Formerly called Menelaus S. Named for Gabriel-Auguste Daubrée (1814–1896), French geologist.

Da Vinci. Near side. 9°N, 45°E. 38 km. In the area of Palus Somnii. Has low walls. Named for Leonardo da Vinci (1452–1519), Italian scientist.

Davisson. Far side. 38°S, 175°W. 87 km. On the eastern rim of Leibnitz, between Mare Ingenii and Apollo. Named for Clinton Davisson (1881–1958), American physicist.

Davy. Near side. 12°S, 8°W. 35 km. A ring formation on the eastern edge of the Mare Nubium. Has irregular walls and a gap in its north wall. It has a low central peak. Named for Sir Humphrey Davy (1778–1829), British scientist.

Dawes. Near side. 17°N, 26°E. 18 km. Between Mare Serenitatis and Mare Tranquillitatis. Distinct. Named for William R. Dawes (1799–1868), British astronomer.

Dawson. Far side. 67°S, 134°W. 45 km. North of Zeeman and south of Fizeau. Named for John Dawson (1820–1899), Canadian geologist.

Debes. Near side. 29°N, 52°E. 31 km. Outside Cleomedes. It is composed of two rings joined together. Named for Ernest Debes (1840–1923), German cartographer.

Debye. Far side. 50°N, 177°W. 122 km. SW of Birkhoff, and SE of D'Alembert. Named for Peter Debye (1884–1966), Dutch physicist.

Dechen. Near side. 46°N, 67°W. 12 km. In the NW area of Oceanus Procellarum. Not very bright. Named for Heinrich von Dechen (1800–1889), German geologist.

De Forest. Far side. 76°S, 162°W. 58 km. Between Zeeman and Schrödinger. Named for Lee de Forest (1873–1961), American inventor.

De Gasperis. Near side. 26°S, 50°W. 30 km. Formerly called Cavendish D. South of Mersenius, in the area west of the Mare Humorum. Quite regular. Named for Annibale De Gasperis (1819–1892), Italian astronomer.

De Gasperis, Rimae. Near side. 25°S, 50°W. 130 km long. A system of rills in the area of De Gasperis (q.v.), in association with which it was named.

Delambre. Near side. 2°S, 18°E. 52 km. In the area of Mare Tranquillitatis. Polygonal, with high terraced walls, it has a low central peak and a bright crater on the summit of the north wall. Named for Jean Baptiste Delambre (1749–1822), French astronomer.

De La Rue. Near side. 67°N, 56°E. 136 km. Adjoins Endymion to the NW. Has very low, broken walls. Named for Warren de la Rue (1815–1889), British astronomer.

Delaunay. Near side. 22°S, 3°E. 46 km. Near Faye, in the area of Albategnius. Irregular. Named for Charles Delaunay (1816–1872), French astronomer.

De L'Isle. Near side. 30°N, 35°W. 25 km. Also spelled Delisle. Forms a pair with Diophantus, on the Oceanus Procellarum. Has a central peak. Named for Joseph Nicolas Delisle (1688–1768), French astronomer.

Dellinger. Far side. 7°S, 140°E. 81 km. South of Pannekoek, and NW of Gagarin, in the area south of Mendeleev. Named for John H. Dellinger (1886–1962), American radio engineer.

Delmotte. Near side. 27°N, 60°E. 33 km. North of Mare Crisium. Not prominent. Named for Gabriel Delmotte (1876–1950), French selenographer.

Delporte. Far side. 16°S, 121°E. 46 km. NW of Tsiolkovskiy. Named for Augustin Delporte (1844–1891), Belgian astronomer.

Deluc. Near side. 55°S, 3°W. 47 km. In the area of Clavius. Has moderate-sized walls. Named for Jean André Deluc (1727–1817), Swiss geologist.

Dembowski. Near side. 3°N, 7°E. 26 km. East of Sinus Medii. Has low walls. Named for Ercole Dembowski (1812–1881), Italian astronomer.

Democritus. Near side. 62°N, 35°E. 39 km. In the highlands north of Mare Frigoris. Very deep. Named for Democritus (c.460–357 B.C.), Greek philosopher.

Demonax. Near side. 85°S, 35°E. 114 km. In the area of Boguslawsky. Quite regular. Named for Demonax (fl. 125 B.C.), Greek philosopher.

De Moraes. Far side. 49°N, 143°E. 54 km. Immediately SW of Van Rhijn, in the area NW of Campbell. Named for Luciano de Moraes, the 20th century Portuguese geologist.

De Morgan. Near side. 3°N, 15°E. 10 km. In the uplands west of Mare Tranquillitatis. Bright. Named for Augustus De Morgan (1806–1871), British mathematician.

Denning. Far side. 16°S, 143°E. 44 km. NW of Gagarin and NE of Tsiolkovskiy. Named for William F. Denning (1848–1931), British astronomer.

De Roy. Far side. 55°S, 99°W. 44 km. NW of Hausen, and west of Arrhenius. Named for Felix De Roy (1883–1942), Belgian astronomer.

Desargues. Near side. 70°N, 73°W. 85 km. Named for Gérard Desargues (1592–1662), French mathematician.

Descartes. Near side. 12°S, 16°E. 48 km. NE of Abulfeda. Has low, broken walls. Named for René Descartes (1596–1650), French mathematician-philosopher.

Deseilligny. Near side. 21°N, 21°E. 6 km. On Mare Serenitatis. Distinct. Named for Jules Deseilligny (1868–1918), French selenographer.

De Sitter. Near side. 80°N, 40°E. 65 km. Named for Willem de Sitter (1872–1934), Dutch astronomer.

Deslandres. Near side. 32°S, 61°W. 234 km. Formerly called Hörbiger. Also known as Hell Plain (Hell [q.v.] is on its interior). A huge plain in the form of a ruined enclosure. Irregular, it has many craterlets, craters and hills. Lexell (q.v.) breaks in on it on the south, to the west of Walter. Named for Henri Deslandres (1853–1948), French astronomer.

Deutsch. Far side. 24°N, 111°E. 66 km. SE of Lomonosov, and to the east of Joliot. Named for Armin Deutsch (1918–1969), American astronomer.

De Vico. Near side. 20°S, 60°W. 20 km. West of Gassendi. Deep. Named for Francesco de Vico (1805–1848), Italian astronomer.

Deville, Cape. Near side. 43°N, 1°E. 20 km long. Also called Promontorium Deville. Near Cape Agassiz, in the Mare Imbrium. Named for Charles

Saint-Clair Deville (1814–1876), French volcanologist.

De Vries. Far side. 20°S. 177°W. 60 km. SE of Aitken, and SW of Korolev. Named for Hugo de Vries (1848–1935), Dutch botanist.

Dewar. Far side. 3°S, 166°E. 50 km. North of Stratton, and north of the point where Keeler and Heaviside meet. Named for Sir James Dewar (1842–1923), British physicist.

Diderot. Far side. 20°S, 121°E. 20 km. On the SE rim of Fermi, just to the west of Tsiolkovskiy. Named for Denis Diderot (1713–1784), French philosopher.

Dionysius. Near side. 3°N, 17°E. 18 km. On the edge of the Mare Tranquillitatis. Brilliant. Named for Dionysius Periegetes (fl. c. 4th century A.D.), Greek poet.

Diophantus. Near side. 28°N, 34°W. 18 km. Forms a pair with De L'Isle, on the Oceanus Procellarum. Has a central peak. Named for Diophantus (fl. c. A.D. 250), Greek mathematician.

Dirichlet. Far side. 10°N, 151°W. 47 km. South of the western rim of Mach, and north of the extreme eastern edge of Korolev. Named for Peter Dirichlet (1805–1859), German mathematician.

Dobrovol'skiy. Far side. 13°S, 130°E. 38 km. South of the eastern rim of Perepel'kin, in the area NW of Gagarin and SW of Mendeleev. Named for Georgiy T. Dobrovol'skiy (1928–1971), USSR cosmonaut.

Doerfel. Far side. 69°S, 108°W. 68 km. NE of Zeeman, and west of the southern portion of Bailly. Named for Georg Dörffel (Doerfel) (1643–1688), German astronomer.

Dollond. Near side. 10°S, 14°E. 11 km. West of Theophilus. It borders a large ghost-crater. Named for John Dollond (1706–1761), British telescope-maker.

Doloris, Lacus. Near side. 17°N, 9°E. 110 km. Means "Lake of Pain" in Latin.

Donati. Near side. 21°S, 5°E. 36 km. Forms a pair with Faye, south of Albategnius. Irregular, it has a central peak. Named for Giovanni Battista Donati (1826–1873), Italian astronomer.

Donner. Far side. 31°S, 98°E. 58 km. To the immediate NE of Mare Australe. Named for Anders S. Donner (1873–1949), Finnish astronomer.

Doppelmayer. Near side. 28°S, 41°W. 64 km. A ring formation in the Mare Humorum. It has a central peak of 2500 feet, cut in two by a ravine. Named for Johann Gabriel Doppelmayr (Doppelmayer) (c.1671–1750), German astronomer.

Doppelmayer, Rimae. Near side. 26°S, 45°W. 130 km. A rill system in the area of Doppelmayer (q.v.), in association with which it was named.

Doppler. Far side. 13°S, 160°W. 90 km. Breaks into the southern rim of Korolev, to the NW of Galois. Named for Christian Doppler (1803–1853), German physicist.

Dorsa (plural of Dorsum). A dorsum is a ridge or scarp. (*See* **Cloos, Dorsum.**)

Douglass. Far side. 35°N, 122°W. 49 km. South of the western rim of Landau, in the area SW of Frost. Named for Andrew E. Douglass (1867–1962), American astronomer.

Dove. Near side. 47°S, 32°E. 30 km. In the area of Janssen. Has low walls. Named for Heinrich Dove (1803–1879), German physicist.

Draper. Near side. 18°N, 22°W. 8 km. South of Pytheas, in the Mare Imbrium. Named for Henry Draper (1837–1882), American celestial photographer.

Drebbel. Near side. 41°S, 49°W. 30 km. In the area of Schickard. Well-formed. Named for Cornelis Van Drebbel (1572–1634), Dutch natural philosopher.

Dreyer. Far side. 10°N, 97°E. 62 km. East of the Mare Marginis, and NE of the Mare Smythii. Named for John Dreyer (1852–1926), Dutch astronomer.

Drude. Far side. 39°S, 91°W. 25 km. South of the Mare Orientale, and NE of Mendel. Named for Paul Drude (1863–1906), German physicist.

Dryden. Far side. 33°S, 157°W. 52 km. In the NW sector of Apollo. Named for Hugh Dryden (1898–1965), American physicist.

Drygalski. Near side. 80°S, 55°W. 163 km. Adjoins Legentil, in the area of Bailly. Named for Erich von Drygalski (1865–1949), German polar explorer.

Dubiago. Near side. 51 km. Also spelled Dubyago. In the area of the Mare Smythii. Regular. Named for Dmitriy Dubiago (1850–1918), Russian astronomer.

Dufay. Far side. 5°N, 170°E. 39 km. SW of Valier, and east of Mandelstam, in the area between Mare Moscoviense and Korolev. Named for Jean Dufay (1896–1967), French astronomer.

Dugan. Far side. 65°N, 103°E. 51 km. SW of Schwarzschild, and north of Compton. Named for Raymond Dugan (1878–1940), American astronomer.

Dunér. Far side. 45°N, 179°E. 63 km. SW of D'Alembert. Named for Nils Dunér (1839–1914), Swedish astronomer.

Dunthorne. Near side. 30°S, 32°W. 16 km. On the edge of the Palus Epidemiarum. Has broad walls. Named for Richard Dunthorne (1711–1775), British astronomer.

Dyson. Far side. 61°N, 121°W. 63 km. East of Stebbins, and north of the western edge of Landau. Named for Sir Frank Dyson (1868–1939), British astronomer.

Dziewulski. Far side. 21°N, 99°E. 63 km. South of Lomonosov, and SE of Joliot. Named for Wladyslaw Dziewulski (1878–1962), Polish astronomer.

Dziewulski, Catena. Far side. 19°N, 100°E. 80 km long. A chain of craters to the south of Joliot, in the area of Dziewulski (q.v.), in association with which it was named.

Eckert. Near side. 17°N, 58°E. 3 km. Named for Wallace Eckert (1902–1971), American celestial mechanician.

Eclipses *see* **Lunar Eclipses**

Eddington. Near side. 21°N, 72°W. 125 km. Named for Sir Arthur Eddington (1882–1944), British astronomer.

Edison. Far side. 25°N, 99°E. 62 km. South of Lomonosov and SE of Joliot. Named for Thomas Alva Edison (1847–1931), American inventor.

Egede. Near side. 49°N, 11°E. 37 km. Near the Alpine Valley. Is lozenge-shaped and has low walls. Named for N. Egede (fl. 1787), Danish navigator.

Ehrlich. Far side. 41°N, 172°W. 31 km. SW of Schneller, and north of Parsons. Named for Paul Ehrlich (1854–1915), German biochemist.

Eichstädt. Near side. 23°S, 80°W. 49 km. In the area of the Mare Orientale. Regular. Named for Lorenz Eichstadt (1596–1660), German mathematician.

Eijkman. Far side. 62°S, 141°W. 55 km. SW of Fizeau, and NE of

Numerov. Named for Christiaan Eijkman (1858–1930), Dutch hygienist.

Eimmart. Near side. 24°N, 65°E. 46 km. Near the edge of the Mare Crisium. Regular. Named for Georg Eimmart (1638–1705), German astronomer.

Einstein. Far and near sides. 18°N, 86°W. 170 km. Named Caramuel on some of the older maps. A vast crater in the area of Otto Struve, north of the Mare Orientale and west of the Oceanus Procellarum. Has a central crater, high walls, and a long ridge on its floor. It is visible on the limb when seen from Earth under ideal conditions. Discovered by Patrick Moore in 1952, and named for Albert Einstein (1879–1955), Swiss physicist.

Einthoven. Far side. 5°S, 110°E. 69 km. East of the Mare Smythii, and SW of Mendeleev. Named for William Einthoven (1860–1927), Dutch physiologist.

Elger. Near side. 35°S, 30°W. 21 km. On the edge of the Palus Epidemiarum. Imperfect, it has low walls. Named for T. Gwyn Elger (1838–1897), lunar cartographer.

Ellerman. Far side. 26°S, 121°W. 47 km. SE of Gerasimovič and Von der Pahlen, in the area to the SW of the Mare Orientale. Named for Ferdinand Ellerman (1869–1940), American astronomer.

Ellison. Far side. 55°N, 108°W. 37 km. East of Birkhoff, and west of the northern portion of the Oceanus Procellarum. Named for Mervyn Ellison (1909–1963), Irish astronomer.

Elmer. Near side. 10°S, 84°E. 17 km. Named for William Elmer (b. 1901), American telescope designer.

Elvey. Far side. 9°N, 101°W. 74 km. SE of Pease, and north of the Mare Orientale. Named for Christian Elvey (1899–1970), American astro-geophysicist.

Emden. Far side. 63°N, 176°W. 110 km. West of Sommerfeld, and south of Roberts. Named for Robert Emden (1862–1940), Swiss astrophysicist.

Encke. Near side. 5°N, 37°W. 28 km. In the area of Kepler, its floor is depressed to 1000 feet below the surrounding Oceanus Procellarum. A high ridge runs along the floor from north to south and splits into two at its north end. Named for Johann Encke (1791–1865), German astronomer.

Endymion. Near side. 55°N, 55°E. 125 km. In the area of the Mare Humboldtianum. Has a darkish floor. Named for the Greek mythological character.

Engelhardt. Far side. 5°N, 159°W. 43 km. Also spelled Englehardt. SE of Lebedinsky, and north of Korolev. Named for Vasiliy Engelhardt (1828–1915), Russian astronomer.

Eötvös. Far side. 36°S, 134°E. 99 km. SE of Tsiolkovskiy and SW of Pavlov, and north of the eastern rim of Roche. Named for Roland von Eötvös (1848–1919), Hungarian physicist.

Epidemiarum, Palus. Near side. 31°S, 26°W. 300 km. A conspicuous dark plain extending out of the Mare Nubium. It contains many rills known as the Ramsden system. Name means "Marsh of Epidemics" in Latin. Named by Schmidt.

Epigenes. Near side. 73°N, 4°W. 55 km. North of the Mare Frigoris. Has several craters on its north and SW crests, and several hills on its floor. It has broad walls. Named for Epigenes (fl. 1st century), Greek astronomer.

Epimenides. Near side. 41°S, 30°W. 27 km. East of Hainzel. Named for Epimenides (fl. 7th and 6th centuries), Cretan poet.

Eppinger. Near side. 9°S, 26°W. 6 km. Formerly called Euclides D. Named for Hans Eppinger (1879–1946), Austrian clinician.

Eratosthenes. Near side. 15°N, 11°W. 58 km. At the very south of the Apennines. It is very deep, and has a complex central mountain. Named for Eratosthenes (c.276–c.196 B.C.), Alexandrian astronomer.

Erro. Far side. 6°N, 98°E. 62 km. NE of Mare Smythii, and NW of Sänger. Named for Luis E. Erro (1897–1955), Mexican astronomer.

Esclangon. Near side. 21°N, 42°E. 16 km. Formerly called Macrobius L. Named for Ernest Esclangon (1876–1954), French astronomer.

Esnault-Pelterie. Far side. 47°N, 142°W. 79 km. NE of Fowler, it borders Schlesinger on the latter's west rim. Named for Robert Esnault-Pelterie (1881–1957), French aeronautics pioneer.

Espin. Far side. 28°N, 109°E. 76 km. SE of Szilard, and east of the northern rim of Joliot. Named for Thomas Espin (1858–1934), British astronomer.

Euclides. Near side. 7°S, 29°W. 11 km. Lies on a bright nimbus, near the Riphaens. Named for Euclid (fl. c.323–285 B.C.), Greek mathematician.

Euctemon. Near side. 76°N, 31°E. 62 km. Named for Euctemon (fl. 5th century B.C.), Greek astronomer.

Eudoxus. Near side. 44°N, 16°E. 67 km. Forms a pair with Aristoteles, south of Mare Frigoris. Has high, prominently-terraced walls, and a circular arrangement of hills is on the floor's southern part. Named for Eudoxus of Cnidus (c.409–c.356 B.C.), Greek astronomer.

Euler. Near side. 23°N, 29°W. 28 km. The center of a minor ray system, in the Mare Imbrium. Named for Leonhard Euler (1707–1783), Swiss mathematician.

Evans. Far side. 10°S, 134°W. 68 km. South of the western portion of Hertzsprung, and east of the southern extremity of Korolev. Named for Sir Arthur Evans (1851–1941), British archeologist.

Evdokimov. Far side. 35°N, 153°W. 50 km. East of the southern portion of Evershed, and SW of Fowler. Named for Nikolay N. Evdokimov (1868–1940), Russian astronomer.

Evershed. Far side. 36°N, 160°W. 67 km. SW of Fowler, and NE of Cockcroft. Named for John Evershed (1864–1956), British solar physicist.

Excellentiae, Lacus. Near side. 36°S, 43°W. 150 km. Means "Lake of Excellence" in Latin.

Explorer Spacecraft. A series of U.S. Moon probes. *Explorer 33:* Launched July 1, 1966. Failed to orbit the Moon. *Explorer 35:* Launched July 19, 1967. Studied Earth's magnetic field. *Explorer 49:* Launched June 10, 1973. Carried out radio astronomy from the far side of the Moon.

Fabbroni. Near side. 19°N, 29°E. 11 km. Formerly called Vitruvius E. Named for Giovanni Fabbroni (1752–1822), Italian physicist.

Fabricius. Near side. 43°S, 42°E. 78 km. Breaks into Janssen. Has a rough floor and a central peak. Named for David Fabricius (1564–1617), German astronomer.

Fabry. Far side. 43°N, 100°E. 179 km. One of the main lunar features, it lies in the NE portion of the Harkhebi enclosure, in the area NW of Mare Moscoviense. Named for Louis Fabry (1862–1939), French astronomer.

Fahrenheit. Near side. 13°N, 62°E. 6 km. Formerly called Picard X. Named for Gabriel Fahrenheit (1686–1736), German physicist.

Faraday. Near side. 42°S, 8°E. 70 km. A large, irregular formation, breaking in on the SW of Stöfler. Named for Michael Faraday (1791–1867), British physicist.

Fauth. Near side. 6°N, 20°W. 12 km. South of Copernicus, on the Oceanus Procellarum. Named for Philipp Fauth (1867–1943), German astronomer.

Faye. Near side. 21°S, 4°E. 37 km. Forms a pair with Donati, south of Albategnius. It is irregular and has a central peak. Named for Hervé Faye (1814–1902), French astronomer.

Fechner. Far side. 58°S, 125°E. 63 km. Part of it is on the Rima Planck, north of Schrödinger. Named for Gustav Fechner (1801–1887), German psychophysicist.

Fecunditatis, Mare. Near side. 8°S, 51°E. 840 km. Connected to the Mare Tranquillitatis, almost at the eastern limb of the Moon. Not regular, it has no high mountain borders and does not have many large craters in it. The Messier objects are in it. Name means "Sea of Fertility" in Latin.

Fedorov. Near side. 28°N, 37°W. 7 km. Named for Yevgeniy Fedorov (b. 1909), Russian astronomer.

Felicitatis, Lacus. Near side. 19°N, 5°E. 90 km. Name means "Lake of Happiness" in Latin.

Fenyi. Far side. 45°S, 105°W. 39 km. NE of Mendel, and SE of Chant, in the area south of the western rim of Mare Orientale. Named for J. Fenyi (1845–1927), Hungarian astronomer.

Feoktistov. Far side. 31°N, 140°E. 23 km. SE of Nijland, and just to the NW of Mare Moscoviense. Named for Konstantin P. Feoktistov (b. 1926), Russian space engineer.

Fermat. Near side. 23°S, 20°E. 39 km. In the area of Altai. Distinct. Named for Pierre de Fermat (1601–1665), French mathematician.

Fermi. Far side. 20°S, 122°E. 238 km. Just NW of Tsiolkovskiy. Named for Enrico Fermi (1901–1954), Italian physicist.

Fernelius. Near side. 38°S, 5°E. 65 km. North of Stöfler. Quite irregular. Named for Jean Fernel (c.1497–1558), French astronomer.

Fersman. Far side. 18°N, 126°W. 143 km. Between Poynting and Weyl, to the north of Hertzsprung. Named for Aleksandr Fersman (1883–1945), Russian mineralogist.

Fesenkov. Far side. 23°S, 135°E. 35 km. SE of Tsiolkovskiy, and NW of Pavlov. Named for Vasiliy Fesenkov (1889–1972), Russian astrophysicist.

Feuillé. Near side. 27°N, 10°W. 9 km. Forms a pair with Beer, on the Mare Imbrium. Named for Louis Feuillé (1660–1732), French astronomer.

Fidei, Sinus. Near side. 18°N, 2°E. 70 km. Means "Bay of Faith" in Latin.

Finsch. Near side. 24°N, 21°E. 4 km. Named for Otto Finsch (1839–1917), German zoologist.

Finsen. Far side. 42°S, 178°W. 73 km. On the SE rim of Leibnitz and the NE rim of Von Kármán. Named for Niels Finsen (1860–1904), Danish physician.

Firmicus. Near side. 7°N, 64°E. 56 km. South of Mare Crisium. Has a dark floor and no central peak. Named for Julius Firmicus Maternus (fl. 4th century A.D.), Italian author.

Firsov. Far side. 4°N, 112°E. 52 km. NW of Abul Wafa, between the Mare Smythii and Mendeleev. Named for Georgiy Firsov (1917–1960), Russian rocket engineer.

Fischer. Far side. 8°N, 142°E. 31 km. South of the eastern rim of Leibnitz, and immediately NE of Von Kármán. Named for Emil Fischer (1852–1919), German chemist.

Fitzgerald. Far side. 27°N, 172°W. 108 km. SW of Cockcroft, and north of Morse, to the east of the Mare Moscoviense. Named for George Fitzgerald (1851–1901), Irish physicist.

Fizeau. Far side. 58°S, 133°W. 108 km. North of Zeeman, and SE of Minkowski. Named for Armand Fizeau (1819–1896), French physicist.

Flammarion. Near side. 3°S, 44°W. 75 km. An irregular, dark-floored plain enclosed by broken walls near the SW border of Sinus Medii, NW of Ptolemaeus. Named for Camille Flammarion (1842–1925), French astronomer.

Flammarion, Rima. Near side. 2°S, 5°W. 80 km. A rill associated with Flammarion (q.v.), in association with which it was named.

Flamsteed. Near side. 5°S, 44°W. 21 km. On the Oceanus Procellarum. Associated with a 100-km ghost-crater. Named for John Flamsteed (1646–1719), British astronomer.

Fleming. Far side. 15°N, 109°E. 130 km. Between Joliot and Mendeleev. Named for Mrs. Williamina Paton Stevens Fleming (1857–1911), Scottish astronomer.

Focas. Far side. 34°S, 94°W. 22 km. To the immediate south of the Mare Orientale, just beyond Montes Rook. Named for Ioannis Focas (1908–1969), Greek astronomer.

Foecunditatis, Mare *see* **Fecunditatis, Mare**

Fontana. Near side. 16°S, 57°W. 31 km. Between Billy and Crüger. It has a central peak. Named for Francesco Fontana (c.1585–1656), Italian lunar cartographer.

Fontenelle. Near side. 63°N, 19°W. 38 km. On the northern edge of the Mare Frigoris. Deep and distinct. Named for Bernard le Bovier de Fontenelle (1657–1757), French philosopher.

Foster. Far side. 23°N, 142°W. 33 km. Immediately south of Joule, in the area to the NW of Hertzsprung. Named for Henry Foster (1797–1831), British geophysicist.

Foucault. Near side. 50°N, 40°W. 23 km. In the area of the Jura Mountains. Bright and deep. Named for Léon Foucault (1819–1868), French physicist.

Fourier. Near side. 30°S, 53°W. 52 km. A ring formation west of the Mare Humorum. It has terraced walls. One peak on the west rises to 9500 feet above the floor. It has a small central crater. Named for Jean Baptiste Fourier (1768–1830), French mathematician.

Fowler. Far side. 43°N, 145°W. 136 km. West of Landau. Its eastern wall is broken by Von Zeipel. Named for Alfred Fowler (1868–1940), British astrophysicist.

Fox. Far side. 1°N, 98°E. 25 km. Breaks into the northern rim of Wyld, in the area just to the east of Mare Smythii. Named for Sidney W. Fox (b. 1912), American biochemist.

Fracastorius. Near side. 21°S, 33°E. 124 km. South of Mare Nectaris. Named for Girolamo Fracastoro (1483–1553), Italian physician.

Fra Mauro. Near side. 6°S, 17°W. 95 km. A ruined ring plain, it forms a group with Bonpland and Parry, on the Mare Nubium. It has many small craters and ridges on its floor and it has low walls. Named for Fra Mauro (d. c.1459), Italian geographer.

Franck. Near side. 23°N, 35°E. 12 km. Formerly called Rømer K. Named for James Franck (1882–1964), German physicist.

Franklin. Near side. 39°N, 48°E. 56 km. SE of Atlas. Regular. Named for Benjamin Franklin (1706–1790), American scientist.

Franz. Near side. 16°N, 40°E. 26 km. On the edge of the Palus Somnii. Has low walls. Named for Julius H. Franz (1847–1913), German astronomer.

Fraunhofer. Near side. 39°S, 59°E. 57 km. South of Furnerius. Its NW wall is broken by craters. Named for Joseph von Fraunhofer (1787–1826), German optician.

Fredholm. Near side. 18°N, 46°E. 15 km. Formerly called Macrobius D. Named for Erik Fredholm (1866–1927), Swedish mathematician.

Fresnel, Cape. Near side. 29°N, 5°E. 20 km. Also called Promontorium Fresnel. Forms the northern end of the Apennines, in the Mare Serenitatis. Named for Augustin Fresnel (1788–1827), French physicist.

Fresnel, Rimae. Near side. 28°N, 4° E. 90 km. A rill system in the area of Cape Fresnel, in association with which it was named.

Freud. Near side. 26°N, 52°W. 3 km. Named for Sigmund Freud (1856–1939), Austrian psychoanalyst.

Freundlich. Far side. 25°N, 171°E. 85 km. SE of Trumpler, and east of the Mare Moscoviense. Named for Erwin Freundlich (1885–1964), German astronomer.

Fridman. Far side. 13°S, 127°W. 104 km. Also spelled Friedmann. South of Hertzsprung, and immediately NE of Joffe. Named for Aleksandr Fridman (1888–1925), Russian mathematician.

Frigoris, Mare. Near side. 55°N, 5°E. 1350 km. A former basin which separates the Alpine region from the highlands around the North Pole. Irregular in shape, it has a light and patchy floor and includes the craters Galle and Protagoras. Name means "The Sea of Cold" in Latin.

Froelich. Far side. 80°N, 110°W. 58 km. South of Lovelace, north of Merrill, and NW of Brianchon, it is one of the largest features north of 70°N. Named for Jack Froelich (1921–1967), American rocket engineer.

Frost. Far side. 37°N, 119°W. 76 km. Breaks in on the southern rim of Landau. Named for Edwin B. Frost (1866–1935), American astronomer.

Furnerius. Near side. 36°S, 60°E. 125 km. Also spelled Furnelius. A walled plain in the Petavius chain, it has a level floor and some small craterlets on it. Its walls are quite broken. Named for Georges Furner (fl. c.1643), French mathematician.

Furnerius, Rima. Near side. 50 km long. A rill in Furnerius (q.v.), in association with which it was named.

G. Bond, Rima. Near side. 33°N, 35°E. 150 km. long. A rill in the area of Bond, G. P. (q.v.), in association with which it was named.

Gadomski. Far side. 36°N, 147°W. 65 km. West of the southern rim of Klute, and south of Fowler. Named for Jan Gadomski (1889–1966), Polish astronomer.

Gagarin. Far side. 20°S, 150°E. 272 km. Between Mendeleev and the Mare Ingenii. Named for Yuriy Gagarin (1934–1968), USSR cosmonaut.

Galen. Near side. 22°N, 5°E. 10 km. Formerly called Aratus A. Named for Galen (c.130–200), Greek physician.

Galilaei. Near side. 10°N, 63°W. 16 km. On the Oceanus Procellarum.

Inconspicuous. Named for Galileo Galilei (1564–1642), Italian astronomer.

Galle. Near side. 56°N, 22°E. 21 km. On the Mare Frigoris. Distinct. Named for Johann Galle (1812–1910), German astronomer.

Galois. Far side. 16°S, 153°W. 207 km. Just SE of Korolev. Named for Évariste Galois (1811–1832), French mathematician.

Galvani. Near side. 50°N, 85°W. 80 km. Named for Luigi Galvani (1737–1798), Italian physicist.

Gambart. Near side. 1°N, 15°W. 25 km. 200 kilometers SSE of Copernicus, on the Oceanus Procellarum. A strange-shaped ring formation with low walls, it has a level floor with a light patch on the south and no central peak. Named for Jean Gambart (1800–1836), French astronomer.

Gamow. Far side. 65°N, 143°E. 116 km. Also spelled Gamov. SW of Schjellerup and west of Avogadro. Named for George Gamow (1904–1968), American physicist.

Ganswindt. Far side. 79°S, 110°E. 75 km. SW of Schrödinger, and north of Idel'son. Named for Hermann Ganswindt (1856–1934), German engineer.

Garavito. Far side. 48°S, 157°E. 75 km. North of Lamarck, and SE of Koch. Named for J. Garavito (1865–1920), Colombian astronomer.

Gardner. Near side. 18°N, 34°E. 18 km. Formerly called Vitruvius A. Named for Lester Gardner (1876–1956), American aeronautics pioneer.

Gärtner. Near side. 60°N, 34°E. 102 km. Named for Christian Gärtner (1750–1813), German geologist.

Gärtner, Rima. 30 km. In Gärtner (q.v.), in association with which it was named.

Gassendi. Near side. 18°S, 40°W. 110 km. A walled plain on the edge of the Mare Humorum. One of the Moon's major features, it has high walls, and a central group of peaks, the highest being 4000 feet. It has on its floor two bright craterlets and between 30 and 40 clefts making up the system of rills known as Rimae Gassendi (q.v.). Named for Pierre Gassendi (1592–1655), French astronomer.

Gassendi, Rimae. Near side. 70 km long. In Gassendi (q.v.), in association with which this rill system was named.

Gaudibert. Near side. 11°S, 37°E. 34 km. On the edge of the Mare Nectaris. Has low walls. Named for Casimir Gaudibert (1823–1901), French selenographer.

Gaudii, Lacus. Near side. 17°N, 13°E. 100 km. Name means "Lake of Joy" in Latin.

Gauricus. Near side. 34°S, 12°W. 79 km. A large walled formation in the Pitatus group. Has an irregular border. Named for Luke Gaurico (1476–1558), Italian astronomer.

Gauss. Near side. 36°N, 80°E. 177 km. Along the limb from the Mare Humboldtianum. Has high walls and a central peak. Named for Karl Gauss (1777–1855), German astronomer.

Gavrilov. Far side. 17°N, 131°E. 60 km. NW of Hoffmeister, and SW of the Mare Moscoviense. Named for Aleksandr Gavrilov (1884–1955), Russian rocket engineer.

Gay-Lussac. Near side. 14°N, 21°W. 26 km. An irregular enclosure north of Copernicus. Named for Joseph Gay-Lussac (1778–1850), French chemist.

Gay-Lussac, Rima. Near side. 13° N, 22°W. 40 km. A rill in the area of Gay-Lussac (q.v.), in association with which it was named.

Geber. Near side. 20°S, 14°E. 45 km. Between Almanon and Abenezra. It is regular and has very regular walls. Named for Geber ibn Aflah (fl. 12th century), Arab astronomer.

Geiger. Far side. 14°S, 158°E. 34 km. East of the northern rim of Gagarin, and south of the western rim of Keeler. Named for Hans Geiger (1882–1947), German physicist.

Geissler. Near side. 3°S, 76°E. 16 km. Formerly called Gilbert D. Named for Heinrich Geissler (1814–1879), German mechanician.

Geminus. Near side. 35°N, 57°E. 86 km. In the area of the Mare Crisium. Has broad terraced walls and a central hill. Named for Geminus (fl. c.70 B.C.), Greek astronomer.

Gemma Frisius. Near side. 34°S, 14°E. 88 km. A great walled plain north of Maurolycus. Goodacre breaks in on it to the north. Its broken walls rise to 14,000 feet above the floor, and it has a nearly central hill on its floor. Named for Reiner Gemma Frisius (1508–1555), Dutch geographer.

Gerard. Near side. 44°N, 75°W. 90 km. West of Sinus Roris. Quite distinct. Named for Gerard of Silteo (fl. 13th century), French astronomer.

Gerasimovič. Far side. 23°S, 124°W. 87 km. Also spelled Gerasimovich. NE of Von der Pahlen, between the Mare Orientale and Apollo. Named for Boris Gerasimovič (1889–1937), Ukrainian astronomer.

Gernsback. Far side. 36°S, 99°E. 48 km. In the NE sector of the Mare Australe, to the SW of Parkhurst. Named for Hugo Gernsback (1884–1967), American science fiction writer.

Gibbs. Near side. 18°S, 84°E. 77 km. Named for Josiah Gibbs (1839–1903), American physicist.

Gilbert. Near side. 3°S, 76°E. 107 km. Named for Grove Gilbert (1843–1918), American geologist.

Gill. Near side. 64°S, 76°E. 66 km. Named for Sir David Gill (1843–1914), Scottish astronomer.

Ginzel. Far side. 14°N, 97°E. 55 km. Breaks into the western rim of the Mare Marginis, north of Dreyer. Named for Friedrich K. Ginzel (1850–1926), German astronomer.

Gioja. Near side. 42 km. In the area of the North Pole. Quite distinct and regular. Named for Flavio Gioja (fl. early 14th century), Italian navigator.

Giordano Bruno. Far side. 36°N, 103°E. 22 km. One of the smaller fresh craters, this one lies between Fabry and Szilard, and has long rays that extend hundreds of kilometers onto the near side of the Moon, west and north of Mare Crisium. The impact that formed this very fresh crater may have taken place in A.D. 1178 (*see* **Phenomena and Discoveries**). Named for Giordano Bruno (c.1548–1600), Italian philosopher.

Glaisher. Near side. 13°N, 49°E. 16 km. On the west border of the Mare Crisium. Obscure. Named for James Glaisher (1809–1903), British meteorologist.

Glasenapp. Far side. 2°S, 138°E. 44 km. Also spelled Glazenap. Just to the south of Mendeleev, and NW of Pannekoek. Named for Sergei P. Glazenap (1848–1937), Russian astronomer.

Glauber. Far side. 11°N, 143°E. 16 km. On the northern rim of Mendeleev. Named for Johann Glauber (1604–1668), German chemist.

Goclenius. Near side. 10°S, 45°E. 72 km. On the edge of the Mare Fecunditatis. Lava-flooded, it has a low central peak. Named for Rudolf Goeckel (Goclenius) (1572–1621), German magnetist.

Goclenius, Rimae. Near side. 8°S, 43°E. 240 km long. A rill system in the area of Goclenius (q.v.), in association with which it was named.

Goddard. Far side, but extends onto the near side as well. 16°N, 90°E. 89 km. Just SW of Al-Biruni, on the eastern rim of the Mare Marginis. Named for Robert H. Goddard (1882–1945), American physicist.

Godin. Near side. 2°N, 10°E. 35 km. Forms a pair with Agrippa, south of the Mare Humorum. Heart-shaped, it has terraced inner slopes and a central hill. On the south is a trumpet-shaped valley, notable at sunrise. Named for Louis Godin (1704–1760), French astronomer.

Goldschmidt. Near side. 75°N, 0°. 120 km. A large ring structure north of the Mare Frigoris. Anaxagoras breaks in on its eastern rim. Has broken walls and several craterlets on its light-colored floor. Named for Hermann Goldschmidt (1802–1866), German astronomer.

Golgi. Near side. 28°N, 60°W. 5 km. Formerly called Schiaparelli D. Named for Camillo Golgi (1844–1926), Italian pathologist.

Golitzyn. Far side. 25°S, 105°W. 36 km. Also spelled Golitsyn. To the immediate SW of the Mare Orientale. Named for Prince Boris Golitzyn (1862–1916), Russian physicist.

Golovin. Far side. 40°N, 161°E. 38 km. South of Langevin, SE of Campbell, and NE of Mare Moscoviense. Named for Nicholas Golovin (1912–1969), American rocket engineer.

Goodacre. Near side. 33°N, 14°E. 46 km. An excellent ring plain east of Aliacensis, it breaks in on Gemma Frisius on the north rim of that plain. It has a low central peak. Named for Walter Goodacre (1856–1938), British lunar cartographer.

Gould. Near side. 19°S, 17°W. 34 km. A ghost-crater (or palimpsest) east of Bullialdus, in the Mare Nubium. Named for Benjamin Gould (1824–1896), American astronomer.

Grachev. Far side. 3°S, 108°W. 35 km. SE of Leuschner, and to the east of the southern sector of Hertzsprung. Named for Andrei Grachev (1900–1964), Russian rocket designer.

Graff. Near side. 42°S, 89°W. 36 km. Named for Kasimir Graff (1878–1950), German astronomer.

Grave. Far side. 17°S, 150°E. 40 km. In the northern portion of Gagarin. Named for Dmitri Grave (1863–1939), Russian mathematician.

Greaves. Near side. 13°N, 53°E. 14 km. Formerly called Lick D. Named for John Greaves (1602–1652), English astronomer.

Green. Far side. 4°N, 133°E. 66 km. To the immediate west of Mendeleev. Named for George Green (1793–1841), British mathematician.

Gregory. Far side. 2°N, 127°E. 67 km. SE of King, and west of Mendeleev. Named for David Gregory (1661–1708), Scottish astronomer.

Gregory, Catena. Far side. 1°S, 130° E. 130 km long. A chain of craters to the SW of Mendeleev, in the area of Gregory (q.v.), in association with which it was named.

Grigg. Far side. 13°N, 130°W. 36 km. SE of Poynting and SW of Fersman, to the immediate north of Hertzsprung. Named for Walter Grigg (1892–1945), American physicist.

Grimaldi. Near side. 6°S, 68°W. 410 km. West of the Oceanus Procellarum. It has low irregular walls, no central peak, and is the darkest point on the Moon. Named for Francesco Grimaldi (1618–1663), Italian astronomer.

Grimaldi, Rimae. Near side. 9°S, 64°W. 230 km long. A rill system in the area of Grimaldi (q.v.), in association with which it was named.

Grissom. Far side. 45°S, 160°W. 59 km. North of Hendrix, and just south of the western rim of Apollo. Named for Virgil Grissom (1926–1967), American astronaut.

Grotrian. Far side. 66°S, 128°E. 38 km. North of Schrödinger, at the southern end of the Rima Planck. Named for W. Grotrian (1890–1954), German astronomer.

Grove. Near side. 40°N, 33°E. 28 km. In the Lacus Somniorum. Bright and deep. Named for Sir William Grove (1811–1896), British physicist.

Gruemberger. Near side. 68°S, 10°W. 94 km. Forms a pair with Cysatus, in the area of Moretus. Pear-shaped, it has high walls and contains a very deep crater. Named for Christoph Gruemberger (1561–1636), Austrian mathematician.

Gruithuisen. Near side. 33°N, 40°W. 16 km. On the Oceanus Procellarum. Bright. Named for Franz von Gruithuisen (1774–1852), German astronomer.

Guericke. Near side. 12°S, 14°W. 64 km. A partially-destroyed ring plain in the Fra Mauro area of the Mare Nubium. It is irregular and has broken walls. A crater lies close under the east wall. Named for Otto von Guericke (1602–1686), German physicist.

Guillaume. Far side. 45°N, 173°W. 57 km. NW of Ehrlich, and east of Chandler, in the area to the SE of D'Alembert. Named for Charles Guillaume (1861–1938), French physicist.

Gullstrand. Far side. 45°N, 130°W. 43 km. NW of Landau, and east of the northern rim of Fowler. Named for Allvar Gullstrand (1862–1934), Swedish ophthalmologist.

Gum. Near side. 40°S, 89°E. 55 km. Named for Colin Gum (1924–1960), Australian astronomer.

Gutenberg. Near side. 8°S. 41°E. 74 km. Near Goclenius, on the edge of the Mare Fecunditatis. Irregular. Named for Johannes Gutenberg (c.1400–1468), German printer.

Gutenberg, Rimae. Near side. 5°S, 38°E. 330 km long. A rill system in the area of Gutenberg (q.v.), in association with which it was named.

Guthnick. Far side. 48°S, 94°W. 36 km. East of Mendel, and NE of De Roy. Named for Paul Guthnick (1879–1947), German astronomer.

Guyot. Far side. 11°N, 117°E. 92 km. To the immediate west of Ostwald, between Mendeleev and the Mare Marginis. Named for Arnold Guyot (1807–1884), American geographer.

Gyldén. Near side. 5°S, 1°E. 47 km. North of Ptolemaeus. A crater-valley abuts it on the west. Its floor is partially filled with lava. Named for Johan Gyldén (1841–1896), Finnish astronomer.

H. G. Wells. Far side. 41°N, 122°E. 103 km. Also called Wells. Between Fabry and Campbell. Named for H. G. Wells (1866–1946), British writer.

Hadley, Mount. Near side. 27°N, 5°E. Also called Mons Hadley. At the northern end of the Apennines. Named for John Hadley (1682–1743), English mathematician.

Hadley, Rima. Near side. 25°N, 3°E. 80 km long. A rill in the area of Mount Hadley (q.v.), in association with which it was named.

Haemus Mountains. Near side. 16° N, 14°E. 400 km. Also called Montes Haemus. Form the southern border of the Mare Serenitatis. Not high, but some peaks rise to 8000 feet. Menelaus and Auwers are on the edge of these mountains. Name means "Balkans" in Latin.

Hagecius. Near side. 60°S, 46°E. 76 km. In the Vlacq group. Its wall is broken by craters. Named for Thaddeus Hayek (1525–1600), Czech astronomer.

Hagen. Far side. 56°S, 135°E. 56 km. NW of Prandtl, and south of Pauli. Named for Johannes Hagen (1847–1930), Austrian mathematician.

Hahn. Near side. 31°N, 74°E. 84 km. Forms a pair with Berosus, in the area of the Mare Crisium, east of Cleomedes. Regular, it has a central peak. Named for Friedrich von Hahn (1741–1805), German astronomer.

Haidinger. Near side. 39°S, 25°W. 22 km. South of the Palus Epidemiarum. Inconspicuous. Named for Wilhelm von Haidinger (1795–1871), Austrian mineralogist.

Hainzel. Near side. 41°S, 34°W. 70 km. North of Schiller. It was formed by two rings coming together. It has high walls, about 9000 feet. It is best seen at sunrise. Named for Paul Hainzel (fl. c.1570), German astronomer.

Haldane. Near side. 2°S, 84°E. 38 km. Named for J. B. S. Haldane (1892–1964), British geneticist.

Hale. Far side. 74°S, 91°E. 84 km. South of Wexler, and north of Amundsen, in the area due west of Schrödinger. Named for George Ellery Hale (1868–1938), American astrophysicist.

Hall. Near side. 34°N, 37°E. 35 km. In the area of the Lacus Somniorum, east of Posidonius. Named for Asaph Hall (1829–1907), American astronomer.

Halley. Near side. 8°S, 6°E. 36 km. Forms a pair with Hind in the Hipparchus group. Regular. Named for Edmund Halley (1656–1742), English astronomer.

Hamilton. Near side. 43°S, 85°W. 57 km. Named for Sir William Rowan Hamilton (1805–1865), Irish mathematician.

Hanno. Near side. 57°S, 73°E. 56 km. In the area of the Mare Australe. Has a darkish floor. Named for Hanno (fl. 5th century B.C.), Carthaginian navigator.

Hansen. Near side. 44°S, 83°E. 40 km. Near Cape Agarum, in the area of the Mare Crisium. Regular. Similar to Alhazen. Named for Peter Andreas Hansen (1795–1874), German astronomer.

Hansky. Far side. 10°S, 97°E. 43 km. Also spelled Hanskiy. To the west of the northern section of Pasteur, and to the east of the southern rim of the Mare Smythii. Named for Aleksey Hansky (1870–1908), Russian astronomer.

Hansteen. Near side. 12°S, 52°W. 45 km. Forms a pair with Billy, near to the southern border of the Oceanus Procellarum. It has terraced walls rising to 3800 feet above the floor. On the floor there are some hills, bright curved ridges, and a craterlet. It is regular. Named for Christopher Hansteen (1784–1873), Norwegian astronomer.

Hansteen, Mons. Near side. 12°S, 50°W. Also called Mount Hansteen. A mountain in the area of Hansteen (q.v.), in association with which it was named.

Hansteen, Rima. Near side. 12°S, 53°W. 25 km long. A rill in the area of Hansteen (q.v.), in association with which it was named.

Harbinger Mountains. Near side. 24°N, 40°W. 90 km in extent. Also known as Montes Harbinger. Not a definite range, but clumps of hills making up part of the circular wall of the Mare Imbrium, between Aristarchus and Sinus Roris. Not very big, the highest peak is 8000 feet. Named descriptively.

Harden. Far side. 6°N, 143°E. 15 km. In the eastern section of Mendeleev. Named for Sir Arthur Harden (1865–1940), British biochemist.

Harding. Near side. 43°N, 70°W. 23 km. In the area of Sinus Roris. Has low walls. Named for Carl Harding (1765–1834), German astronomer.

Haret. Far side. 58°S, 176°W. 29 km. SW of Bhabha, and east of Abbe. Named for Spiru Haret (1851–1912), Rumanian mathematician.

Hargreaves. Near side. 2°S, 64°E. 16 km. Formerly called Maclaurin S. Named for James Hargreaves (1834–1915), British chemist.

Harkhebi. Far side. 40°N, 100°E. 282 km. A huge enclosure in the area north of Joliot. It contains Fabry in its NE portion. Named for Harkhebi (fl. 3rd century B.C.), Egyptian astronomer.

Harpalus. Near side. 53°N, 43°W. 39 km. On the edge of the Mare Frigoris. It is the center of a minor ray system. Deep, it has high walls rising to 16,000 feet on the east and has a bright, central peak. Named for Harpalus (fl. 4th century B.C.), Greek astronomer.

Harriott. Far side. 33°N, 114°E. 56 km. Also spelled Harriot. East of Szilard, and SW of Cantor. Named for Thomas Harriott (1560–1621), English astronomer.

Hartmann. Far side. 3°N, 135°E. 62 km. Breaks into the SW rim of Mendeleev. Named for Johannes Hartmann (1865–1936), German astronomer.

Hartwig. Near side. 6°S, 80°W. 79 km. Named for Ernst Hartwig (1851–1923), German astronomer.

Harvey. Far side. 19°N, 147°W. 60 km. Breaks in on the NE rim of Mach, to the NW of Hertzsprung. Named for William Harvey (1578–1657), English anatomist.

Hase. Near side. 30°S, 63°E. 83 km. South of Petavius. Quite irregular. Named for Johann Hase (1684–1742), German mathematician.

Hatanaka. Far side. 29°N, 122°W. 27 km. East of Bobone, in the area north of Hertzsprung. Named for Hiroshi Hatanaka, the 20th century Japanese physicist.

Hausen. Near side. 65°S, 88°W. 167 km. Named for Christian Hausen (1693–1743), German astronomer.

Hayford. Far side. 13°N, 176°W. 27 km. NE of Sharonov, in the area to the NW of Korolev. Named for John Hayford (1868–1925), American geodesist.

Hayn. Near side. 65°N, 85°E. 87 km. Named for Friedrich Hayn (1863–1928), German astronomer.

Healy. Far side. 32°N, 111°W. 38 km. SW of Winlock, in the area to the SE of Landau. Named for Roy Healy (1915–1968), American rocket designer.

Heaviside. Far side. 10°S, 167°E. 163 km. Between Keeler and Aitken. Named for Oliver Heaviside (1850–1925), British mathematical physicist.

Hecataeus *see* **Hekataeus**

[1]**Hedin.** Far side. 68°N, 123°E. In the SE area of the Schwarzschild enclosure. Named for Sven von Hedin (1865–1952), Swedish scientist.

[2]**Hedin.** Near side. 3°N, 76°W. 143 km. Named for Sven von Hedin (1865–1952), Swedish scientist.

Heinrich. Near side. 25°N, 15°W. 7 km. Formerly called Timocharis A. Named for Helmut Heinrich (b. 1910), German aerodynamicist.

Heinsius. Near side. 39°S, 18°W. 64 km. In the area of Tycho. Irregular, it has three craters on its south wall. Named for Gottfried Heinsius (1709–1769), German astronomer.

Heis. Near side. 32°S, 32°W. 14 km. On the Mare Imbrium. Bright. Named for Eduard Heis (1806–1877), German astronomer.

Hekataeus. Near side. 23°S, 84°E. 127 km. Also spelled Hecataeus. SE of Vendelinus. It has irregular walls and a central peak. Named for Hecataeus of Miletus (fl. late 6th century B.C.), Greek geographer.

Helberg. Far side. 22°N, 102°W. 62 km. NW of Bell, and NE of Robertson, in the area NW of Einstein. Named for Robert Helberg (1906–1967), American engineer.

Helicon. Near side. 40°N, 23°W. 25 km. Forms a pair with Le Verrier, in the area of the Sinus Iridum, on the Mare Imbrium. Regular, it has a central crater on its floor. Named for Helicon (fl. c.400 B.C.), Greek mathematician.

Hell. Near side. 32°S, 8°W. 33 km. In the western part of Deslandres. Has a low central peak. Named for Maximilian Hell (1720–1792), Austrian astronomer.

Hell Plain *see* **Deslandres**

Helmert. Near side. 8°S, 88°E. 27 km. Named for Friedrich Helmert (1843–1917), German astronomer.

Helmholtz. Near side. 72°N, 78°E. 95 km. In the area of Boussingault, in the southern uplands. Quite regular. Named for Hermann von Helmholtz (1821–1894), German physicist.

Henderson. Far side. 5°N, 152°E. 47 km. East of Mendeleev, and immediately NW of Mandelstam. Named for Thomas Henderson (1798–1844), Scottish astronomer.

Hendrix. Far side. 48°S, 161°W. 17 km. South of the eastern rim of Apollo, and NE of Bose. Named for Don Hendrix (1905–1961), American optician.

Henry, Paul. Near side. 24°S, 57°W. 40 km. Also called Henry. Forms a pair with Henry, Prosper (or Prosper Henry). The two are often known as Henry Frères. West of the Mare Humorum. Distinct. Named for Paul Henry (1848–1905), French astronomer.

Henry, Prosper. Near side. 24°S, 59°W. 45 km. Forms a pair with Henry, Paul (or Paul Henry, or Henry), west of the Mare Humorum. See **Henry, Paul** (above) for more details. Named for Prosper Henry (1849–1903), French astronomer.

Henyey. Far side. 13°N, 152°W. 64 km. South of the western rim of Mach, in the area north of the eastern portion of Korolev. Named for Louis G. Henyey (1910–1970), American astronomer.

Heraclides, Cape. Near side. 40°N, 34°W. 50 km. Also called Promontorium Heraclides. In Sinus Iridum. Named for Heraclides Ponticus (c.390–c.338 B.C.), Greek astronomer.

Heraclitus. Near side. 49°S, 6°E. 90 km. In the Cuvier-Licetus group, south of Stöfler. A strange shape, it has a ridge in the center that projects partly into Licetus, which breaks in on it on the north. Named for Heraclitus (c.535–c.475 B.C.), Greek philosopher.

Hercules. Near side. 46°N, 39°E. 69 km. Forms a pair with Atlas. Has bright walls and a deep interior crater. Named for Hercules (Heracles) of Greco-Roman mythology.

Herigonius. Near side. 13°S, 34°W. 15 km. NE of Gassendi. Bright, it has a central peak. Named for Pierre Hérigone (d. c.1643), French mathematician.

Herigonius, Rima. Near side. 13°S, 37°W. 100 km long. A rill in the area of Herigonius (q.v.), in association with which it was named.

Hermann. Near side. 1°S, 57°W. 16 km. East of Lohrmann, on the Oceanus Procellarum. Bright. Named for Hermann the Lame (1013–1054), German astronomer.

Hermite. Near side. 86°N, 87°W. 110 km. Named for Charles Hermite (1822–1901), French mathematician.

Hero. Far side. 1°N, 120°E. 29 km. South of King, and immediately east of Ctesibius, in the area between Mendeleev and the Mare Smythii. Named for Hero (fl. c. A.D. 150), Alexandrian mathematician.

Herodotus. Near side. 23°N, 50°W. 35 km. Forms a pair with Aristarchus. Quite regular, it has a dark, level floor, and narrow walls rising to 4000 feet. Schröter's Valley begins its course inside Herodotus, at the north wall. Named for Herodotus (c.484–c.424 B.C.), Greek historian.

Herodotus, Mons. Near side. 27°N, 53°W. Also called Mount Herodotus. A peak in the area of Herodotus (q.v.), in association with which it was named.

Herschel. Near side. 6°S, 2°W. 41 km. North of Ptolemaeus. Has terraced walls and a large central peak. Named for Sir William Herschel (1738–1822), British astronomer.

Herschel, Caroline. Near side. 34°N, 31°W. 13 km. Also called Herschel, C. and C. Herschel. Forms a group with De l'Isle and Carlini, on the Mare Imbrium. Bright. Named for Caroline Herschel (1750–1848), astronomer sister of William Herschel.

Herschel, John. Near side. 62°N, 41°W. 156 km. Also called Herschel, J. and J. Herschel. A very large ridge-bordered enclosure north of the Mare Frigoris. Its interior has several craters, ridges and hills. Named for Sir John Herschel (1792–1871), British astronomer.

Hertz. Far side. 13°N, 104°E. 90 km. East of the Mare Marginis, and west of the southern rim of Fleming. Named for Heinrich Hertz (1857–1894), German physicist.

Hertzsprung. Far side. 0°, 130°W. 520 km. A huge ringed enclosure, or basin, one of the major features of the far side of the Moon, it lies between Korolev and the Mare Orientale. Its inner section is darker than the outer part of the interior. The outer ring is broken by Michelson to the NE and Vavilov to the SW. Named for Ejnar Hertzsprung (1873–1967), Danish astronomer.

Hesiodus. Near side. 29°S, 16°W. 43 km. Forms a pair with Pitatus, south of the Mare Nubium. A major rill (*see* **Rima Hesiodus,** below), runs SW from it. Named for Hesiod (fl. 735 B.C.), Greek poet.

Hesiodus, Rima. Near side. 30°S, 21°W. 300 km long. A major cleft in the lunar surface, this rill runs SW from Hesiodus (q.v.), in association with which it was named.

Hess. Far side. 54°S, 174°E. 88 km. SW of Boyle, and north of Abbe, in the area south of Von Kármán and NW of Poincaré. Named for Victor F. Hess (1883–1964), Austrian physicist.

Hevel. Near side. 2°N, 67°W. 106 km. Also called Hevelius. In the Grimaldi chain. It has a convex floor containing rills (*see* **Rima Hevelius,** below) and a central peak. Named for Johannes Hevelius (Hevel) (1611–1687), Polish astronomer.

Hevelius, Rima. Near side. 2°N, 66°W. 190 km long. A major rill, one of several in Hevel (q.v.), in association with which it was named.

Heymans. Far side. 75°N, 145°W. 50 km. North of Hippocrates and south of

Poinsot, in the area north of Stebbins. Named for Corneille Heymans (1892–1968), Belgian physiologist.

Hiemalis, Lacus. Near side. 15°N, 14°E. 50 km. Name means "Wintry Lake" in Latin.

Hilbert. Far side. 18°S, 108°E. 170 km. Immediately SE of Pasteur, in the area west of the northern portion of Tsiolkovskiy. Named for David Hilbert (1862–1943), German mathematician.

Hill. Near side. 21°N, 41°E. 16 km. Formerly called Macrobius B. Named for George W. Hill (1838–1914), American astronomer.

Hind. Near side. 8°S, 7°E. 29 km. Forms a pair with Halley, in the Hipparchus group. Regular. Named for John Hind (1823–1895), British astronomer.

Hippalus. Near side. 25°S, 30°W. 58 km. An incomplete ring formation which has the remains of a central peak. Associated with rills (*see* **Hippalus, Rima,** below). Named for Hippalus (fl. c. A.D. 50), Greek navigator.

Hippalus, Rima. Near side. 1°S, 23°E. 180 km long. A major rill, one of several associated with Hippalus (q.v.), in association with which it was named.

Hipparchus. Near side. 6°S, 5°E. 151 km. Forms a pair with Albategnius, east of Ptolemaeus. Horrocks occupies its NW border. It is one of the largest ring formations on the Moon, but is only prominent under a low Sun. It has very broken and disconnected, low walls. Named for Hipparchus (c.160–125 B.C.), Greek astronomer.

Hippocrates. Far side. 71°N, 146°W. 60 km. North of Stebbins, and NE of Kirkwood. Named for Hippocrates (c.460–c.377 B.C.), Greek physician.

Hirayama. Far side. 6°S, 93°E. 139 km. Breaks into the SE rim of the Mare Smythii, just over on the far side of the Moon. Named for Kiyotsugo Hirayama (1874–1943), Japanese astronomer.

Hoffmeister. Far side. 15°N, 137°E. 45 km. North of the western portion of Mendeleev, and SW of the Mare Moscoviense. Named for Friedrich L. C. Hoffmeister (1892–1968), German astronomer.

Hogg. Far side. 34°N, 122°E. 38 km. South of Kidinnu, and SE of Cantor, in the area between Mare Moscoviense and Fabry. Named for Arthur R. Hogg (1903–1966), Australian astronomer.

Hohmann. Far side. 18°S, 94°W. 17 km. South of Maunder, and west of Kopff, in the central portion of the Mare Orientale. Named for Walter Hohmann (1880–1945), German engineer.

Holden. Near side. 19°S, 63°E. 47 km. South of Vendelinus. Deep. Named for Edward S. Holden (1846–1914), American astronomer.

Holetschek. Far side. 28°S, 151°E. 39 km. South of Gagarin, east of Pavlov, and NW of Ingenii. Named for Johann Holetschek (1846–1923), Austrian astronomer.

Hommel. Near side. 54°S, 33°E. 125 km. In the southern uplands. Has two large craters on the floor. Named for Johann Hommel (1518–1562), German astronomer.

Honoris, Sinus. Near side. 12°N, 18° E. 100 km. Name means "Bay of Honor" in Latin.

Hooke. Near side. 41°N, 55°E. 37 km. West of Messala. Quite regular. Named for Robert Hooke (1635–1703), English physicist.

Hopmann. Far side. 51°S, 160°E. 89 km. Formerly called Lamarck. North of Poincaré and immediately south of Garavito. Named for Josef Hopmann (b. 1890), German astronomer.

Hörbiger *see* **Deslandres**

Hornsby. Near side. 24°N, 12°E. 3 km. Named for Thomas Hornsby (1733–1810), British astronomer.

Horrebow. Near side. 59°N, 41°W. 24 km. Forms a pair with Robinson, in the area of the Mare Frigoris. It is outside John Herschel (*see* **Herschel, John**). Named for Peder Horrebow (1679–1764), Danish astronomer.

Horrocks. Near side. 4°S, 6°E. 31 km. A bright, regular crater on the NW border of Hipparchus. Named for Jeremiah Horrocks (c.1617–1641), English astronomer.

Hortensius. Near side. 6°N, 28°W. 15 km. On the Oceanus Procellarum. Bright. Named for Martinus Hortensius (1605–1639), Dutch astronomer.

Houtermans. Near side. 9°S, 87°E. 30 km. Named for Fritz Houtermans (b. 1903), German physicist.

Houzeau. Far side. 18°S, 124°W. 71 km. South of the eastern portion of Hertzsprung, in the area between the Mare Orientale and Korolev. Named for Jean Charles Houzeau de Lehaie (1820–1888), Belgian astronomer.

Hubble. Near side. 22°N, 87°E. 81 km. Named for Edwin P. Hubble (1889–1953), American astronomer.

Huggins. Near side. 41°S, 2°W. 65 km. Breaks in on Orontius. Irregular. Named for Sir William Huggins (1824–1910), British astronomer.

Humason. Near side. 31°N, 57°W. 4 km. Formerly called Lichtenberg G. Named for Milton L. Humason (1891–1972), American astronomer.

Humboldt, W. Near side. 27°S, 81°E. 207 km. Also called Humboldt. East of Petavius. Irregular, it has rills on the floor. Named for Wilhelm von Humboldt (1767–1835), German philologist.

Humboldtianum, Mare. Near side. 56°N, 80°E. 305×410 km. Also known as Humboldt's Sea (its translation from Latin). A regular mare on the limb of the Moon. Named for Alexander von Humboldt (1769–1859), German scientist.

Hume. Far side. 5°S, 90°E. 24 km. Just on the far side of the Moon, in Mare Smythii. Named for David Hume (1711–1776), Scottish philosopher.

Humorum, Mare. Near side. 23°S, 38°W. 423×460 km. A minor circular mare, the same size as England, and just over 4 billion years old. It contains Puiseux crater, and many bays and rills. It shows striking examples of faulting, but its floor is essentially featureless. Name means "The Sea of Humors" in Latin.

Hutton. Far side. 37°N, 169°E. 50 km. NW of Shajn, NE of the Mare Moscoviense, and SE of Campbell. Named for Charles Hutton (1737–1823), British mathematician.

Huxley. Near side. 20°N, 4°W. 4 km. Formerly called Wallace B. Named for Thomas Huxley (1825–1895), British biologist.

Huygens, Mount. Near side. 20°N, 3°W. Also called Mons Huygens. 18,000 feet high. The highest mountain in the Apennines. Named for Christiaan Huygens (1629–1695), Dutch astronomer.

Hyginus. Near side. 8°N, 6°E. 9 km. A large walled plain which breaks in on the west wall of Orontius. Nasireddin breaks in on its west wall. It has low walls which slope down gently to the floor and the remains of a central peak. Named for Gaius Julius Hyginus (fl. 1st century B.C.), Roman mathematician.

Hyginus, Rima. Near side. 8°N, 6°E. 220 km long. Also known as Hyginus Rille and Hyginus Cleft. Part crater-chain and part cleft, it is curved like a string of beads, and has crater-like enlargements running along it. Visible with a very small telescope, it is in the area of Hyginus, the crater (in association with which it was named).

Hypatia. Near side. 4°S, 23°E. 40 km. South of the Mare Tranquillitatis. It is triangular, and has low walls. Named for Hypatia (d. 415), Alexandrian philosopher.

Hypatia, Rimae. Near side. 25°S, 29°W. 240 km long. A system of rills. Named for Hypatia (d. 415), Alexandrian philosopher.

Ibn Battuta. Near side. 7°S. 50°E. 12 km. Formerly called Goclenius A. Named for Ibn Battuta (c.1304–c.1377), Arab traveler.

Ibn Firnas. Far side. 7°N, 122°E. 90 km. Immediately NE of King, in the area west of Mendeleev. Named for Abbas ibn Firnas (d. 887), Arab scholar.

Ibn-Rushd. Near side. 12°S, 22°E. 33 km. Formerly called Cyrillus B. Named for Ibn Rushd (Averroës), (1126–1198), Arab philosopher.

Ibn Yunis. Far side. 14°N, 91°E. 58 km. Also spelled Ibn Yunus. NW of Ginzel, on the NE rim of the Mare Marginis. Named for Ibn Yunis (950–1009), Arab astronomer.

Icarus. Far side. 6°S, 173°W. 96 km. Just to the east of Daedalus, between Korolev and Mendeleev. Named for the Greek mythological character.

Ideler. Near side. 49°S, 22°E. 39 km. SE of Maurolycus. Distinct. Named for Christian Ideler (1766–1846), German astronomer.

Idel'son. Far side. 81°S, 114°E. 60 km. NE of Amundsen, and just south of the western rim of Schrödinger, it is one of the most southerly lunar features. Named for Naum Idel'son (1885–1951), Russian astronomer.

Imbrium, Mare. Near side. 36°N, 16°W. 1300 km diameter. Gilbert in 1600 called it Regio Magna Orientalis. The largest "regular" mare, it is circular in type and dominates the NW part of the near side of the Moon. The Apennines separate it from the Mare Vaporum, and it is bordered by the Alps, the Juras, the Carpathians, as well as the Apennines. This mare contains the Spitsbergen Mountains, the Teneriffe Mountains, Archimedes, and Lambert, among other features. It is larger than Great Britain and France combined and is just under 4 billion years old. It is either volcanic or impactual in origin. It is 7 km deeper at its center than at its periphery. Name means "The Sea of Showers" in Latin.

Ingalls. Far side. 4°S, 153°W. 38 km. The most easterly crater within the Korolev enclosure (c.f. Krylov). Named for Albert Ingalls (1888–1958), American telescope maker.

Ingenii, Mare. Far side. 34°S, 163°E. 350 km. Between Apollo and the Mare Australe. One of the major features on the far side of the Moon, it is not really a mare at all. It is an irregular formation with a darkish floor. Name means "Sea of Character" in Latin.

Inghirami. Near side. 47°S, 69°W. 91 km. In the Schickard area. Regular, it has a central peak. Named for Giovanni Inghirami (1779–1851), Italian astronomer.

Inghirami, Vallis. Near side. 44°S, 73°W. 140 km long. A valley in the area of Inghirami (q.v.), in association with which it was named.

Innes. Far side. 28°N, 119°E. 43 km. East of the southern rim of Seyfert, in the area between Joliot and Mare Moscoviense. Named for Robert Innes (1861–1933), British astronomer.

Insularum, Mare. Near side. 7°N, 22°W. 900 km. Means "Sea of Islands" in Latin.

Ioffe *see* **Joffe.**

Iridum, Sinus. Near side. 45°N, 32°W. 200 km. Means "The Bay of Rainbows" in Latin.

Isaev. Far side. 17°S, 147°E. 90 km. In the NW part of Gagarin. Named for Aleksey Isaev (1908–1971), Russian engineer.

Isidorus. Near side. 8°S, 33°E. 42 km. Forms a pair with Capella, outside the Mare Nectaris. Deep. Named for Isidore of Seville (c.560–636), Spanish encyclopedist.

Izsak. Far side. 23°S, 117°E. 30 km. West of the southern rim of Tsiolkovskiy, and NE of the Mare Australe. Named for Imre Izsak (1929–1965), American astronomer.

Jackson. Far side. 22°N, 163°W. 71 km. SW of Mineur, in the area north of Korolev. Named for John Jackson (1887–1958), Scottish astronomer.

Jacobi. Near side. 57°S, 11°E. 68 km. Forms a pair with Cuvier, in the Heraclitus group. Quite distinct, there is a prominent crater in the center of its floor. Named for Moritz Jacobi (1801–1874), German physicist.

Jansen. Near side. 13°N, 29°E. 24 km. In the Mare Tranquillitatis. Has low walls and a darkish floor. Named for Zacharias Jansen (1588–c.1630), Dutch telescope inventor.

Jansen, Rima. Near side. 15°N, 29°E. 35 km long. A rill in the area of Jansen (q.v.), in association with which it was named.

Jansky. Near side. 8°N, 89°E. 73 km. Named for Karl Jansky (1905–1950), American radio engineer.

Janssen. Near side. 45°S, 41°E. 190 km. A great ruin in the southern uplands. Fabricius breaks into its northern rim. Named for Pierre Janssen (1824–1907), French astronomer.

Janssen, Rimae. Near side. 140 km long. In Janssen (q.v.), in association with which this rill system was named.

Jeans. Far side. 53°S, 91°E. 79 km. East of the southern rim of Lyot, in the area NW of Schrödinger. Named for Sir James Jeans (1877–1946), British astronomer.

Jenkins. Near side. 0°, 78°E. 38 km. Formerly called Schubert Z. Named for Charles Francis Jenkins (1867–1934), American inventor.

Jenner. Far side. 42°S, 96°E. 72 km. In the southern portion of the Mare Australe, between Hamilton and Lamb. Named for Edward Jenner (1749–1823), British physician.

Joffe. Far side. 15°S, 129°W. 87 km. Also spelled Ioffe. Between Fridman and Belopol'skiy, and between Hertzsprung and Apollo. Named for Abram Ioffe (1880–1960), Russian physicist.

Joliot. Far side. 26°N, 94°E. 143 km. Just over on the far side of the Moon, between Fabry and the Mare Smythii. Named for Frédéric Joliot-Curie (1900–1958), French physicist.

Joule. Far side. 27°N, 144°W. 97 km. Between Hertzsprung and Fowler. Has a darkish floor containing craterlets. Named for James P. Joule (1818–1889), British physicist.

Joy. Near side. 25°N, 7°E. 6 km. Formerly called Hadley A. Named for Alfred H. Joy (1882–1973), American astronomer.

Jules Verne. Far side. 36°S, 146°E. 134 km. Between Pavlov and Koch, to the west of the Mare Ingenii. Named for Jules Verne (1828–1905), French novelist.

Julius Caesar. Near side. 9°N, 15°E. 91 km. A large, imperfect formation in the area of the Mare Vaporum. It has several low hills and craterlets, scattered about the floor's surface. The floor is very dark. This feature is one of the darkest areas on the Moon. It has low, irregular walls. Named for Julius Caesar (c.102–44 B.C.), Roman general.

Jura Mountains. Near side. 46°N, 38°W. 380 km long. Also called Montes Jura. They make up part of the circular wall of the Mare Imbrium, and border Sinus Iridum. Named by Debes after the European mountain chain.

Kaiser. Near side. 36°N, 6°E. 52 km. A large, well-marked ring formation north of Stöfler. It has two craters on its floor, and two chains of craterlets, but no central peak. Named for Frederik Kaiser (1808–1872), Dutch astronomer.

Kamerlingh Onnes. Far side. 15°N, 116°W. 67 km. East of the southern rim of Fersman, to the NE of Hertzsprung. Named for Heike Kamerlingh Onnes (1853–1926), Dutch physicist.

Kane. Near side. 63°N, 26°E. 55 km. North of the Mare Frigoris. Quite regular. Named for Robert J. Kane (1809–1890), Irish chemist.

Kant. Near side. 11°S, 20°E. 33 km. A prominent deep ring plain, west of Theophilus. The inner walls are terraced and the large, bright central peak has a summit pit. Named for Immanuel Kant (1724–1804), German philosopher.

Kao. Near side. 7°S, 88°E. 34 km. Named for Shih Kung Kao (b. 1918), Chinese atmospheric scientist.

Kapteyn. Near side. 13°S, 70°E. 49 km. East of Langrenus. Not prominent. Named for Jacobus Kapteyn (1851–1922), Dutch astronomer.

Kármán, Von *see* **Von Kármán**

Karpinskiy. Far side. 73°N, 166°E. 93 km. East of Seares, and south of the western rim of Plaskett. Named for Aleksandr Karpinskiy (1847–1936), Russian geologist.

Karrer. Far side. 52°S, 142°W. 52 km. South of Riedel, and north of Minkowski. Named for Paul Karrer (1889–1971), Swiss organic chemist.

Kästner. Near side. 6°S, 80°E. 105 km. In the area of the Mare Smythii. Distinct. Named for Abraham Kästner (1719–1800), German mathematician.

Katchal'skiy. Far side. 6°N, 116°E. 32 km. NW of King, and SE of Lobachevsky, in the area between Mendeleev and and Mare Smythii.

Kearons. Far side. 12°S, 113°W. 23 km. Breaks into the NW rim of Mare Orientale, between Grachev and Lewis. Named for William Kearons (1878–1948), American astronomer.

Keeler. Far side. 10°S, 162°E. 169 km. On the NW border of Heaviside, to the SW of Korolev. Named for James E. Keeler (1857–1900), American astronomer.

Kekulé. Far side. 16°N, 138°W. 94 km. West of the southern portion of Poynting and east of the southern rim of Mach, to the NW of Hertzsprung. Named for Friedrich August Kekulé von Stradonitz (1829–1896), German chemist.

Keldysh. Near side. 51°N, 44°E. 33 km. Formerly called Hercules A. Named for Mstislav Keldysh (1911–1978), Russian mathematician.

Kelvin, Cape. Near side. 27°S, 33°W. 50 km. Also called Promontorium Kelvin. Just south of Hippalus, in the Mare Humorum. Named for Lord Kelvin (1824–1907), British mathematical physicist.

Kelvin, Rupes. Near side. 28°S, 33° W. 150 km long. A long cliff-like scarp in the area of Cape Kelvin (q.v., above), in association with which it was named.

Kepinski. Far side. 29°N, 127°E. 31 km. NW of Vernandsky, in the area west of the Mare Moscoviense. Named for Felicjan Kepinski (b. 1885), Polish astronomer.

Kepler. Near side. 8°N, 38°W. 32 km. The center of an extensive ray system on the Oceanus Procellarum. Bright, it has terraced walls and a central hill. Named for Johann Kepler (1571–1630), German astronomer.

Khwolson. Far side. 14°S, 112°E. 54 km. Also spelled Khvol'son. A heart-shaped crater south of the western rim of Meitner, east of the southern portion of Pasteur and west of Kondratyuk. Named for Orest Khvol'son (1852–1934), Russian physicist.

Kibaltchitch. Far side. 2°N, 147°W. 93 km. The name is spelled in a variety of ways, others being Kibal'chich, Kibal'chitch, Kibaltchich, etc. SE of Tsander, with which it forms a pair, between Hertzsprung and Korolev. Named for Nikolay Kibaltchich (1853–1881), Russian rocket revolutionary.

Kidinnu. Far side. 36°N, 123°E. 56 km. South of H. G. Wells, and SE of Cantor, in the area between Mare Moscoviense and Fabry. Named for Cidenas (Kidinnu), (b. c.343 B.C.), Babylonian astronomer.

Kies. Near side. 26°S, 22°W. 46 km. In the area of Bullialdus, on the Mare Nubium. It has very low walls a mountain spur projects from the outside of its south wall. Named for Johann Kies (1713–1781), German mathematician.

Kiess. Near side. 6°S, 84°E. 63 km. Named for Carl C. Kiess (b. 1887), American astrophysicist.

Kimura. Far side. 57°S, 118°E. 29 km. South of Cassegrain, and north of the western rim of Schrödinger. Named for Hisashi Kimura (1870–1943), Japanese astronomer.

Kinau. Near side. 60°S, 15°E. 42 km. In the Jacobi group. Has high walls and a central peak. Named for C. A. Kinau (fl. c.1850), Bohemian astronomer.

King. Far side. 5°N, 120°E. 77 km. One of the smaller fresh craters, to the NE of Abul Wafa, between Mendeleev and Mare Smythii. Well-formed, it has terraced walls. Named for Edward S. King (1861–1931), American astronomer.

Kirch. Near side. 39°N, 6°W. 12 km. On the Mare Imbrium. Bright. Named for Gottfried Kirch (1639–1710), German astronomer.

Kircher. Near side. 67°S, 45°W. 73 km. In the Bettinus chain, in the area of Bailly. Has walls on the south rising to 18,000 feet above the depressed floor. Named for Athanasius Kircher (c.1601–1680), German polymath.

Kirchhoff. Near side. 30°N, 39°E. 25 km. The larger of two craters west of Newcomb, in the area of Cleomedes. Named for Gustav Kirchhoff (1824–1887), German physicist.

Kirkwood. Far side. 69°N, 157°W. 68 km. Immediately NE of Sommerfeld. Named for Daniel Kirkwood (1814–1895), American astronomer.

Klaproth. Near side. 70°S, 26°W. 119 km. A walled plain. There are low ridges and several craterlets on its interior. Named for Martin Klaproth (1743–1817), German chemist.

Kleimenov. Far side. 33°S, 141°W. 55 km. Also spelled Kleymenov. Immediately east of the NE rim of Apollo, and to the west of the northern portion of Chebyshev. Named for Ivan Kleimenov (1898–1938), Russian engineer.

Klein. Near side. 12°N, 3°E. 44 km. A regular ring formation breaking into the SE wall of Albategnius. Has a central peak. Named for Hermann Klein (1844–1914), German astronomer.

Kleymenov *see* **Kleimenov**

Klute. Far side. 37°N, 142°W. 75 km. East of the northern rim of Gadomski, and SE of Fowler. Named for Daniel Klute (1921–1964), American engineer.

Knox-Shaw. Near side. 5°S, 80°E. 12 km. Formerly called Banachiewicz F. Named for Harold Knox-Shaw (b. 1885), British astronomer.

Koch. Far side. 43°S, 150°E. 96 km. South of the eastern rim of Jules Verne, east of Roche, and SW of the Mare Ingenii. Named for Robert Koch (1843–1910), German bacteriologist.

Kohlschütter. Far side. 15°N, 154°E. 53 km. NE of Mendeleev, and SE of the Mare Moscoviense. Named for Arnold Kohlschütter (1883–1969), German astronomer.

Kolhörster. Far side. 10°N, 115°W. 98 km. NE of Michelson, in the area NE of Hertzsprung. Named for Werner Kolhörster (1887–1946), German astronomer.

Komarov. Far side. 25°N, 153°E. 78 km. In the eastern portion of the Mare Moscoviense, SE of Titov. Named for Vladimir Komarov (1927–1967), Russian cosmonaut.

Kondratyuk. Far side. 15°S, 115°E. 106 km. East of the southern rim of Pasteur and NE of Hilbert, in the area to the NW of Tsiolkovskiy. Named for Yuriy Kondratyuk (1900–1942), Russian rocket pioneer.

König. Near side. 24°S, 25°W. 23 km. In the area of Bullialdus, in the Mare Nubium. Deep. Named for Rudolf König (1865–1927), Austrian astronomer.

Konstantinov. Far side. 20°N, 159°E. 66 km. SE of the Mare Moscoviense, and SW of Freundlich. Named for Konstantin Konstantinov (1817–1871), Russian rocket engineer.

Kopff. Far side. 17°S, 90°W. 42 km. It actually straddles the limb of the Moon, being on the far and the near sides, but most of it falls on the far side, in the eastern portion of the Mare Orientale, SE of Maunder, and just west of the Rook Mountains. Named for August Kopff (1882–1960), German astronomer.

Korolev. Far side. 5°S, 157°W. 453 km. A huge ringed enclosure, one of the major features on the far side of the Moon, it lies SW of Hertzsprung and contains Krylov and Ingalls. Named for Sergey Korolev (1907–1966), Russian mechanician.

Kosberg. Far side. 20°S, 150°E. 15 km. In the center of Gagarin. Named for Semyin Kosberg (1903–1965), Russian engineer.

Kostinskiy. Far side. 14°N, 118°E. 75 km. North of Guyot, and south of Olcott. Named for Sergey Kostinskiy (1867–1936), Russian astronomer.

Kovalevskaya. Far side. 31°N, 129° W. 111 km. On the NE of Bobone, with which it forms a pair, to the SW of Landau. Named for Sonya Kovalevskaya (1850–1891), Russian mathematician.

Koval'skiy. Far side. 22°S, 101°E. 49 km. SE of Sklodowska, and south of the western rim of Pasteur. Named for Marian Koval'skiy (1821–1884), Russian astronomer.

Krafft. Near side. 17°N, 73°W. 51 km. Named for Wolfgang Krafft (1743–1814), German astronomer.

Kramers. Far side. 53°N, 128°W. 62 km. NW of Weber, and east of Birkhoff. Named for Hendrik Kramers (1894–1952), Dutch theoretical physicist.

Krasnov. Near side. 30°S, 80°W. 41 km. Named for Aleksandr Krasnov (1866–1907), Russian astronomer.

Krasovskiy. Far side. 4°N, 176°W. 59 km. NW of Congreve and SE of Stein, in the area NW of Korolev. Named for Theodosy N. Krasovskiy (1878–1948), Russian mathematician.

Kreiken. Near side. 9°S, 85°E. 23 km. Named for E. A. Kreiken (fl. 1933), Indonesian astronomer.

Krieger. Near side. 29°N, 46°W. 22 km. In the area of Aristarchus. Distinct, it has walls broken by craterlets. Named for Johann Krieger (1865–1902), German astronomer.

Krogh. Near side. 9°N, 66°E. 20 km. Formerly called Auzout B. Named for August Krogh (1874–1946), Danish physiologist.

Krusenstern. Near side. 26°S, 6°E. 47 km. In the area of Werner. It is not prominent and is bordered by ridges. Named for Admiral Ivan Krusenstern (1770–1846), Russian hydrographer.

Krylov. Far side. 9°S, 157°W. 49 km. An interior crater of the huge enclosure Korolev (cf. Ingalls), it is regular, well-marked, and has a central peak. A row of craters runs east from it to the wall of Korolev. Named for Aleksey Krylov (1863–1945), Russian mathematician.

Kugler. Far side. 53°S, 104°E. 66 km. NW of Priestly, in the area NW of Schrödinger. Named for F. X. Kugler (1862–1929), German philologist.

Kuiper. Near side. 10°S, 23°W. 7 km. Formerly called Bonpland E. Named for Gerard Kuiper (1905–1973), American astronomer.

Kulik. Far side. 42°N, 155°W. 58 km. West of Fowler, and east of Schneller. Named for Leonid Kulik (1883–1942), Russian mineralogist.

Kundt. Near side. 11°S, 11°W. 11 km. Formerly called Guericke C. Named for August Kundt (1839–1894), German physicist.

Kunowsky. Near side. 3°N, 32°W. 18 km. East of Encke, on the Oceanus Procellarum. Has a low central ridge. Named for Georg Kunowsky (1786–1846), German astronomer.

Kuo Shou Ching. Far side. 8°N, 134°W. 34 km. Breaks into the NW rim of Hertzsprung, south of the western rim of Poynting. Named for Kuo Shou Ching (1231–1316), Chinese astronomer.

Kurchatov. Far side. 38°N, 142°E. 105 km. SW of Wiener and SE of Bridgman, in the area SW of Campbell. Named for Igor Kurchatov (1903–1960), Russian physicist.

Kurchatov, Catena. Far side. 37°N, 136°E. 220 km long. A chain of craters in the proximity of Kurchatov (q.v.), in association with which it was named. North of Nijland, in the area NW of the Mare Moscoviense.

Lacaille. Near side. 24°S, 1°E. 68 km. Also spelled La Caille. In the area of Werner. Irregular. Named for Nicolas de Lacaille (1713–1762), French astronomer.

Lacchini. Far side. 41°N, 107°W. 58 km. South of Stefan, and east of Landau. Named for Giovanni Lacchini (1884–1967), Italian astronomer.

Lachi (plural of Lacus). A lacus is a lake-like area. (*See* **Aestatis, Autumnii, Bonitatis, Doloris, Excellentiae, Felicitatis, Gaudii, Hiemalis, Lenitatis, Luxuriae, Mortis, Oblivionis, Odii, Perseverantiae, Solitudinis, Somniorum, Spei, Temporis, Timoris, Veris.**)

La Condamine *see* **Condamine**

Lacroix. Near side. 38°S, 59°W. 38 km. North of Schickard. Quite regular, it has a central peak. Named for Sylvestre Lacroix (1765–1843), French mathematician.

Lade. Near side. 1°S, 10°E. 56 km. In the highlands, south of Godin. Has low walls. Named for Heinrich von Lade (1817–1904), German selenographer.

Lagalla. Near side. 45°S, 23°W. 85 km. Abuts on Wilhelm I. Pear-shaped, it has low, broad terraced walls. Named for Iulio Caesare Lagalla (1576–1624), Italian physicist.

Lagrange. Near side. 33°S, 72°W. 160 km. West of the Mare Humorum. It has low walls and a rough floor. Named for Joseph Lagrange (1736–1813), French mathematician.

La Hire, Mount. Near side. 28°N, 25°W. 5000 feet. Also known as Mons La Hire. Just NW of Lambert, in the Mare Imbrium. Bright, it has a summit craterlet. Named for Philippe de la Hire (1640–1718), French astronomer.

Lalande. Near side. 4°S, 8°W. 24 km. In the area of Ptolemaeus. Very deep, it has bright terraced walls rising to 6000 feet above the floor, and a low central peak. Named for Joseph de Lalande (1732–1807), French astronomer.

Lamarck *see* **Hopmann**

Lamarck. Near side. 23°S, 70°W. 115 km. Named for Jean Baptiste Lamarck (1744–1829), French naturalist. Not to be confused with Hopmann (q.v.).

Lamb. Far side. 43°S, 101°E. 104 km. The largest crater in the southern portion of the Mare Australe. Named for Sir Horace Lamb (1849–1934), British mathematician.

Lambert. Near side. 26°N, 21°W. 30 km. Has broad walls, finely terraced on the inside, and has a central craterlet on a long ridge. Named for Johann Lambert (1728–1777), German mathematician.

Lamé. Near side. 15°S, 65°E. 84 km. On the NE wall of Vendelinus. Well-formed. Named for Gabriel Lamé (1795–1870), French mathematician.

Lamèch. Near side. 43°N, 13°E. 13 km. In the area of Eudoxus. Has very low, irregular walls. Named for Félix Lamèch (1894–1962), French selenographer.

Lamont. Near side. 5°N, 23°E. 175 km. A low and imperfect ring formation in the area of Arago, in the Mare Tranquillitatis. Has low walls. Named for Johann von Lamont (1805–1879), German astronomer.

Lampland. Far side. 31°S, 131°E. 65 km. SE of Tsiolkovskiy, and SW of Pavlov. Named for Carl Otto Lampland (1873–1951), American astronomer.

Landau. Far side. 42°N, 119°W. 221 km. North of Hertzsprung. Much deformed by intruding craters, the most prominent of which is Wood on its NW rim. Named for Lev Landau (1908–1968), Russian physicist.

Lander. Far side. 15°S, 132°E. 40 km. SE of Perepelkin, and NE of Tsiolkovskiy. Named for William Lander (fl. 1833), British astronomer.

Landsberg. Near side. 0°, 26°W. 39 km. Also spelled Lansberg. On the Mare Nubium. Isolated, it has massive walls and a central mountain with several peaks on it. It has a huge, crescent-shaped terrace on its inner east slope. Named for Grigoriy Landsberg (1890–1957), Russian physicist.

Landsteiner. Near side. 31°N, 15°W. 6 km. Formerly called Timocharis F. Named for Karl Landsteiner (1868–1943), American pathologist.

Lane. Far side. 9°S, 132°E. 55 km. SW of Mendeleev, and NW of Chauvenet, in the area north of the eastern rim of Tsiolkovskiy. Named for Jonathan Lane (1819–1880), American physicist.

Langemak. Far side. 10°S, 119°E. 102 km. NE of Meitner, in the area between Pasteur and Mendeleev. Named for Georgy E. Langemak (1898–1938), Russian rocket designer.

Langevin. Far side. 44°N, 162°E. 58 km. South of D'Alembert, and east of the southern rim of Campbell. Named for Paul Langevin (1872–1946), French physicist.

Langley. Near side. 51°N, 86°W. Named for Samuel Langley (1834–1906), American astronomer.

Langmuir. Far side. 36°S, 129°W. 91 km. Breaks into the SE rim of Chebyshev, and into the west rim of Brouwer, to the east of Apollo. Named for Irving Langmuir (1881–1957), American chemist.

Langrenus. Near side. 9°S, 61°E. 132 km. In the Petavius chain, on the eastern edge of the Mare Fecunditatis. Has massive walls and a central peak. Named for Michael von Langren (c. 1600–1675), Belgian selenographer.

La Paz. Near side. 24°S, 64°W. 19 km. Formerly called Byrgius A. On the west rim of Byrgius. Very bright. Perhaps named for Lincoln Lapaz (b. 1897), American mathematician.

La Peyrouse. Near side. 10°S, 78°E. 78 km. Also spelled La Pérouse. Forms a pair with Ansgarius, east of the Mare Fecunditatis. Distinct. Named for Jean François La Pérouse (1741–1788), French naturalist.

Laplace, Cape. Near side. 46°N, 26°W. 50 km. Also known as Promontorium Laplace. In Sinus Iridum. Named for Pierre Laplace (1749–1827), French astronomer.

Larmor. Far side. 32°N, 180°. 97 km. SE of Shajn, and NW of Fitzgerald. Named for Sir Joseph Larmor (1857–1942), Irish mathematician.

Lassell. Near side. 16°S, 8°W. 23 km. An irregular low-walled ring in the area of Alphonsus, in the Mare Nubium. Has a small central peak. Named for William Lassell (1799–1880), British astronomer.

Laue. Far side. 28°N, 97°W. 87 km. SW of Röntgen, in the area NW of Einstein. Named for Max von Laue (1879–1960), German physicist.

Lauritsen. Far side. 27°S, 96°E. 87 km. South of Sklodowska, and north of the Mare Australe. Named for Charles C. Lauritsen (1892–1968), American physicist.

La Voisier. Near side. 36°N, 70°W. 70 km. Also spelled Lavoisier. West of the Oceanus Procellarum. Well-formed. Named for Antoine Lavoisier (1743–1794), French chemist.

Lawrence. Near side. 7°N, 43°E. 24 km. Formerly called Taruntius M. Named for Ernest O. Lawrence (1901–1958), American physicist.

Leakey. Near side. 3°S, 37°E. 13 km. Formerly called Censorinus F. Named for Louis Leakey (1903–1972), British anthropologist.

Leavitt. Far side. 46°S, 140°W. 67 km. SE of Apollo, and SW of Buffon. Named for Henrietta Leavitt (1868–1921), American astronomer.

Lebedev. Far side. 48°S, 108°E. 112 km. SE of the Mare Australe, and SW of Van der Waals. Named for Pyotr Lebedev (1866–1911), Russian physicist.

Lebedinskiy. Far side. 8°N, 165°W. 62 km. East of Zhukovskiy, in the area NW of Korolev. Named for Aleksandr Lebedinskiy (1913–1967), Russian astrophysicist.

Lebesgue. Near side. 5°S, 89°E. 11 km. Named for Henri Lebesgue (1875–1941), French mathematician.

Lee. Near side. 31°S, 41°W. 41 km. An incomplete ring structure on the south edge of the Mare Humorum. Damaged by lava. Named for John Lee (1783–1866), British astronomer.

Leeuwenhoek. Far side. 30°S, 179°W. 117 km. East of the southern rim of Van de Graaff, and north of Leibnitz. Named for Antonius von Leeuwenhoek (1632–1723), Dutch naturalist.

Legendre. Near side. 29°S, 70°E. 79 km. West of the Humboldt area. Has a central ridge. Named for Adrien Legendre (1752–1833), French mathematician.

Legentil. Near side. 73°S, 80°E. 113 km. Also spelled Le Gentil. South of Bailly. Distinct. Named for Guillaume le Gentil de la Galaisière (1725–1792), French astronomer.

Lehmann. Near side. 40°S, 56°W. 53 km. In the Schickard area. Irregular. Named for Jacob Lehmann (1800–1863), German astronomer.

Leibnitz. Far side. 38°S, 178°E. 236 km. To the SE of the Mare Ingenii. Named for Gottfried von Leibniz (sometimes spelled Leibnitz; 1646–1716), German mathematician (and see "A Note...," page xv).

Leibnitz Mountains. Near side. Found not to be mountains at all (*see also* **D'Alembert Mountains**), and the name was given to a feature on the far side (*see* **Leibnitz,** above).

Lemaître. Far side. 62°S, 150°W. 91 km. SW of Fizeau, and NW of Zeeman. Named for Abbe Georges Lemaître (1894–1966), Belgian physicist.

Le Monnier. Near side. 26°N, 31°E. 61 km. Has a smooth floor. Named for Pierre Lemonnier (1715–1799), French astronomer.

Lenitatis, Lacus. Near side. 14°N, 12°E. 80 km. Name means "The Lake of Smoothness" in Latin.

Lenz. Far side. 3°N, 102°W. 21 km. NW of Leuschner, in the area east of Hertzsprung. Named for Emil Lenz (1804–1865), Russian physicist.

Leonov. Far side. 19°N, 148°E. 34 km. On the southern rim of the Mare Moscoviense. Named for Aleksey Leonov (b. 1934), Russian cosmonaut.

Lepaute. Near side. 33°S, 34°W. 16 km. On the edge of the Palus Epidemiarum. Distinct. Named for Nicole Lepaute (1723–1788), French mathematician.

Letronne. Near side. 10°S, 43°W. 119 km. A ruined ring, south edge of Oceanus Procellarum. It has a low central peak and its north wall is destroyed. Named for Jean Antoine Letronne (1787–1848), French archeologist.

Leucippus. Far side. 29°N, 116°W. 56 km. NW of Parenago, in the area south of Landau. Named for Leucippus (fl. c.500 B.C.), Greek philosopher.

Leuschner. Far side. 2°N, 109°W. 49 km. At the SE end of the Catena Leuschner, to the east of Hertzsprung, and in the area to the NW of the Mare Orientale. Named for Armin Leuschner (1868–1953), American astronomer.

Leuschner, Catena. Far side. 6°N, 111°W. 210 km. Looks like a chain of craters, in the area of Leuschner (q.v.), in association with which it was named.

Le Verrier. Near side. 40°N, 20°W. 20 km. Also spelled Leverrier. Forms a pair with Helicon on the Mare Imbrium. Dark and distinct. Named for Urbain Leverrier (1811–1877), French astronomer.

Levi-Civita. Far side. 24°S, 143°E. 107 km. SW of Gagarin, and SE of Pirquet, in the area north of Pavlov. Named for Tullio Levi-Civita (1873–1941), Italian mathematician.

Lewis. Far side. 19°S, 114°W. 43 km. On the western edge of the Mare

Orientale, and to the SE of Houzeau. Named for Gilbert Lewis (1875–1946), American physical chemist.

Lexell. Near side. 36°S, 4°W. 63 km. A partial ring, open in the north, which breaks in on the south of Deslandres. Has a dark interior and the remains of a small central hill. Named for Anders Lexell (1740–1784), Swedish astronomer.

Ley. Far side. 43°N, 154°E. 80 km. Breaks in on the SE rim of Campbell. Named for Willy Ley (1906–1969), German-American engineer.

Liapunov *see* **Lyapunov**

Licetus. Near side. 47°S, 6°E. 75 km. Breaks in on the north side of Heraclitus, and it is depressed well below the level of that feature. In the area of Stöfler. Irregular, it has a central peak. Named for Fortunio Liceti (1577–1657), Italian physician.

Lichtenberg. Near side. 32°N, 68°W. 20 km. The center of a minor ray system on the edge of the Oceanus Procellarum. Named for Georg Lichtenberg (1742–1799), German physicist.

Lick. Near side. 12°N, 53°E. 31 km. On the edge of the Mare Crisium. Incomplete. Named for James Lick (1796–1876), American businessman-astronomer.

Liebig. Near side. 24°S, 48°W. 37 km. Formerly called Mersenius A. West of the Mare Humorum. Has moderate walls. Named for Justus von Liebig (1803–1873), German chemist.

Liebig, Rupes. Near side. 25°S, 46° W. 180 km long. A scarp in the area of Liebig (q.v.), in association with which it was named.

Lilius. Near side. 54°S, 6°E. 61 km. In the Jacobi group. Has steep, high, finely-terraced walls, an excellent central peak, and several craterlets on its floor. Named or Aloysius Lilius (d. 1576), Italian astronomer.

Lindbergh. Near side. 5°S, 53°E. 13 km. Formerly called Messier G. Named for Charles Lindbergh (1902–1974), American aviator.

Lindblad. Far side. 70°N, 99°W. 66 km. SW of Brianchon, and north of Smoluchowski. Named for Bertil Lindblad (1895–1965), Swedish astronomer.

Lindenau. Near side. 32°S, 25°E. 53 km. A walled formation in the Rabbi Levi group. Has finely-terraced walls rising to 1200 feet on the east. There is a group of low hills near the center of the floor. Named for Bernard von Lindenau (1779–1854), German astronomer.

Lindsay. Near side. 7°S, 13°E. 32 km. Formerly called Dollond C. Named for James B. Lindsay (1799–1862), Scottish electrical engineer.

Linné. Near side. 28°N, 12°E. 2 km. One of the most famous features on the Moon, it is a craterlet surrounded by nimbus on the Mare Serenitatis. Under high light it appears as a white spot, and under low angle illumination it looks like a craterlet. It was the center of a major astronomical controversy in the 1860s (*see* **Phenomena and Discoveries**). Named for Karl von Linné (Linnaeus), (1707–1778), Swedish naturalist.

Liouville. Near side. 3°N, 73°E. 16 km. Formerly called Dubiago S. Named for Joseph Liouville (1809–1882), French mathematician.

Lippershey. Near side. 26°S, 10°W. 7 km. In the Pitatus area, on the Mare Nubium. Irregular. Named for Hans Lippershey (d. c.1619), Dutch optician.

Lippmann. Far side. Named for Gabriel Lippmann (1845–1921), French physicist. This feature was renamed Boltzmann (q.v.).

Lipskiy. Far side. 2°S, 179°W. 80 km. SE of Coriolis, between Korolev and Mendeleev. Named for Vladimir Lipskiy (1863–1937), Russian botanist.

Littrow. Near side. 22°N, 31°E. 31 km. On the edge of the Mare Serenitatis. Irregular. Named for Joseph von Littrow (1781–1840), Austrian astronomer.

Littrow, Rimae. Near side. 23°N, 30°E. 180 km long. A rill system in the area of Littrow (q.v.), in association with which it was named.

Lobachevskiy. Far side. 10°N, 113°E. 85 km. SW of Guyot, and east of Moiseev. It is slightly polygonal in outline, but has fairly regular walls and has a group of central elevations. Named for Nikolas Lobachevskiy (1793–1856), Russian mathematician.

Lockyer. Near side. 46°S, 37°E. 34 km. Intrudes into Janssen. Has bright walls. Named for Sir Joseph Lockyer (1836–1920), British astronomer.

Lodygin. Far side. 18°S, 147°W. 63 km. SE of Galois, in the area SE of Korolev, and SW of Hertzsprung. Named for Aleksandr Lodygin (1847–1923), Russian electrical engineer.

Loewy. Near side. 23°S, 33°W. 24 km. On the east edge of the Mare Humorum. Distinct. Named for Maurice Loewy (1883–1907), French astronomer.

Lohrmann. Near side. 1°S, 67°W. 31 km. Between Grimaldi and Hevel. Has a central peak. Named for Wilhelm Lohrmann (1796–1840), German selenographer.

Lohse. Near side. 14°S, 60°E. 42 km. On the north wall of Vendelinus. Deep, it has a central peak. Named for Wilhelm Lohse (1845–1915), German astronomer.

Lomonosov. Far side. 27°N, 98°E. 93 km. Breaks in on the NE rim of Joliot. Named for Mikhail Lomonosov (c.1711–1765), Russian scientist.

Longomontanus. Near side. 50°S, 21°W. 145 km. A great walled plain, one of the largest on the Moon, it lies in the Clavius area. It has broken, complex walls, and a dark floor with much detail, including a central group of hills. Named for Christian Severin (Longomontanus) (1562–1647), Danish astronomer.

Lorentz. Far side. 34°N, 100°W. 371 km. Between Nernst and Berkner, to the SE of Landau. Named for Hendrik Lorentz (1853–1928), Dutch mathematical physicist.

Louville. Near side. 44°N, 47°W. 36 km. In the Jura Mountains. Has low walls and a darkish floor. Named for Jacques Louville (1671–1732), French astronomer.

Love. Far side. 6°S, 129°E. 85 km. South of the western rim of Prager, in the area SW of Mendeleev. Named for Augustus Love (1863–1940), British mathematician.

Lovelace. Far side. 82°N, 107°W. 55 km. North of Froelich, and south of Hermite, it is one of the closest features to the North Pole. Named for W. Randolph Lovelace (1907–1965), American physician.

Lovell. Far side. 39°S, 149°W. 34 km. In the SE portion of Apollo. Named for Jim Lovell (b. 1928), American astronaut.

Lowell. Far side. 13°S, 103°W. 66 km. On the NE rim of the Mare Orientale. Named for Percival Lowell (1855–1916), American astronomer.

Lubbock. Near side. 4°S, 42°E. 14 km. On the west edge of the Mare Fecunditatis. Quite bright. Named for Sir John Lubbock (1803–1865), British astronomer.

Lubiniezky. Near side. 18°S, 24°W. 44 km. A ruined ring formation in the Bullialdus area of the Mare Nubium. Has low walls broken on the south. Named for Stanislas Lubiniezky (1623–1675), Polish astronomer.

Lucian. Near side. 14°N, 37°E. 7 km. Formerly called Maraldi B. Named for Lucian (c. A.D. 120–c.200), Roman satirist.

Lucretius. Far side. 9°S, 121°W. 63 km. At the SE end of the Catena Lucretius, to the SE of Hertzsprung, and to the west of the northern portion of the Mare Orientale. Named for Lucretius (c.96–55 B.C.), Roman poet.

Lucretius, Catena. Far side. 6°S, 125°W. 240 km long. A long chain of craters extending from the southern rim of the interior enclosure of Hertzsprung to Lucretius ([q.v.], in association with which it was named), or from 4°S, 128°W to 8°S, 122°W.

Ludwig. Far side. 8°S, 97°E. 23 km. SE of Hirayama, just to the east of the southern portion of the Mare Smythii. Named for Karl Ludwig (1816–1895), German physiologist.

Luna Spacecraft. A long series of USSR Moon probes. Originally called Lunik.

Luna 1: Launched January 2, 1959. On January 4 it passed within 5955 km of the Moon, proving that there is no appreciable lunar magnetic field. Signals were lost 62 hours after it passed the Moon. It then went into a never-ending 446-day orbit around the Sun. Luna 1 hinted that humans could fly to the Moon.

Luna 2: Launched September 12, 1959. On September 14 it landed at 30°N, 1°W, near the Mare Serenitatis, at 2 mins 24 secs after midnight (Moscow time), which was 2 mins 24 secs later than expected. This was the first direct hit on the Moon by a man-made object.

Luna 3: Launched October 4, 1959. At 6:30 a.m. on October 7 the first photographic images were taken of the far side of the Moon, from a range of 70,400 km. Until that time only a maximum of 59 percent of the Moon's surface had been seen. Two cameras were used for 40 mins. On October 10, 1959, Luna 3 was at its apogee, 292,000 miles from Earth. On October 18, 1959, it was at its perigee, 29,000 miles from Earth. At this point it sent its pictures back to Earth. On October 24, 1959, the USSR gave out the pictures taken by Luna 3. All contact was lost with the spacecraft, and it disappeared.

Luna 4: Launched April 2, 1963. Missed the Moon by 8529 km. Earlier that year, on January 4, a rocket went up from the USSR. It was unnamed, and unsuccessful.

Luna 5: Launched May 9, 1965. On May 12, it crash-landed on the Moon at 31°S, 8°E, in the Mare Imbrium.

Luna 6: Launched June 8, 1965. On June 11 it missed the Moon by 161,000 km.

Luna 7: Launched October 4, 1965. Crash-landed at 9°N, 40°W, in the Oceanus Procellarum.

Luna 8: Launched December 3, 1965. Crash-landed at 9°06'N, 63°18' W, in the Oceanus Procellarum.

Luna 9: Launched January 31, 1966. On February 3 it made the first "soft landing" on the Moon, in the area of the Oceanus Procellarum, at 7°06'N, 64°24'W. It relayed to Earth closeup and panoramic pictures from the lunar surface.

Luna 10: Launched March 31, 1966. It became the first lunar satellite, making 460 orbits of the Moon. It got to within 350 km of the lunar surface, and contact with Earth was maintained for two months.

Luna 11: Launched August 24, 1966. It got to within 159 km of the Moon, and orbited. On October 1, 1966, it lost contact with Earth.

Luna 12: Launched October 22,

1966. It orbited the Moon. Lost contact with Earth on January 19, 1967.

Luna 13: Launched December 21, 1966. Similar in history to Luna 9, landing at 18°54'N, 62°W, in the Oceanus Procellarum. It also tested the hardness of the lunar soil. On December 27, 1966, it lost contact with Earth.

Luna 14: Launched April 7, 1968. Orbited the Moon, and got to within 160 km of the lunar surface.

Luna 15: Launched July 13, 1969. Made 52 lunar orbits and crash-landed in the Mare Crisium, at 17°N, 60°E. It was an unsuccessful attempt to bring back lunar samples.

Luna 16: Launched September 12, 1970. On September 20 it landed in the Mare Fecunditatis, at 0°41'S, 56°18'E. It was the first unmanned spacecraft to return lunar soil to Earth, picking up 100 grams of material and lifting off from the Moon after 26½ hours there. On September 24, 1970, Luna 16 was recovered in Kazakhstan (Earth).

Luna 17: Launched November 10, 1970. It deployed Lunokhod 1 (*see* **Lunokhod Spacecraft**).

Luna 18: Launched September 2, 1971. Made 54 lunar orbits and crash-landed in the Mare Fecunditatis, at 3°18'N, 56°30'E.

Luna 19: Launched September 28, 1971. It made over 4000 lunar orbits. Contact with Earth was maintained for over a year.

Luna 20: Launched February 14, 1972. It had a history similar to Luna 16, landing 120 km north of that craft's impact point, south of the Mare Crisium, at 3°30'N, 56°36'E. It collected highlands soil samples, and on February 25 returned to Earth.

Luna 21: Launched January 8, 1973. It had a history similar to Luna 20, but landed in Le Monnier. It deployed Lunokhod 2.

Luna 22: Launched May 29, 1974. Orbited the Moon. Ceased transmissions on November 6, 1975.

Luna 23: Launched October 28, 1974. On November 6 it landed in the southern part of the Mare Crisium. It was an unsuccessful probe. It ceased transmissions on November 9, 1975.

Luna 24: Launched August 9, 1976. Similar in history to Luna 20, it landed in the Mare Crisium, at 12°45'N, 62° 12'E, on August 18. It drilled down to 2 meters and obtained samples. On August 19 it lifted off and got back to Earth on August 22, 1976.

Lunar Eclipses. Following are 122 notable lunar eclipses recorded since the dawn of history (P=partial; T= total): 1135 B.C. The Chinese observed a lunar eclipse, the first on record. 413 B.C. lunar eclipse important in Sparta's defeat of Athens. A.D. 1110 a very dark lunar eclipse. 1504 lunar eclipse important in Columbus's story. The Moon almost disappeared in 1588 during a lunar eclipse. December 9, 1601, a very dark lunar eclipse. June 15, 1620, Kepler watched the Moon disappear during a lunar eclipse. December 9, 1620, the moon was invisible during a lunar eclipse. April 14, 1642, Hevelius observed the Moon disappear during a lunar eclipse. December 23, 1703, a very bright and red eclipse of the Moon. May 18, 1761, Wargentin observed the Moon become invisible in a total lunar eclipse. June 10, 1816, Beer and Mädler saw the Moon become invisible in a total lunar eclipse. March 19, 1848, the Moon turned blood red during a very bright lunar eclipse. October 4, 1884, almost total lunar eclipse. 1885 dark lunar eclipse seen from Tasmania. October 16, 1902, unusually dark eclipse. April 11, 1903, a dark lunar eclipse. October 6, 1903, a very bright lunar eclipse. March 22, 1913, a very dark lunar eclipse. September 15, 1913, a very dark lunar eclipse. March 2, 1923, P. August 25, 1923, P. February 20, 1924, T. August 14, 1924, T. February 8/9, 1925, P. August 4, 1925, P. June 15, 1927, T. December 8,

1927, T. June 3, 1928, T. November 27, 1928, T. April 13, 1930, P. October 7, 1930, P. April 2, 1931, T. September 26, 1931, T. March 22, 1932, P. September 14, 1932, P. January 30, 1934, P. July 26, 1934, P. January 19, 1935, T. July 16, 1935, T. January 8, 1936, T. July 4, 1936, P. November 18, 1937, P. May 14, 1938, T. November 7/8, 1938, T. May 3, 1939, T. October 28, 1939, P. March 13, 1941, P. September 5, 1941, P. March 2/3, 1942, T. August 26, 1942, T. February 20, 1943, P. August 15, 1943, P. June 25, 1945, P. December 18/19, 1945, T. June 14, 1946, T. December 8, 1946, T. June 3, 1947, P. April 23, 1948, P. April 13, 1949, T. October 6/7, 1949, T. April 2, 1950, T. September 26, 1950, T. February 10/11, 1952, P. August 5, 1952, P. January 29/30, 1953, T. July 26, 1953, T. July 15/16, 1954, P. January 18/19, 1955, T. November 29, 1955, P. May 24, 1956, P. November 18, 1956, T. May 13/14, 1957, T. November 7, 1957, T. May 3, 1958, P. March 24, 1959, P. March 13, 1960, T. September 5, 1960, T. March 2, 1961, P. August 26, 1961, P. July 6/7, 1963, P; fingers of light seen on the Moon. December 30, 1963, unusually dark total lunar eclipse. January 24/25, 1964, T. December 19, 1964, T. June 13/14, 1965, P. April 24, 1967, T. October 18, 1967, T, very bright. April 13, 1968, T. October 6, 1968, T. February 21, 1970, P. August 17, 1970, P. February 10, 1971, T. August 6, 1971, T. January 30, 1972, T. July 26, 1972, P. December 10, 1973, unusually dark partial lunar eclipse. June 4, 1974, P. November 29, 1974, T. May 25, 1975, T. November 18/19, 1975, T. May 13, 1976, 7:50 p.m. GMT, P. April 4, 1977, 4:21 a.m. GMT, P. March 24, 1978, 4:25 p.m. GMT, T. September 16, 1978, 7:03 p.m. GMT, T. March 13, 1979, 9:10 p.m. GMT, P. September 6, 1979, 10:54 a.m. GMT, T. July 17, 1981, 4:48 a.m. GMT, P. January 9, 1982, 7:56 p.m. GMT, T. July 6, 1982, 7:30 a.m. GMT, T. December 30, 1982, 11:26 a.m. GMT, T. June 25, 1983, 8:25 a.m. GMT, P. May 4, 1985, 7:57 p.m. GMT, T. October 28, 1985, 5:43 p.m. GMT, T. April 24, 1986, 12:44 p.m. GMT, T. October 17, 1986, 7:19 p.m. GMT, T. October 1, 1987, P. March 3, 1988, 4:14 p.m. GMT, P. August 27, 1988, 11:05 a.m. GMT, P. February 20, 1989, 3:37 p.m. GMT, T. August 17, 1989, 3:09 a.m. GMT, T. February 9, 1990, 7:13 p.m. GMT, T. August 6, 1990, 2:12 p.m. GMT, P.

Lunar Landings. Following is a list of the major Moon landings, manned and unmanned, in chronological order (see spacecraft names for details). September 14, 1959, Luna 2 (crash). April 26, 1962, Ranger 4 (crash). February 2, 1964, Ranger 6 (crash). July 31, 1964, Ranger 7 (crash). February 20, 1965, Ranger 8 (crash). March 24, 1965, Ranger 9 (crash). May 12, 1965, Luna 5 (crash). October 7, 1965, Luna 7 (crash). December 6, 1965, Luna 8 (crash). February 3, 1966, Luna 9 ("soft"). June 1966, Surveyor 1 ("soft"). September 1966, Surveyor 2 (crash). November 9, 1966, Orbiter 2 (crash). December 24, 1966, Luna 13 ("soft"). February 25, 1967, Orbiter 3 (crash). April 1967, Surveyor 3 (crash). July 1967, Surveyor 4 (crash). September 1967, Surveyor 5 ("soft"). November 1967, Surveyor 6 ("soft"). January 1968, Surveyor 7 ("soft"). January 31, 1968, Orbiter 5 ("soft"). July 20, 1969, Apollo 11 (manned). July 21, 1969, Luna 15 (crash). November 19, 1969, Apollo 12 (manned). September 20, 1970, Luna 16 ("soft"). November 17, 1970, Luna 17 ("soft"). February 5, 1971, Apollo 14 (manned). July 30, 1971, Apollo 15 (manned). September 1971, Luna 18 (crash). February 21, 1972, Luna 20 ("soft"). April 21, 1972, Apollo 16 (manned). December 11, 1972, Apollo 17 (manned). January 16, 1973, Luna 21 ("soft"). November 6, 1974, Luna

23 ("soft"). August 18, 1976, Luna 24 ("soft").

Lundmark. Far side. 39°S, 152°E. 113 km. SE of Jules Verne, and SW of the Mare Ingenii. Named for Knut Lundmark (1889–1958), Swedish astronomer.

Lunicus, Sinus. Near side. 32°N, 1°W. 100 km. Named in Latin for the Luna spacecraft.

Lunokhod Spacecraft. USSR wheeled vehicles deployed onto the Moon's surface by various Luna spacecraft. They were controlled from Earth. The program ran from November 17, 1970, to June 3, 1973, when the USSR announced the end of the Lunokhod program. *Lunokhod 1:* Deployed by Luna 17 (*see* **Luna spacecraft**) onto the Moon on November 17, 1970, the first wheeled vehicle landed on the Moon. It touched down at 38°18'N, 35°W, in the Mare Imbrium. It covered 6.54 miles (10.54 km) on gradients up to 30 degrees in the Mare Imbrium. It weighed 756 kg and operated for 11 months. It returned 20,000 photos and over 200 panoramic pictures. It became nonfunctional on October 4, 1971. *Lunokhod 2:* Deployed by Luna 21, near Le Monnier, 180 km from Apollo 17's site. Obtained 86 panoramic pictures, and over 80,000 TV pictures. It traveled 37 km, and finished operating in mid–May 1973.

Luther. Near side. 33°N, 24°W. 10 km. In the northern portion of the Mare Serenitatis. Distinct. Named for C. Robert Luther (1822–1900), German astronomer.

Lütke. Far side. 17°S, 123°E. 39 km. SE of Delporte, and NW of Tsiolkovskiy. Named for Feodor P. Lütke (1797–1882), Russian Arctic explorer.

Luxuriae, Lacus. Far side. 19°N, 176°E. 50 km. SE of Buys-Ballot, and NE of Anderson, in the area between Mare Moscoviense and Korolev. Name means "Lake of Luxury" in Latin.

Lyapunov. Near side. 26°N, 89°E. 66 km. Also spelled Liapunov. Named for Aleksandr Lyapunov (1857–1918), Russian mathematician.

Lyell. Near side. 14°N, 41°E. 32 km. On the western edge of the Palus Somnii. Has a darkish floor. Named for Sir Charles Lyell (1797–1875), Scottish geologist.

Lyman. Far side. 65°S, 162°E. 84 km. NE of Schrödinger and due west of Rayleigh, in the area south of Poincaré. Named for Chester Lyman (1814–1890), American astronomer.

Lyot. Near side. 50°S, 84°E. 141 km. Named for Bernard Lyot (1897–1952), French astronomer.

McAdie. Far side. 2°N, 92°E. 45 km. In the NE extremity of the Mare Smythii, just NE of Purkyně. Named for Alexander McAdie (1863–1943), Scottish meteorologist.

McClure. Near side. 15°S, 50°E. 24 km. In the Goclenius area, on the Mare Fecunditatis. Bright. Named for Sir Robert McClure (1807–1873), Irish scientific explorer.

McDonald. Near side. 30°N, 21°W. 8 km. Formerly called Carlini B. Named for William J. McDonald (1844–1926), American financier who gave the money for the McDonald Observatory.

Mach. Far side. 18°N, 149°W. 182 km. One of the main features on the far side of the Moon. Between Korolev and Joule. Named for Ernst Mach (1838–1916), Austrian physicist.

McKeller. Far side. 16°S, 171°W. 52 km. Also spelled McKellar. SW of Korolev and south of Amici. Named for Andrew McKellar (1910–1960), Canadian astronomer.

McLaughlin. Far side. 47°N, 93°W. 79 km. SW of Galvan, and east of

Stefan. Named for Dean B. McLaughlin (1901–1965), American astronomer.

Maclaurin. Near side. 2°S, 68°E. 50 km. West of the Mare Smythii. Has a concave floor and uneven walls. Named for Colin Maclaurin (1698–1746), Scottish mathematician.

Maclear. Near side. 11°N, 20°E. 20 km. On the Mare Tranquillitatis. Has a darkish floor. Named for Thomas Maclear (1794–1879), Irish astronomer.

Maclear, Rimae. Near side. 13°N, 20°E. 110 km. A system of rills in the area of Maclear (q.v.), in association with which it was named.

McMath. Far side. 18°N, 167°W. 86 km. West of Bredikhin, and NW of Korolev. Named for Robert R. McMath (1891–1962), American astronomer.

MacMillan. Near side. 24°N, 8°W. 7 km. Formerly called Archimedes F. Named for William MacMillan (1871–1948), American astronomer.

McNally. Far side. 22°N, 127°W. 48 km. NW of Comstock, and SE of Bobone, in the area north of Hertzsprung. Named for Paul McNally (1890–1955), American astronomer.

Macrobius. Near side. 21°N, 46°E. 64 km. In the area of the Mare Crisium. Has high walls and a compound central peak. Named for Ambrosius Theodosius Macrobius (fl. early 5th century A.D.), Roman grammarian.

Mädler. Near side. 11°S, 30°E. 28 km. In the Mare Nectaris. Irregular. Named for Johann von Mädler (1794–1874), German astronomer.

Maestlin. Near side. 5°N, 41°W. 7 km. Near Encke, in the Oceanus Procellarum. Obscure. Named for Michael Maestlin (1550–1631), German astronomer.

Magelhaens. Near side. 12°S, 44°E. 41 km. On the edge of the Mare Fecunditatis. Has a darkish floor. Named for Ferdinand Magelhãens (Magellan) (c.1480–1521), Portuguese navigator.

Maginus. Near side. 50°S, 6°W. 163 km. An excellent example of a walled plain, in the Clavius area. It has ruined, irregular walls, and broad inner slopes. Has a group of hills just west of center on its floor. The floor has several crater pits, hills and craterlets. Maginus is invisible at full moon. Named for Giovanni Magini (1555–1617), Italian astronomer.

Main. Near side. 81°N, 9°E. 46 km. Forms a pair with Challis, in the area of the North Pole. Named for Robert Main (1808–1878), British astronomer.

Mairan. Near side. 42°N, 43°W. 40 km. In the area of the Jura Mountains. Bright and irregular, it has high walls rising to 15,000 feet above the floor on the west. Named for Jean de Mairan (1678–1771), French physicist.

Maksutov. Far side. 41°S, 169°W. 83 km. Between Nishina and Oppenheimer, in the area to the west of the southern rim of Apollo. Named for Dmitriy Maksutov (1896–1964), Russian astronomer.

Malapert. Near side. 85°S, 13°E. 69 km. Named for Charles Malapert (1581–1630), Flemish mathematician.

Mallet. Near side. 45°S, 53°E. 58 km. In the area of the Rheita Valley. Inconspicuous. Named for John W. Mallet (1832–1912), American chemist.

Malyy. Far side. 22°N, 105°E. 41 km. East of Dziewulski, in the area to the NE of the Mare Marginis. Named for Aleksandr Malyy (1907–1961), Russian rocket engineer.

Mandelstam. Far side. 4°N, 156°E. 179 km. Also spelled Mandel'stam,

Mandel'shtam. SE of Henderson, in the area due east of Mendeleev. Named for Leonid Mandelstam (1879–1944), Russian physicist.

Manilius. Near side. 15°N, 9°E. 39 km. A banded crater, the center of a faint minor ray system, on the edge of the Mare Vaporum. Two dark bands extend from the center to the east wall. It has brilliant walls and a central peak. It is very bright under a high sun. Named for Marcus Manilius (fl. early 1st century A.D.), Roman astrologer.

Manners. Near side. 5°N, 20°E. 15 km. In the Arago area of the Mare Tranquillitatis. Bright. Named for Russell H. Manners (1800–1870), British astronomer.

Manzinus. Near side. 68°S, 25°E. 98 km. In the Boguslawsky area. Has high, terraced walls. Named for Carlo Manzini (1599–1677), Italian astronomer.

Mapping the Moon. Democritus was the first to propose that the Moon has mountains. He was right. That was in the 4th century B.C. About A.D. 80 Plutarch wrote *De Face in Orbe Lunae* (On the Face in the Orb of the Moon), in which he described the Moon as Earthlike, with mountains and ravines, and native inhabitants. Around 1600, William Gilbert drew the first lunar map, but it was not until the invention of the telescope in 1609 that the real possibilities of lunar cartography opened up. In July 1609 Thomas Harriott drew the first lunar map based on telescopic observation. This map showed several identifiable features, and was much more accurate than, for example, Galileo's map of the following year. Galileo's 1610 map was really five drawings of the Moon published in his magazine *Nuncius Siderius*. The original drawings are 8 cm in diameter. That year also, Galileo made the first serious attempts to measure the heights of lunar mountains.

It wasn't long before other astronomers began observing and mapping the Moon with the aid of ever more sophisticated telescopes. The first lunar map of any use was published on page 58 of Scheiner's book *Disquisitiones Mathematicae de Controversiis et Novitatibus Astronomiciis* in 1619. The original drawing was 92 mm in diameter, and was the first to depict identifiable features such as the Maria Smythii, Crisium, Serenitatis, Tranquillitatis, Fecunditatis, and Nectaris, and the craters Maurolycus, Walter, Eudoxus, Theophilus, Petavius, Posidonius, and Lacus Somniorum. In 1620 a lunar map appeared in Malapert's *Oratio*.

In 1634 Claude Mellan's *Carte de la Lune* appeared, the most sophisticated lunar map to that date. Between 1634 and 1638 Mellan made several accurate drawings of the Moon under the direction of Pierre Gassendi. In 1643 F. Fontana's lunar map (24 cm in the original drawing) was first reproduced in M. Hirtzgärtner's *Detectio Dioptrica Corporum Planetarum Verorum* in Frankfurt. In 1644 Argoli's map of the Moon appeared in *Pansodion Sphaericum,* and in 1645 M. F. Van Langren's very sophisticated lunar map appeared in his *Selenographia Langreniana.* His original drawing was 35 cm. Also in 1645, A. M. Schyrlaeus de Rheita's map of the Moon appeared in his *Opus Theologiae, Philosophiae et Verbi dei Praeconibus Utile et Incundum.* His original drawing was 18 cm. In 1646 Fontana's map appeared again in his *Novae Coelestium Terrestriumque Rerum Observationes.* In 1647 Hevelius drew his lunar map. He named several features, only a few of which are still in use. In 1648 appeared his third lunar map (29 cm in the original drawing) in his *Selenographia Sive Lunae Descriptio.*

The second half of the 17th century saw a continuation of lunar mapping. In 1651 William Gilbert's map of half a century earlier was published, and in the same year Riccioli produced a map based on his pupil Grimaldi's observations of the more than 200 features he named. Most of these names are still in use, including Mare Imbrium, Mare Tranquillitatis and Sinus Iridum. This map appeared in his *Almagestum Novum.* In 1655 Borel and Müller both produced lunar maps, and in 1671 Cherubin published his. In 1676 Francisci produced his map, and then in 1680 came the most magnificent lunar map to that date, Cassini's 21¼-inch map, prepared by Leclerc de Paligny under Cassini's direction, and engraved by Mellan. In 1696 Eimmart came out with the last major Moon map of the century.

In 1750 Tobias Mayer, in his *Bericht von den Mondskugeln,* described his micrometric measurements of 23 lunar features. Mayer was the pioneer in this field. Thirteen years after Mayer's death, in 1775, his 8-inch lunar map was published, and for over half a century this was to remain the best. He drew the Moon with south at the top, and introduced coordinates. In 1778 J. H. Schröter first described lunar rills, and in 1780–83 J. H. Lambert's lunar map based on micrometric measurements in stereographic projection was published. In 1791 Schröter, in his *Selenotopographische Fragmente,* gave positional measurements and heights of several lunar mountains.

In 1824 the first sections of Wilhelm Lohrmann's large, accurate lunar map were published. In 1835 his largest lunar map, 385 mm in diameter, was published in Leipzig. In 1837 Wilhelm Beer and Johann Mädler prepared a new, large lunar map, the first to be divided into four quadrants. It was 97.5 cm in diameter, and shows all the details that can be seen with a 4-inch refractor. It remained the best map of the Moon until 1878. In 1838 *Der Mond,* written by Beer and Mädler, was published. It contained a full description of the entire visible surface of the Moon. In 1839 F. W. Bessel made the first accurate measurements of the Moon with a heliometer. That same year Daguerre photographed the Moon—unsuccessfully (*see* **Photography**). In 1841–43 Julius Schmidt made six drawings of the Moon, and in 1876 *The Moon,* written by E. Neison (Edward Nevill) was published. It contained a map based on Mädler's, with a description of every named formation.

In 1878 Schmidt's *Charte der Gebirge des Mondes* was published in Berlin, based on his observations between 1840 and 1874. This was the best lunar map up to its time, and one of the best ever, even in hindsight. It consisted of 25 sections printed on separate sheets. The whole was 194.9 cm in diameter, and 33,000 individual features were recorded. It introduced the lunar nomenclature pretty much as we know it today. The heights of over 3000 lunar mountains were measured. In 1896 T. Gwyn Elger drew his lunar map, and in 1897 the Lick Observatory produced its great photographic atlas of the Moon, based on photos taken with the Observatory's 36-inch refractor.

In 1900 L. Weinek's *Photographischer Mond-Atlas* was produced in Prague. It consisted of 100 sheets covering most of the visible surface of the Moon. In 1904 W. H. Pickering produced a lunar atlas showing each region of the Moon under five different conditions of illumination. In 1909 the great photographic atlas of the Observatoire National de Paris was finished. It was called *Atlas Photographique de la Lune.* In 1910 Walter Goodacre's lunar map was published in London, based on photographic positional measurements by S. A. Saunder. It was printed on 25 sheets, and the whole was 192.5 cm in diameter. In 1912 *J. N. Krieger's Mond-Atlas* was produced in Vienna and in 1930 Goodacre was back with the publication of his book containing a detailed lunar map and a full account of each named formation. In 1935 the I.A.U.

(International Astronomical Union) issued a map drawn by W. H. Wesley and M. A. Blagg.

Lunar maps and atlases continued to be produced, but the true landmark was the first photographic session taken of the far side of the Moon, on October 7, 1959, by Luna 3 (*see* **Luna spacecraft**). Until that time only 59 percent of the Moon had been seen from Earth. That year, 1959, H. P. Wilkins published his lunar map of 100 inches to the Moon's diameter, and Gerard P. Kuiper produced the best lunar atlas to that date, *Atlas of the Moon,* in Chicago. In 1964 Ranger 7 plummeted into the Mare Nubium, but before it did it sent back to Earth 4308 high-quality photos, and for the first time the surface of the Moon could be studied from very close range. The photos covered an area about the size of France. In 1969 H. R. Hatfield's *The Amateur Astronomer's Photographic Lunar Atlas* was published in London, and also in that year men landed on the Moon. From then on lunar mapping almost reached the height of sophistication. This entry acknowledges a great debt to that most exciting and provocative of astronomers, Patrick Moore, and to his 1976 book *New Guide to the Moon.*

Maraldi. Near side. 19°N, 35°E. 40 km. In the northern portion of the Mare Tranquillitatis. Distinct. Named for Giovanni Maraldi (1709–1788), Italian astronomer.

Maraldi, Mons. Near side. 20°N, 35°E. A mountain in the area of Maraldi (q.v.), in association with which it was named.

Marci. Far side. 22°N, 169°W. 25 km. SE of Morse and west of Jackson, in the area east of Buys-Ballot. Named for Johannes Marci of Kronland (1595–1667), Czech physicist.

Marco Polo. Near side. 15°N, 2°W. 28 km. In the area of the Apennines. Irregular, it has a darkish floor. Named for Marco Polo (c.1254–c.1324), Venetian traveler.

Marconi. 9°S, 145°E. 73 km. SW of Chaplygin, and SE of Dellinger, in the area SE of Mendeleev. Named for Guglielmo Marconi (1874–1937), Italian electrician.

Marginis, Mare. Near side. 13°N, 87°E. 360 km. Its Latin name is "The Marginal Sea," because it is on the limb of the Moon and is never well-seen from Earth. Orbiter and Apollo pictures prove it to be a true mare, of the Crisium (q.v.) type, but less well defined.

Maria. Plural of mare, a lunar "sea." Although there is no water on the Moon, early astronomers thought these were seas. (*See* **Anguis, Australe, Cognitum, Crisium, Fecunditatis, Frigoris, Humboldtianum, Humorum, Imbrium, Ingenii, Insularum, Marginis, Moscoviense, Nectaris, Nubium, Orientale, Serenitatis, Smythii, Spumans, Tranquillitatis, Undarum, Vaporum**.)

Marinus. Near side. 50°S. 75°E. 58 km. In the area of the Mare Australe. Distinct, it has a central peak. Named for Marinus (fl. 2nd century A.D.), Greek geographer.

Mariotte. Far side. 29°S, 140°W. 66 km. Due east of Barringer, and NE of Kleimenov, in the area immediately NE of Apollo. Named for Edmé Mariotte (c.1620–1684), French physicist.

Marius. Near side. 12°N, 51°W. 41 km. Forms a pair with Reiner, in the Oceanus Procellarum. Has a bright border, rising to 4000 feet above its floor. It has a low central peak. Named for Simon Mayr (Marius) (1573–1624), German astronomer.

Marius, Rima. Near side. 17°N, 49°W. 200 km long. A rill in the area of

Marius (q.v.), in association with which it was named.

Markov. Near side. 53°N, 63°W. 40 km. Named for Andrei Markov (1856–1922), Russian mathematician.

Marth. Near side. 31°S, 29°W. 7 km. In the Palus Epidemiarum. Named for A. Marth (1828–1897), German astronomer.

Maskelyne. Near side. 2°N, 30°E. 24 km. In the Mare Tranquillitatis. Has a low central peak. Named for Nevil Maskelyne (1732–1811), British astronomer.

Mason. Near side. 43°N, 30°E. 34 km. Forms a pair with Plana, in the area of Bürg. Named for Charles Mason (c.1730–1787), British astronomer.

Maunder. Far side. 14°S, 94°W. 55 km. In the north central part of the Mare Orientale. Named for Edward Maunder (1851–1928), Irish astronomer.

Maupertuis. Near side. 50°N, 27°W. 46 km. An irregular mountain enclosure, in the Juras. Named for Pierre de Maupertuis (1698–1759), French astronomer.

Maurolycus. Near side. 42°S, 14°E. 114 km. A great enclosure east of Stöfler, this is one of the major features of the Moon. It has huge ramparts, a rough floor, and a high central mountain with several peaks. Named for Francesco Maurolico (1494–1575), Italian astronomer.

Maury. Near side. 37°N, 40°E. 18 km. In the Atlas area. Bright, and deep. Named for Antonia Maury (1866–1952), American astronomer.

Maxwell. Far side. 30°N, 98°E. 115 km. NE of Joliot, and north of Lomonosov. Named for James Clerk Maxwell (1831–1879), Scottish physicist.

Mayer, C. Near side. 63°N, 17°E. 38 km. North of the Mare Frigoris. Rhomboidal in shape. Named for Christian Mayer (1719–1783), German astronomer.

Mayer, T. Near side. 16°N, 29°W. 33 km. Also called T. Mayer, and Tobias Mayer. An excellent crater at the east end of the Carpathians. Has a central peak. Named for Tobias Mayer (1723–1762), German astronomer.

Medii, Sinus. Near side. 3°N, 3°E. 350 km. The craterlets Bruce and Blagg are on it. Its name in Latin means "The Central Bay."

Mee. Near side. 44°S, 35°W. 132 km. A large mountain walled plain with low broken walls, to the SE of Hainzel, on which it abuts. Named for Arthur Mee (1860–1926), Scottish astronomer.

Mees. Far side. 14°N, 96°W. 51 km. West of Einstein, and east of Nobel, in the area north of the Mare Orientale. Named for Charles E. K. Mees (1882–1960), American chemist.

Meggers. Far side. 24°N, 123°E. 53 km. NW of Vernandsky, and NE of Olcott, in the area NW of Mendeleev and SW of the Mare Moscoviense. Named for William F. Meggers (1888–1966), American physicist.

Meitner. Far side. 11°S, 113°E. 87 km. To the immediate east of Pasteur, and SW of Langemak. Named for Lise Meitner (1878–1968), Austrian physicist.

Mendel. Far side. 49°S, 110°W. 138 km. SW of the Mare Orientale, and NE of Boltzmann. Named for Gregor Mendel (1822–1884), Austrian geneticist.

Mendeleev. Far side. 6°N, 141°E. 330 km. South of the Mare Moscoviense, between Fabry and the Mare Ingenii, it is one of the major features on the far side of the Moon. Named for

Dmitri Mendeleev (1834–1907), Russian chemist.

Mendeleev, Catena. Far side. 12°N, 140°E. 130 km. A chain of craters which extends NE from the northern rim of Mendeleev (q.v.), in association with which it was named.

Menelaus. Near side. 16°N, 16°E. 27 km. In the Haemus Mountains. Brilliant, it has an interior peak. Named for Menelaus (fl. 1st century A.D.), Greek astronomer.

Menelaus, Rimae. Near side. 17°N, 17°E. 140 km long. A rill system in the area of Menelaus (q.v.), in association with which it was named.

Menzel. Near side. 3°N, 37°E. 3 km. Named for Donald Menzel (1901–1976), American astronomer.

Mercator. Near side. 29°S, 26°W. 47 km. Forms a pair with Campanus, in the area of the Mare Humorum. Has a dark floor, with craterlets. Named for Gerardus Mercator (1512–1594), Flemish geographer.

Mercator, Rupes. Near side. 30°S, 23°W. 180 km. A scarp in the area of Mercator (q.v.), in association with which it was named.

Mercurius. Near side. 56°N, 65°E. 68 km. In the area of the Mare Humboldtianum. Has a low central peak. Named for Girolamo Mercurio (c.1550–1615), Italian physician.

Merrill. Far side. 75°N, 116°W. 57 km. NW of Niepce, and south of Froelich. Named for Paul Merrill (1887–1961), American astronomer.

Mersenius. Near side. 21°S, 49°W. 84 km. Close to the NE border of the Mare Humorum. The walls rise to 7000 feet on the west, higher on the north, and the inner walls are terraced. It has a distinctly convex floor, on which are craterlets. There is an extensive rill system to the west of it (*see* **Mersenius, Rimae,** below). Named for Marin Mersenne (Mersenius) (1588–1648), French mathematician.

Mersenius, Rimae. Near side. 20°S, 45°W. 230 km long. A rill system in the area of Mersenius (q.v.), in association with which it was named.

Mesentsev. Far side. 72°N, 129°W. 90 km. Also spelled Mezentsev. Immediately west of Niepce, in the area NE of Birkhoff. Named for Yuriy Mezentsev (1929–1965), Russian engineer.

Meshcerskiy. Far side. 12°N, 125°E. 65 km. Borders the NE rim of Ostwald, to the NW of Mendeleev. Named for Ivan Meshcerskiy (1859–1935), Russian mechanician.

Messala. Near side. 39°N, 60°E. 124 km. In the area of the Mare Humboldtianum. It is rectangular and has low, broken walls. Named for Masha'alla (Messahala, Messala), (fl. 762–c.815), Arab astrologer.

Messier. Near side. 2°S, 48°E. 11 km. On the Mare Fecunditatis. Named for Charles Messier (1730–1817), French astronomer.

Messier, Rima. Near side. 1°S, 45°E. 100 km long. A rill in the area of Messier (q.v.), in association with which it was named.

Metchnikiff. Far side. 11°S, 149°W. 60 km. Also spelled Mechnikov. NE of Das, NW of Paschen, and SW of Sechenov, in the area just to the east of the southern rim of Korolev. Named for Élie Metchnikiff (1845–1916), Russian bacteriologist.

Metius. Near side. 40°S, 44°E. 88 km. Forms a pair with Fabricius, in the Janssen group. Distinct. Named for Jacobus Metius (d. 1628), Dutch telescope maker.

Meton. Near side. 74°N, 25°E. 122 km. Near Scoresby, in the area of the

North Pole. One of the largest formations on the Moon, it has a light gray interior, a smooth floor, and a small peak near the north rampart. Named for Meton (fl. 5th century B.C.), Greek astronomer.

Michelson. Far side. 6°N, 121°W. 126 km. Breaks the NE rim of Hertzsprung. Named for Albert A. Michelson (1852–1931), American physicist.

Michelson, Catena. Far side. 2°N, 115°W. 280 km long. A chain of craters between Hertzsprung and Leuschner, it extends from Michelson crater ([q.v.], in association with which it was named), in a SE fashion toward Grachev, or from 6°N, 120°W to 3°S, 108°W.

Milanković. Far side. 77°N, 170°E. 105 km. South of the western rim of Plaskett, and NW of Riccò. Named for Milutin Milanković (1879–1958), Yugoslav geophysicist.

Milichius. Near side. 10°N, 30°W. 12 km. On the Oceanus Procellarum. Bright. Named for Jacob Milich (1501–1559), German physicist.

Miller. Near side. 39°S, 1°E. 61 km. A ring plain which breaks in on the north wall of Nasireddin, in the Orontius group. Quite distinct, it has a central mountain with several peaks. Named for William A. Miller (1817–1870), British astronomer.

Millikan. Far side. 47°N, 121°E. 98 km. NE of Fabry, and north of H. G. Wells. Named for Robert A. Millikan (1868–1953), American physicist.

Mills. Far side. 9°N, 156°E. 32 km. East of the northern rim of Mendeleev, and NE of Henderson. Named for Mark Mills (1917–1958), American physicist.

Milne. Far side. 31°S, 113°E. 262 km. Between Chrétien and Scaliger, to the NE of the Mare Australe. Named for Edward A. Milne (1896–1950), British astronomer.

Mineur. Far side. 25°N, 162°W. 73 km. NE of Jackson, and SE of Cockcroft. Named for Henri Mineur (1899–1954), French astronomer.

Minkowski. Far side. 56°S, 145°W. 104 km. Between Chebyshev and Schrödinger, and between Lemaître and Riedel, to the NW of Fizeau, and to the east of Stoney. Named for Hermann Minkowski (1864–1909), German mathematician.

Minnaert. Far side. Named for Marcel Minnaert (1893–1970), Belgian astronomer. This feature had its name changed to Rayleigh (q.v.).

Mitchell. Near side. 50°N, 20°E. 30 km. Distinct. Abuts on Aristoteles. Named for Maria Mitchell (1818–1889), American astronomer.

Mitra. Far side. 18°N, 155°W. 92 km. Immediately west of Mach. Named for S. K. Mitra (1890–1963), Indian physicist.

Möbius. Far side. 16°N, 101°E. 50 km. Immediately to the SE of Popov, in the area just to the NE of the Mare Marginis. Named for August Möbius (1790–1868), German astronomer.

Mohorovičić. Far side. 19°S, 165°W. 51 km. SW of Korolev, and NW of Apollo. Named for Andrija Mohorovičić (1857–1936), Yugoslav meteorologist.

Moigno. Near side. 66°N, 29°E. 37 km. Named for François Moigno (1804–1884), French mathematician.

Moiseev. Far side. 9°N, 103°E. 60 km. Due east of Dreyer, in the area east of the Mare Marginis. Named for Nikolay Moiseev (1902–1955), Russian astronomer.

Moissan. Far side. 5°N, 137°E. 22 km. In the extreme eastern part of

Mendeleev. Named for Henri Moissan (1852–1907), French chemist.

Möltke. Near side. 1°S, 24°E. 7 km. On the northern edge of the Mare Tranquillitatis. Distinct. Named for Helmuth Möltke (1800–1891), German field-marshal.

Monge. Near side. 19°S, 48°E. 37 km. On the edge of the Mare Fecunditatis. Quite irregular. Named for Gaspard Monge (1746–1818), French mathematician.

Montanari. Near side. 46°S, 20°W. 77 km. In the area of Longomontanus. Distorted, it has a craterlet on its floor. Named for Geminiano Montanari (1633–1687), Italian astronomer.

Montgolfier. Far side. 47°N, 160°W. 88 km. Teamed with Woltjer to its south. NW of Fowler. Named for the Montgolfier brothers, French balloonists: Jacques Étienne (1745–1799), and Joseph Michel (1740–1810).

Moore. Far side. 37°N, 178°W. 55 km. East of Champollion, and west of Parsons. Named for Joseph Moore (1878–1949), American astronomer.

Moretus. Near side. 70°S, 8°W. 114 km. An excellent ring structure, in the southern uplands. It has massive walls, and a dark floor, and its central peak rises to 700 feet (the highest central mountain on the Moon, according to Mädler). Named for Theodore Moretus (1602–1667), Flemish mathematician.

Morley. Near side. 3°S, 65°E. 14 km. Formerly called Maclaurin R. Named for Edward Morley (1838–1923), British chemist.

Moro, Mons. Near side. 12°S, 20°W. A mountain. Named for Antonio-Lazzaro Moro (1687–1764), Italian geologist.

Morozov. Far side. 5°N, 127°E. 43 km. Just west of Mendeleev. Named for Nikolay Morozov (1854–1946), Russian scientist.

Morse. Far side. 22°N, 175°W. 77 km. SW of Fitzgerald, and east of Buys-Ballot. Named for Samuel Morse (1791–1872), American inventor.

Mortis, Lacus. Near side. 44°N, 27°E. 150 km. A small, darkish plain near Bürg. Name means "The Lake of Death" in Latin.

Moscoviense, Mare. Far side. 27°N, 147°E. Also known as Mare Mosquense. Between Mendeleev and Campbell, it is one of the major features on the far side of the Moon and was one of the first features on the far side to be identified. It was shown as a dark patch on the Luna 3 photos of 1959. It has a dark floor, an outer ring, and contains Titov. Name means "The Sea of Moscow" in Latin.

Moseley. Far side. 23°N, 95°W. 90 km. Immediately NE of Bell, to the NW of Einstein. Named for Henry Moseley (1801–1872), British scientific writer.

Mösting. Near side. 1°S, 6°W. 25 km. Forms a pair with Sömmering, in the area of the Sinus Medii. Very deep, it has an inconspicuous central peak. Named for Johann von Mösting (1759–1843), the Danish statesman-astronomer.

Mouchez. Near side. 78°N, 27°W. 82 km. Named for Ernest Mouchez (1821–1852), French astronomer.

Moulton. Far side. 61°S, 97°E. 50 km. Immediately south of Chamberlin, along the Rima Schrödinger, NW of Schrödinger. Named for Forest Moulton (1872–1952), American astronomer.

Mountains *see* **Agricola, Alps, Altai Scarp, Ampère, Apennines, Archimedes, Argaeus, Mont Blanc** (under B), **Bradley, Carpathians, Caucasus, Cordilleras, D'Alembert,**

Hadley, Haemus, Hansteen, Harbinger, Herodotus, Huygens, Jura, La Hire, Leibnitz, Maraldi, Moro, Penck, Percy, Pico, Piton, Pyrenees, Riphaens, Rook, Rümker, Schneckenberg, Secchi, Serao, Soviet, Spitsbergen, Stag's-Horn, Straight Range, Straight Wall, Taurus, Teneriffe, Urals, Usov, Vinogradov, Wolff.

Müller. Near side. 7°S, 3°E. 22 km. In the area of Ptolemaeus. Quite regular. Named for Paul H. Müller (1899–1965), Swiss physiologist.

Murchison. Near side. 5°N, 0°. 58 km. Forms a pair with Pallas, on the edge of the Sinus Medii. Irregular, it has complete low walls on the west but broken ones on the south. Named for Sir Roderick Murchison (1792–1871), Scottish geologist.

Mutis. Near side. 63°S, 30°E. 78 km. In the southern uplands. Has two large craters on its floor. Named for José Mutis (1732–1808), Spanish astronomer.

Nagaoka. Far side. 20°N, 154°E. 47 km. Just to the SE of the Mare Moscoviense, and west of Konstantinov. Named for Hantaro Nagaoka (1865–1950), Japanese physicist.

Nansen. Far side. 81°N, 91°E. 122 km. Between Peary and Schwarzschild, it is the largest feature north of 80°N, and thus appropriately near the North Pole, because it was named for Fridtjof Nansen (1861–1930), Norwegian Arctic explorer.

Naonobu. Near side. 5°S, 58°E. 35 km. Formerly called Langrenus B. Named for Kano Naonobu (1607–1650), Japanese painter.

Nasireddin. Near side. 41°S, 0°. 52 km. An excellent crater in the Orontius group. Quite distinct, it has regular terraced walls and a central crater on its floor. Named for Nasir ed-Din al-Tusi (1201–1274), Arab mathematician.

Nasmyth. Near side. 52°S, 53°W. 77 km. In the Phocylides group. Quite regular, it has no central peak. Named for James Nasmyth (1808–1890), British astronomer.

Nassau. Far side. 25°S, 177°E. 77 km. Just to the NE of Van de Graaff. Named for Jason J. Nassau (1892–1965), American astronomer.

Naumann. Near side. 35°N, 62°W. 10 km. In the northern part of the Oceanus Procellarum. Has bright walls. Named for Karl F. Naumann (1797–1873), German mineralogist.

Neander. Near side. 31°S, 40°E. 50 km. In the area of the Rheita Valley. Well formed. Named for Michael Neander (1529–1581), German mathematician.

Nearch. Near side. 58°S, 39°E. 76 km. In the area of Vlacq. Has craterlets on its floor. Named for Nearch (fl. 325 B.C.), friend of Alexander the Great.

Nebularum, Palus. Near side. 38°N, 1°E. Part of the Mare Imbrium. An old naming, it has been left off some modern maps. Name means "The Marsh of Mists" in Latin.

Necho. Far side. 5°S, 123°E. 31 km. NE of Langemak, between Mendeleev and Pasteur. Named for Necho II of Egypt (d. 593 B.C.), pharaoh who sponsored navigation.

Nectaris, Mare. Near side. 14°S, 34°E. 350 km. Just over 4 billion years old, there is much faulting here, and it is basically circular, but distorted. The Altai Scarp represents part of its system. On the SE edge are Theophilus and the bays of Beaumont and Fracastorius. Rosse crater is on it. Name means "The Sea of Nectar" in Latin.

Neison. Near side. 68°N, 28°E. 53 km. In the area of Meton. Regular, it has no central peak. Named for E. Neison (Edward Nevill) (1851–1938), British astronomer.

Neper. Near side. 7°N, 83°E. 137 km. In the area of the Mare Marginis and the Mare Smythii. Deep. Named for John Napier (Neper) (1550–1617), Scottish mathematician.

Nernst. Far side. 36°N, 95°W. 119 km. On the NW rim of Röntgen, with which it forms a pair, in the area to the NW of Einstein. Named for Walther Nernst (1864–1941), German physical chemist.

Neujmin. Far side. 27°S, 125°E. 100 km. Directly south of the western rim of Tsiolkovskiy. Named for Grigoriy Neujmin (1886–1946), Russian astronomer.

Neumayer. Far side. 62°S, 75°E. 76 km. In the area of Boussingault. Distinct. Named for Georg von Neumayer (1826–1909), German geophysicist.

Newcomb. Near side. 30°N, 44°E. 41 km. In the Cleomedes area. Its south wall is broken by a crater. Named for Simon Newcomb (1835–1909), American astronomer.

Newton. Near side. 78°S, 20°W. 79 km. In the area of Moretus. Irregular and unusually deep. Named for Sir Isaac Newton (1642–1727), English mathematician.

Nicholson. Near side. 26°S, 85°W. 38 km. Named for Seth Nicholson (1891–1963), American astronomer.

Nicolaev *see* **Nikolayev**

Nicolai. Near side. 42°S, 26°E. 42 km. In the area of Janssen. Regular. Named for Friedrich Nicolai (1793–1846), German astronomer.

Nicollet. Near side. 22°S, 12°W. 15 km. In the Mare Nubium, west of Birt. Distinct. Named for Joseph Nicollet (1786–1843), French mathematician.

Nielsen. Near side. 32°N, 52°W. 10 km. Formerly called Wollaston C. Named for Niels Nielsen (1865–1931), Danish mathematician.

Niepce. Far side. 72°N, 120°W. 58 km. Just south of Merrill, in the area to the NE of Birkhoff. Named for Joseph Niepce (1765–1833), French inventor.

Nijland. Far side. 33°N, 134°E. 36 km. Between Mare Moscoviense and H. G. Wells, in the area to the SW of Kurchatov. Named for Albertus Nijland (1868–1936), Dutch astronomer.

Nikolayev. Far side. 35°N, 151°E. 41 km. Also spelled Nicolaev. Just to the north of the eastern half of Mare Moscoviense, and south of Campbell. Named for Andrian G. Nikolayev (b. 1929), Russian cosmonaut.

Nishina. Far side. 45°S, 171°W. 66 km. Just SW of Maksutov, in the area to the east of Von Kármán. Named for Yoshio Nishina (1890–1951), Japanese physicist.

Nobel. Far side. 15°N, 101°W. 49 km. West of Einstein and north of Elvey, in the area to the NE of Hertzsprung. Named for Alfred Nobel (1833–1896), Swedish chemist.

Nobili. Near side. 2°N, 76°E. 42 km. Formerly called Schubert Y. Named for Leopoldo Nobili (1784–1835), Italian physician.

Nöggerath. Near side. 49°S, 45°W. 31 km. In the area of Schiller. Has low walls. Named for Johann Nöggerath (1788–1877), German geologist.

Nonius. Near side. 35°S, 4°E. 70 km. A large formation which breaks in on the wall of Walter, NE of Kaiser, in the area of Stöfler. Quite regular, it has broken walls and the interior has many ridges and large low rings. Named for

Pedro Nunes (Nonius) (1492–1577), Portuguese cosmographer.

Norman. Near side. 11°S, 30°W. 10 km. Formerly called Euclides B. Named for Robert Norman (fl. late 16th century), English navigator.

Nöther. Far side. 66°N, 114°W. 67 km. Also spelled Noether. NE of Dyson and SE of Niepce, in the area NE of Birkhoff. Named for Amalie Nöther (1882–1935), German mathematician.

Nubium, Mare. Near side. 19°S, 14°W. 750 km. One of the major lunar maria, the name means (and it is also called) "The Sea of Clouds" in Latin. It is lighter, patchier, and much less regular than the Mare Imbrium. Craters on it include Bullialdus and the Fra Mauro group. Part of it is also called Mare Insularum (q.v.), and another part of it (10°S, 23°W, and 340 km's worth) was renamed Mare Cognitum where Apollo 12 came down. However, this Mare Cognitum is not universally accepted, by any means.

Numerov. Far side. 71°S, 161°W. 106 km. NW of Zeeman and NE of Schrödinger. Named for Boris Numerov (1891–1943), Russian astronomer.

Nunn. Far side. 5°N, 91°E. 19 km. NW of Babcock, and SE of Jansky, just outside the NE rim of Mare Smythii. Named for Sir Thomas Nunn (b. 1870), British mathematician.

Nušl. Far side. 32°N, 167°E. 62 km. West of Shajn, and east of the northern sector of the Mare Moscoviense. Named for Frantisek Nušl (1867–1925), Czech astronomer.

Oblivionis, Lacus. Far side. 21°S, 168°W. 50 km. Between Sniadecki and Mohorovičić, in the area NW of Apollo and SW of Korolev. Name means "The Lake of Oblivion" in Latin.

Obruchev. Far side. 39°S, 162°E. 72 km. Breaks in on the southern rim of the Mare Ingenii. Named for Vladimir Obruchev (1863–1904), Russian geologist.

Oceanus. The only "oceanus" on the Moon is the Oceanus Procellarum (q.v.). It is the largest irregular "sea" on the surface and is much larger than the largest mare, or "sea."

O'Day. Far side. 31°S, 157°E. 71 km. Fairly prominent crater breaking into the NW rim of Mare Ingenii. Named for Marcus O'Day (1897–1961), American rocket engineer.

Odii, Lacus. Near side. 19°N, 7°E. 70 km. Name means "The Lake of Hatred" in Latin.

Oenopides. Near side. 57°N, 64°W. 67 km. Near Sinus Roris, in the area of the limb of the Moon. Has high walls. Named for Oenopides of Chios (fl. 5th century B.C.), Greek astronomer.

Oersted. Near side. 43°N, 47°E. 42 km. On the edge of the Lacus Somniorum. Quite irregular. Named for Hans Oersted (1777–1851), Danish physicist.

Ohm. Far side. 18°N, 114°W. 64 km. Between Weyl and Alter, NE of Hertzsprung. A smaller fresh crater, it is remarkable in that one ray stretches from it onto the near side of the Moon, passing north of Aristarchus and on to Timocharis. Named for Georg Ohm (1787–1854), German physicist.

Oken. Near side. 44°S, 76°E. 72 km. In the area of the Mare Australe. Has a darkish floor. Named for Lorenz Oken (1779–1851), German naturalist.

Olbers. Near side. 7°N, 76°W. 75 km. In the area of Grimaldi. It is the center of a major ray system. Named for Heinrich Olbers (1758–1840), German astronomer.

Olcott. Far side. 20°N, 117°E. 82 km. A major crater NW of Mendeleev, and SE of Joliot. There is terracing here.

Named for William T. Olcott (1873–1936), American writer on astronomy.

Olivier. Far side. 59°N, 138°E. 69 km. NW of Størmer and NE of Volterra, in the area SE of Schwarzschild. Named for Guillaume Olivier (1756–1814), French naturalist.

Omar Khayyám. Far side. 58°N, 102°W. 70 km. North of Chapman, and east of Birkhoff. Named for Omar Khayyám (c.1050–c.1123), Persian poet-astronomer.

Opelt. Near side. 16°S, 17°W. 49 km. A ghost crater east of Bullialdus, in the Mare Nubium. Named for Friedrich Opelt (1794–1863), German financier.

Opelt, Rima. Near side. 13°S, 18°W. 70 km long. A rill in the area of Opelt (q.v.), in association with which it was named.

Oppenheimer. Far side. 35°S, 166°W. 206 km. Between Apollo and Leibnitz. Named for J. Robert Oppenheimer (1904–1967), American physicist.

Oppolzer. Near side. 1°S, 1°W. 40 km. On the edge of the Sinus Medii. Has low walls. Named for Theodor von Oppolzer (1841–1886), Czech astronomer.

Oppolzer, Rima. Near side. 1°S, 2°E. 110 km long. A rill in the area of Oppolzer (q.v.), in association with which it was named.

Orbiter Spacecraft. A series of U.S. Moon probes. *Orbiter 1:* Launched August 10, 1966. A successful photographic lunar probe, it stopped photographing the Moon on August 29, and on October 29, 1966, crashed into the Moon at 6°42'N, 162°E. *Orbiter 2:* Launched November 7, 1966. A successful photographic lunar probe, it transmitted 422 pictures before crash-landing at 4°S, 98°E. It photographed Copernicus obliquely from 150 miles away, but from only 28 miles above the Moon's surface. This was called "The Picture of the Century," and was the best lunar view up to that time. *Orbiter 3:* Launched February 4, 1967. Returned 307 photos before crashing at 14°36'N, 91°42'W. It was a success. *Orbiter 4:* Launched May 4, 1967. A successful photographic lunar probe, it sent back 326 photos. *Orbiter 5:* Launched August 1, 1967. A successful photographic lunar probe, it was control-landed onto the Moon at 0°, 70°W.

Oresme. Far side. 43°S, 169°E. 77 km. SE of the Mare Ingenii and west of the northern half of Von Kármán. Named for Nicole Oresme (c.1323–1382), French mathematician.

Orientale, Mare. The only major mare which straddles the limb of the Moon, being mostly on the far side, but visible from Earth during favorable librations. 19°S, 95°W. 965 km. To the west of Eichstädt and Rocca, the Rook Mountains and the Cordillera Mountains make up its outer and inner ringwall respectively. It is probably between three and eight billion years old, and was discovered by Wilkins and Moore in 1938. Name means "The Eastern Sea" in Latin.

Orlov. Far side. 26°S, 175°W. 81 km. East of Nassau, in the area east of the northern portion of Van de Graaff. Named for Aleksandr Orlov (1880–1954), Russian astronomer.

Orontius. Near side. 40°S, 4°W. 122 km. A large, irregular formation NE of Tycho. Once nearly circular, but distorted by Huggins, it has several craterlets and pits on its interior. Named for Oronce Fine (1494–1555), French mathematician.

Ostwald. Far side. 11°N, 122°E. 113 km. A major crater just east of Guyot, in the area to the NW of Mendeleev. Named for Wilhelm Ostwald (1853–1932), German chemist.

Palisa. Near side. 9°S, 7°W. 33 km. An obscure ringed formation on the edge of a larger ring, in the area of Alphonsus. Has low ramparts and some craterlets on the interior. Named for Johann Palisa (1848–1925), Czech astronomer.

Palitzsch. Near side. 28°S, 64°E. 41 km. In actuality this is a crater-chain. Named for Johann Palitzsch (1723–1788), German astronomer.

Palitzsch, Vallis. Near side. 25°S, 65°E. 110 km long. A valley in the area of Palitzsch (q.v.), in association with which it was named.

Pallas. Near side. 5°N, 2°W. 46 km. Forms a pair with Murchison, in the area of Sinus Medii. An excellent telescopic object, it has a bright central peak. Named for Peter Simon Pallas (1741–1811), German naturalist.

Palmieri. Near side. 29°S, 48°W. 41 km. In the Mare Humorum area. Has a darkish floor. Named for Luigi Palmieri (1807–1896), Italian mathematician.

Palmieri, Rimae. Near side. 28°S, 47°W. 150 km. A rill system in the area of Palmieri (q.v.), in association with which it was named.

Paludes. Plural of palus. A palus is a swamp, or swamplike area. (*See* **Epidemiarum, Nebularum, Putredinis, Somnii.**)

Paneth. Far side. 63°N, 95°W. 65 km. Just north of Smoluchowski, in the area to the west of Pythagoras. Named for Friedrich Paneth (1887–1958), German chemist.

Pannekoek. Far side. 4°S, 140°E. 71 km. South of Mendeleev and NW of Gagarin. Named for Antonie Pannekoek (1873–1960), Dutch astronomer.

Papaleski. Far side. 10°N, 164°E. 98 km. Also spelled Popaleski. SE of the Mare Moscoviense and east of the northern rim of Mendeleev. Named for Nikolay Papaleski (1880–1947), Russian radiophysicist.

Paracelsus. Far side. 23°S, 163°E. 84 km. East of Barbier and north of the Mare Ingenii. Named for Philippus Paracelsus (1493–1541), German-Swiss physician.

Paraskevopoulos. Far side. 50°N, 150°W. 94 km. SW of Carnot, in the area south of Birkhoff. Named for John Paraskevopoulos (1889–1951), Greek astronomer.

Parenago. Far side. 26°N, 109°W. 94 km. Immediately west of Berkner. Named for Pavel Parenago (1906–1960), Russian astronomer.

Parkhurst. Far side. 34°S, 103°E. 97 km. Just outside the NE border of the Mare Australe, to the NE of Gernsback. Named for John Parkhurst (1861–1925), American astronomer.

Parrot. Near side. 15°S, 3°E. 70 km. In the area of Albategnius. Very irregular. Named for Georg Parrot (1767–1852), German physicist.

Parry. Near side. 8°S, 16°W. 48 km. A ring plain with broken walls, it forms a group with Fra Mauro and Bonpland, on the Mare Nubium. Quite regular, it has a central crater on its floor and one on the east wall. Named for Charles C. Parry (1823–1890), American naturalist.

Parry, Rimae. Near side. 8°S, 17°W. 300 km. A rill system in the area of Parry (q.v.), in association with which it was named.

Parsons. Far side. 37°N, 171°W. 41 km. East of Moore, in the area NW of Cockcroft. Named for John W. Parsons (1913–1952), American rocket engineer.

Pascal. Near side. 74°N, 70°W. 106 km. Named for Blaise Pascal (1623–1662), French geometrician.

Paschen. Far side. 14°S, 141°W. 133 km. Between Hertzsprung and Apollo. Named for Louis Paschen (1865–1947), German spectroscopist.

Pasteur. Far side. 12°S, 105°E. 235 km. Between the Mare Smythii and Tsiolkovskiy. Named for Louis Pasteur (1822–1895), French chemist.

Patsayev. Far side. 17°S, 133°E. 55 km. Also called Patsaev. NE of Tsiolkovskiy and west of Gagarin. Named for Viktor Patsayev (1933–1971), USSR cosmonaut.

Pauli. Far side. 45°S, 137°E. 84 km. Breaks in on the southern rim of Roche. Named for Wolfgang Pauli, Jr. (1900–1958), Austrian physicist.

Pavlov. Far side. 29°S, 142°E. 141 km. SW of Gagarin and SE of Tsiolkovskiy, in the area NW of Jule Verne. Named for Ivan Pavlov (1849–1936), Russian physiologist.

Pawsey. Far side. 44°N, 145°E. 60 km. West of Campbell and north of Wiener. Named for Joseph L. Pawsey (b. 1908), Australian astronomer.

Peary. Near side. 89°N, 33°E. 74 km. Named for Robert E. Peary (1856–1920), American arctic explorer.

Pease. Far side. 13°N, 106°W. 39 km. NE of Kolhörster and SW of Nobel, in the area SW of Einstein. Named for Francis Pease (1881–1938), American astronomer.

Peek. Near side. 3°N, 87°E. 13 km. Named for Frank W. Peek (1881–1933), American electrical engineer.

Peirce. Near side. 18°N, 53°E. 19 km. In the Mare Crisium. Quite regular. Named for Benjamin Peirce (1809–1880), American mathematician.

Peirescius. Near side. 46°S, 71°E. 62 km. In the Mare Australe area. Quite irregular. Named for Nicolas de Peiresc (1580–1637), French astronomer.

Penck, Mons. Near side. 10°S, 22°E. A mountain named for Albrecht Penck (1858–1945), German geographer.

Pentland. Near side. 64°S, 12°E. 56 km. Near Curtius, in the southern uplands. Has high walls and a central peak. Named for Joseph B. Pentland (1797–1873), Irish geologist.

Percy Mountains. Near side. 18°S, 43°W. This is an unofficial name and it is not a major range. It forms the NW border of the Mare Humorum. Named for John Percy (1817–1889), British metallurgist.

Perel'man. Far side. 24°S, 106°E. 47 km. NW of Scaliger, in the area NE of the Mare Australe. Named for Yakov Perel'man (1882–1942), Russian rocket engineer.

Perepelkin. Far side. 10°S, 128°E. 97 km. Due east of Langemak, in the area to the SW of Mendeleev and north of Tsiolkovskiy. Named for Yevgeniy Perepelkin (1906–1940), Russian astrophysicist.

Perkin. Far side. 47°N, 176°W. 62 km. East of Chandler, in the area between Fowler and Campbell. Named for Sir William Perkin (1838–1907), British chemist.

Perrine. Far side. 42°N, 129°W. 86 km. South of Gullstrand, in the area between Fowler and Landau. Named for Charles D. Perrine (1867–1951), American astronomer.

Perseverantiae, Lacus. Near side. 8°N, 62°E. 70 km. Name means "The Lake of Perseverance" in Latin.

Petavius. Near side. 25°S, 61°E. 177 km. One of a great chain of craters, it has high walls, a central peak, and an interior rill system (*see* **Petavius, Rimae,** next page). Named for Dionysius Petavius (1583–1652), French chronicler.

Petavius, Rimae. Near side. 80 km. In the crater Petavius (see on previous page), in association with which it was named.

Petermann. Near side. 74°N, 66°E. 73 km. Named for August Petermann (1822–1878), German geographer.

Peters. Near side. 68°N, 29°E. 15 km. Named for Christian Peters (1813–1890), American astronomer.

Petit. Near side. 2°N, 63°E. 5 km. Formerly called Apollonius W. Named for Pierre Petit (1598–1677), French astronomer.

Petrie. Far side. 45°N, 108°E. 34 km. Just to the NE of Fabry and west of Rayet. Named for Flinders Petrie (1853–1942), British egyptologist.

Petropavlovskiy. Far side. 37°N, 115°W. 63 km. Hemmed in between Rasumov and Frost, just outside the southern border of Landau. Named for Boris Petropavlovskiy (1898–1933), Russian rocket designer.

Petrov. Near side. 61°S, 88°E. 49 km. Named for Vassiliy Petrov (1761–1834), Russian physicist.

Pettit. Near side. 28°S, 87°W. 35 km. Named for Edison Pettit (1890–1962), American astronomer.

Petzval. Far side. 63°S, 113°W. 90 km. South of Boltzmann, and NE of Zeeman. Named for Józeph Petzval (1807–1891), Hungarian mathematician.

Phenomena and Discoveries. Following is a chronological list of some of the major happenings in the lunar field.

8th century B.C., Anaximander described the Moon as a circle 19 times larger than the Earth, shaped like a chariot-wheel, the rim of which is hollow and full of fire.

5th century B.C., Xenophanes declared that there were several moons. 4th century B.C., Democritus was the first to propose that the Moon has mountains. 2nd century B.C., Hipparchus discovered the Moon's eccentric orbit, the motions of perigee and node, and the inclination of the orbital plane to the ecliptic.

2nd century A.D., Ptolemy discovered the Moon's (perturbation of orbit due to the gravity of the sun). c.577, Gregory of Tours saw a light on the Moon. July 18, 1178, Gervase of Canterbury saw flames leaping out of the Moon. 1611, William Lower of Wales observed the Moon telescopically. 1655, Robert Hooke proposed that the lunar craters were formed by the collapse of huge gas bubbles. 1693, Cassini discovered the laws governing lunar optical librations (the apparent oscillation of the Moon as it moves), and stated that the Moon's rotation is synchronous.

May 4, 1973, Herschel reported active volcanoes on the Moon. He was wrong. April 19 and 20, 1787, Herschel again reported volcanoes. He was wrong again. December 1787, D'Angos of Malta observed a luminous point on the Moon. April 9–11, 1788, Schröter observed a bright spot 26" north of the rim of Aristarchus. September 26, 1788, from 4:30 to 4:45 a.m. (German time), Schröter saw a very bright spot on the Moon, 1'18" SW of Plato. October 15, 1789, Schröter saw meteors (probably) hitting the Moon. October 22, 1790, Herschel saw about 150 small, round, bright red, luminous points when the Moon was totally eclipsed. He also claimed that the Moon is inhabited. 1796, Laplace proposed that the Moon was formed from a gaseous ring thrown off by the contracting Earth.

February 4–6, 1821, a "volcano" was seen erupting on the Moon for three successive nights, in the area of Aristarchus. Confirmed by Olbers, but as reflected light rather than volcanoes. 1822, Franz von Paula Gruithuisen "discovered" a lunar city on the edge of the Sinus Medii and described it as "a collection of dark gigantic ramparts" about 23 miles in diameter. He called it "a work of art." Actually, they are lunar ridges. 1824, Gruithuisen put forward the theory that the lunar craters were caused by bombardment. 1831, Mädler described the Linné crater. 1834, Lohrmann described the Linné crater. August 25, 1835, Richard Locke of the *New York Sun* began a series of hoax articles, claiming that Herschel had discovered life on the Moon (*see* Bibliography). August 28, 1835, Locke described Herschel's discovery of bat-men on the Moon. September 16, 1835, the *Sun* admitted the hoax.

October 16, 1866, Julius Schmidt found that the Linné crater was no longer there (*see* above, 1831 and 1834). This contradicted Mädler's long-held view that the Moon is dead, and from that moment interest in the Moon was reawakened on Earth. February 11, 1867, Angelo Secchi confirmed that Linné was now just a white patch. May 1867, Mädler reviewed Linné, and found it just as he had in 1831, despite the reports of other astronomers (*see* above, 1866, 1867). For an explanation of this, *see* the entry under Linné. 1868, Schwabe suggested the presence of belts of vegetation on the lunar mountains. November 2, 1871, W. R. Birt was the first to see sparkling lights on the Moon. August 27, 1883, the Moon seemed green after the Krakatoa eruption on Earth at that time. January 17, 1884, from Stockholm the Moon seemed green for three minutes. February 14, 1884, from Kalmar, Sweden, the Moon turned green for three minutes. 1885, Ericson of Norway put forward the theory that the Moon is made of ice. 1892, G. K. Gilbert's theory that bombardment caused the lunar craters was published (*see also* 1824, above). 1896, Cerulli proposed the idea of lunar canals. 1897, R. D. M. Verbeck proposed that tektites came from the Moon.

May 1902, Pickering claimed that there is snow on the Moon. 1910, Simon Newcomb (*see* Bibliography) proposed that no change had ever taken place on the Moon's surface. January 4, 1912, the smallest perigee in the 20th century: 216,398 miles (348,259 km) from the center of the Moon to the center of the Earth. 1912, Pickering rediscovered lunar "canals" (*see* above, 1896). These were an optical illusion. 1913, Hans Hörbiger in his book *Glazial-Kosmogonie* (*see also* Bibliography) claimed that the Moon is ice and that it is spiraling toward Earth. 1917, D. P. Beard proposed that the lunar craters are coral atolls. 1932, R. Barker was the first to describe lunar domes. 1938, Wilkins and Moore discovered the Mare Orientale. 1938, Sir Harold Spencer Jones measured "tidal acceleration" at −22 arc seconds per century^2. 1938, C. Davisson proposed a connection between earthquake frequency and the phases of the Moon.

1944, Josiah Spurr proposed that the large lunar craters are calderas (volcanic collapse structures). He named the overall structural pattern in the Moon's crust as "the lunar grid system." 1946, Z. Bay of Hungary obtained the first radar echoes from the Moon. 1949, R. P. Baldwin published his theory that meteorite bombardment formed the lunar craters. 1949, Sixto Ocampo of Spain offered the theory that one-time inhabitants of the Moon had blown themselves up with an atomic bomb. September 26, 1950, as seen from Britain, the Moon seemed to turn blue and grew very bright. This was due to sulfur particles in the upper atmosphere caused by a fire in British Columbia, Canada. 1951, K. Kordylewski in Poland began his search for minor Earth moons. 1952, H. H. Nininger suggested that Messier and Messier A were craters formed by a meteorite. 1955, Horst Gerstenkorn proposed that the Moon was captured by Earth. 1955, Dr. Thomas Gold published his theory that the lunar maria were filled with soft dust, into which a probe would sink. He was wrong. October 4, 1955, N. A. Kozyrev detected the emission lines of hydrogen from the area of Aristarchus.

November 3, 1958, the first photographic confirmation of TLP (Transient Lunar Phenomena) was made by N. A. Kozyrev, at the Crimean Astrophysical Observatory, of an event in Alphonsus. 1959, Gerard Kuiper announced his "discovery" of extinct volcanoes on the Moon. October 23, 1959, N. A. Kozyrev saw a red glow in Alphonsus. March 6, 1961, Kordylewski discovered his two faint "clouds" (*see* Part Two of this book, under **Toro**) moving in the same orbit as the Moon. April 6, 1961, Kordylewski saw these "clouds" again. They have never been confirmed. July 6–7, 1963, fingers of light were seen on the Moon during a partial lunar eclipse. October 30, 1963, a TLP (*see* 1958, above) was observed in the area of Aristarchus by J. Greenacre and J. Barr at the Lowell Observatory. 1967, Patrick Moore and B. Middlehurst's first comprehensive catalog of TLP reports (*see* 1958, above) was published by NASA. July 17, 1972, a one-ton meteorite hit the moon. March 2, 1984, the largest apogee in the 20th century: 252,718 miles (406,711 km) from the center of the Moon to the center of the Earth.

Phillips. Near side. 26°S, 78°E. 124 km. West of Humboldt. Has a central ridge. Named for Theodore Phillips (1868–1942), British astronomer.

Philolaus. Near side. 75°N, 33°W. 71 km. Forms a pair with Anaximenes, NE of Fontenelle, in the Mare Frigoris area. Deep and regular, it has terraced walls of 12,000 feet. Named for Philolaus (fl. 5th century B.C.), Greek philosopher.

Phocylides. Near side. 54°S, 58°W. 114 km. In the Schickard group. Has a lot of floor detail. Named for Jan Fokker (Johannes Phocylides) (1618–1651), Dutch astronomer.

Photography. Following is a chronological list of some of the major moments in lunar photography.

1839, François Arago predicted photography of the Moon. 1839, Daguerre photographed the Moon, unsuccessfully. March 23, 1840, J. W. Draper of New York made a daguerrotype of the Moon, using a long-focus 5-inch reflector. The image was one inch in diameter, and light and dark areas were recorded. 1851, J. A. Whipple made a series of daguerrotypes of the Moon, showing its different phases. They were shown at the Great Exhibition. 1852–1857, Warren de la Rue's photographs of the Moon were the best taken to that date. 1857, W. C. Bond and J. A. Whipple produced the most detailed photographs of the Moon to date.

October 7, 1959, at 6:30 a.m. the first photographic images of the hidden side of the Moon were taken by Luna 3 (*see* **Luna Spacecraft**), from a range of 43,750 miles (70,400 km). Two cameras were used for 40 minutes. Until that time only 59 percent at best had been seen of the Moon's surface. On October 18, 1959, from a distance of 29,000 miles from Earth, the pictures were sent back to Moscow. On October 24, 1959, the USSR gave out the photos.

July 31, 1964, Ranger 7 sent back 4308 photos of the Moon before it crashed (*see* **Ranger Spacecraft**). February 20, 1965, Ranger 8 sent back 7137 photos. March 24, 1965, Ranger 9 sent back 5814 photos. July 27, 1965, Zond 3 (*see* **Zond Spacecraft**) sent back 25 pictures of the far side of the Moon, from 2,200,000 km out in space. February 3, 1966, Luna 9 (*see* **Luna Spacecraft**) sent back closeups of the Moon. May 30, 1966, Surveyor 1 (*see* **Surveyor Spacecraft**) sent back

11,237 photos of the lunar surface. November 9, 1966, Orbiter 2 (*see* **Orbiter Spacecraft**) transmitted 422 pictures. February 1967, Orbiter 3 was a successful photographic probe. Returned 307 photos. April 1967, Surveyor 3 returned 6315 photos. May 1967, Orbiter 4 returned 326 photos. August 1967, Orbiter 5 was a successful photographic probe. September 1967, Surveyor 5 sent back 18,006 photos. November 1967, Surveyor 6 sent back 30,065 photos.

January 1968, Surveyor 7 returned 21,274 photos. November 1968, Zond 6 filmed the far side of the Moon. December 1968, views of the lunar surface were televised to Earth by Apollo 8 (*see* **Apollo Spacecraft**). August 1969, Zond 7 photographed the far side in color from 2000 km. October 1970, Zond 8 took color photos of the Moon. November 17, 1970, Lunokhod 1 (*see* **Lunokhod Spacecraft**) returned 20,000 photos, and over 200 panoramic pictures. January 16, 1973, Lunokhod 2 obtained 86 panoramic pictures, and over 80,000 television pictures.

Piazzi. Near side. 36°S, 68°W. 101 km. In the Schickard area. Has very broken walls. Named for Giuseppe Piazzi (1746–1826), Italian astronomer.

Piazzi Smyth. Near side. 42°N, 3°W. 13 km. On the Mare Imbrium. Bright. Named for Charles Piazzi Smyth (1819–1900), Scottish astronomer.

Picard. Near side. 15°N, 55°E. 23 km. The largest crater on the Mare Crisium. Has a central hill. Named for Jean Picard (1620–1682), French astronomer.

Piccolomini. Near side. 30°S, 32°E. 88 km. At the end of the Altai Scarp. Has high walls and a central peak. Named for Alessandro Piccolomini (1508–1578), Italian astronomer.

Pickering. Near side. 3°S, 7°E. 15 km. In the Hipparchus area. Distinct. Named for William Pickering (1858–1938) and Edward Pickering (1846–1919), American astronomers.

Pico, Mount. Near side. 46°N, 9°W. 8000 feet. Also known as Mons Pico. A triple-peaked mountain mass 100 miles south of Plato, in the Mare Imbrium. Bright and isolated, it has broad slopes. Its foothills are studded with pits and craterlets. Named by Schröter for Giovanni Pico della Mirandola (1463–1494), Italian philosopher.

Pictet. Near side. 43°S, 7°W. 62 km. Just east of Tycho. Quite regular. Named for Marc Pictet (1752–1825), Swiss astronomer.

Pikel'ner. Far side. 48°S, 123°E. 47 km. SE of Van der Waals, and SW of Roche. Named for Solomon B. Pikel'ner (fl. 1940s), Russian chemist.

Pingré. Near side. 59°S, 74°W. 89 km. Named for Alexandre-Gui Pingré (1711–1796), French astronomer.

Pioneer Spacecraft. Only the first 4 Pioneers sent from the United States were particularly relevant to the Moon effort. *Pioneer 1:* Launched October 11, 1958. It reached 113,000 km from Earth and sent data for 43 hours. *Pioneer 2:* Launched November 9, 1958. It failed at the third stage. *Pioneer 3:* Launched December 6, 1958. Reached 106,000 km. *Pioneer 4:* Launched March 3, 1959. On March 5, 1959, it passed within 60,000 km of the Moon.

Pirquet. Far side. 20°S, 140°E. 65 km. East of Tsiolkovskiy, and west of Gagarin, in the area NW of Pavlov. Named for Guido von Pirquet (1880–1966), Austrian space scientist.

Pitatus. Near side. 30°S, 14°W. 97 km. An excellent ring plain connected to Hesiodus by passes, on the south edge of the Mare Nubium. Eroded, it has a dark floor and a central hill. Named for Pietro Pitati (fl. c.1550), Italian astronomer.

Pitatus, Rimae. Near side. 100 km. A series of rills in Pitatus (q.v.), in association with which it was named.

Pitiscus. Near side. 51°S, 31°E. 82 km. In the southern uplands. The walls are narrow in places. Named for Bartholomeo Pitiscus (1561–1613), German mathematician.

Piton, Mount. Near side. 41°N, 1°W. 7000 feet. Also called Mons Piton. An imposing isolated mountain, well to the SE of Pico, near Cape Agassiz, in the Mare Imbrium. It has a summit craterlet and is bright and easy to find. Named for El Pitón, the peak on Tenerife, in the Canary Islands.

Pizzetti. Far side. 35°S, 119°E. 45 km. East of Tyndall and NW of Coblentz, in the area to the NE of the Mare Australe. Named for P. Pizzetti (1860–1918), Italian geodesist.

Plana. Near side. 42°N, 28°E. 44 km. Forms a pair with Mason, in the area of Bürg. Has a darkish floor. Named for Giovanni Plana (1781–1864), Italian astronomer.

Planck. Far side. 58°S, 136°E. 344 km. An enormous enclosure due north of Schrödinger. Named for Max Planck (1858–1947), German physicist.

Planck, Vallis. Far side. 57°S, 125°E. 480 km long. Also called Rima Planck. A rill radiating NW out of Schrödinger. It runs from 65°S, 129°E to 54°S, 125°E. In the area of Planck (q.v.), in association with which it was named.

Planté. Far side. 10°S, 163°E. 38 km. In the SE portion of Keeler. Named for Gaston Planté (1834–1889), French physicist.

Plaskett. Far side. 82°N, 175°E. 110 km. SW of Rozhdestvensky, it is one of the major features north of 80°N. Named for John S. Plaskett (1865–1941), Canadian astronomer.

Plato. Near side. 51°N, 9°W. 101 km. A regular walled plain, in the area of the Alps, just on the north border of the Mare Imbrium. One of the Moon's major features, it has a smooth, very dark gray floor, and a tiny craterlet in the center of the floor. Best seen at sunrise. Named for Plato (428–347 B.C.), Greek philosopher.

Plato, Rimae. Near side. 51°N, 2°W. A system of unrelated, scattered rills in the area of Plato (q.v.), in association with which it was named.

Playfair. Near side. 23°S, 9°E. 48 km. Connected to Apianus by a mountainous arm, in the area of Abenezra. Quite regular. Named for John Playfair (1748–1819), Scottish mathematician.

Plinius. Near side. 15°N, 24°E. 43 km. Between Mare Serenitatis and Mare Tranquillitatis. Isolated, it has almost circular, finely terraced walls and central craters. It also has an undetermined object in the center of its floor. Named for Pliny (A.D. 23–79), Roman naturalist.

Plinius, Rimae. Near side. 17°N, 24°E. 120 km long. A rill system in the area of Plinius (q.v.), in association with which it was named.

Plummer. Far side. 25°S, 155°W. 73 km. Between Korolev and Apollo. Named for William E. Plummer (1849–1928), British astronomer.

Plutarch. Near side. 25°N, 75°E. 68 km. NE of the Mare Crisium. Has a central peak. Named for Plutarch (b. c. A.D. 16), Greek historian.

Poczobutt. Far side. 57°N, 99°W. 209 km. NE of Cannizzaro, and south of Smoluchowski. Named for Martinus de Poczobutt (1729–1810), Polish astronomer.

Pogson. Far side. 42°S, 111°E. 50 km. Just to the east of the southern border of the Mare Australe. Named for Norman Pogson (1829–1891), British astronomer.

Poincaré. Far side. 57°S, 161°E. 319 km. NE of Schrödinger and SW of Von Kármán. Named for Jules H. Poincaré (1854–1912), French mathematician.

Poinsot. Far side. 79°N, 147°W. 68 km. South of Rozhdestvensky and NW of Merrill. Named for Louis Poinsot (1777–1859), French mathematician.

Poisson. Near side. 30°S, 11°E. 42 km. A very irregular formation in the area of Aliacensis. Named for Siméon Poisson (1781–1840), French mathematician.

Polybius. Near side. 22°S, 26°E. 41 km. In the area of Theophilus and Catharina. Distinct. Named for Polybius (c.204–c.122 B.C.), Greek historian.

Polzunov. Far side. 26°N, 115°E. 67 km. NE of Deutsch and south of Seyfert. Named for Ivan Polzunov (1728–1766), Russian engineer.

Pomortsev. Near side. 1°N, 67°E. 23 km. Formerly called Dubiago P. Named for Mikhail Pomortsev (1851–1916), Russian aerologist.

Poncelet. Near side. 76°N, 51°W. 69 km. Named for Jean Poncelet (1788–1867), French mathematician.

Pons. Near side. 25°S, 22°E. 41 km. In the area of Altai. Has very thick walls. Named for Jean-Louis Pons (1761–1831), French astronomer.

Pontanus. Near side. 28°S, 15°E. 58 km. An irregular formation in the area of Altai. Has a low, broken border, a dark floor, and a central peak. Named for Giovanni Pontano (1426–1503), Italian scholar.

Pontécoulant. Near side. 69°S, 65° E. 91 km. In the southern uplands. Has high walls. Named for Philippe, Comte de Pontécoulant (1795–1847), French astronomer.

Popov. Far side. 17°N, 99°E. 65 km. East of Al-Biruni, in the area just to the NE of the Mare Marginis. Named for Aleksandr Popov (1859–1906), Russian physicist.

Porter. Near side. 56°S, 10°W. 52 km. Inside Clavius. Very distinct, it has a central peak. Named for Russel W. Porter (1871–1949), American telescope manufacturer.

Posidonius. Near side. 32°N, 30°E. 95 km. On the edge of the Mare Serenitatis. Has narrow walls and much floor detail. Named for Posidonius (fl. early 1st century B.C.), Greek philosopher.

Posidonius, Rimae. Near side. 70 km. In the crater Posidonius (q.v.), in association with which this rill system was named.

Poynting. Far side. 17°N, 133°W. 126 km. The name is sometimes seen as Poyning. Between Kekulé and Fersman, to the north of Hertzsprung. Named for John H. Poynting (1852–1914), British physicist.

Prager. Far side. 4°S, 131°E. 60 km. SW of Mendeleev and north of Tsiolkovskiy. Named for Richard Prager (1838–c.1943), German astronomer.

Prandtl. Far side. 60°S, 141°E. 91 km. Due north of Schrödinger, and SW of Poincaré. Named for Ludwig Prandtl (1875–1953), German physicist.

Priestly. Far side. 57°S, 108°E. 52 km. Also spelled Priestley. West of Kimura, and SE of Kugler, in the area SW of Schrödinger. Named for Joseph Priestley (1733–1804), British natural philosopher (and see "A Note...," page xv).

Prinz. Near side. 26°N, 44°W. 47 km. NE of Aristarchus, in the Oceanus Procellarum. Incomplete. Named for Wilhelm Prinz (1857–1910), German astronomer.

Prinz, Rimae. Near side. 27°N, 43° W. 80 km long. A rill system in the area of Prinz (q.v.), in association with which it was named.

Procellarum, Oceanus. Near side. 20°N, 55°W. Has a diameter of 2000 km, or an area of 2 million square miles. A huge, but not well-formed circular mare, or "sea," it is lighter and patchier than the Mare Imbrium on the west. Name means "The Ocean of Storms" in Latin.

Proclus. Near side. 16°N, 47°E. 28 km. West of the Mare Crisium. Bright, it has a low central peak. Named for Proclus (c.410–485), Greek philosopher.

Proctor. Near side. 46°S, 5°W. 52 km. In the area of Maginus. Quite regular. Named for Richard Proctor (1837–1888), British astronomer.

Protagoras. Near side. 56°N, 7°E. 22 km. In the Mare Frigoris. Bright and regular. Named for Protagoras of Abdera (c.481–c.411 B.C.), Greek sophist.

Ptolemaeus. Near side. 14°S, 3°W. 153 km. A huge, almost perfect walled plain, which forms a trio with Alphonsus and Arzachel. Lyot and other craters lie on its detailed floor, which is gray and smooth. A perfect hexagon. Named for Ptolemy (fl. 1st half of the 2nd century A.D.), Alexandrian astronomer.

Puiseux. Near side. 28°S, 39°W. 25 km. Near Doppelmayer, on the Mare Humorum. Has very low walls. Named for Pierre Puiseux (1855–1928), French astronomer.

Pupin. Near side. 24°N, 11°W. 2 km. Formerly called Timocharis K. Named for Michael Pupin (1858–1935), American physicist.

Purbach. Near side. 25°S, 2°W. 118 km. A huge, rhomboidal walled plain in the Walter group. Has a nearly central ridge. Named for Georg Peurbach (Purbach) (1423–1461), Austrian astronomer.

Purkyně. Far side. 1°S, 95°E. 49 km. Immediately west of Wyld, on the eastern border of the Mare Smythii. Named for Jan Purkyně (1787–1869), Czech physiologist.

Putredinis, Palus. Near side. 27°N, 1°W. 180 km. Part of the Mare Imbrium, NW of Mount Hadley, and to the west of Archimedes. Name means "The Marsh of Decay" in Latin.

Pyrenees Mountains. Near side. 14°S, 41°E. 250 km long. Also called Montes Pyrenaei. Not a definite range, but clumps of moderate hills bordering Mare Nectaris to the east, between Gutenberg and Bohnenberger. Named by Mädler after the Pyrenees in Europe.

Pythagoras. Near side. 65°N, 65°W. 130 km. A large walled plain, NW of Sinus Iridum, near to the limb of the Moon. One of the largest of the Moon's ring formations, it has high, terraced walls of much splendor, with peaks rising to 17,000 feet. It has an excellent central mountain group on the floor. Named for Pythagoras (d. c.497 B.C.), Greek mathematician.

Pytheas. Near side. 21°N, 20°W. 20 km. A very bright rhomboidal ring plain on the Mare Imbrium. It is the center of a light ray system and has a brilliant central peak. Named for Pytheas (fl. 2nd half of the 4th century B.C.), Greek astronomer.

Quételet. Far side. 43°N, 135°W. 55 km. SW of Gullstrand, and just east of Von Zeipel, in the area east of Fowler.

Named for Lambert Quételet (1796–1874), Belgian astronomer.

Rabbi Levi. Near side. 35°S, 24°E. 81 km. SW of Piccolomini. An irregular walled formation, one of a group of six. Named for Rabbi Levi ben Gerson (1288–1344), French astronomer (and see "A Note...," page xv).

Racah. Far side. 14°S, 180°. 64 km. NE of Aitken, in the area SW of Korolev. Named for Giulio Racah (1909–1965), Israeli physicist.

Raimond. Far side. 14°N, 159°W. 70 km. SW of Mach and north of Korolev. Named for J. J. Raimond (1903–1961), Dutch astronomer.

Raman. Near side. 27°N, 55°W. 11 km. Formerly called Herodotus D. Named for Sir Chandrasekhara Raman (1888–1970), Indian physicist.

Ramsay. Far side. 40°S, 145°E. 82 km. Just south of Jules Verne and just NE of Roche, in the area SW of the Mare Ingenii. Named for Sir William Ramsay (1852–1916), Scottish chemist.

Ramsden. Near side. 33°S, 32°W. 25 km. On the edge of the Palus Epidemiarum. There are rills nearby (*see* **Ramsden, Rimae,** below). Named for Jesse Ramsden (1735–1800), British telescope manufacturer.

Ramsden, Rimae. Near side. 33°S, 31°W. 130 km long. A rill system in the area of Ramsden (see above).

Ranger Spacecraft. A United States program of unmanned space probes. *Ranger 1:* Launched August 23, 1961; did not approach the Moon. *Ranger 2:* Launched November 18, 1961; a complete failure. *Ranger 3:* Launched January 26, 1962; missed the Moon by 36,800 km on January 28, 1962. *Ranger 4:* Launched April 23, 1962. On April 26, 1962, its guidance instruments and cameras failed, and it landed on the far side of the Moon, at 15°30'S, 130°42'W. *Ranger 5:* Launched October 18, 1962; missed the Moon by 725 km. *Ranger 6:* Launched January 30, 1964. On February 2, 1964, it hit the Moon at 12°N, 21°30'E, but no photos received. *Ranger 7:* Launched July 28, 1964. On July 31, 1964 it crash-landed near Guericke crater, in the Mare Cognitum area of the Mare Nubium, at 10° 42'S, 20°42'W. Before it did, it sent back over 4308 high-quality photos, and for the first time the surface of the Moon could be studied from very close range. Four cameras were used for just over 15 minutes, as the craft plunged toward the Moon, and the photos covered an area about the size of France. It kept photographing until 0.19 of a second before impact, and showed a region of 105 feet by 150 feet as it took its last photos. Ranger 7 was the first spacecraft to obtain high-resolution (1-meter) television pictures. *Ranger 8:* Launched February 17, 1965. It had a fate similar to that of Ranger 7, sending back 7137 photos before impact in the Mare Tranquillitatis, at 2°42'N, 24° 48'E. *Ranger 9:* Launched March 21, 1965. It had a fate similar to that of Ranger 7 and Ranger 8, sending back 5814 photos before impact in the plain of Alphonsus, at 12°54'S, 2°24'W, in the highland region of the Moon.

Rankine. Near side. 4°S, 71°E. 9 km. Named for Alexander Rankine (1881–1956), British physicist.

Raspletin. Far side. 22°S, 152°E. 49 km. On the SE rim of Gagarin. Named for Aleksandr Raspletin (b. 1908), Russian radio engineer.

Rasumov. Far side. 39°N, 114°W. 70 km. Also spelled Razumov. Breaks in on the SE rim of Landau. Named for Vladimir Razumov (1890–1967), Russian engineer.

Rayet. Far side. 45°N, 114°E. 27 km. East of the northern portion of Fabry, NW of H. G. Wells. Named for Georges Rayet (1839–1906), French astronomer.

Rayleigh. Far side. 67°S, 179°E. 118 km. Previously called Minnaert (q.v. for origin of name). A major feature bordering on the NW rim of Antoniadi, to the NE of Schrödinger. Extends over onto the near side. Named for 3rd Baron Rayleigh (J. W. Strutt) (1842–1909), British physicist.

Réaumur. Near side. 2°S, 1°E. 53 km. In the area of the Sinus Medii. Has low walls. Named for René Réaumur (1683–1757), French physicist.

Réaumur, Rima. Near side. 3°S, 3°E. 30 km long. A rill in the area of Réaumur (q.v.), in association with which it was named.

Recht. Far side. 10°N, 124°E. 20 km. SE of Ostwald, in the area west of the northern rim of Mendeleev. Named for Pierre Recht (b. 1915), Belgian physician.

Recta, Rupes *see* **Straight Wall**

Recti, Montes *see* **Straight Range**

Regiomontanus. Near side. 28°S, 0°. 124 km. Distorted between Walter and Purbach. Prominent and irregular, it has complex ramparts and has a central peak with a crater on its side. Named for Johann Müller (Regiomontanus) (1436–1476), German astronomer.

Regnault. Near side. 54°N, 88°W. 47 km. Named for Henri Regnault (1810–1878), French chemist.

Reichenbach. Near side. 30°S, 48°E. 71 km. In the Rheita area. Irregular. "Reichenbach Valley," a crater chain, is to the SE. Named for Georg von Reichenbach (1772–1826), German telescope manufacturer.

Reimarus. Near side. 46°S, 55°E. 48 km. In the Rheita Valley area. Irregular. Named for Hermann Reimarus (1694–1768), German philosopher.

Reiner. Near side. 7°N, 55°W. 30 km. Forms a pair with Marius, on the Oceanus Procellarum. Isolated, it has bright terraced walls rising to 10,000 feet above the floor. The floor is dark with a low central peak and two hills on it. Named for Vincentio Reineri (d. 1648), Italian mathematician.

Reinhold. Near side. 3°N, 23°W. 43 km. SW of Copernicus, in the Oceanus Procellarum. Isolated, it has walls rising to 9000 feet above the floor on the west, and on the inner slope of its wall is a regular terrace. Named for Erasmus Reinhold (1511–1553), German mathematician.

Repsold. Near side. 50°N, 70°W. 107 km. One of a group, in the area west of Sinus Roris. Named for Adolf Repsold (1806–1871), German telescope manufacturer.

Respighi. Near side. 3°N, 72°E. 19 km. Formerly called Dubiago C. Named for Lorenzo Respighi (1824–1889), Italian astronomer.

Rhaeticus. Near side. 0°, 5°E. 46 km. In the area of the Sinus Medii. Has low walls. Named for George Rheticus (Rhaeticus) (1514–1574), Austrian astronomer.

Rheita. Near side. 37°S, 47°E. 70 km. West of Furnerius. Has sharp crests. Associated with the Rheita Valley (see following entry). Named for Anton de Rheita (1597–1660), Bohemian astronomer.

Rheita, Vallis. Near side. 40°S, 48°E. 500 km long. 15 miles wide at its greatest. Also called the Rheita Valley, although it is not a true valley, rather a crater chain. In the southern highlands. Named in association with Rheita (q.v.).

Riccioli. Near side. 3°S, 75°W. 146 km. Forms a pair with Grimaldi. Has broken walls and very dark patches on its floor. Has no central peak. Named for Giambattista Riccioli (1598–1671), Italian astronomer.

Riccius. Near side. 37°S, 26°E. 71 km. A walled formation in the Rabbi

Levi group. It has broken walls and a crater on it south wall. It has several craters on its rough floor. Named for Matteo Ricci (1552–1610), Italian astronomer.

Riccò. Far side. 75°N, 177°E. 65 km. SE of Milanković and west of Thiessen. Named for Annibale Riccò (1844–1919), Italian astrophysicist.

Richards. Far side. 8°N, 140°E. 17 km. In the northern portion of Mendeleev. Named for Theodore W. Richards (1868–1928), American chemist.

Richardson. Far side. 31°N, 100°E. 161 km. Between Szilard and Lomonosov, in the area NE of Joliot. Named for Owen Richardson (1879–1959), British physicist.

Riedel. Far side. 49°S, 140°W. 47 km. Due south of Leavitt, in the area SE of Apollo and west of Mendel. Named for Klaus Riedel (1910–1944), German rocket engineer.

Riemann. Near side. 39°N, 89°E. 110 km. Straddles the near and far sides of the Moon. Due north of Joliot and SW of Fabry. Named for Bernhard Riemann (1826–1866), German mathematician.

Rills *see* **Rimae**

Rimae. A rima (or rill, or rille) is a narrow furrow, or ditch, on the Moon, less than two miles wide and inconspicuous from Earth (this is the rule, and true most of the time). (*See* **Agatharchides, Alphonsus, Apollonius, Archimedes, Archytas, Ariadaeus, Aristarchus, Arzachel, Atlas, Billy, Birt, Bode, Boscovich, Bradley, Bürg, Calippus, Cardanus, Cauchy, Chacornac, Cleomedes, Conon, Daniell, Darwin, De Gasperis, Doppelmayer, Flammarion, Fresnel, Furnerius, G. Bond, Gärtner, Gassendi, Gay-Lussac, Goclenius, Grimaldi, Gutenberg, Hadley, Hansteen, Herigonius, Hesiodus, Hevelius, Hippalus, Hyginus, Hypatia, Jansen, Janssen, Littrow, Maclear, Marius, Menelaus, Mersenius, Messier, Opelt, Oppolzer, Palmieri, Parry, Petavius, Pitatus, Plato, Plinius, Posidonius, Prinz, Ramsden, Réaumur, Ritter, Rømer, Schröter, Sharp, Sirsalis, Sosigenes, Sulpicius Gallus, Theaetetus, Triesnecker, Zupus.**)

Riphaen Mountains. Near side. 6°S, 26°W. 150 km long. Also called Montes Riphaeus. A short range in the Mare Nubium, near Euclides. Less than 3000 feet high, they are possibly the remains of the ramparts of a destroyed crater. The Ural Mountains are really part of these. Named for the ancient Greek mountains.

Ritchey. Near side. 11°S, 9°E. 25 km. East of Albategnius. Has broken walls. Named for George Ritchey (1864–1945), American astronomer.

Rittenhouse. Far side. 74°S, 107°E. 27 km. To the immediate west of Schrödinger and due north of Ganswindt. Named for David Rittenhouse (1732–1796), American astronomer.

Ritter. Near side. 2°N, 19°E. 29 km. Forms a pair with Sabine, near the border of the Mare Tranquillitatis. Has narrow walls and a central hill. Named for August Ritter (1826–1908), German astrophysicist.

Ritter, Rimae. Near side. 3°N, 18°E. 100 km long. A rill system in the area of Ritter (q.v.), in association with which it was named.

Ritz. Far side. 16°S, 92°E. 51 km. NW of Sklodowska, in the area south of the eastern rim of the Mare Smythii. Named for Walter Ritz (1878–1909), Swiss physicist.

Roberts. Far side. 71°N, 175°W. 90 km. NW of Kirkwood, and SE of

Karpinsky. Named for Isaac Roberts (1829–1904), British astronomer.

Robertson. Far side. 22°N, 105°W. 88 km. A crater between Sternberg and Laue, to the immediate south of Berkner, in the area NE of Hertzsprung. Named for Howard P. Robertson (1903–1961), American physicist.

Robinson. Near side. 59°N, 46°W. 24 km. A deep crater, similar to Horrebow, in the Mare Frigoris area. Distinct, it has a smooth floor, terraced walls and a craterlet on its west wall. Named for Romney Robinson (1792–1882), Irish astronomer.

Rocca. Near side. 15°S, 72°W. 90 km. South of Grimaldi. Has irregular walls. Named for Giovanni Rocca (1607–1656), Italian mathematician.

Roche. Far side. 42°S, 135°E. 146 km. SW of Jules Verne, west of Koch, and SE of Tsiolkovskiy. Pauli breaks in on its southern rim. Named for Édouard Roche (1820–1883), French celestial mechanician.

Rømer. Near side. 27°N, 37°E. 40 km. In the area of Taurus. Has a very massive central peak with a summit pit. Named for Ole Rømer (1644–1710), Danish astronomer.

Rømer, Rimae. Near side. 27°N, 35°E. 110 km long. A rill system in the area of Rømer (q.v.), in association with which it was named.

Röntgen. Far side. 33°N, 91°W. 126 km. Immediately SE of Nernst, in the area north of Einstein. Named for Wilhelm Röntgen (1845–1923), German physicist.

Rook Mountains. Near side. 40°S, 83°W. 900 km long. Also known as Montes Rook. A huge limb range forming the outer wall of the Mare Orientale. Named for Lawrence Rooke (1622–1662), English astronomer.

Roris, Sinus. Near side. 51°N, 50°W. 500 km. Forms the "outlet" of the Oceanus Procellarum into the Mare Frigoris. Its surface looks like the oceanus. Rümker is on it. Name means "The Bay of Dews" in Latin.

Rosenberger. Near side. 55°S, 43°E. 96 km. In the Vlacq group. Has a darkish floor and a central peak. Named for Otto Rosenberger (1800–1890), German astronomer.

Ross. Near side. 12°N, 22°E. 25 km. On the Mare Tranquillitatis. Has a central peak. Named for Frank Ross (1874–1966), American astronomer.

Rosse. Near side. 18°S, 35°E. 12 km. On the Mare Nectaris. Bright. Named for the 3rd Earl of Rosse (William Parsons) (1800–1867), British astronomer.

Röst. Near side. 56°S, 34°W. 49 km. Forms a pair with Weigel, in the Schiller area. Quite regular. Named for Johann Röst (1688–1727), German astronomer.

Rothmann. Near side. 31°S, 28°E. 42 km. In the Altai area. Quite deep and quite regular. Named for Christoph Rothmann (d. c.1605), German astronomer.

Rowland. Far side. 57°N, 163°W. 164 km. West of Birkhoff. Named for Henry A. Rowland (1848–1901), American physicist.

Rozhdestvensky. Far side. 86°N, 155°W. 179 km. Also spelled Rozhdestvenskiy. Between Hermite and Plaskett, near the North Pole. Named for Dmitriy Rozhdestvenskiy (1876–1940), Russian physicist.

Rumford. Far side. 29°S, 170°W. 62 km. SE of Sniadecki, NE of Leibnitz, and west of the northern rim of Apollo. Named for Benjamin Thompson (Count Rumford) (1753–1814), American physicist.

Rümker. Near side. 41°N, 58°W. A semiruined plateau on Sinus Roris, NE of Aristarchus, on the extreme north of the Oceanus Procellarum. Named for Karl Rümker (1788–1862), German astronomer.

Rümker, Mons. Near side. 41°N, 58°W. A mountain in the area of Rümker (q.v.), in association with which it was named.

Runge. Near side. 2°S, 87°E. 39 km. Named for Carl Runge (1856–1927), German mathematician.

Rupes. Or scarps. (*See* **Cauchy, Kelvin, Liebig, Mercator, Recta, Straight Wall.**)

Russell. Near side. 26°N, 75°W. 103 km. Named for Henry Norris Russell (1877–1957), American astronomer.

Rutherford. Far side. 11°N, 137°E. 14 km. Just NW of Mendeleev. Named for Ernest Rutherford (1871–1937), British physicist.

Rutherfurd. Near side. 61°S, 12°W. 48 km. Breaks in on the southern rim of Clavius. Distinct, it has a central peak. Named for Lewis Rutherfurd (1816–1892), American astronomer.

Rydberg. Far side. 47°S, 96°W. 50 km. East of the northern rim of Mendel and immediately NW of Guthnick, in the area south of the Mare Orientale. Named for Johannes Rydberg (1854–1919), Swedish physicist.

Rynin. Near side. 37°N, 86°E. The name Rynin was originally given to the 76 km crater on the NE border of Stefan but the name was relocated to a crater SW of Fabry and NW of Joliot, on the near side. Named for Nikolay Rynin (1877–1942), Russian space writer.

Sabatier. Near side. 13°N, 79°E. 10 km. Named for Paul Sabatier (1854–1941), French organic chemist.

Sabine. Near side. 2°N, 20°E. 30 km. Forms a pair with Ritter, near the SE border of the Mare Tranquillitatis. Has narrow walls and a central hill. Named for Sir Edward Sabine (1788–1883), British astronomer.

Sacrobosco. Near side. 24°S, 17°E. 98 km. A great walled plain in the Altai area. Irregular, it has broad, high walls, and has several craters in it, two having a central peak. Named for Johannes de Sacrobosco (c.1200–1256), English astronomer.

Šafařik. Far side. 10°N, 177°E. 28 km. SE of Sharonov, and due north of Stein, in the area to the NW of Korolev. Named for Vojtech Šafařik (1829–1902), Slovak astronomer.

Saha. Far side. 2°S, 103°E. 99 km. SE of Wyld, in the area east of the Mare Smythii. Named for Meghnad N. Saha (1894–1956), Indian physicist.

St. John. Far side. 10°N, 150°E. 68 km. NE of Mendeleev and south of the Mare Moscoviense. Named for Charles Edward St. John (1857–1935), American astronomer.

Sampson. Near side. 30°N, 16°W. 2 km. Named for Ralph Sampson (1866–1939), Irish astronomer.

Sanford. Far side. 32°N, 139°W. 55 km. Immediately west of Teisserenc and NE of Joule. Named for Roscoe Sanford (1883–1958), American astronomer.

Sänger. Far side. 4°N, 102°E. 75 km. Also spelled Saenger. North of Saha, SE of Erro, in the area to the east of the northern border of the Mare Smythii. Named for Eugen Sänger (1905–1964), Bohemian rocket pioneer.

Santbech. Near side. 21°S, 44°E. 64 km. East of Fracastorius. Has a darkish floor. Named for Daniel Santbech (fl. c.1561), Dutch astronomer.

Santos-Dumont. Near side. 28°N, 5°E. 9 km. Formerly called Hadley B. Named for Alberto Santos-Dumont (1873–1932), Brazilian airship pioneer.

Sarabhai. Near side. 25°N, 21°E. 8 km. Formerly called Bessel A. Named for Seraphion (Sarabhai) (fl. 2nd half of the 9th century), Syrian physician.

Sarton. Far side. 49°N, 121°W. 69 km. Due north of Landau and NW of Stefan. Named for George Sarton (1884–1956), American science historian.

Sasserides. Near side. 39°S, 9°W. 90 km. An irregular enclosure north of Tycho. Named for Gellio Sasserides (1562–1612), Danish astronomer.

Saunder. Near side. 4°S, 9°E. 45 km. East of Hipparchus. Has low walls. Named for Samuel A. Saunder (1852–1912), British astronomer.

Saussure. Near side. 43°S, 4°W. 54 km. A walled depression near the south wall of Orontius, north of Maginus. Has bright, terraced walls rising to 8000 feet in the east. Has a dark interior and a double craterlet just west of its center. Named for Horace Saussure (1740–1799), Swiss geologist.

Scaliger. Far side. 27°S, 109°E. 84 km. Name sometimes seen as Scalinger. Between Titius and Schaeberle, in the area SE of the Mare Smythii. Named for Joseph Scaliger (1540–1609), French chronologist.

Schaeberle. Far side. 26°S, 117°E. 63 km. SW of Tsiolkovskiy and east of Scaliger. Named for John Schaeberle (1853–1924), American astronomer.

Scheele. Near side. 9°S, 38°W. 5 km. Formerly called Letronne D. Named for Karl W. Scheele (1742–1786), Swedish chemist.

Scheiner. Near side. 60°S, 28°W. 110 km. A large walled plain which forms a pair with Blancanus in the Clavius area. Has high, prominently terraced walls. Seven craters are on its floor. Named for Christoph Scheiner (1573–1650), German astronomer.

Schiaparelli. Near side. 23°N, 59°W. 24 km. On the Oceanus Procellarum. Distinct. Named for Giovanni Schiaparelli (1835–1910), Italian astronomer.

Schickard. Near side. 44°S, 54°W. 227 km. One of the Moon's largest walled plains, it has an average wall height of 4500 feet and on the west peaks rise to 9500 feet. There are three large ring plains on the interior. Named for Wilhelm Schickard (1592–1635), German astronomer.

Schiller. Near side. 52°S, 39°W. 179 km. An elongated, trough-like feature in the Schickard area. Elliptical, it was formed by two rings coming together. Named for Julius Schiller (d. c.1627), German astronomer.

Schjellerup. Far side. 69°N, 157°E. 62 km. NW of Avogadro, and east of Schwarzschild. Named for Hans Schjellerup (1827–1887), Danish astronomer.

Schlesinger. Far side. 47°N, 138°W. 97 km. Immediately east of Esnault-Pelterie, in the area just NE of Fowler. Named for Frank Schlesinger (1871–1943), American astronomer.

Schliemann. Far side. 2°S, 155°E. 80 km. NW of Ventris between Keeler and Mendeleev. Named for Heinrich Schliemann (1822–1890), German archeologist.

Schlüter. Near side. 6°S, 83°W. 89 km. Named for Heinrich Schlüter (1815–1844), German astronomer.

Schmidt. Near side. 1°N, 19°E. 11 km. In the area of Sabine and Ritter, on the Mare Tranquillitatis. Bright. Named for Johann Schmidt (1825–1884), German astronomer.

Schneckenberg, Mount. Near side. 9°N, 9°E. A strange "spiral mountain" near Rima Hyginus, in the SE part of the Mare Vaporum. It is not well seen from Earth.

Schneller. Far side. 42°N, 164°W. 55 km. SW of Woltjer and due west of Fowler. Named for Herbert Schneller (1901–1967), German astronomer.

Schömberger. Near side. 76°N, 30°E. 85 km. In the area of Boguslawsky. Regular. Named for Georg Schömberger (1579–1645), German mathematician.

Schönfeld. Far side. 45°N, 98°W. 26 km. Due east of Stefan and SW of McLaughlin. Named for Eduard Schönfeld (1828–1891), German astronomer.

Schorr. Far side. 19°S, 90°E. 53 km. It straddles the near and far sides of the Moon, south of the eastern portion of the Mare Smythii, and north of Curie. Named for Richard Schorr (1867–1951), German astronomer.

Schrödinger. Far side. 75°S, 133°E. 312 km. A large, fresh crater, almost a basin, the largest lunar feature south of 70° south. Vallis Schrödinger and Vallis Planck radiate from it. Named for Erwin Schrödinger (1887–1961), Austrian physicist.

Schrödinger, Vallis. Far side. Runs from 62°S, 99°E to 71°S, 114°E. A valley radiating from the large Schrödinger crater (q.v.), in association with which it was named.

Schröter. Near side. 3°N, 7°W. 35 km. In the Sinus Medii area. Has low walls. Named for Johann Schröter (1745–1816), German astronomer.

Schröter, Rima. Near side. 1°N, 6°W. 40 km. A rill in the area of Schröter (q.v.), in association with which it was named.

Schröteri, Vallis. Near side. 26°N, 52°W. 150 km long. Also known as Schröter's Valley. It is not in the area of Schröter crater, but it is named for Johann Schröter (*see* **Schröter,** above).

Schubert. Near side. 3°N, 70°E. 54 km. In the Mare Smythii area. Distinct. Named for Theodor F. von Schubert (1789–1865), Russian geodesist.

Schumacher. Near side. 42°N, 55°E. 61 km. In the area of Messala. Quite distinct. Named for Heinrich Schumacher (1780–1850), German astronomer.

Schuster. Far side. 4°N, 147°E. 103 km. Breaks in on the eastern rim of Mendeleev. Named for Arthur Schuster (1851–1934), German physicist.

Schwabe. Near side. 65°N, 46°E. 25 km. Named for Heinrich Schwabe (1789–1875), German astronomer.

Schwarzschild. Far side. 71°N, 120°E. 235 km. Between Nansen and Volterra, it is the largest feature north of 70° north. Named for Karl Schwarzschild (1873–1916), German astrophysicist.

Scoresby. Near side. 77°N, 15°E. 56 km. In the polar uplands. Deep and prominent, it has a central peak. Named for William Scoresby (1789–1857), British physicist.

Scott. Near side. 82°S, 43°E. 108 km. Named for Robert F. Scott (1868–1912), British polar explorer.

Seares. Far side. 74°N, 145°E. 112 km. West of Karpinsky, and east of the northern sector of Schwarzschild. Named for Frederick H. Seares (1873–1964), American astronomer.

Secchi. Near side. 2°N, 43°E. 23 km. In the Mare Fecunditatis. Has bright walls and a central peak. Named for Pietro Angelo Secchi (1818–1878), Italian astronomer.

Secchi Mountains. Near side. 3°N, 43°E. 50 km long. Also known as Montes Secchi. In the area of Secchi (q.v.), in association with which they were named.

Sechenov. Far side. 7°S, 143°W. 62 km. SE of Timiryazev, between the southern portion of Korolev and the southern rim of Hertzsprung. Named for Ivan Sechenov (1829–1905), Russian physiologist.

Seeliger. Near side. 2°S, 1°E. 9 km. North of Hipparchus. Irregular. Named for Hugo Seeliger (1849–1924), German astronomer.

Segers. Far side. 47°N, 128°E. 17 km. NE of H. G. Wells and east of Millikan. Named for Carlos Segers (1900–1967), Argentine astronomer.

Segner. Near side. 59°S, 48°W. 67 km. Forms a pair with Zucchius, in the area of Schiller. Distinct, it has a small central peak. A peak on the west wall casts a notable shadow. Named for János Segner (1704–1777), Hungarian mathematician.

Seidel. Far side. 33°S, 152°E. 62 km. Between Jules Verne and O'Day, in the area just west of the Mare Ingenii. Named for Philipp von Seidel (1821–1896), German astronomer.

Seleucus. Near side. 21°N, 66°W. 43 km. On the Oceanus Procellarum. Has terraced walls and a central peak. Named for Seleucus (fl. 2nd century B.C.), Babylonian astronomer.

Seneca. Near side. 27°N, 80°E. 47 km. Named for Lucius Seneca (c.4 B.C.–A.D. 65), Roman philosopher.

Serao. Near side. 17°N, 6°W. A mountain crater between Ampère and Wolff, in the Apennines. Named for Francesco Serao (1702–1783), Italian physician.

Serenitatis, Mare. Near side. 30°N, 17°E. 690×885 km. One of the most perfect of the "regular" maria, it is just over 4 billion years old. It is bordered in part by the Caucasus Mountains and by the Haemus Mountains. It has a smooth floor, but with many ridges, and Linné, Bessel, Deseilligny and Luther craterlets are on it. Name means "The Sea of Serenity" in Latin.

Seyfert. Far side. 29°N, 114°E. 110 km. SE of Szilard and east of Joliot. Named for Carl Seyfert (1911–1960), American astronomer.

Shajn. Far side. 33°N, 172°E. 93 km. Also spelled Shayn. East of Nušl and NE of Trumpler, in the area east of the northern rim of the Mare Moscoviense. Named for Gregoriy Shayn (1892–1956), Russian astronomer.

Shaler. Near side. 33°S, 85°W. 48 km. Named for Nathaniel Shaler (1841–1906), American geologist.

Shapley. Near side. 9°N, 57°E. 23 km. Formerly called Picard H. Named for Harlow Shapley (b.1885), American astronomer.

Sharonov. Far side. 13°N, 173°E. 74 km. East of Spencer Jones, in the area NE of Mandelstam. Named for Vsevolod Sharonov (1901–1964), Russian astronomer.

Sharp. Near side. 46°N, 40°W. 40 km. In the Jura Mountains. Deep, its inner east slope is terraced and it has a small central peak. Named for Abraham Sharp (1651–1742), British mathematician.

Sharp, Rima. Near side. 45°N, 51°W. 210 km long. A rill in the area of Sharp (q.v.), in association with which it was named.

Shatalov. Far side. 24°N, 140°E. 22 km. In the western rim of the Mare Moscoviense. Named for Vladimir A. Shatalov (b. 1927), USSR cosmonaut.

Sheepshanks. Near side. 59°N, 17°E. 25 km. North of the Mare Frigoris. Quite regular. Named for Richard Sheepshanks (1794–1855), British astronomer.

Sherrington. Far side. 11°S, 118°E. 18 km. Between Meitner and Langemak, in the area to the NW of Tsiolkovskiy. Named for Sir Charles Sherrington (1861–1952), British physiologist.

Shi Shen. Far side. 76°N, 105°E. 43 km. Just south of Nansen and NE of Schwarzschild. Named for Shi Shen (fl. 4th century B.C.), Chinese astronomer.

Shirakatsi. Far side. 12°S, 129°E. 51 km. SE of Perepelkin and north of Tsiolkovskiy. Named for Anania Shirakatsi (c.620–c.687), Armenian astronomer.

Short. Near side. 76°S, 5°W. 71 km. A ring formation in the Moretus group. Deep, with high walls. On its floor is a small bright craterlet with a little hill on its south edge. Named for James Short (1710–1768), Scottish telescope manufacturer.

Shuckburgh. Near side. 43°N, 53°E. 39 km. In the Cepheus group. Quite regular. Named for Sir George Shuckburgh-Evelyn (1751–1804), British mathematician.

Siedentopf. Far side. 22°N, 135°E. 61 km. West of the southern inner border of Mare Moscoviense. Named for Henry Siedentopf (1906–1963), German astronomer.

Sierpinski. Far side. 27°S, 155°E. 69 km. SE of Gagarin and east of the northern rim of Pavlov. Named for Waclaw Sierpinski (1882–1969), Polish mathematician.

Sikorsky. Far side. 66°S, 103°E. 99 km. On the Rima Schrödinger, to the NW of Schrödinger crater and SE of Chamberlin. Named for Igor Sikorsky (1889–1972), American aeronautical engineer.

Silberschlag. Near side. 6°N, 13°E. 13 km. Near Ariadaeus. Bright. Named for Johann Silberschlag (1716–1791), German mathematician.

Simpelius. Near side. 75°S, 15°E. 70 km. In the Moretus area. Deep. Named for Hugh Sempill (Simpelius) (1596–1654), Scottish mathematician.

Sinas. Near side. 9°N, 32°E. 12 km. On the Mare Tranquillitatis. Not prominent. Named for Simon Sinas (1810–1876), Greek financier.

Sinuses. Bays in the maria. (*See* **Aestuum, Amoris, Asperitatis, Concordiae, Fidei, Honoris, Iridum, Lunicus, Roris, Successus.**)

Sirsalis. Near side. 13°S, 60°W. 42 km. Just outside the Oceanus Procellarum. Associated with a great rill (*see* **Sirasalis, Rimae,** below). Named for Girolamo Sirsalis (1584–1654), Italian astronomer.

Sirsalis, Rimae. Near side. 14°S, 60°W. 330 km long. A great rill system in the area of Sirsalis (q.v.), in association with which it was named. It runs from the Oceanus Procellarum to Byrgius.

Sisakian. Far side. 41°N, 109°E. 34 km. Also spelled Sisakyan. SE of Fabry and north of Szilard. Named for Norair Sisakian (1907–1966), USSR biochemist.

Sklodowska. Far side. 18°S, 159°E. 131 km. SE of the Mare Smythii and NE of Curie. Named for Marja Sklodowska (later Marie Curie) (1867–1934), Polish-French chemist.

Slipher. Far side. 50°N, 160°E. 69 km. Breaks in on the SW rim of D'Alembert. Named for Vesto M. Slipher (1875–1969), American astronomer.

Slocum. Near side. 3°S, 89°E. 13 km. Named for Harvey Slocum (1887–1961), American engineer.

Smithson. Near side. 2°N, 54°E. 6 km. Formerly called Taruntius N.

Named for James Smithson (c.1765–1829), British chemist.

Smoluchowski. Far side. 60°N, 96°W. 83 km. Borders on the SW rim of Paneth, SW of Pythagoras. Named for Marian Smoluchowski (1872–1917), Polish physicist.

Smythii, Mare. Near side. 3°S, 80°E. 360 km. A limb mare, some of it goes over onto the far side of the Moon. It is of the Mare Crisium type. Seen well only from probes. A good guide to it is Schubert crater (46 miles wide). Named for Charles Piazzi Smyth (1819–1900), astronomer royal for Scotland.

Snellius. Near side. 29°S, 56°E. 83 km. Forms a pair with Stevinus, in the Furnerius area. Has high walls and a central peak. Named for Willebrord Snellius (1581–1626), Dutch mathematician.

Snellius, Vallis. Near side. 31°S, 59°E. 500 km. In the area of Snellius (q.v.), in association with which this valley was named.

Sniadecki. Far side. 22°S, 169°W. 43 km. NE of Orlov, and SW of Korolev, in the area NW of Apollo. Named for Jan Sniadecki (1756–1830), Polish astronomer.

Soddy. Far side. 0°, 122°E. 43 km. SW of Mendeleev and west of Gregory. Named for Frederick Soddy (1877–1956), British chemist.

Solitudinis, Lacus. Far side. 27°S, 104°E. 120 km. Between Titius and Lauritsen, in the area south of Pasteur. Name means "The Lake of Solitude" in Latin.

Somerville. Near side. 8°S, 65°E. 15 km. Formerly called Langrenus J. Named for Mary Somerville (1780–1872), British mathematician.

Sommerfeld. Far side. 65°N, 161°W. 148 km. NW of Birkhoff. Named for Arnold Sommerfeld (1868–1951), German physicist.

Sömmering. Near side. 0°, 7°W. 28 km. Forms a pair with Mösting, in the Sinus Medii area. Has low broken walls and a dark interior. Named for Samuel Sömmering (1755–1830), German anatomist.

Somnii, Palus. Near side. 15°N, 46°E. 240 km. An extension of the Mare Tranquillitatis, bounded on the NE and SW by rays from Proclus. Has a brownish/greenish/yellowish color, different from Tranquillitatis. Name means "The Marsh of Sleep" in Latin.

Somniorum, Lacus. Near side. 37°N, 35°E. 230 km. A bay leading out of the Mare Serenitatis. On its southern edge is Posidonius. There are delicate rills here. Daniell is here, too. Its floor is much lighter and patchier than Serenitatis. Name means "The Lake of Dreamers" in Latin.

Sosigenes. Near side. 9°N, 18°E. 18 km. On the edge of the Mare Tranquillitatis. It is bright, and has a low central peak. Named for Sosigenes (fl. 1st century B.C.), Alexandrian astronomer.

Sosignes, Rimae. Near side. 7°N, 19°E. 150 km long. A rill system in the area of Sosigenes (q.v.), in association with which it was named.

South. Near side. 57°N, 50°W. 108 km. A walled plain which forms a pair with Babbage, between Pythagoras and Harpalus, in the Mare Frigoris area. Bounded by ridges, it has low, broken walls, and a rough interior with many ridges crossing it. It has no central peak or crater. Named for James South (1785–1867), British astronomer.

Soviet Mountains. Far side. A huge range stretching from Vestine (34°N, 94°E) in the north to Tsiolkovskiy (21°S, 128°E) in the south. Also known as Montes Sovietici. Recorded by

Luna 3 in 1959. Named by the Russians and shown on early maps. The disappointing news was that it was only a bright ray, not a mountain range at all, so the name has been expunged from more modern maps.

Spallanzani. Near side. 46°S, 25°E. 32 km. West of Janssen. Has low walls. Named for Lazzaro Spallanzani (1729–1799), Italian biologist.

Spei, Lacus. Near side. 43°N, 65°E. 80 km. Name means "The Lake of Hope" in Latin.

Spencer Jones. Far side. 13°N, 166°E. 85 km. Immediately north of Papaleski, with which it forms a pair, to the NE of Mendeleev and to the SE of Mare Moscoviense. Named for Sir Harold Spencer Jones (1890–1960), British astronomer.

Spiru Haret. Far side. 59°S, 176°W. NW of Cabannes and east of Poincaré. Named for Spiru Haret (1851–1912), Romanian mathematician.

Spitsbergen Mountains. Near side. 34°N, 5°E. 60 km long. Also called Montes Spitsbergen. A mountain clump, or a series of bright little hills, lying on the edge of a very obscure ghost-ring, north of Archimedes, in the Mare Imbrium. Named after the Arctic archipelago on Earth.

Spörer. Near side. 4°S, 2°W. 28 km. North of Ptolemaeus and Herschel. Partly lava-filled. Named for Gustav Spörer (1822–1895), German astronomer.

Spumans, Mare. Near side. 1°N, 65°E. 130 km. South of Apollonius, it is not a true mare. Name means "The Foaming Sea" in Latin.

Spurr. Near side. 28°N, 1°W. 13 km. Formerly called Archimedes K. Named for Josiah Spurr (1870–1950), American geologist.

Stadius. Near side. 11°N, 14°W. 69 km. A ghost-ring east of Copernicus. A low, old and eroded formation, it has broken walls and many crater pits on the interior. Named for Georg Stadius (c.1550–1593), Austrian astronomer.

Stag's-Horn Mountains. Near side. 27°S, 5°W. Also known as Archimedes Mountains and Montes Archimedes. A clump of hills which form part of an ancient ring at the south end of the Straight Wall, near Thebit, in the Mare Nubium. Named for their shape.

Stark. Far side. 25°S, 134°W. 50 km. SE of Tsiolkovskiy and west of the northern portion of Pavlov. Named for Johannes Stark (1874–1957), German physicist.

Stearns. Far side. 35°N, 163°E. 37 km. NE of Steno, in the area NE of the Mare Moscoviense. Named for Carl L. Stearns (b. 1892), American astronomer.

Stebbins. Far side. 65°N, 143°W. 135 km. Immediately north of Birkhoff. Named for Joel Stebbins (1878–1966), American astronomer.

Stefan. Far side. 46°N, 109°W. 116 km. East of Wegener, in the area NE of Landau. Named for Josef Stefan (1835–1893), Austrian physicist.

Stein. Far side. 7°N, 179°E. 34 km. Just east of Valier, in the area to the NW of Korolev. Named for Johan Stein (1871–1951), Dutch astronomer.

Steinheil. Near side. 50°S, 48°E. 67 km. Forms a pair with Watt, to the SW of Janssen. Named for Karl von Steinheil (1801–1870), German astronomer.

Steklov. Far side. 37°S, 105°W. 36 km. NE of Chant, in the area to the south of the western portion of the Mare Orientale. Named for Vladimir Steklov (1864–1926), Russian mathematician.

Steno. Far side. 33°N, 162°E. 32 km. East of the northern rim of the Mare Moscoviense. Named for Nicolaus Steno (1638–c.1687), Danish astronomer.

Sternberg. Far side. 19°N, 117°W. 70 km. SE of Comstock, in the area NE of Hertzsprung. Named for Pavel Sternberg (1865–1920), Russian astronomer.

Stetson. Far side. 40°S, 119°W. 65 km. West of Chant and east of Buffon, in the area to the east of the southern border of Apollo. Named for Harlan T. Stetson (1885–1964), American astronomer.

Stevinus. Near side. 33°S, 54°E. 75 km. Forms a pair with Snellius, in the Furnerius area. Has high walls and a central peak. Named for Simon Stevin (Stevinus) (1548–1620), Belgian mathematician.

Stewart. Near side. 2°N, 67°E. 13 km. Formerly called Dubiago Q. Named for Balfour Stewart (1828–1887), Scottish physicist.

Stiborius. Near side. 34°S, 32°E. 44 km. South of Piccolomini, in the Altai area. Has a central peak. Named for Andreas Stiborius (c.1470–1515), German astronomer.

Stöfler. Near side. 41°S, 6°E. 126 km. A large, irregular enclosure SE of Walter. Faraday breaks in on it on the SW. It has a level, darkish floor. Named for Johann Stöffler (Stöfler) (1452–1531), German astronomer.

Stokes. Near side. 52°N, 88°W. 51 km. Named for Sir George Stokes (1819–1903), Irish mathematician.

Stoletov. Far side. 45°N, 155°W. 42 km. Just east of Woltjer, in the area just NW of Fowler. Named for Aleksandr Stoletov (1839–1896), Russian physicist.

Stoney. Far side. 56°S, 156°W. 45 km. SW of Baldet, and east of Bhabha. Named for George Stoney (1826–1911), Irish physicist.

Størmer. Far side. 57°N, 145°E. 69 km. North of Van Rhijn, and NW of D'Alembert. Named for Fredrik Størmer (1874–1957), Norwegian mathematician.

Strabo. Near side. 62°N, 55°E. 55 km. Near De la Rue. It is the center of a minor ray system. Named for Strabo (c.63 B.C.–c. A.D. 24), Greek geographer.

Straight Range. Near side. 22°S, 7°W. 90 km long. Also called Montes Recti. Between Plato and Cape Laplace, in the Mare Imbrium. It is fairly bright and very regular, even though it has abrupt endings. Less than 6000 feet. There is nothing else like it on the Moon. Named for its straightness.

Straight Wall. Near side. 22°S, 8°W. Also known as Rupes Recta. The most famous fault on the Moon, it runs from Stag's-Horn Mountains north for 110 km, and is one of the Moon's major features. It used to be thought of as sheer, vertical cliffs, but in 1955 it was proved to be at a 40 degree angle. The surface drops sharply to the west. After full moon it is seen as a bright line near the edge of the Mare Nubium, not far from Thebit. Before full moon it is seen as a dark line. Named for its straightness.

Stratton. Far side. 6°S, 165°E. 71 km. Just NE of Keeler and NW of Heaviside. Named for Frederick Stratton (1881–1960), British astronomer.

Street. Near side. 46°S, 10°W. 58 km. South of Tycho. Quite regular. Has no central peak. Named for Thomas Street (1622–1689), Irish astronomer.

Strömgren. Far side. 22°S, 133°W. 62 km. Just north of Von der Pahlen, in the area NE of Apollo. Named for Svante Strömgren (1870–1947), Danish astronomer.

Struve. Near side. 43°N, 65°W. 18 km. Adjoins Messala. Lies on a dark patch. Named for Wilhelm von Struve (1819–1905), Russian astronomer.

Struve, Otto. Near side. 25°N, 75°W. 170 km. On the west edge of the Oceanus Procellarum. Named for Otto Struve (b. 1897), American astronomer.

Subbotin. Far side. 29°S, 135°E. 68 km. North of Eötvös, just to the SW of Pavlov. Named for Mikhail Subbotin (1893–1966), Russian astronomer.

Successus, Sinus. Near side. 1°N, 58°E. 100 km. Name means "The Bay of Success" in Latin.

Suess. Near side. 4°N, 48°W. 8 km. West of Encke, on the Oceanus Procellarum. Obscure. Named for Eduard Suess (1831–1914), Austrian geologist.

Sulpicius Gallus. Near side. 20°N, 12°E. 12 km. On the Mare Serenitatis. Very bright. Named for Gaius Sulpicius Gallus (fl. 170–164 B.C.), Roman astronomer.

Sulpicius Gallus, Rimae. Near side. 21°N, 10°E. 90 km long. A rill system in the area of Sulpicius Gallus (q.v.), in association with which it was named.

Sumner. Far side. 37°N, 109°E. 50 km. NE of Szilard and SE of Fabry. Named for Thomas H. Sumner (1807–1876), American geographer.

Sumner, Catena. Far side. 38°N, 112°E. 220 km long. A chain of craters in the area of Sumner crater (q.v.), in association with which it was named. It extends in a NW–SE direction from 40°N, 107°E to 36°N, 118°E, in the area SE of Fabry.

Sundman. Far side. 11°N, 91°W. 41 km. SW of Einstein, and SE of Mees. Named for Karl Sundman (1873–1949), Finnish astronomer.

Surveyor Spacecraft. A series of U.S. probes to the Moon. *Surveyor 1:* Launched May 30, 1966. The first U.S. space probe to "soft" land on the Moon. Landed north of Flamsteed, at 2°30'S, 43°12'W. First craft to relay panoramic and closeup pictures from the lunar surface. Sent back 11,237 photos. *Surveyor 2:* Launched September 20, 1966. Because of a guidance failure, it crash-landed at 5°N, 25°W, near Copernicus. *Surveyor 3:* Launched April 17, 1967. It had a history similar to Surveyor 1, and landed at 2°54'S, 23°18'W, in the Oceanus Procellarum, 612 km east of the Surveyor 1 site, near the future Apollo 12 site. It was the first craft to dig trenches on the Moon, during its soil studies. It returned 6315 photos. *Surveyor 4:* Launched July 14, 1967. A failure, it crash-landed at 0° 24'N, 1°18'W, in the Sinus Medii. *Surveyor 5:* Launched September 8, 1967. A successful photographic probe, it had a history similar to Surveyor 1. It landed at 1°24'N, 23°12'E, in the Mare Tranquillitatis, 25 km from the future Apollo 11 site. It was the first craft to analyze lunar mare soil, and sent back 18,006 photos. *Surveyor 6:* Launched November 7, 1967. It had a history similar to Surveyor 1. It landed on the Sinus Medii, at 0°30'N, 1°24'W and conducted soil studies. It sent back 30,065 photos. *Surveyor 7:* Launched January 7, 1968. Had a history similar to Surveyor 1. It made the first "soft" landing in the lunar highlands, landing on the north rim of Tycho, at 40°54'S, 11°30'W. It sent back 21,274 photos.

Sven Hedin. Near side. 5°N, 75°W. West of Hevel. Irregular, it has broken walls. Named for Sven von Hedin (1865–1952), Swedish scientist.

Swann. Far side. 52°N, 112°E. 42 km. SE of Compton, and NW of

Millikan. Named for William Swann (1884–1962), British physicist.

Swasey. Near side. 5°S, 90°E. 24 km. Named for Ambrose Swasey (1846–1937), American telescope manufacturer.

Swift. Near side. 19°N, 54°E. 11 km. Formerly called Peirce B. Named for Jonathan Swift (1667–1745), British satirist.

Sylvester. Near side. 83°N, 80°W. 58 km. Named for James J. Sylvester (1814–1897), British mathematician.

Szilard. Far side. 34°N, 106°E. 127 km. SE of Fabry. Named for Leo Szilard (1898–1964), American physicist.

Tacchini. Near side. 5°N, 86°E. 40 km. Formerly called Neper K. Named for Pietro Tacchini (1838–1905), Italian astronomer.

Tacitus. Near side. 16°S, 19°E. 40 km. In the area of Catharina. Polygonal, it has terraced walls. There are two craters on its floor, and the floor has a central crater pit. Named for Tacitus (c. A.D. 55–117), Roman historian.

Taenarium, Cape *see* **Aenarium, Cape**

Talbot. Near side. 2°S, 85°E. 12 km. Named for William Talbot (1800–1877), British mathematician.

Tamm. Far side. 4°S, 146°E. 38 km. NW of Chaplygin and SE of Mendeleev. Named for Igor Y. Tamm (1895–1971), Russian physicist.

Tannerus. Near side. 56°S, 22°E. 29 km. Near Mutis, in the southern uplands. Has a central peak. Named for Adam Tanner (1572–1632), German mathematician.

Taquet. Near side. 17°N, 19°E. 7 km. Also spelled Tacquet. Near Menelaus, just in the Mare Serenitatis. Bright. Named for André Tacquet (1612–1660), Flemish mathematician.

Taruntius. Near side. 6°N, 48°E. 56 km. A concentric crater with a central peak, in the Mare Fecunditatis. Has quite low walls. Named for Taruntius (fl. c.86 B.C.), Roman astrologer.

Taurus Mountains. Near side. 28°N, 35°E. 500 km long. Also known as Montes Taurus. More a hilly upland, or mountain clumps, extending from the Berzelius area to the area of Rømer, east of the Mare Serenitatis. Named for the range in Asia Minor.

Taylor. Near side. 5°S, 17°E. 42 km. Forms a pair with Taylor A (a subsidiary, yet to be given its own identity), in the area of Delambre. Elliptical, it has a large central peak. Named for Brook Taylor (1685–1731), English mathematician.

Tebbutt. Near side. 10°N, 54°E. 32 km. Formerly called Picard G. Named for John Tebbutt (1834–1916), Australian astronomer.

Teisserenc de Bort. Far side. 32°N, 136°W. 62 km. Also called Teisserenc. Just east of Sanford and SW of Charlier. Named for Léon Philippe Teisserenc de Bort (1855–1913), French meteorologist.

Tempel. Near side. 4°N, 12°E. 45 km. In the uplands west of the Mare Tranquillitatis. Bright. Named for Ernst Tempel (1821–1889), German astronomer.

Temporis, Lacus. Near side. 46°N, 57°E. 250 km. Name means "Lake of Time" in Latin.

ten Bruggencate. Far side. 9°S, 134° E. 59 km. Just east of Lane, in the area south of the western rim of Mendeleev. Named for P. ten Bruggencate (1901–1961), German astronomer.

Teneriffe Mountains. 110 km. Also called Montes Teneriffe. Mountain clumps of little peaks south of Plato in the Mare Imbrium, near Pico, on the border of "Ancient Newton," the ghost-ring between Pico and Plato. They may have formed part of the wall of "Ancient Newton" (which is now destroyed), but probably the mountains are of a much later origin. They are bright. Named for the Tenerife (formerly Teneriffe) range in the Canary Islands.

Tereshkova. Far side. 28°N, 147°E. 31 km. Also spelled Terashkova. Just west of Titov, in the central portion of the Mare Moscoviense. Named for Valentina Tereshkova (b. 1937), USSR cosmonaut.

Tesla. Far side. 38°N, 125°E. 43 km. Just SE of H. G. Wells and NE of Kidinnu. Named for Nikola Tesla (1857–1943), American physicist.

Thales. Near side. 59°N, 41°E. 32 km. The center of a major ray system near Strabo. Named for Thales (c.640–c.546 B.C.), Greek astronomer.

Theaetetus. Near side. 37°N, 6°E. 25 km. On Palus Nebularum. Very deep, it is 5000 feet below the surrounding terrain, and has a low central peak. Named for Theaetetus (c.417–369 B.C.), Greek mathematician.

Theaetetus, Rimae. Near side. 33°N, 6°E. 50 km long. A rill system in the area of Theaetetus (q.v.), in association with which it was named.

Thebit. Near side. 22°S, 4°W. 57 km. Near Arzachel, on the edge of the Mare Nubium. Named for Thabit (Thebit) ibn Qurra (836–901), Arab astronomer.

Theiler. Near side. 13°N, 83°E. 8 km. Named for Max Theiler (1899–1972), American physiologist.

Theon Junior. Near side. 2°S, 16°E. 18 km. Forms a pair with Theon Senior, near Delambre. Bright. Named for Theon of Alexandria (fl. 2nd half of the 4th century), Alexandrian astronomer.

Theon Senior. Near side. 1°S, 15°E 18 km. Forms a pair with Theon Junior. Bright. Named for Theon of Smyrna (fl. early 2nd century A.D.), Alexandrian astronomer.

Theophilus. Near side. 12°S, 26°E. 100 km. Forms a chain with Cyrillus and Catharina, on the edge of the Mare Nectaris. Polygonal, and very deep, its massive walls rise 3½ miles above the interior. It has an excellent, bright central mountain with several peaks, one of them rising 6000 feet above the floor. Named for Theophilus (fl. 12th century), German metallurgist.

Theophrastus. Near side. 17°N, 39°E. 9 km. Formerly called Maraldi M. Named for Theophrastus (c.372–c. 287 B.C.), Greek philosopher.

Thiele. Far side. 40°N, 134°W. 33 km. South of Quételet, and due west of Landau. Named for Thorvald Thiele (1838–1910), Danish astronomer.

Thiessen. Far side. 75°N, 169°W. 67 km. NW of Hippocrates and NE of Karpinskiy. Named for E. Thiessen (1914–1961), German astronomer.

Thomson. Far side. 32°S, 166°E. 112 km. The largest crater in the Mare Ingenii. Named for Joseph J. Thomson (1856–1940), British physicist.

Tikhomirov. Far side. 25°N, 162°E. 65 km. SW of Trumpler and east of the Mare Moscoviense. Named for Viktor Tikhomirov (b. 1912), Russian radio engineer.

Tikhov. Far side. 62°N, 172°E. 83 km. SE of Avogadro, and NE of D'Alembert. Named for Gavriel Tikhov (1875–1960), Russian astrophysicist.

Tiling. Far side. 53°S, 132°W. 38 km. South of Fizeau, and SE of Minkowski.

Named for Reinhold Tiling (1890–1933), German rocket pioneer.

Timaeus. Near side. 63°N, 1°W. 33 km. On the edge of the Mare Frigoris. Bright. Named for Timaeus (fl. 400 B.C.), Greek philosopher.

Timiryazev. Far side. 5°S, 147°W. 53 km. Just NW of Sechenov, between Korolev and Hertzsprung. Named for Kliment Timiryazev (1843–1920), Russian plant physiologist.

Timocharis. Near side. 17°N, 13°W. 34 km. The center of an extensive but faint ray system on the Mare Imbrium. A perfect crater, it has broad walls, finely terraced on the inside, and the floor has a central crater and some low hills. Named for Timocharis (c.320–260 B.C.), Greek astronomer.

Timoleon. Near side. 35°N, 75°E. 130 km. Forms a pair with Gauss. Quite distinct. Named for Timoleon (c.411–337 B.C.), Greek general.

Timoris, Lacus. Near side. 39°S, 28°W. 130 km. Name means "Lake of Fear" in Latin.

Tiselius. Far side. 7°N, 176°E. 54 km. Just west of Stein, in the area NW of Korolev. Named for Arne Tiselius (1902–1971), Swedish analytical chemist.

Tisserand. Near side. 21°N, 48°E. 37 km. In the Mare Crisium area. Regular, it has no central peak. Named for François Tisserand (1845–1896), French astronomer.

Titius. Far side. 27°S, 101°E. 73 km. NE of Lauritsen and south of Kovalskiy, in the area just NE of the Mare Australe. Named for Johann D. Titius (1729–1796), German astronomer.

Titov. Far side. 28°N, 150°E. 32 km. In the eastern portion of the Mare Moscoviense. Named for Gherman Titov (b. 1935), USSR cosmonaut.

Tolansky. Near side. 9°S, 16°W. 13 km. Formerly called Parry A. Named for Samuel Tolansky (b. 1907), British physicist.

Torricelli. Near side. 5°S, 29°E. 23 km. In the Mare Nectaris. Irregular. Named for Evangelista Torricelli (1608–1647), Italian physicist.

Toscanelli. Near side. 28°N, 47°W. 7 km. Formerly called Aristarchus C. Named for Paolo dal Pozzo Toscanelli (1397–1482), Italian astronomer.

Townley. Near side. 3°N, 63°E. 19 km. Formerly called Apollonius G. Named for Richard Towneley (Townley) (1629–1707), English natural philosopher.

Tralles. Near side. 28°N, 53°E. 43 km. On the wall of Cleomedes. Very deep. Named for Johann Tralles (1763–1822), German physicist.

Tranquillitatis, Mare. Near side. 9°N, 30°E. 800 km. One of the major maria on the Moon, it is also called "The Sea of Tranquility." This is where Armstrong and Aldrin landed. It joins the following maria: Serenitatis, Vaporum, Nectaris, and Fecunditatis. It is lighter and patchier than Serenitatis, and less regular in shape. Craters on it include Cauchy, Sinas, Maskelyne, Jansen, and Arago.

Triesnecker. Near side. 4°N, 4°E. 26 km. In the Mare Vaporum area. It is associated with a major rill system (*see* following entry). Named for Franz von Triesnecker (1745–1817), German astronomer.

Triesnecker, Rimae. Near side. 5°N, 5°E. 200 km long. A major rill system, in the area of Triesnecker (q.v.), in association with which it was named.

Trouvelot. Near side. 49°N, 6°E. 9 km. In the Alpine Valley area. Quite bright. Named for Étienne Trouvelot (1827–1895), French astronomer.

Trumpler. Far side. 28°N, 168°E. 77 km. NE of Freundlich, and south of Nušl, in the area east of the Mare Moscoviense. Named for Robert Trumpler (1886–1956), American astronomer.

Tsander. Far side. 5°N, 149°W. 171 km. NW of Kibaltchich, with which it forms a pair, between Hertzsprung and Korolev. Named for Fridrikh A. Tsander (1887–1933), Russian rocket pioneer.

Tsiolkovskiy. Far side. 21°S, 129°E. 180 km. Between Mendeleev and the Mare Australe. Isolated, it is one of the larger fresh craters and is the most prominent of the lava-flooded craters. It has an extradark floor. Named for Konstantin E. Tsiolkovskiy (1857–1935), Russian scientist.

Tsu Chung-Chih. Far side. 17°N, 144°W. 28 km. SE of Mach, and west of Kekulé. Named for Tsu Ch'ung-Chih (429–500), Chinese mathematician.

Tucker. Near side. 6°S, 88°E. 7 km. Named for George Tucker (1775–1861), British science fiction writer.

Turner. Near side. 2°S, 13°W. 12 km. Near Gambart, in the Mare Nubium. Deep. Named for Herbert Turner (1861–1930), British astronomer.

Tycho. Near side. 43°S, 11°W. 85 km. At full moon this is the most prominent lunar feature and is the center of the most important ray system on the Moon. It is circular, and has a central peak, and terraced walls. Named for Tycho Brahe (1546–1601), Danish astronomer.

Tyndall. Far side. 35°S, 117°E. 18 km. West of Pizzetti, in the area east of the northern portion of the Mare Australe. Named for John Tyndall (1820–1893), Irish physicist.

Ukert. Near side. 8°N, 1°E. 23 km. On the edge of the Mare Vaporum. Bright-walled, it has rills nearby. Named for Friedrich Ukert (1780–1851), German geographer.

Ulugh Beigh. Near side. 33°N, 82°W. 54 km. West of the Oceanus Procellarum. Has high walls and a central peak. Named for Ulugh Beigh (1394–1449), Mongol astronomer.

Undarum, Mare. Near side. 7°N, 67°E. 220 km. A patch of dark lava, rather than a well-defined "sea," SE of the Mare Crisium, east of Firmicus and Apollonius. Easily seen from Earth, it is very dark near full moon. Name means "The Sea of Waves" in Latin.

Ural Mountains. Near side. 2°S, 22°W. An extension of the Riphaens, they lie to the north of that range. Named after the range in the USSR.

Usov, Mons. Near side. 12°N, 63°E. A mountain. Named for Mikhail Usov (1883–1939), Russian geologist.

Vaisala. Near side. 26°N, 48°W. 8 km. Formerly called Aristarchus A. Named for Yrjö Vaisala (1891–1971), Finnish astronomer.

Valier. Far side. 7°N, 174°E. 68 km. Just west of Stein, between Korolev and the Mare Moscoviense. Named for Max Valier (1895–1930), Austrian engineer.

Valles. Plural of vallis. A vallis is a valley, although sometimes the term is used incorrectly as far as the Moon goes. (*See* **Alpes, Baade, Bohr, Bouvard, Inghirami, Palitzsch, Planck, Rheita, Schrödinger, Schröteri, Snellius**.)

Van Albada. Near side. 9°N, 64°E. 22 km. Formerly called Auzout A. Named for Lieuwe Van Albada (b. 1868), Dutch optician.

Van Biesbroeck. Near side. 29°N, 46°W. 10 km. Formerly called Krieger B. Named for George Van Biesbroeck (b. 1880), Belgian astronomer.

Van de Graaff. Far side. 27°S, 172°E. 234 km. A footprint-shaped depression about 4 km deep, NE of the Mare Ingenii. Extremely interesting in that it is associated with a strong magnetic anomaly, showing greater radioactivity than its surroundings, possibly indicating buried volcanic rock. Named for Robert Van de Graaff (1901–1967), American physicist.

Van den Bergh. Far side. 31°N, 159°W. 42 km. Just east of Cockcroft, and south of Evershed. Named for Johannes Van den Bergh (1824–1890), Dutch engineer.

Van den Bos. Far side. 5°S, 146°E. 22 km. SE of Mendeleev and just to the south of Tamm. Named for Willem Van den Bos (b. 1896), American astronomer.

Van der Waals. Far side. 44°S, 119°E. 101 km. Between Lamb and Roche, in the area east of the southern border of the Mare Australe. Named for Johannes D. Van der Waals (1837–1923), Dutch physicist.

Van Gent. Far side. 16°N, 160°E. 44 km. NE of Kohlschütter and NW of Spencer Jones, in the area SE of the Mare Moscoviense. Named for H. Van Gent (1900–1947), Dutch astronomer.

Van Gu. Far side. 11°S, 139°W. 53 km. Also called Wan-Hoo. North of Paschen and SW of Hertzsprung.

Van Maanen. Far side. 36°N, 127°E. 60 km. East of Kidinnu, and SE of Tesla, in the area between H. G. Wells and the Mare Moscoviense. Named for Adrian Van Maanen (1884–1946), Dutch-American astronomer.

Van Rhijn. Far side. 52°N, 145°E. 46 km. South of Størmer and west of D'Alembert. Named for Pieter Van Rhijn (1886–1960), Dutch astronomer.

Van Vleck. Near side. 2°S, 78°E. 31 km. Formerly called Gilbert M. Named for John Van Vleck (1899–1980), American physicist.

Van Wijk. Far side. 63°S, 119°E. 32 km. South of Kimura, and NW of Grotrian, in the area to the north of the western rim of Schrödinger. Named for Nicolaas Van Wijk (1880–1942), Dutch philologist.

Van't Hoff. Far side. 62°N, 133°W. 93 km. East of the south rim of Stebbins and NE of Birkhoff. Named for Jacobus van't Hoff (1852–1911), Dutch physical chemist.

Vaporum, Mare. Near side. 14°N, 5°E. 230 km. Between Copernicus and the Mare Serenitatis, this is one of the minor maria. Dark. Name means "The Sea of Vapors" in Latin.

Vasco da Gama. Near side. 15°N, 85°W. 96 km. West of the Oceanus Procellarum. Has a central ridge. Named for Vasco da Gama (c.1469–1524), Portuguese navigator.

Vashakidze. Far side. 44°N, 93°E. 44 km. West of Fabry, and NE of Rynin. Named for Mikhail Vashakidze (1909–1956), Russian astronomer.

Vavilov. Far side. 1°S, 139°W. 99 km. Breaks the SW rim of Hertzsprung. Named for Sergey Vavilov (1891–1951), Russian physicist.

Vega. Near side. 45°N, 63°E. 76 km. In the area of the Mare Australe. Deep. Named for Georg von Vega (1754–1802), Austrian mathematician.

Vendelinus. Near side. 16°S, 62°E. 147 km. In the Petavius chain. Irregular, and broken. Named for Godefroi Vendelinus (1580–1667), Flemish astronomer.

Vening Meinesz. Far side. 0°, 163°E. 87 km. South of Mandel'stam and north of Keeler. Named for Felix Vening-Meinesz (1887–1966), Dutch engineer.

Ventris. Far side. 5°S, 158°E. 95 km. SE of Schliemann and NW of Keeler.

Named for Michael Ventris (1922–1956), British cryptographer.

Veris, Lacus. Near side. 13°S, 87°W. 540 km. Name means "Lake of Truth" in Latin.

Vernadskiy. Far side. 23°N, 130°E. 92 km. SW of the Mare Moscoviense and SE of Meggers. Named for Vladimir Vernadskiy (1863–1945), Russian mineralogist.

Verne, Jules *see* **Jules Verne**

Vertregt. Far side. 20°S, 171°E. 171 km. To the east of Gagarin and NE of the Mare Ingenii. Aitken breaks in on its NE rim.

Very. Near side. 26°N, 25°E. 5 km. Formerly called Le Monnier B. Named for Frank Very (1852–1927), American astronomer.

Vesalius. Far side. 3°S, 115°E. 62 km. SE of Buisson and NE of Einthoven, in the area between Mendeleev and the Mare Smythii. Named for Andreas Vesalius (1514–1564), Flemish anatomist.

Vestine. Far side. 34°N, 94°E. 96 km. SW of Fabry and north of Joliot. Named for Ernest H. Vestine (1906–1968), American geophysicist.

Vetchinkin. Far side. 10°N, 131°E. 98 km. NW of Mendeleev and SW of Hoffmeister. Named for Vladimir P. Vetchinkin (1888–1950), Russian aerodynamicist.

Viète. Near side. 29°S, 57°W. 87 km. West of the Mare Humorum. Has a small, low central hill, and several craterlets on its floor. Named for François Viète (1540–1603), French mathematician.

Vil'ev. Far side. 6°S, 144°E. 46 km. SE of Pannekoek, and west of Chaplygin. Named for Mikhail Vil'ev (1893–1919), Russian astronomer.

Vinogradov, Mons. Near side. 22°N, 32°W. Named for Aleksandr Vinogradov (1895–1975), Russian geochemist.

Virchow. Near side. 10°N, 84°E. 17 km. Formerly called Neper G. Named for Rudolf Virchow (1821–1902), German scientist.

Virtanen. Far side. 15°N, 177°E. 44 km. Just east of Anderson and NW of Stein. Named for Artturi Virtanen (1895–1973), Finnish biochemist.

Vitello. Near side. 30°S, 38°W. 42 km. On the south edge of the Mare Humorum. Has a bright inner ring not quite concentric with the main wall. Has a central peak. Named for Witelo (Vitello) (c.1230–c.1276), Polish optician.

Vitruvius. Near side. 18°N, 31°E. 30 km. Between Mare Serenitatis and Mare Tranquillitatis. Has low but not quite bright walls. Named for Pollio Vitruvius (fl. 1st century B.C.), Roman architect-engineer.

Viviani. Far side. 5°N, 117°E. 27 km. West of King and south of Guyot. Named for Vincenzo Viviani (1622–1703), Italian mathematician.

Vlacq. Near side. 53°S, 39°E. 89 km. One of a group of six, SW of Janssen. Deep, it has a central peak. Named for Adriaan Vlacq (1600–1667), Dutch mathematician.

Vogel. Near side. 15°S, 6°E. 27 km. SE of Albategnius. Named for Hermann Vogel (1841–1907), German astrophysicist.

Volkov. Far side. 14°S, 132°E. 41 km. SW of Chauvenet and NE of Tsiolkovskiy. Named for Vladislav Volkov (1935–1971), USSR cosmonaut.

Volta. Near side. 54°N, 85°W. 113 km. Named for Alessandro Volta (1745–1827), Italian physicist.

Volterra. Far side. 57°N, 131°E. 52 km. NE of Millikan and east of the southern rim of Compton. Named for Vito Volterra (1860–1940), Italian mathematician.

Von Behring. Near side. 8°S, 72°E. 39 km. Formerly called Maclaurin F. Named for Emil A. von Behring (1854–1917), German immunologist.

Von Bekesy. Far side. 52°N, 127°E. 96 km. South of Volterra and NE of Millikan. Named for Georg von Bekesy (1899–1972), American physiologist.

Von der Pahlen. Far side. 25°S, 133°W. 57 km. South of Strömgren, in the area south of Hertzsprung and west of the Mare Orientale. Named for Emanuel von der Pahlen (1882–1952), German astronomer.

Von Kármán. Far side. 45°S, 176°E. 179 km. SW of Leibnitz and SE of the Mare Ingenii. Named for Theodor von Kármán (1881–1963), American physicist.

Von Neumann. Far side. 40°N, 153°E. 78 km. South of Campbell and north of the eastern rim of the Mare Moscoviense. Named for John Von Neumann (1903–1957), American mathematician.

Von Zeipel. Far side. 42°N, 142°W. 83 km. Breaks the east wall of Fowler. Named for E. H. von Zeipel (1873–1959), Swedish astronomer.

Voskresenskiy. Near side. 28°N, 88°W. 50 km. Named for Leonid Voskresenskiy (1913–1965), Russian rocket designer.

Walker. Far side. 26°S, 162°W. 33 km. To the north of the west wall of Apollo. Named for Sears Cook Walker (1805–1853), American astronomer.

Wallace. Near side. 10°N, 9°W. 26 km. An imperfect ring formation in the Apennines, in the Mare Imbrium. Has very low walls. Named for Alfred Wallace (1823–1913), British scientist.

Wallach. Near side. 5°N, 32°E. 6 km. Formerly called Maskelyne H. Named for Otto Wallach (1847–1931), German chemist.

Walter. Near side. 33°S, 1°E. 140 km. A rhomboidal walled plain which forms a trio with Regiomontanus and Purbach, outside the Mare Nubium. It has massive walls and very complex ramparts, and has a central mountain with two craters in it. Notable under morning illumination. Named for Bernard Walter (1430–1504), German astronomer.

Wan-Hoo *see* **Van Gu**

Wargentin. Near side. 50°S, 60°W. 84 km. In the Schickard group. Has a familiar plateau. Named for Pehr Wargentin (1717–1783), Swedish astronomer.

Warner. Near side. 4°S, 87°E. 35 km. Named for Edward Warner (1894–1958), American aeronautical engineer.

Waterman. Far side. 26°S, 128°E. 76 km. Immediately south of Tsiolkovskiy. Named for Alan T. Waterman (1892–1967), American physicist.

Watson. Far side. 63°S, 124°W. 62 km. SW of Boltzmann and west of Petzval, in the area north of Zeeman. Named for James C. Watson (1838–1880), Canadian astronomer.

Watt. Near side. 50°S, 51°E. 66 km. Forms a pair with Steinheil, SW of Janssen. Named for Sir Robert Watson Watt (1892–1973), Scottish physicist.

Watts. Near side. 9°N, 46°E. 15 km. Formerly called Taruntius D. Named for William W. Watts (1860–1947), British geologist.

Webb. Near side. 1°S, 60°E. 22 km. The center of a minor ray system, on the edge of the Mare Fecunditatis. Has a darkish floor and a central peak. Named for Thomas W. Webb (1806–1885), British astronomer.

Weber. Far side. 50°N, 124°W. 43 km. Forms a pair with Sarton, in the area north of Landau and south of Dyson. Named for Wilhelm Weber (1804–1891), German physicist.

Wegener. Far side. 45°N, 113°W. 88 km. Squeezed in between Landau and Stefan. Has an asymmetrical floor. Named for Alfred Wegener (1880–1930), German geophysicist.

Weierstrass. Near side. 1°S, 77°E. 33 km. Formerly called Gilbert N. Named for Karl Weierstrass (1815–1897), German mathematician.

Weigel. Near side. 58°S, 39°W. 36 km. Forms a pair with Röst, in the Schiller area. Quite regular. Named for Christian Weigel (1748–1831), German chemist.

Weinek. Near side. 28°S, 37°E. 32 km. In the area of Altai, NE of Piccolomini. Has a darkish floor. Named for Ladislav Weinek (1848–1913), Hungarian astronomer.

Weiss. Near side. 32°S, 20°W. 66 km. In the Pitatus group. Very irregular. Named for Edmund Weiss (1837–1917), Austrian astronomer.

Wells, H. G. *see* **H. G. Wells**

Werner. Near side. 28°S, 3°E. 70 km. Forms a pair with Aliacensis. Very regular, it has high walls and a central peak. Named for Johan Werner (1468–1528), German astronomer.

Wexler. Far side. 69°S, 90°E. 52 km. North of Hale. Its southern rim is due west of the northern rim of Schrödinger. Named for Harry Wexler (1911–1962), American meteorologist.

Weyl. Far side. 16°N, 120°W. 115 km. East of Fersman, and NW of Kamerlingh Onnes, in the area NE of Hertzsprung. Named for Hermann Weyl (1885–1955), German mathematician.

Whewell. Near side. 4°N, 14°E. 14 km. In the uplands, west of the Mare Tranquillitatis. Bright. Named for William Whewell (1794–1866), British scientist.

White. Far side. 48°S, 149°W. 39 km. South of the eastern part of Apollo. Named for Edward H. White (1930–1967), American astronaut.

Wichmann. Near side. 8°S, 38°W. 10 km. On the Oceanus Procellarum. Associated with a large ghost-crater. Named for Moritz Wichmann (1821–1859), German astronomer.

Widmanstätten. Near side. 6°S, 85° E. 46 km. Named for Aloys von Widmanstätten (1754–1849), Austrian mineralogist.

Wiechert. Far side. 84°S, 165°E. 41 km. Also spelled Wiechart. East of Amundsen and south of Schrödinger, on the way to the South Pole. Named for Emil Wiechert (1861–1928), German geophysicist.

Wiener. Far side. 41°N, 146°E. 114 km. To the immediate NE of Kurchatov, in the area NW of Mare Moscoviense and SW of Campbell. Named for Norbert Wiener (1894–1964), American mathematician.

Wildt. Near side. 9°N, 76°E. 11 km. Formerly called Condorcet K. Named for Rupert Wildt (1905–1976), German-American astronomer.

Wilhelm I. Near side. 43°S, 20°W. 107 km. Also called Wilhelm. An irregular ring formation in the area of Longomontanus. It has an uneven floor and uneven walls. Named for Wilhelm IV of Hesse (1797–1888), German astronomer.

Wilkins. Near side. 30°S, 20°E. 57 km. In the Rabbi Levi group. Irregular. Formerly called Zagut by W. Goodacre, it was renamed for Percy Wilkins (1896–1960), Welsh astronomer.

Williams. Near side. 42°N, 37°E. 36 km. In the Lacus Somniorum area. Not prominent. Named for Arthur S. Williams (1861–1938), British astronomer.

Wilsing. Far side. 22°S, 155°W. 74 km. South of Galois, between Apollo and Korolev. Named for Johannes Wilsing (1856–1943), German astronomer.

Wilson. Near side. 69°S, 33°W. 70 km. Near Bailly, in the Bettinus chain. Regular, and deep, it has very high walls, a crater on the inner slopes on the west, and a low ridge on the floor. It has no central peak. Named for Alexander Wilson (1714–1786), Scottish astronomer.

Winkler. Far side. 42°N, 179°W. 23 km. SE of Chandler and NE of Champollion. Named for Johannes Winkler (1897–1947), German rocket engineer.

Winlock. Far side. 35°N, 106°W. 64 km. NE of Healy, in the area SE of Landau. Named for Joseph Winlock (1826–1875), American astronomer.

Winthrop. Near side. 11°S, 44°W. 18 km. Formerly called Letronne P. Named for John Winthrop (1714–1779), American astronomer.

Wöhler. Near side. 38°S, 31°E. 27 km. Near the Rabbi Levi group. Quite regular. Named for Friedrich Wöhler (1800–1882), German chemist.

Wolf. Near side. 23°S, 17°W. 25 km. In the southern part of the Mare Nubium. Irregular, it has low walls. Named for Max J. C. Wolf (1863–1932), German astronomer.

Wolff, Mount. Near side. 17°N, 7°W. 12,000 feet high, or more. Also known as Mons Wolff. Between Ampère and Eratosthenes, in the Apennines. Named for Christian von Wolff (1679–1754), German philosopher.

Wollaston. Near side. 31°N, 47°W. 10 km. North of the Harbinger Mountains. Bright. Named for William Wollaston (1766–1828), British chemist.

Woltjer. Far side. 45°N, 160°W. 47 km. Teamed with Montgolfier to its north. West of Fowler. Named for Jan Woltjer (1891–1946), Dutch astronomer.

Wood. Far side. 44°N, 121°W. 78 km. Breaks into the NW rim of Landau. Named for Robert W. Wood (1868–1955), American physicist.

Wright. Near side. 31°S, 88°W. 40 km. Named for Thomas Wright (1711–1786), British astronomer.

Wroblewski. Far side. 24°S, 153°E. 22 km. SE of Gagarin and SW of Cyrano. Named for Zygmunt von Wroblewski (1845–1888), Polish physicist.

Wrottesley. Near side. 24°S, 57°E. 57 km. In the Petavius group. Has a twin-peaked central mountain. Named for John, 2nd Baron Wrottesley (1798–1867), British astronomer.

Wurzelbauer. Near side. 34°S, 16° W. 88 km. A large ringed formation in the Pitatus group. Nearly circular, it has a very complex border and an uneven floor. Named for Johannes von Wurzelbauer (1651–1725), German astronomer.

Wyld. Far side. 1°S, 98°E. 94 km. To the east of the Mare Smythii and NW of Saha. Named for James Wyld (1913–1953), American rocket pioneer.

Xenophanes. Near side. 57°N, 77° W. 120 km. On the Moon's limb, near Sinus Roris. Has high walls and a central peak. Named for Xenophanes (c. 570–c.480 B.C.), Greek philosopher.

Xenophon. Far side. 23°S, 122°E. 25 km. To the west of the southern rim of

Tsiolkovskiy. Named for Xenophon (c.430–358 B.C.), Greek historian.

Yablochkov. Far side. 61°N, 127°E. 99 km. South of the eastern rim of Schwarzschild, and north of Volterra. Named for Tikhon Yablochkov (1848–1906), Russian historian.

Yamamoto. Far side. 59°N, 161°E. 77 km. North of D'Alembert, and south of Avogradro. Named for I. Yamamoto (1889–1959), Japanese astronomer.

Yangel'. Near side. 17°N, 5°E. 9 km. Formerly called Manilius F. Named for Mikhail Yangel' (1911–1971), Russian rocket designer.

Yerkes. Near side. 15°N, 52°E. 36 km. On the west edge of the Mare Crisium. Irregular, it has low walls. Named for Charles T. Yerkes (1837–1905), American observatory founder.

Young. Near side. 42°S, 51°E. 72 km. In the Rheita Valley area. Irregular. Named for Charles A. Young (1834–1908), American astronomer.

Zach. Near side. 61°S, 5°E. 71 km. East of Clavius. Quite deep, it has walls rising to over 13,000 feet. Quite regular. Named for Franz von Zach (1754–1832), Hungarian astronomer.

[1]**Zagut** *see* **Wilkins**

[2]**Zagut.** Near side. 32°S, 22°E. 84 km. A walled formation. A large ring plain in the Rabbi Levi group breaks in on its floor on the NW. Irregular, it has a crater near the center of its floor. Named for Abraham Zacuto (Zagut) (c.1450–c.1522), Spanish astronomer.

Zahringer. Near side. 60°N, 40°E. 11 km. Formerly called Taruntius E. Named for Joseph Zahringer (b. 1929), German physicist.

Zanstra. Far side. 3°N, 125°E. 43 km. Between Gregory and King, and between Mendeleev and the Mare Smythii. Named for Herman Zanstra (1894–1972), Dutch astronomer.

Zasyadko. Far side. 4°N, 94°E. 11 km. Breaks into the NE rim of Babcock, on the NE side of the Mare Smythii. Named for D. Zasyadko (1779–1837), Russian rocket pioneer.

Zeeman. Far side. 75°S, 135°W. 184 km. The second largest lunar feature south of 70° south (*see also* **Schrödinger**). Named for Pieter Zeeman (1865–1943), Dutch physicist.

Zelinskiy. Far side. 29°S, 167°E. 54 km. Immediately north of Thomson, between the southern portion of Van de Graaff and the NW portion of the Mare Ingenii. Named for Nikolay Zelinskiy (1861–1953), Russian chemist.

Zeno. Near side. 45°N, 73°E. 65 km. Named for Zeno (fl. 5th century B.C.), Greek philosopher.

Zernike. Far side. 18°N, 168°E. 49 km. NW of Anderson, and SW of Buys-Ballot. Named for Fritz Zernike (1888–1966), Dutch physicist.

Zhiritskiy. Far side. 25°S, 120°E. 35 km. SW of Tsiolkovskiy and NE of Schaeberle. Named for Georgiy Zhiritskiy (1893–1966), Russian aeronautical engineer.

Zhukovskiy. Far side. 7°N, 167°W. 81 km. Immediately west of Lebedinskiy, with which it forms a pair, in the area NW of Korolev. Named for Nikolay Zhukovskiy (1847–1921), Russian mechanician.

Zinger. Far side. 57°N, 176°E. 44 km. Also spelled Tsinger. North of the eastern rim of D'Alembert and SE of Avogadro. Named for Nikolay Zinger (1842–1918), Russian astronomer.

Zinner. Near side. 27°N, 59°W. 4 km. Formerly called Schiaparelli B. Named for Ernst Zinner (1886–1970), German astronomer.

Zöllner. Near side. 8°S, 19°E. 47 km. A large, elliptical enclosure NW of Theophilus. It has low, broad walls with some craters on them. Named for Johann Zöllner (1834–1882), German astronomer.

Zond Spacecraft. A series of USSR Moon probes. Only those listed are relevant. *Zond 3:* Launched July 18, 1965. Photographed the far side of the Moon, sending back 25 pictures. Got to within 9219 km of the surface. It sent back the photos on July 27, when it was 2,200,000 km from Earth. *Zond 4:* Launched March 2, 1968; purpose and outcome unknown. *Zond 5:* Launched September 14, 1968. It carried plants, seeds, insects, and tortoises. It orbited the Moon and got to within 1950 km. On September 21 it returned to Earth, landing in the Indian Ocean. *Zond 6:* Launched November 10, 1968. Orbited the Moon, and filmed the far side. Got to within 2420 km of the surface. On November 17 it returned to Earth. *Zond 7:* Launched August 7, 1969; flew around the Moon, and photographed the far side in color, from 2000 km; returned to Earth. *Zond 8:* Launched October 20, 1970. Flew around the Moon, and took color pictures. On October 27 it splashed down on Earth in the Indian Ocean, where it was picked up.

Zsigmondy. Far side. 59°N, 105°W. 66 km. Between Smoluchowski and Birkhoff, in the area NW of the Oceanus Procellarum. Named for Richard Zsigmondy (1865–1929), German colloid chemist.

Zucchius. Near side. 61°S, 50°W. 64 km. Also spelled Zuchius. Forms a pair with Segner, in the Schiller area. Distinct, it is the center of a minor ray system, and has a central mountain with several peaks. Named for Niccolò Zucchi (1586–1670), Italian mathematician.

Zupus. Near side. 17°S, 52°W. 38 km. South of Billy. Irregular, it has low walls and a very dark floor. Named for Giovanni Zupi (1590–1650), Italian astronomer.

Zupus, Rimae. Near side. 15°S, 53° W. 120 km long. A rill system in the area of Zupus (q.v.), in association with which it was named.

Zwicky. Far side. 16°S, 168°E. 135 km. South of Heaviside, and west of Aitken. Named for Fritz Zwicky (1898–1974), American physicist.

Lunar Bibliography

The works chosen here are presented chronologically and represent significant advances in human understanding of and attitudes toward the Moon. Omitted are numerous adequate, even excellent, works that are duplicative or retrospective.

De Face in Orbe Lunae. Plutarch. c. A.D. 80. The Moon is described as Earthlike, with mountains and ravines, and inhabitants (*see also* **Mapping** entry).

True History. Lucian. 2nd century A.D. A satire, in which a ship is carried from the Earth to the Moon in 7 days.

De Phenomenis in Orbe Lunae. Iulio Caesare La Galla. 1612. The first real nonfiction book about the Moon.

Disquisitiones Mathematicae de Controversiis et Novitatibus Astronomiciis. Scheiner. 1619 (*see* **Mapping** entry).

Oratio. Malapert (1620 (*see* **Mapping** entry).

Somniorum. Johann Kepler. 1634. The hero is carried to the Moon by demon-power. Life on the Moon is described.

The Discovery of the World in the Moon. John Wilkins. 1638. He said that the Moon is inhabited and that England should claim it.

The Man in the Moon. Francis Godwin. 1638. A man is flown to the Moon on a raft pulled by wild geese. He is met by a race of musically-talking giants.

Detectio Dioptrica Corporum Planetarum Verorum. M. Hirtzgärtner. 1643 (*see* **Mapping** entry).

Selenographia Langreniana. M. F. Van Langren. 1645 (*see* **Mapping** entry).

Opus Theologiae, Philosophiae et Verbi Dei Praeconibus Utile et Incundum. A. M. Schyrlaeus de Rheita. 1645.

Novae Coelestium Terrestriumque Rerum Observationes. F. Fontana. 1646 (*see* **Mapping** entry).

Selenographia Sive Lunae Descriptio. Hevelius. 1647. Danzig (*see* **Mapping** entry).

Almagestum Novum. Riccioli. 1651. Bologna (*see* **Mapping** entry).

Voyage to the Moon. Cyrano. 1656. A comedy.

Bericht von den Mondskugeln. Tobias Mayer. 1750 (*see* **Mapping** entry).

Selenotopographische Fragmente. J. H. Schröter. 1791. Lilienthal (*see* **Mapping** entry).

Der Mond. Wilhelm Beer and Johann Mädler. 1838 (*see* **Mapping** entry).

Moon Hoax. Richard Adams Locke. 1859. A book about the 1835 hoax (*see* **Phenomena and Discoveries** entry).

From the Earth to the Moon. Jules Verne. 1865. A novel.

The Moon. A. Proctor. 1873.

The Moon. E. Neison 1876 (*see* **Mapping** entry).

The Moon. J. Nasmyth and J. Carpenter. 1903.

The Moon. G. P. Serviss, 1908.

Astronomy for Everyone. Simon Newcomb. 1910. He wrote that no change ever takes place on the Moon's surface.

Glazial-Kosmogonie. Hans Hörbiger. 1913. He claimed that the Moon is ice, that its glacial covering is 150 miles deep, and that the Moon is spiraling toward Earth. He said that the Moon was captured by Earth 13–14,000 years ago, and this led to cataclysms on Earth, one of which submerged Atlantis.

Physics and Astronomy of the Moon. ed. Zdenek Kopal. 1962.

New Guide to the Moon. Patrick Moore. 1976.

The Moon Observer's Handbook. Fred Price. 1988.

Part II

Photographs

Checklist of Moons Depicted

Apollo 11 view of the full moon, from 160,000 km, July 21, 1969, during the spacecraft's journey home; aboard Apollo 11 were astronauts Neil Armstrong, Buzz Aldrin and Michael Collins.

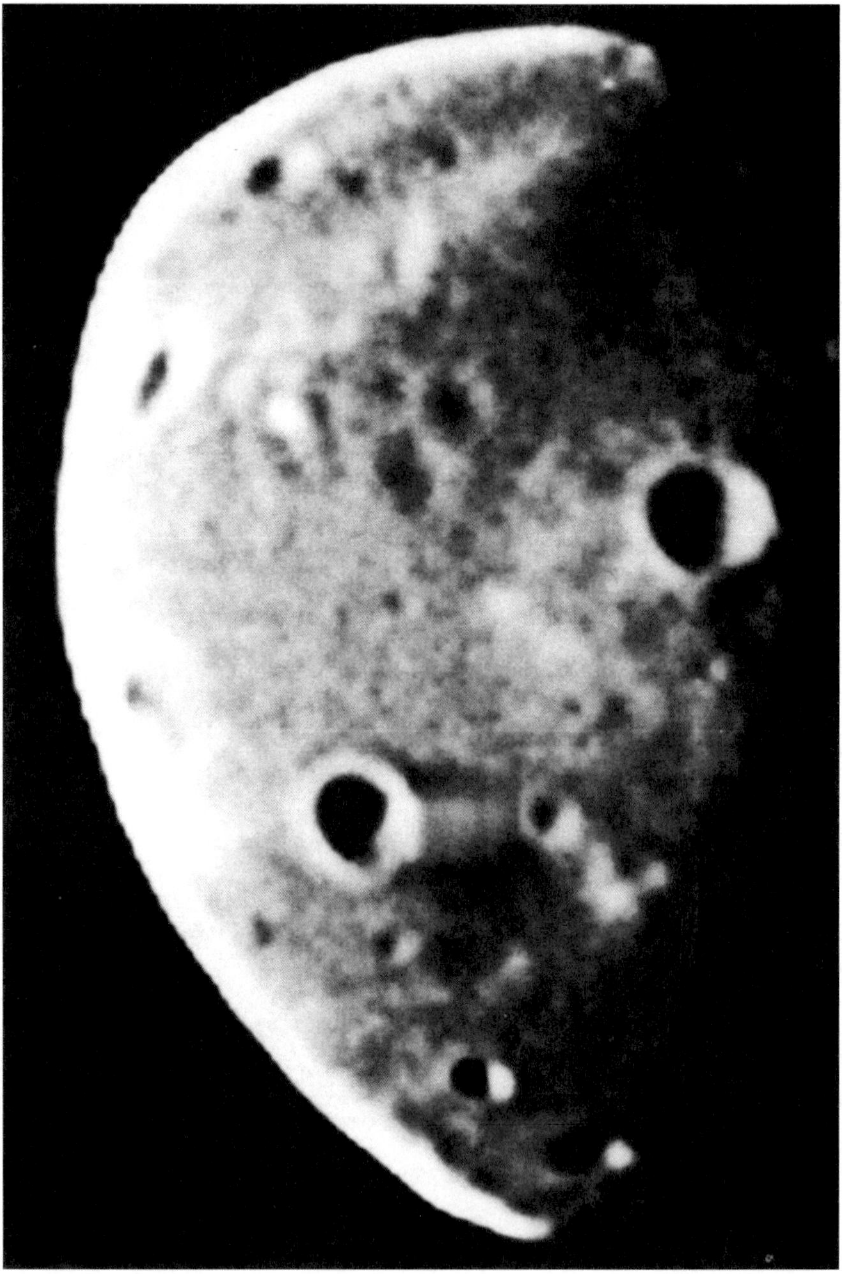

Opposite: **The best photo of Deimos, Mars's smaller moon, taken by Viking Orbiter 1 from 3300 km. Mars would be to the left (that is, toward the bottom of the page).**

This page, top: **The Moon taken by Apollo 16, May 2, 1972.** ***Bottom:*** **The Moon taken by Galileo Spacecraft at 7 p.m. PST on December 8, 1990. On the right is Oceanus Procellarum. The dark spots in the center are Mare Orientale.**

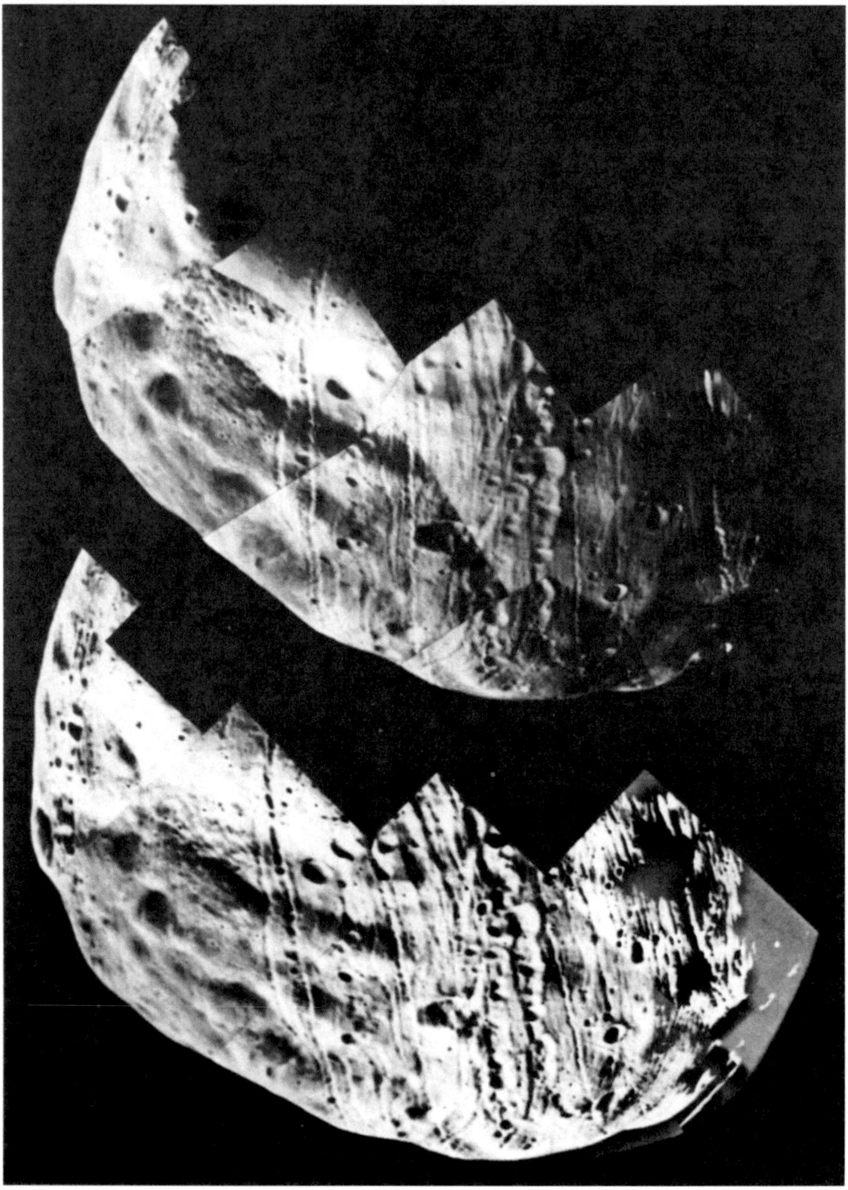

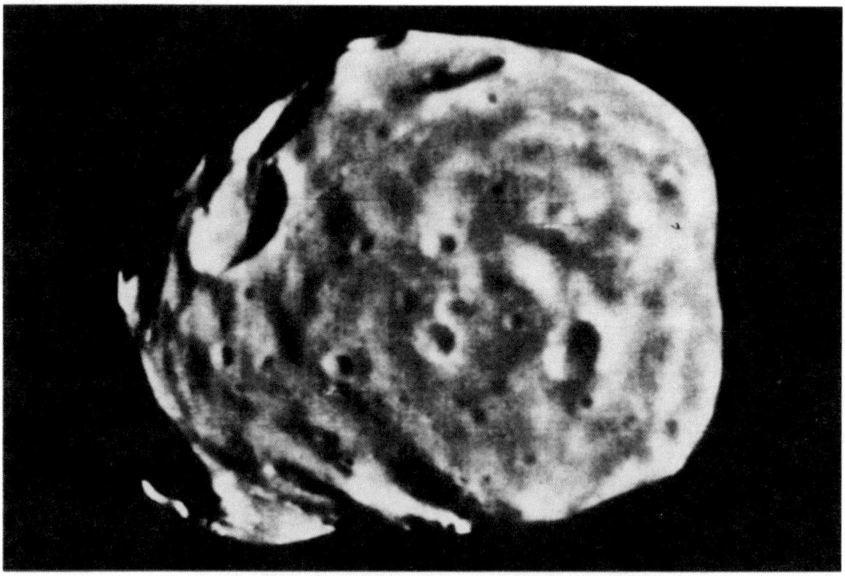

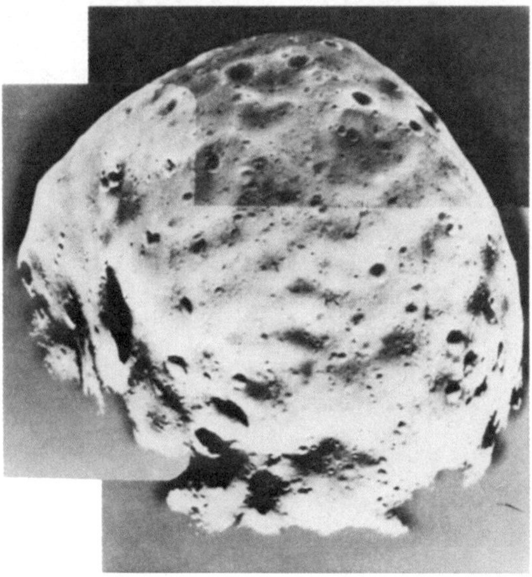

Opposite: **A near-encounter (300 km) photomosaic of Phobos, the larger Martian moon, taken May 27, 1977, by Viking Orbiter 1. The version at bottom is from raw imaging data; at top, computer-enhanced. The crater Stickney is near the bottom.**

This page: **Phobos.** ***Top:*** **A 20×24 km portion taken by Phobos 2 Spacecraft on February 21, 1989, from 440 km. Stickney is partly visible in the bottom left corner.** ***Bottom:*** **A photomosaic taken by Viking Orbiter 1 from 480 km on February 22, 1977. Large crater at bottom left is Hall, within which lies the South Pole.**

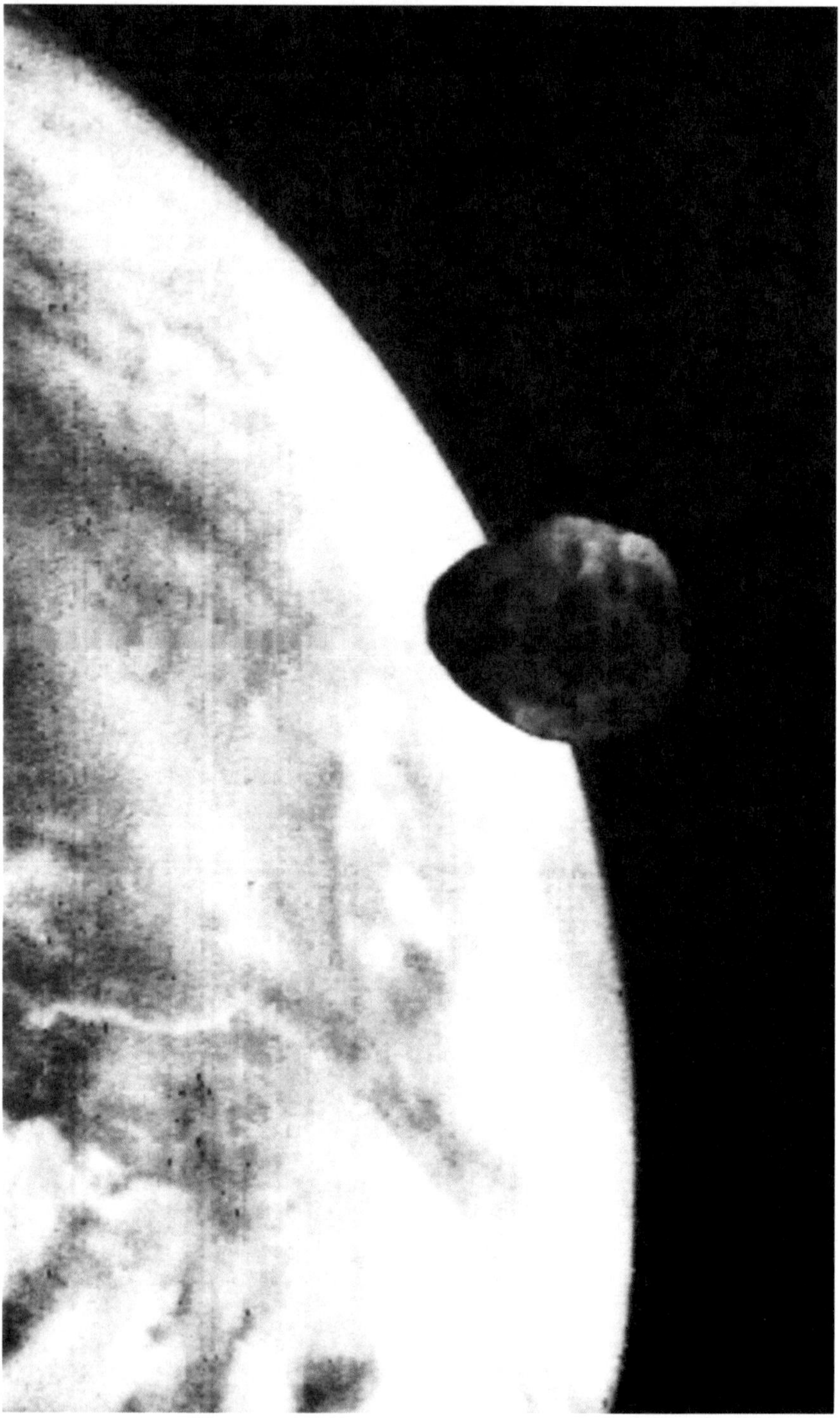

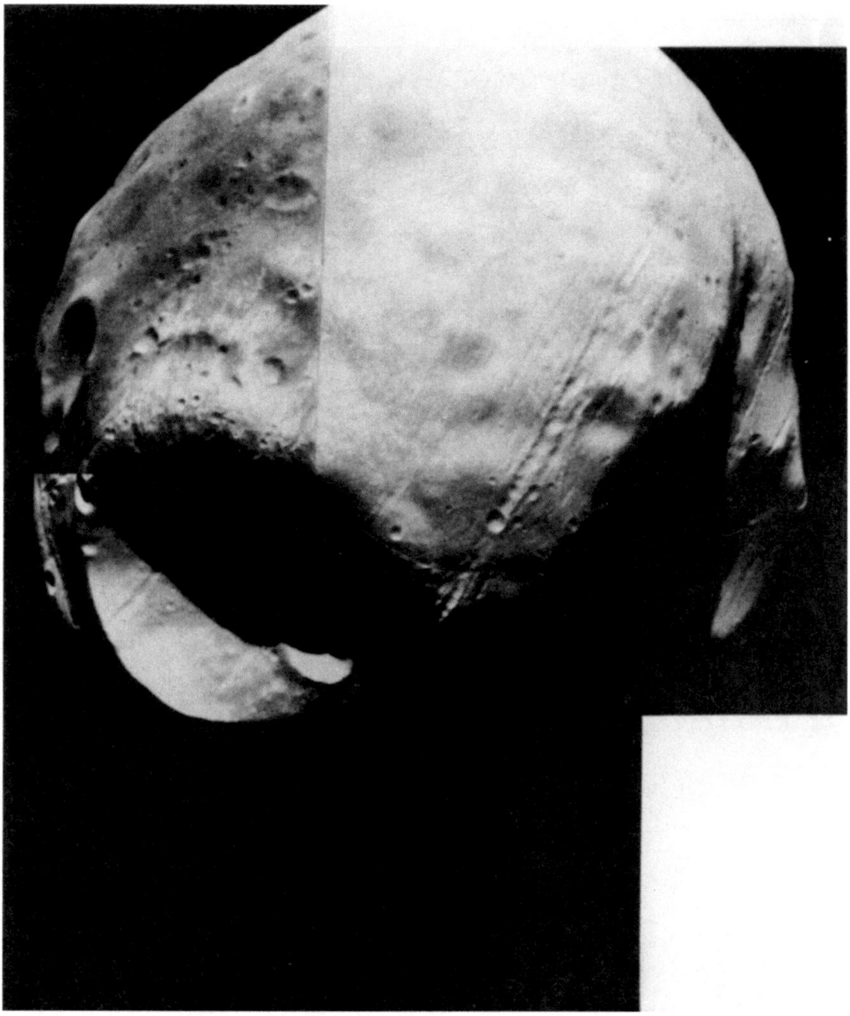

Opposite: **Phobos from 320 km, with Mars about 6000 km in the background, taken by Phobos 2 on February 21, 1989. Even though the image of Phobos has been enhanced and made 4 times brighter, it still appears dark relative to Mars.**

This page: **Phobos, photographed from 612 km by Viking Orbiter 1 on October 19, 1978. This photomosaic shows the moon's front side which always faces Mars from about 10 degrees below the equator with north at the top. Stickney is at left. Kepler Ridge is casting a shadow in the southern hemisphere which partially covers the large crater Hall at the bottom.**

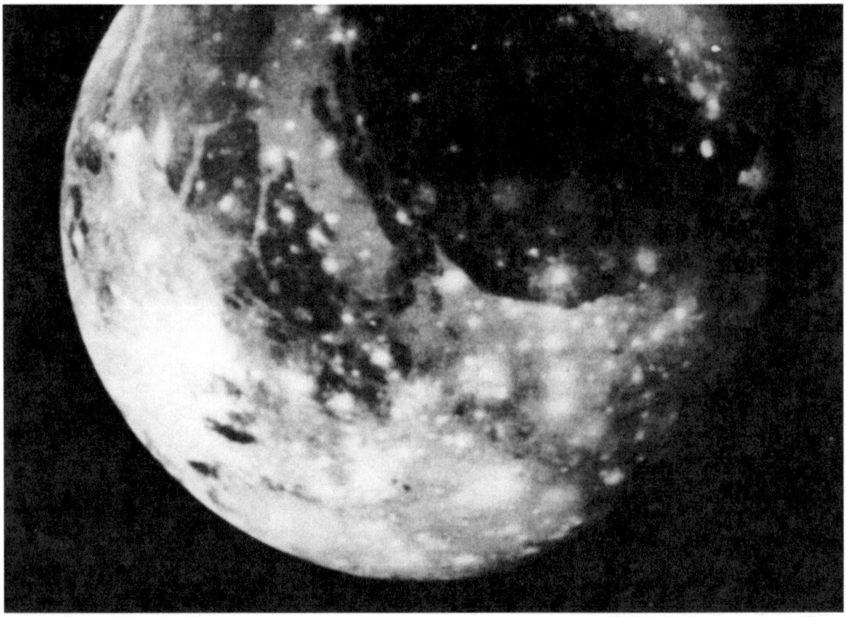

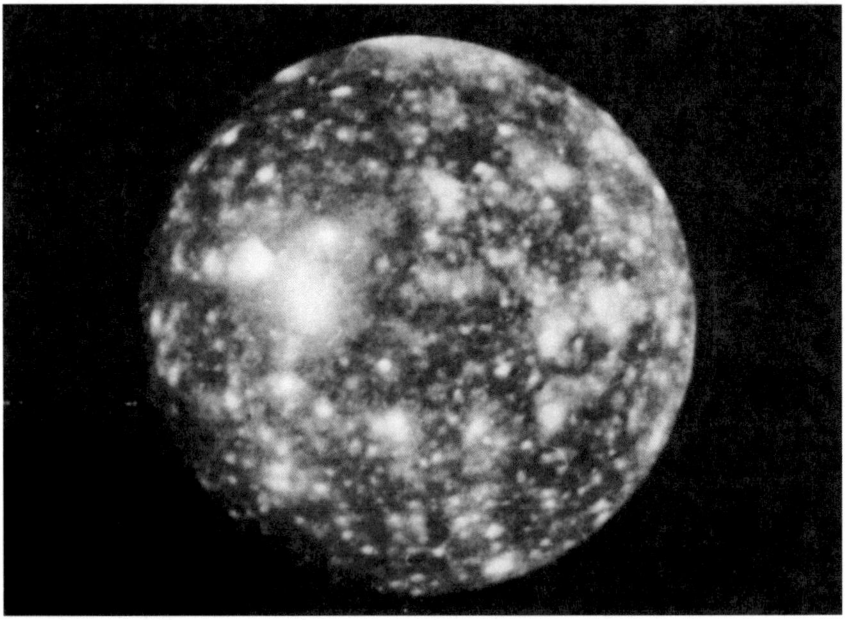

Top: **Jupiter's Ganymede, taken by Voyager from 1.2 million km.** ***Bottom:*** **Jupiter's Callisto, taken by Voyager from 2,300,800 km.**

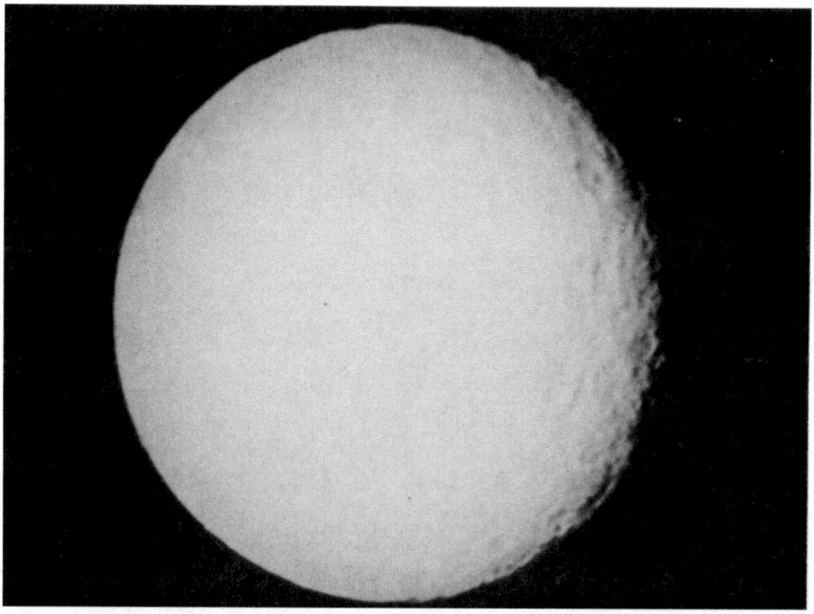

Top: **Saturn's Tethys. Note huge canyon system. Taken by Voyager.** ***Bottom:*** **Saturn's Dione, taken by Voyager from 162,000 km on November 12, 1980.**

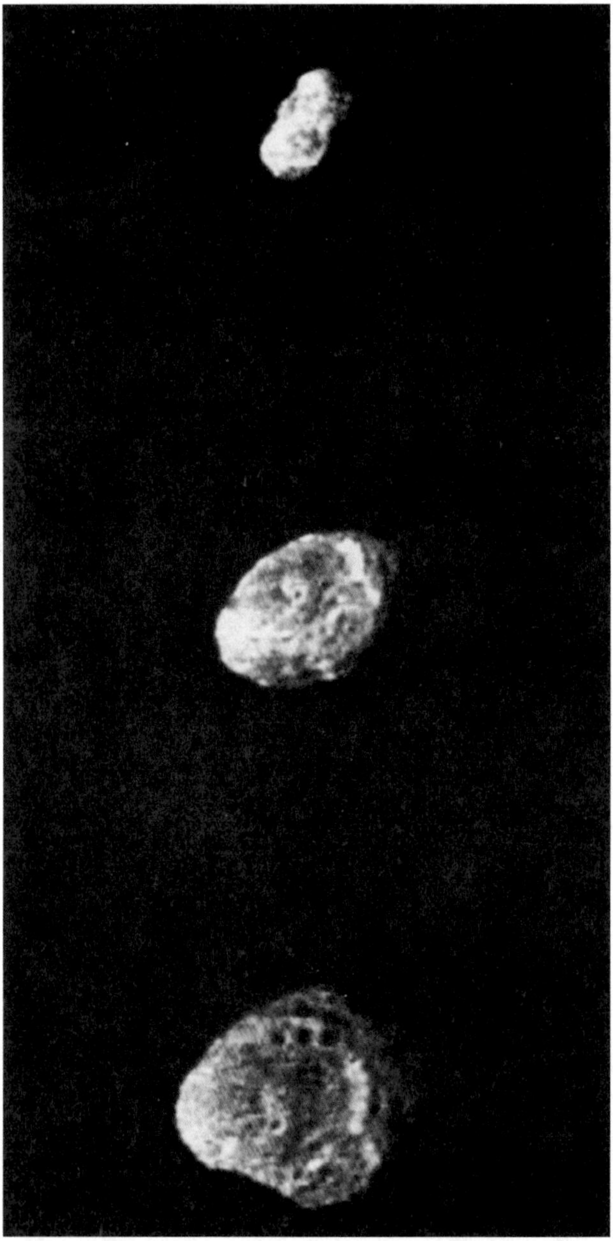

Three views of Saturn's Hyperion taken as Voyager 2 flew by. They were taken (from top) the morning of August 23, 1981, from a range of 1.2 million km, the morning of August 24 from 700,000 km, and at noon on August 24 from 500,000 km.

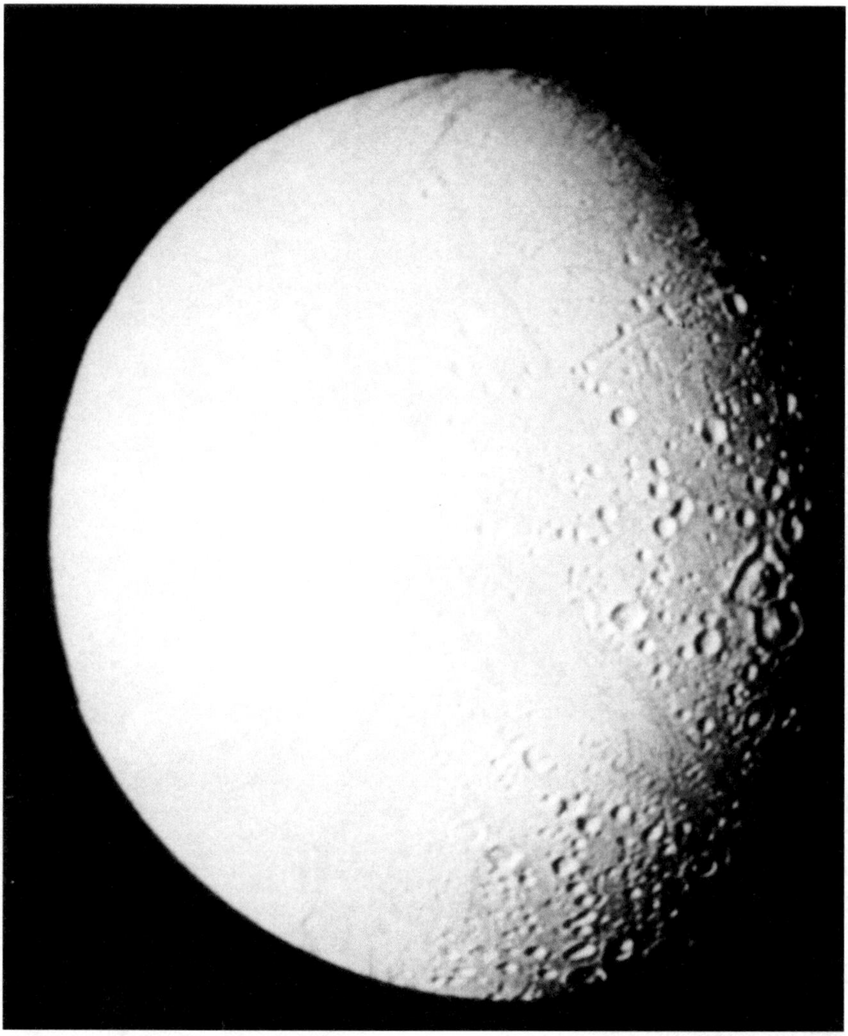

Saturn's Enceladus, 502 km in diameter, taken from 74,000 km out on August 25, 1981, by Voyager 2, launched in 1977 from Kennedy Space Center in Florida.

Saturn's Mimas, a heavily cratered moon about 394 km in diameter, taken by Voyager 1 from 129,000 km on November 12, 1980.

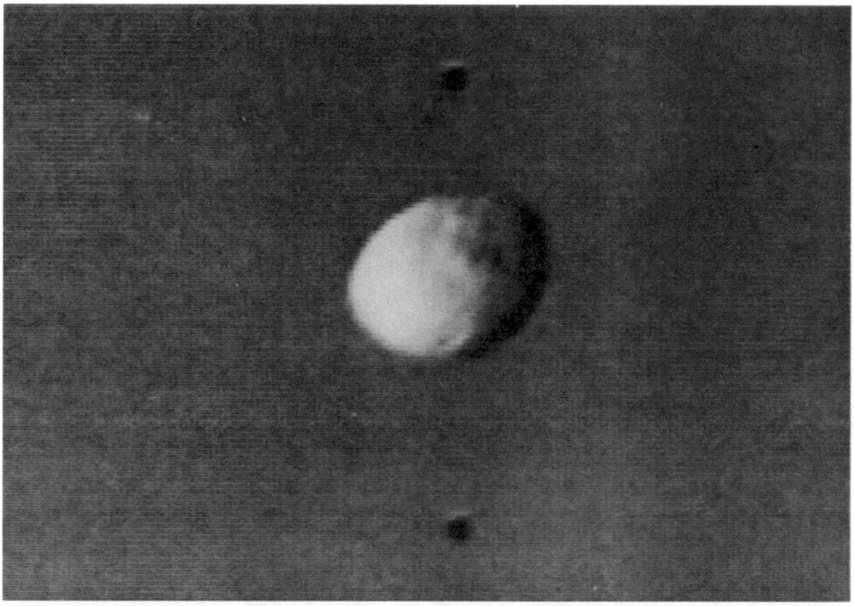

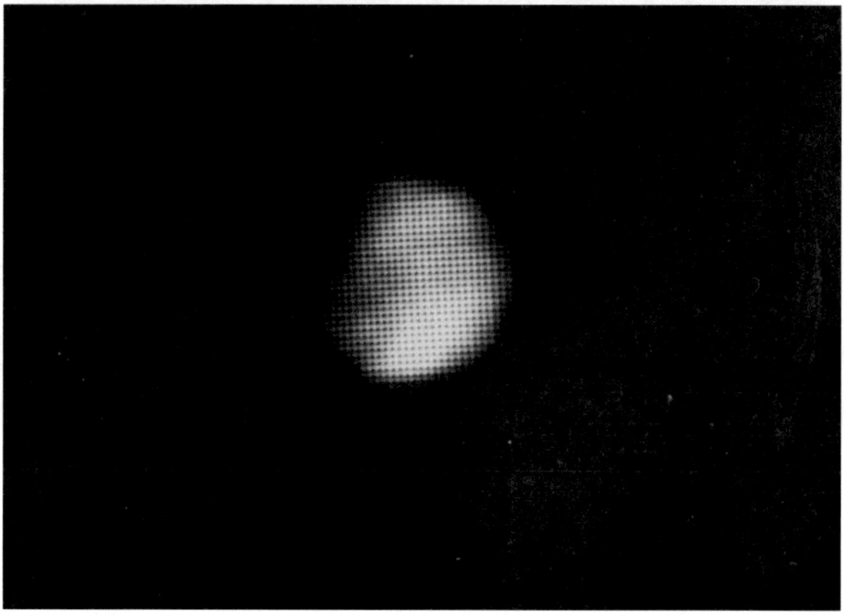

Top: **Janus, in transit across Saturn, taken by Voyager 1 on November 12, 1980, from 611,000 km.** ***Bottom:*** **Saturn's Phoebe, taken by Voyager 2 on September 4, 1981, from 2.2 million km.**

Saturn's F-ring and its inner shepherding satellite Prometheus (originally 1980 S27), taken by Voyager 2 on August 25, 1981, from 365,000 km. The moon is elongated and irregular, with its longest axis pointing toward the center of Saturn (toward the lower right).

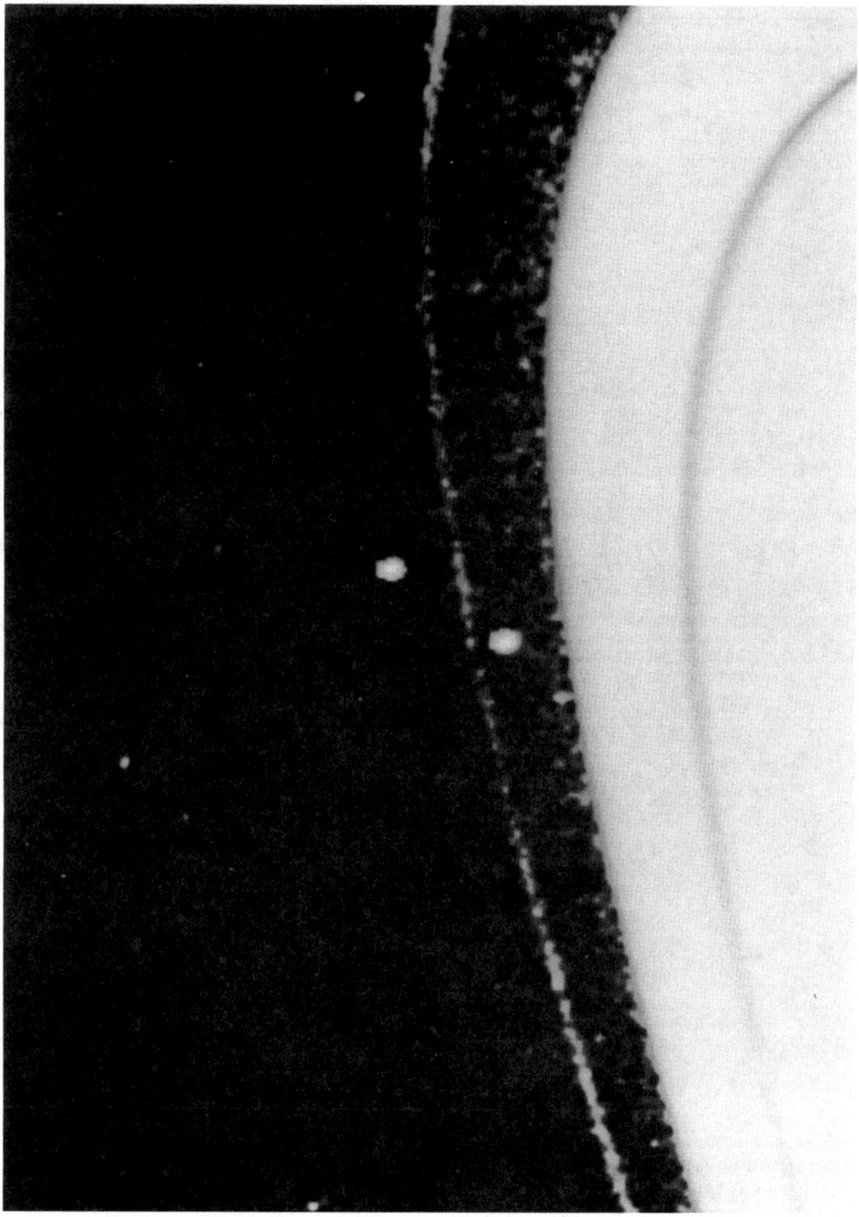

Voyager 2 shot showing Saturn's F-ring being shepherded by Prometheus on the inside of the ring and Pandora on the outside. Photo taken August 15, 1981, from 10.5 million km. Prometheus revolves around the planet slightly faster than Pandora and laps that satellite every 25 days. The two are here less than 1,800 km apart.

Above: On October 25, 1980, Voyager 1 took this enhanced image from 25 million km. It shows the two newly discovered moons of Saturn, Prometheus (at left) and Pandora (at top). The F-ring is barely visible in the top left corner. Circular black spots in the rings are reseau marks engraved on the camera.

Opposite, top: High-resolution mosaic of Ariel, the most detailed view of that Uranian moon taken by Voyager 2, on January 24, 1986, from 128,000 km, showing numerous faults and valleys. *Bottom:* A computer mosaic of Uranus's Miranda images at high resolution, taken by Voyager 2 on January 24, 1986, from ranges between 30,000 and 40,000 km, showing varied geologic regions.

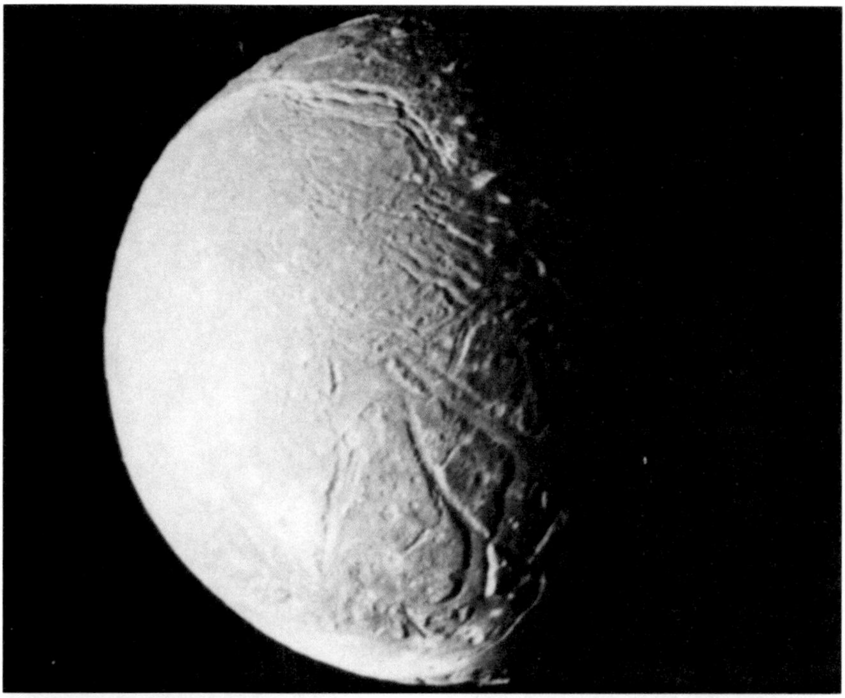

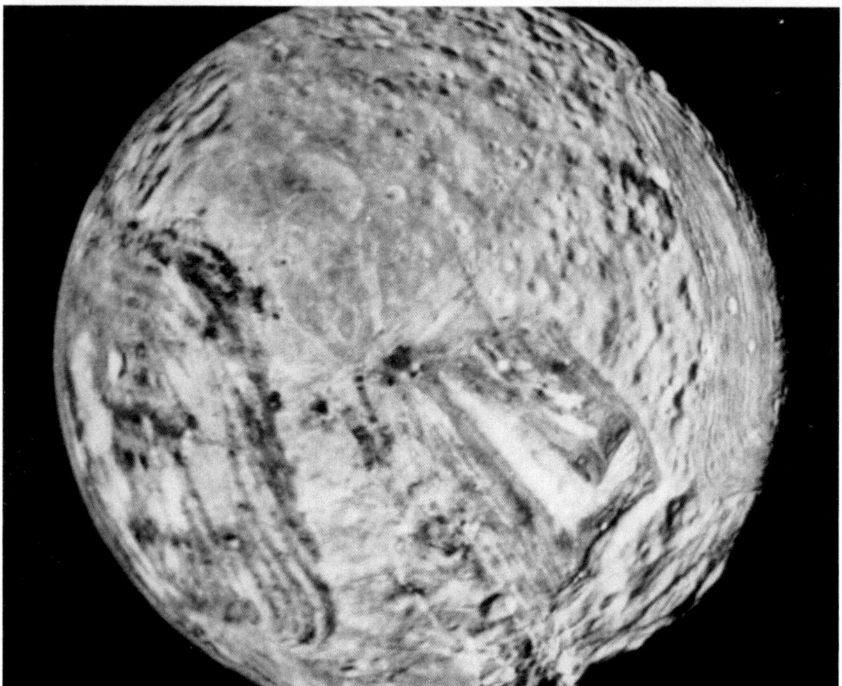

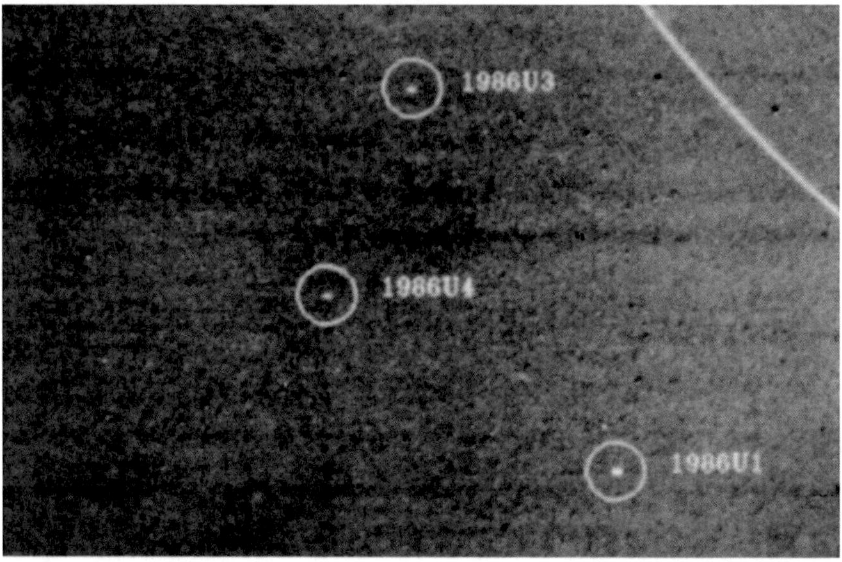

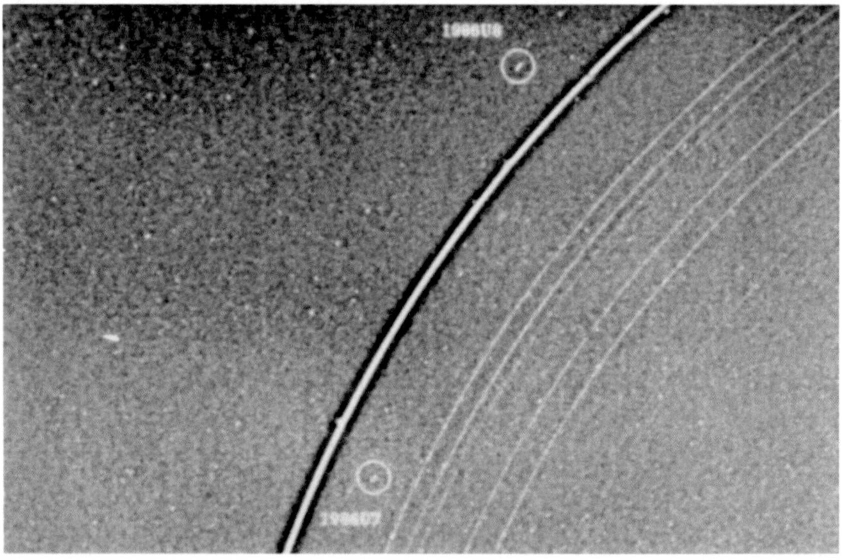

This page, top: Three of the moons discovered in the Uranian system by Voyager 2, January 18, 1986; range 7.68 million km: 1986 U1 (Portia), 1986 U4 (Rosalind) and 1986 U3 (Cressida). *Bottom:* Uranus's 1986 U7 (Cordelia) and 1986 U8 (Ophelia) with the epsilon-ring, taken by Voyager 2 on January 21, 1986, from 4 million km.

Opposite, top: Uranus's Oberon, taken at high resolution, by Voyager 2 on January 24, 1986, from 655,000 km. *Bottom:* Uranus's Puck, the only photo of what was first called 1985 U1, by Voyager 2, on January 24, 1986, from 500,000 km.

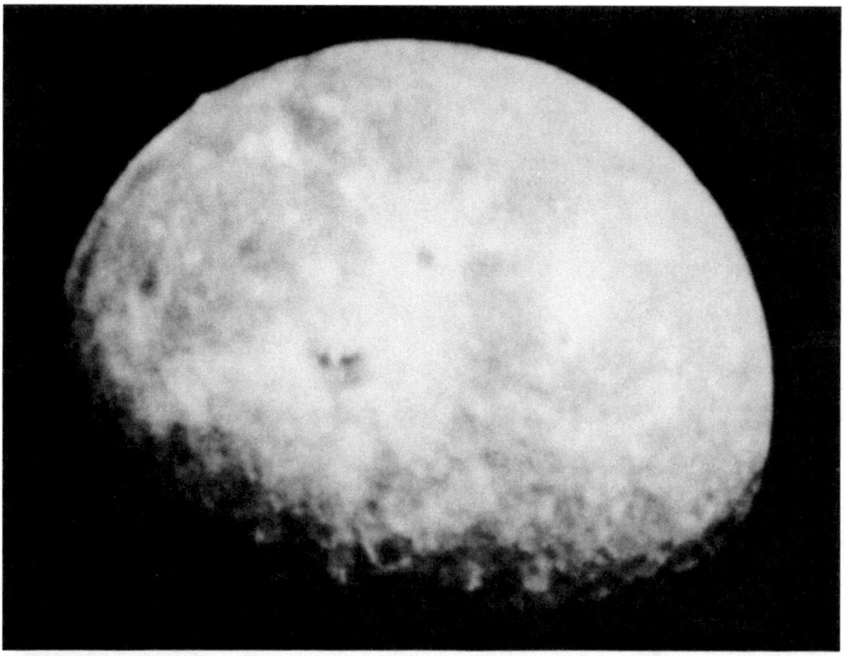

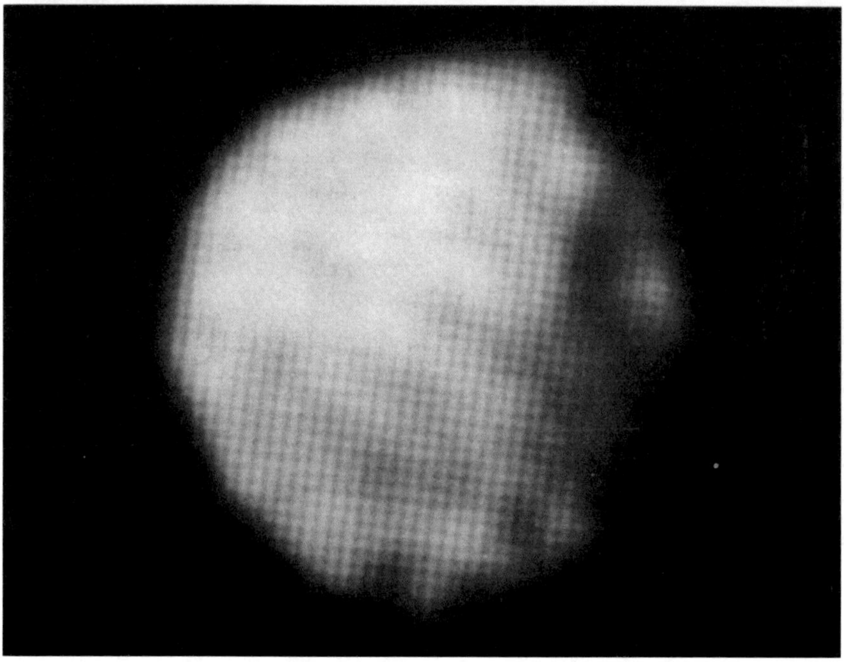

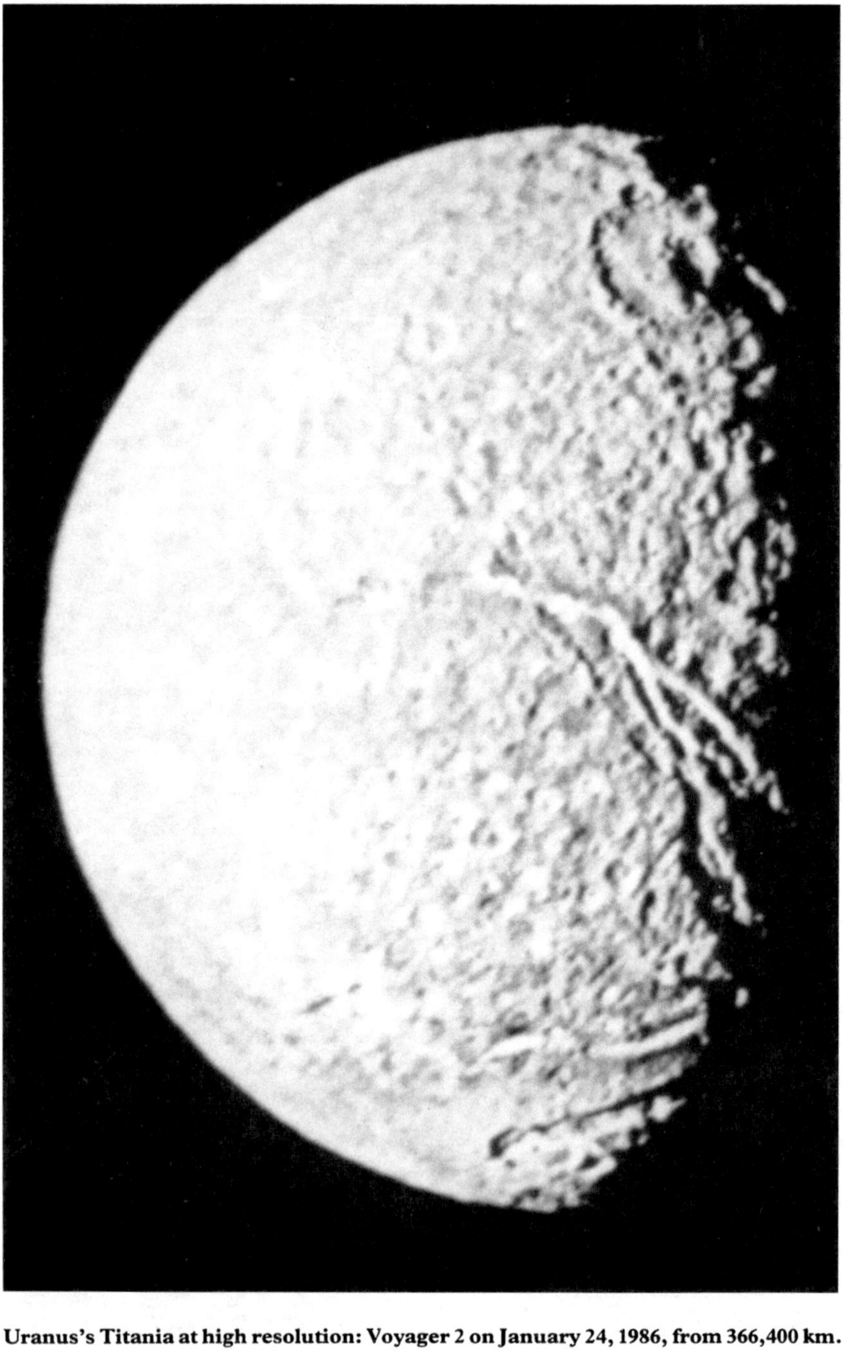

Uranus's Titania at high resolution: Voyager 2 on January 24, 1986, from 366,400 km.

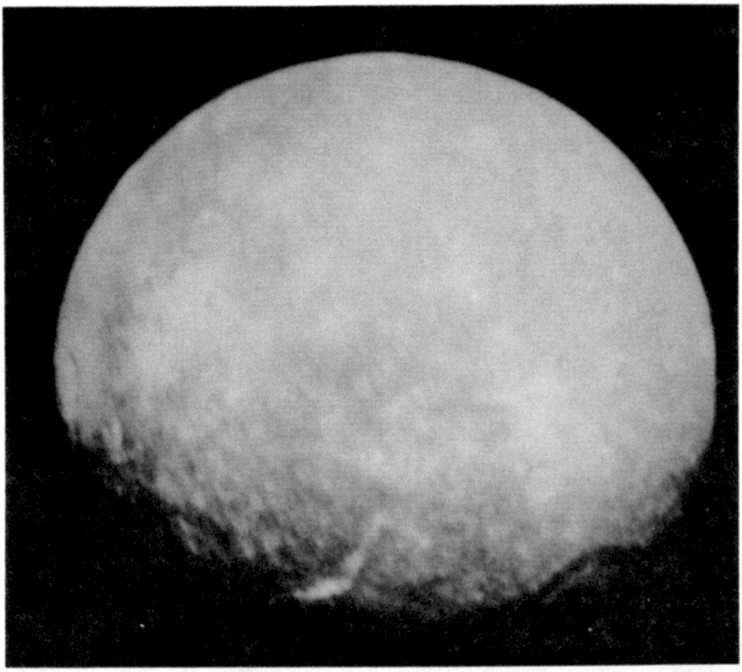

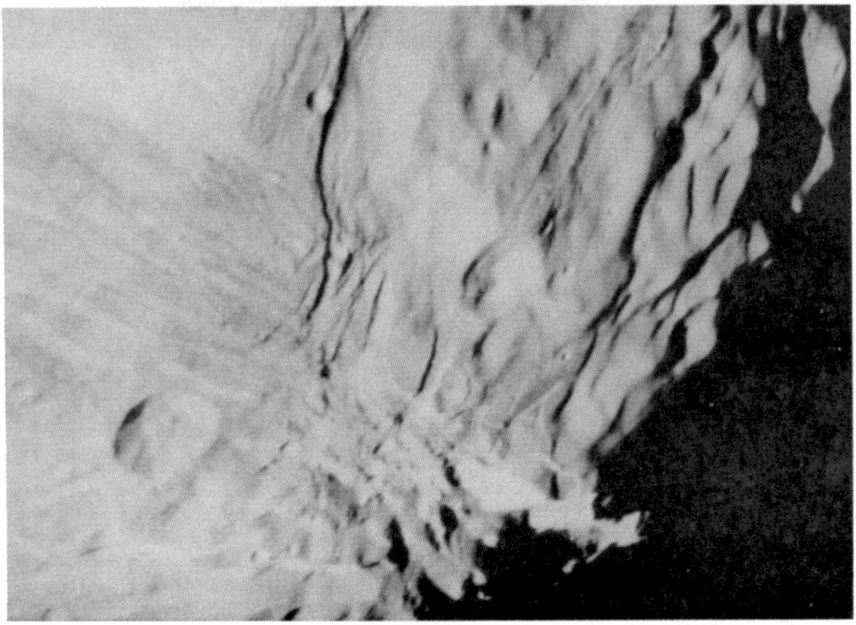

Top: Composite of Uranus's Titania, from images taken by Voyager 2 on January 24, 1986, from 480,000 km. *Bottom:* Uranus's Miranda, taken at high resolution by Voyager 2 on January 24, 1986, from 35,200 km.

This page, top: **Uranus's Umbriel, taken at high resolution by Voyager 2 on January 24, 1986, from 554,000 km. *Bottom:* The outer rings of Uranus, taken by Voyager 2 on January 23, 1986, from 1.44 million km. The outer and brightest ring is the epsilon-ring. Cordelia is seen as the elongated bright shield midway between the epsilon-ring and the left of the two fainter rings at right (the delta-ring). The moon appears elongated because its orbital motion smeared its image during the long exposure.**

Opposite: **Miranda. *Top:* Taken at high resolution by Voyager 2 on January 24, 1986, from 33,600 km. *Bottom:* Taken by Voyager 2 shortly before the spacecraft's closest approach, on January 24, 1986, from a range of 30,400 km.**

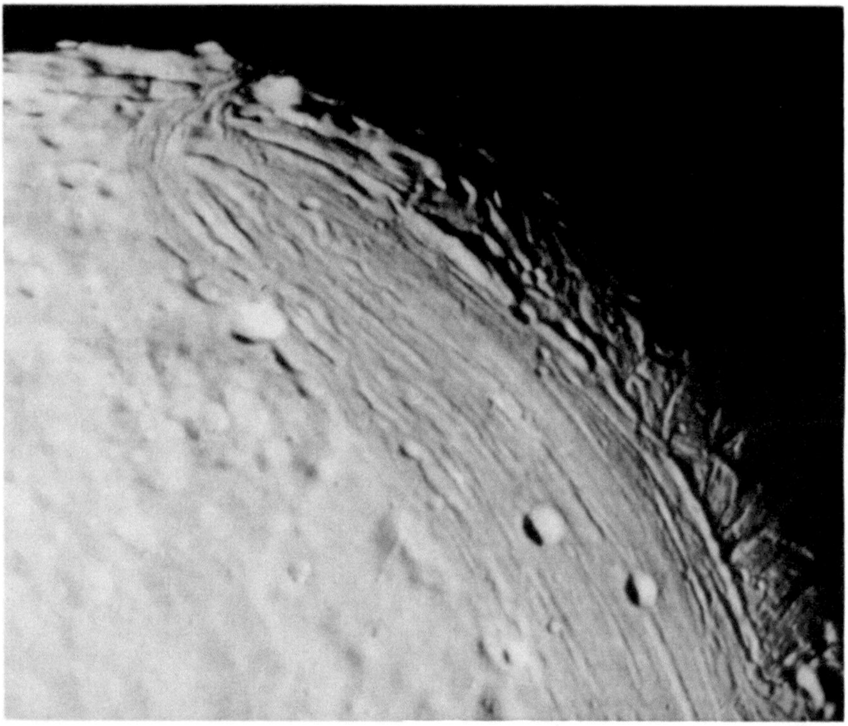
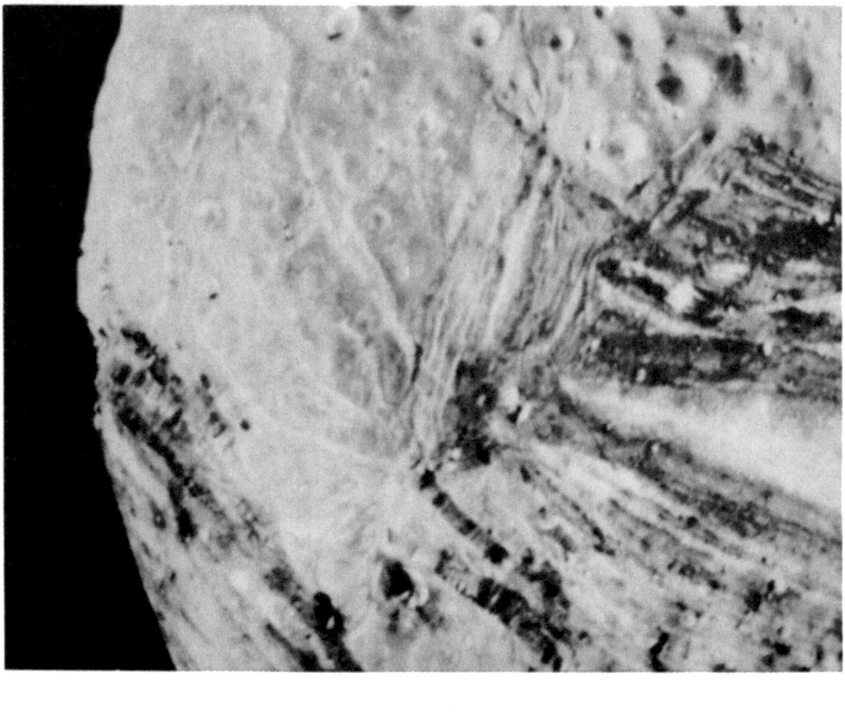

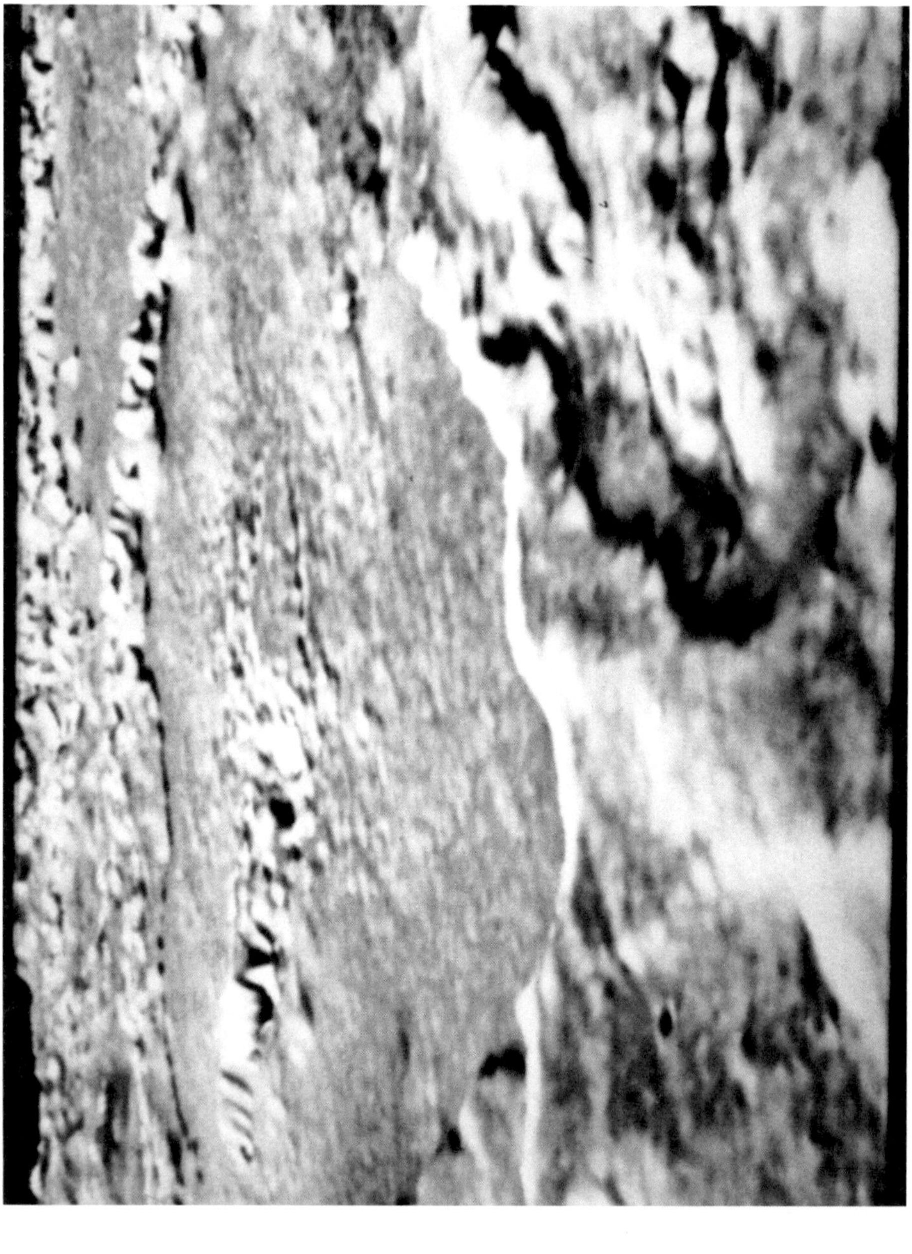

Computer-generated perspective view of one of the caldera-like depressions on Neptune's Triton.

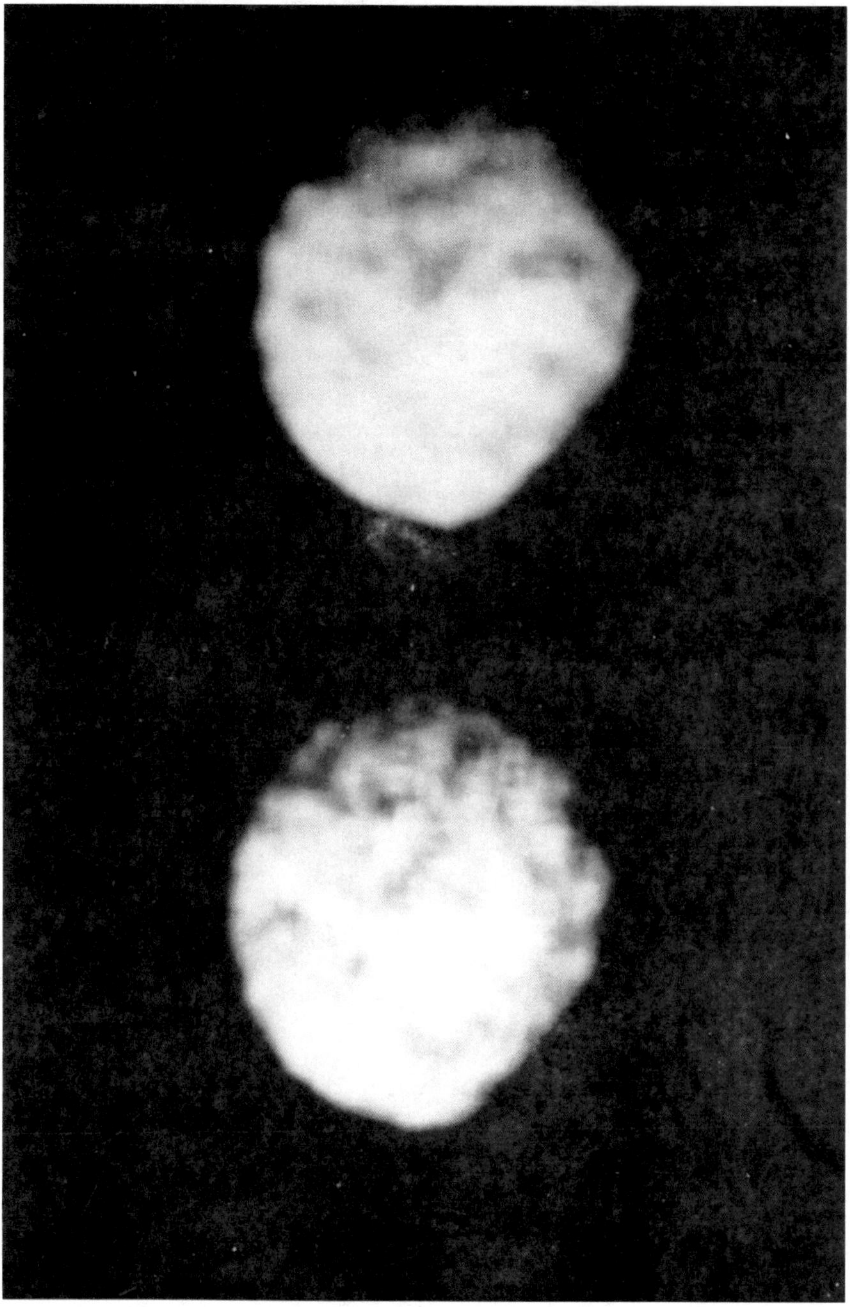

Two views of 1989 N2 (Neptune), dark irregular moon discovered by Voyager 2.

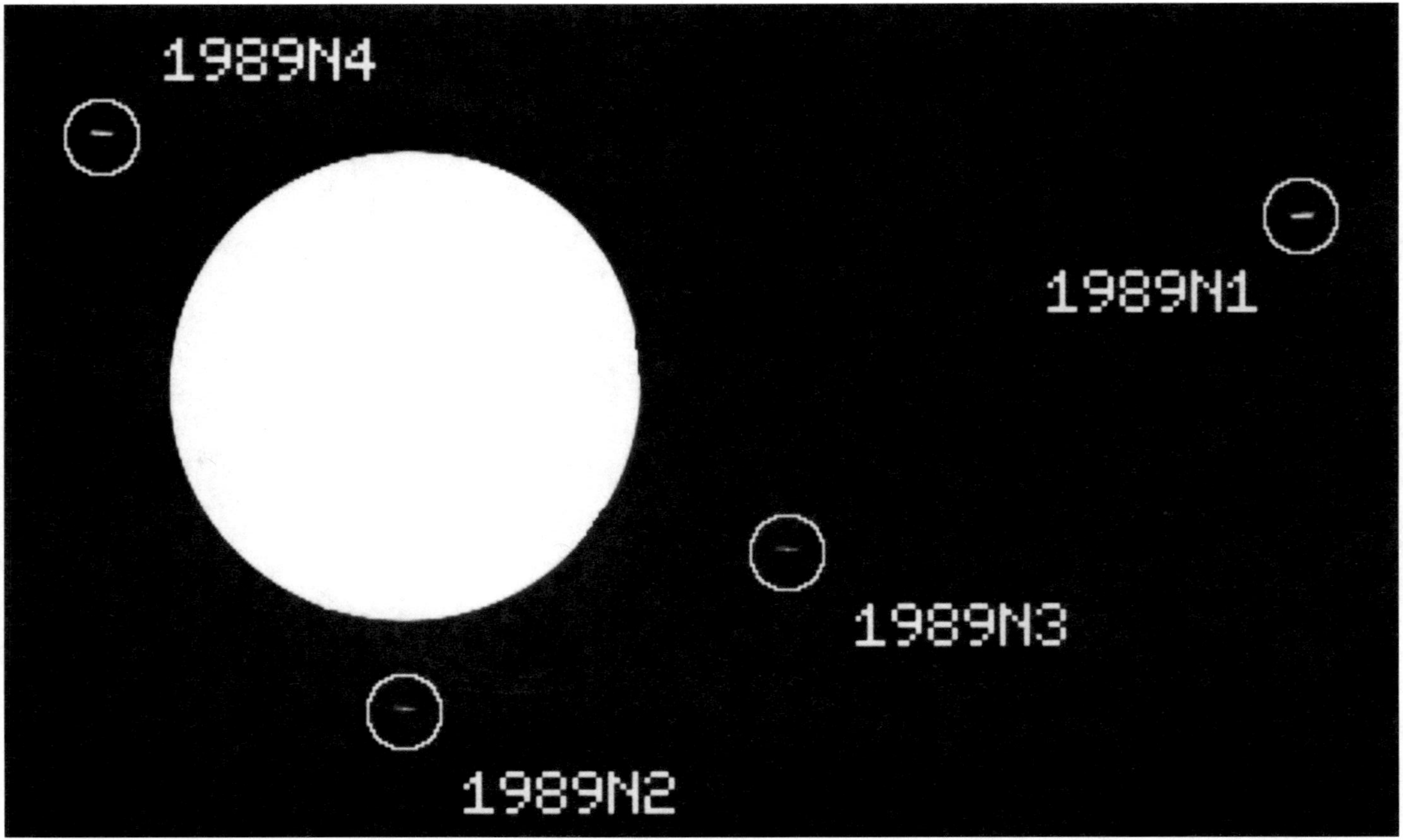
1989N4
1989N1
1989N3
1989N2

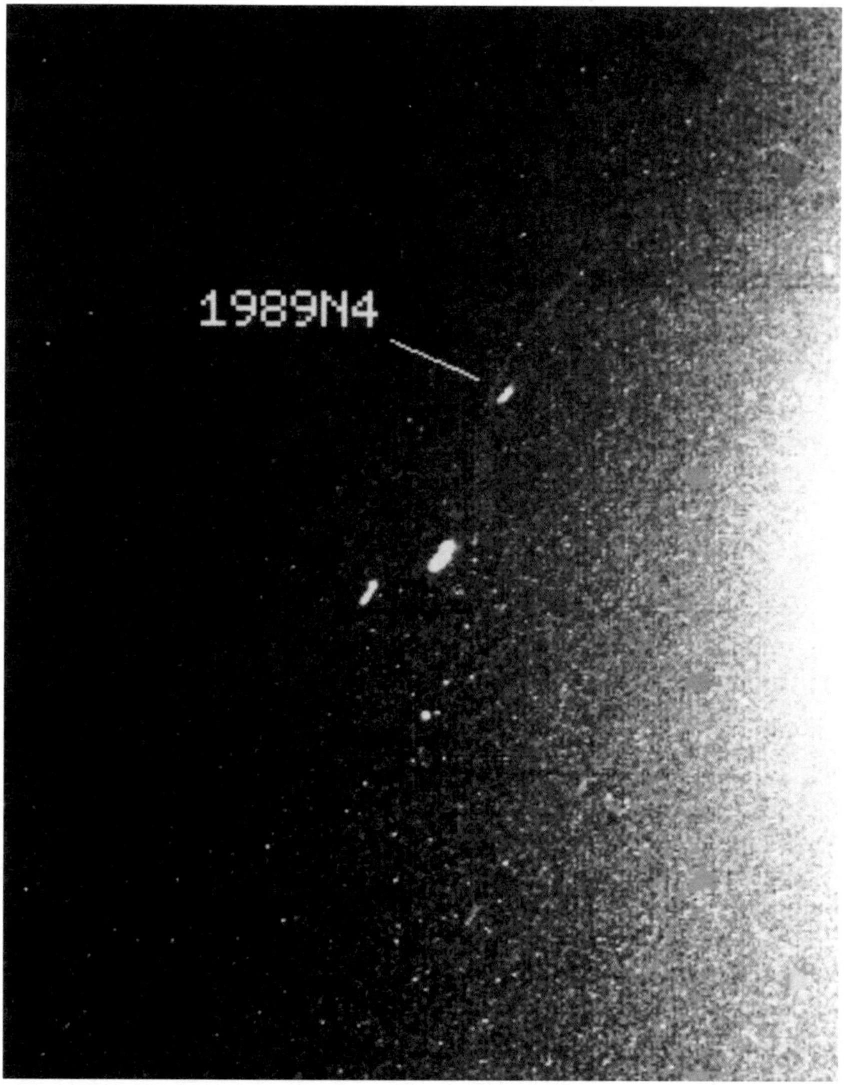

Opposite: This image, captured by the Voyager 2 spacecraft, was used to confirm the discovery of three new satellites orbiting Neptune. The 46-second exposure was taken by Voyager 2's narrow angle camera through a clear filter on July 30, 1989, from about 37.3 million km. The large globe of the planet itself is severely overexposed and appears pure white. The image has been computer-processed to accentuate the new moons, which otherwise would be hard to distinguish from their background. Each of the moons appears as a small streak, an effect caused by movement of the spacecraft during the long exposure.

Above: Voyager 2 took this photo, August 11, 1989, of 1989 N4. Also visible is a ring just outside the small moon's orbit. Neptune's glare is to the right.

On August 21, 1989, Voyager 2 was 4.8 million km from Neptune when it took this 61-second exposure. This image, which is extremely computer-enhanced, shows Despina at bottom right as the large, elongated white object.

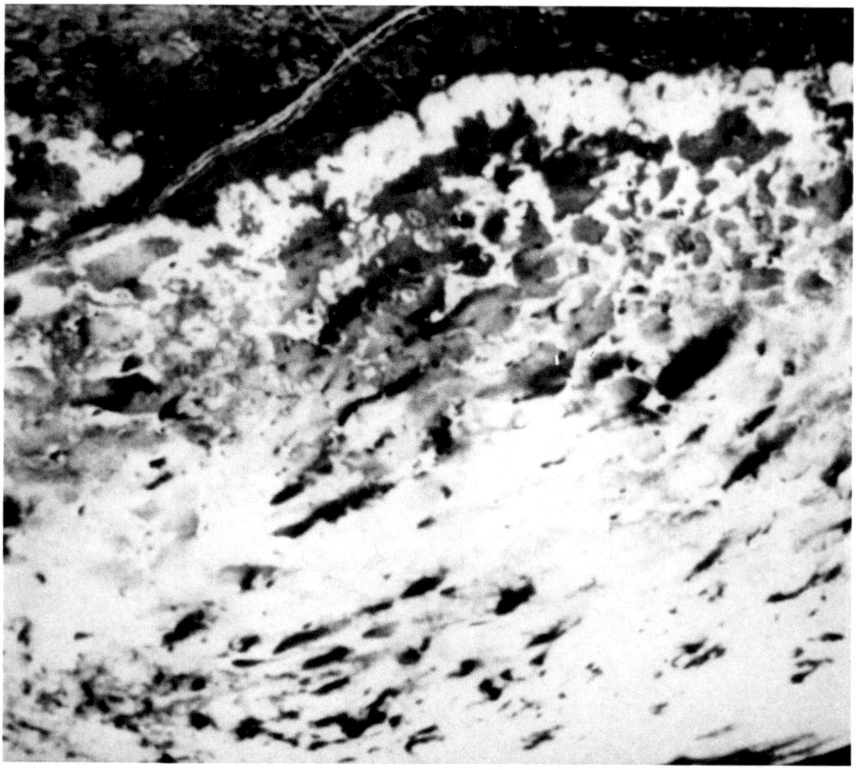

South polar terrain of Neptune's Triton. About 50 dark plumes mark what may be ice volcanoes.

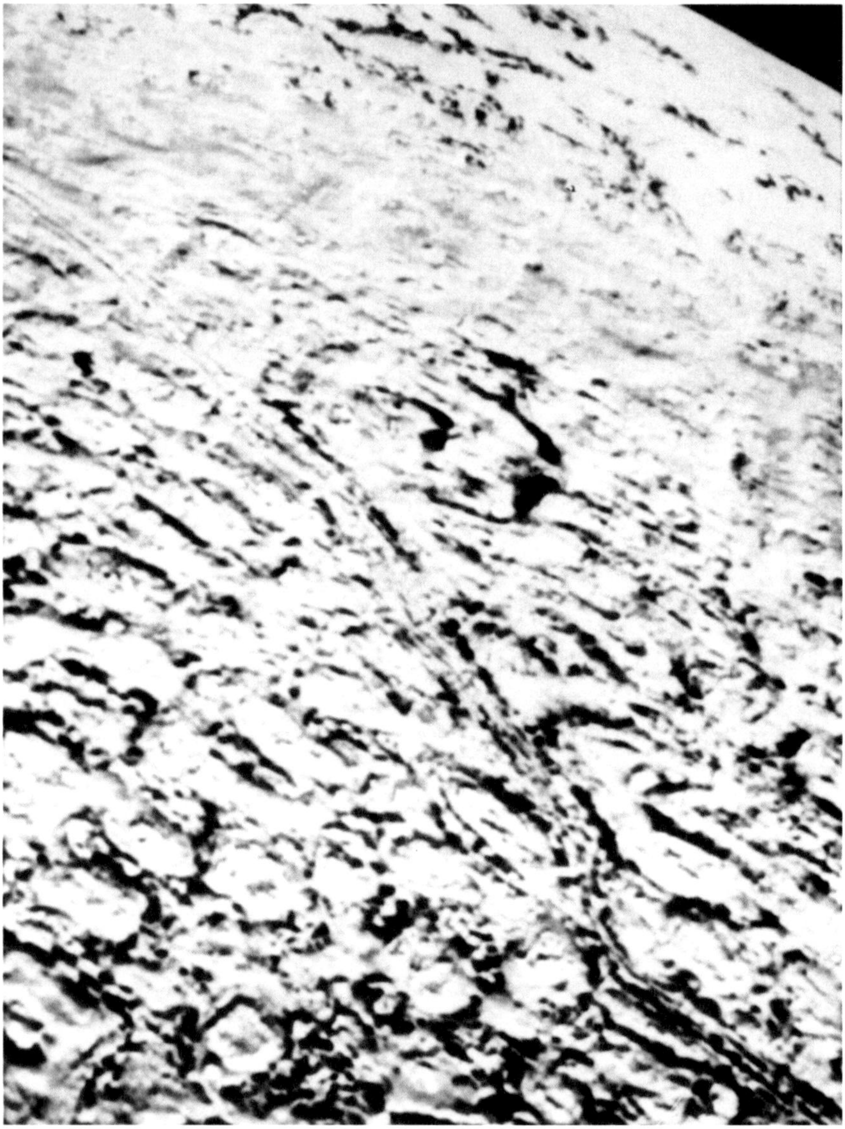

Neptune's Triton from 40,000 km, taken by Voyager 2. Depressions may be caused by melting and collapsing of icy surface.

Neptune's Triton, taken by Voyager 2 from 128,000 km.

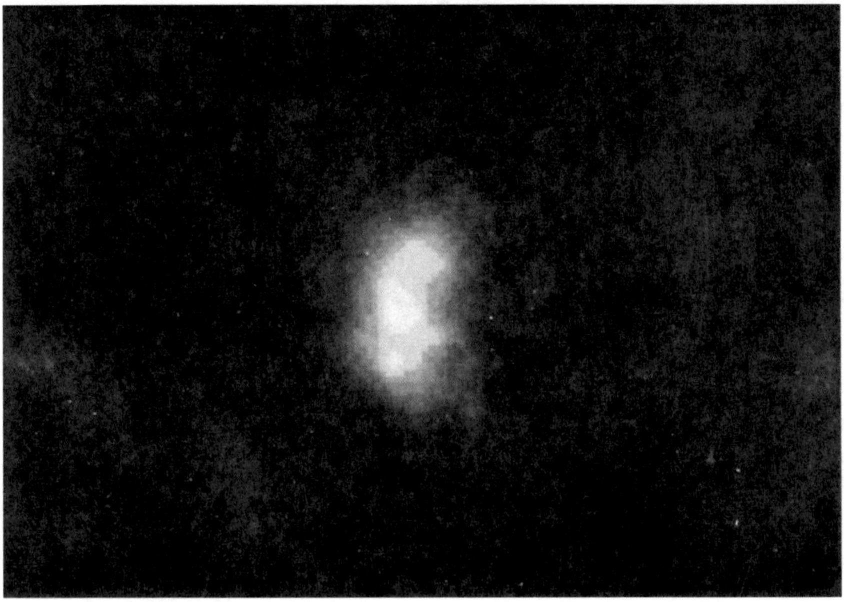

Top: **Neptune's satellite 1989 N1, discovered by Voyager 2.** ***Bottom:*** **Neptune's Nereid, taken by Voyager 2 on August 24, 1989, from 4.7 million km. With a resolution of 43 km per pixel, this image has sufficient detail to show size and albedo. Nereid is about 170 km across and reflects about 12 percent of the incident light.**

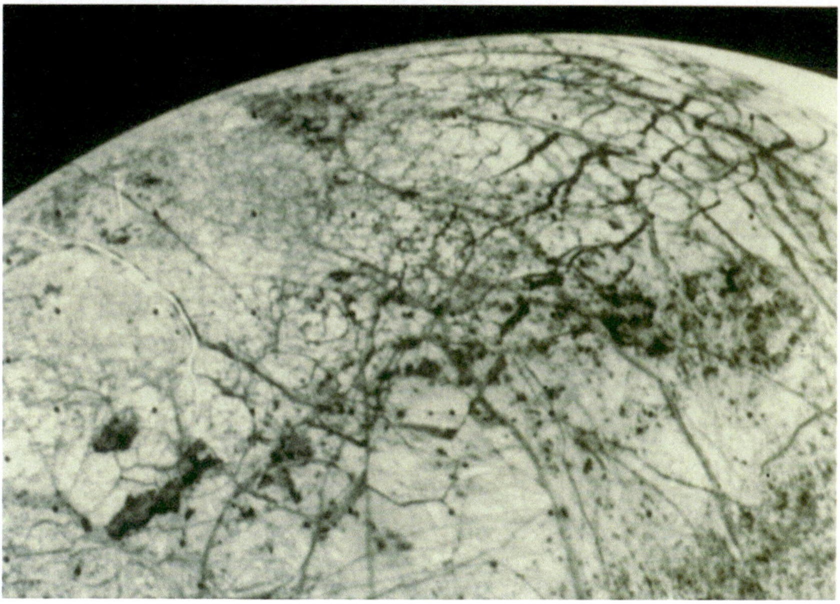

Top: Full Moon from Apollo 17, December 1972; one-third of surface visible is the lunar far side. *Bottom:* Closeup of Jupiter's Europa from 240,000 km, 1979.

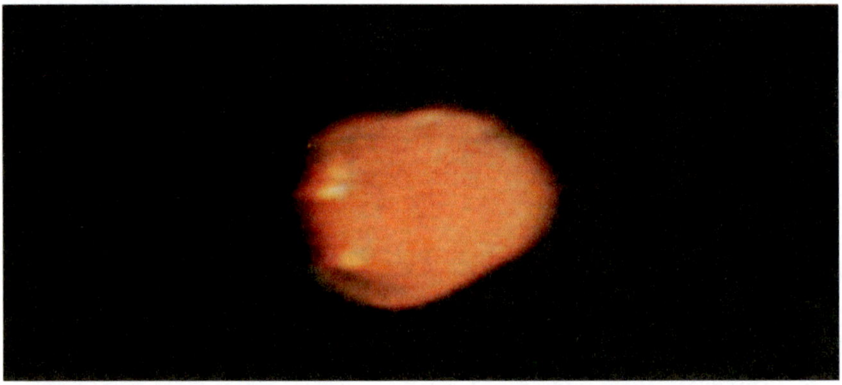

This page, top: Europa, smallest of Jupiter's moons, taken from 1.92 million km, 1979. *Bottom:* Tiny Amalthea, 125 km by 160 km, Jupiter's innermost, zips around the planet every 12 hours; taken from 408,000 km, March 4, 1979, by Voyager 1.

Opposite, top: Jupiter's Ganymede, from 242,900 km, 1979. *Bottom:* Photomosaic of Jupiter's Callisto, composed of 9 frames taken from 392,000 km, 1979.

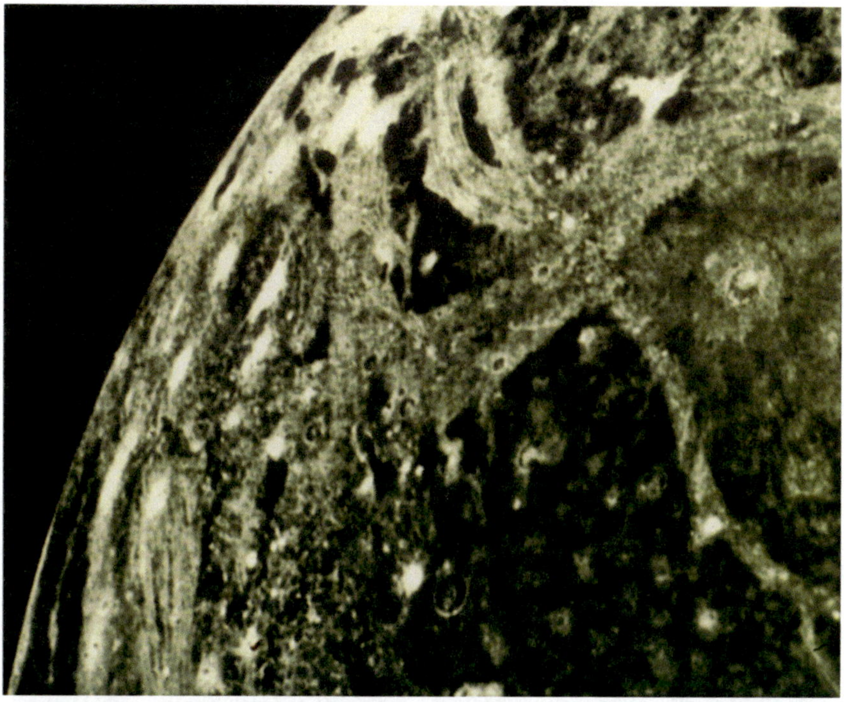

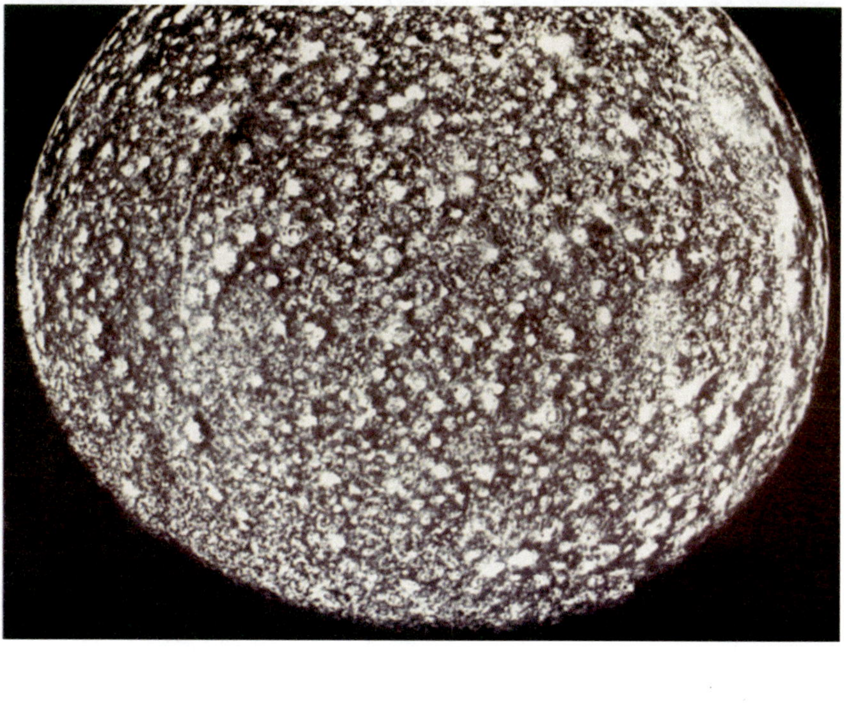

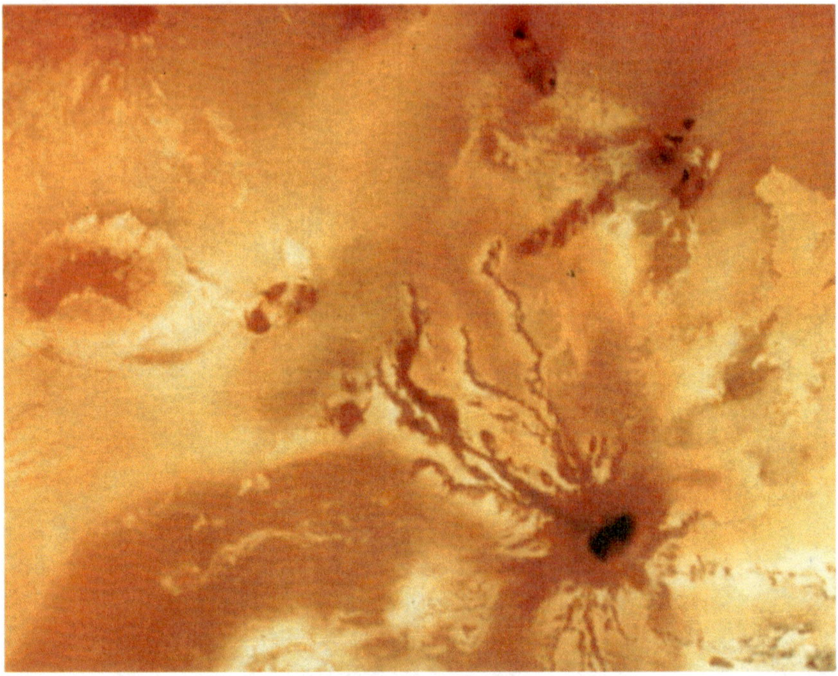

Top: **Jupiter's Io, from 123,350 km, 1979.** ***Bottom:*** **Massive volcano at horizon of Io, debris to height of 160 km, 1979.**

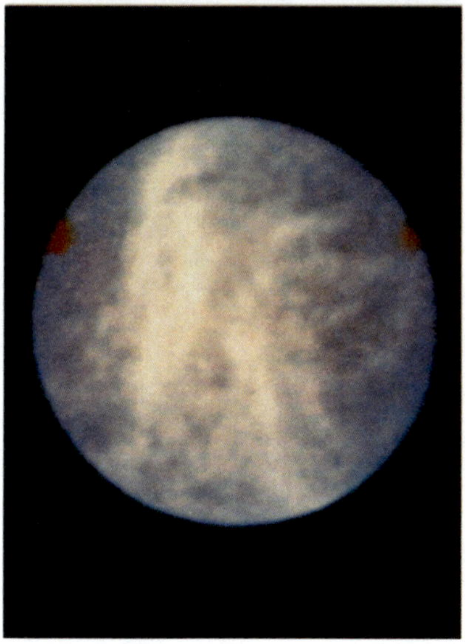

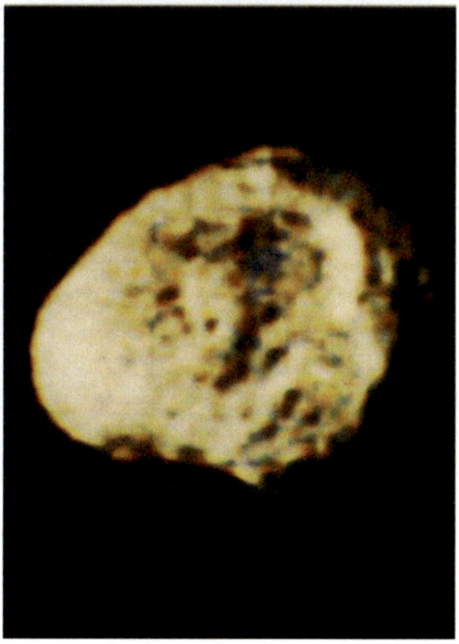

Top: **Montage of Saturnian system: Dione front, Tethys, Mimas right, Enceladus at left of ring, Rhea, Titan top right.** ***Bottom, left:*** **Rhea, from 1.7 million km, November 11, 1980.** ***Right:*** **Saturn's Hyperion, 375 km across, August 24, 1981.**

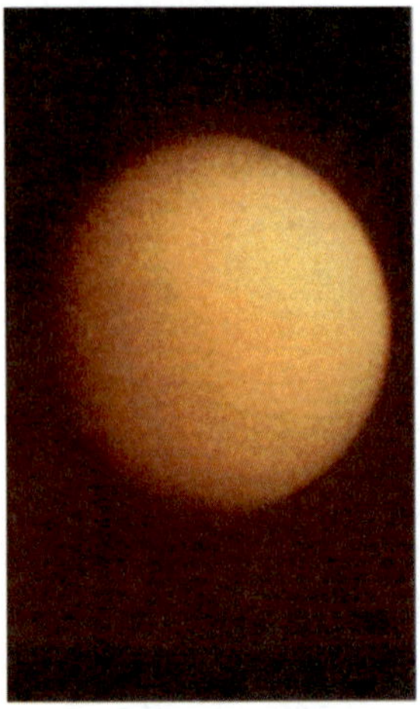

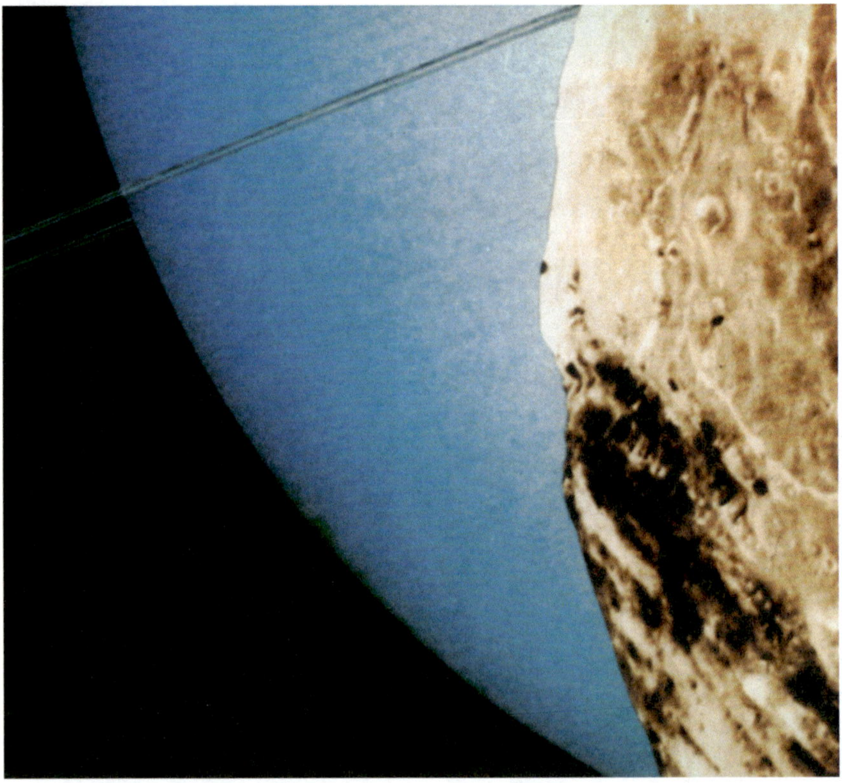

This page, top left: Saturn's cloud-covered Titan. *Right:* Titan and thick haze, from 435,000 km, November 12, 1980. *Bottom:* Montage simulates view over horizon of Miranda toward Uranus and rings 104,000 km away; Voyager 2, January 1986.

Opposite, top: "Chevron" on Uranus's Miranda from 41,600 km; January 24, 1986. *Bottom:* High-resolution mosaic of Neptune's Triton; August 1989; both Voyager 2.

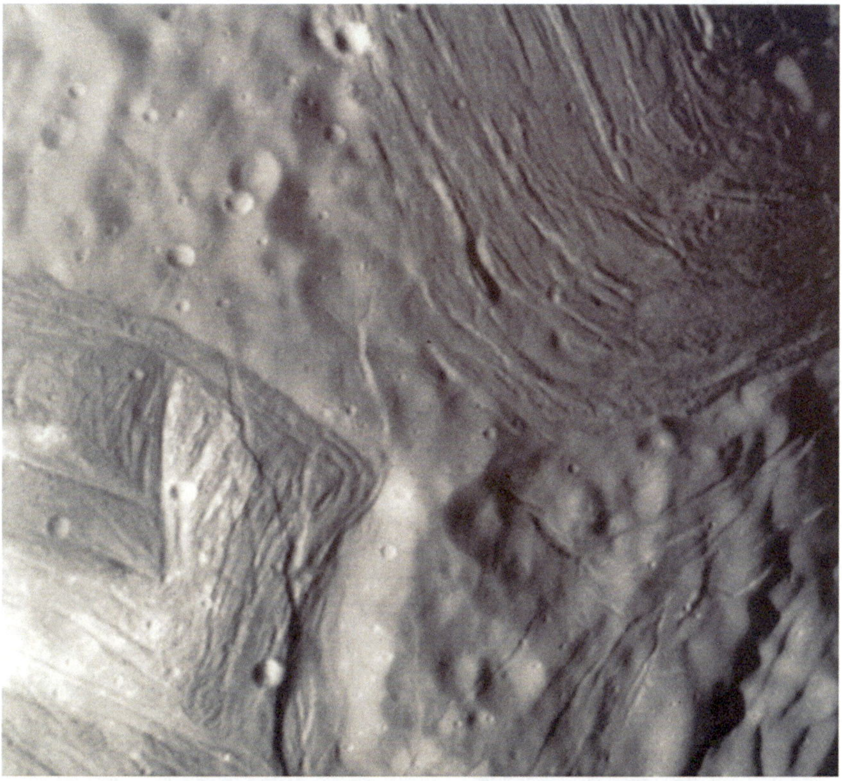

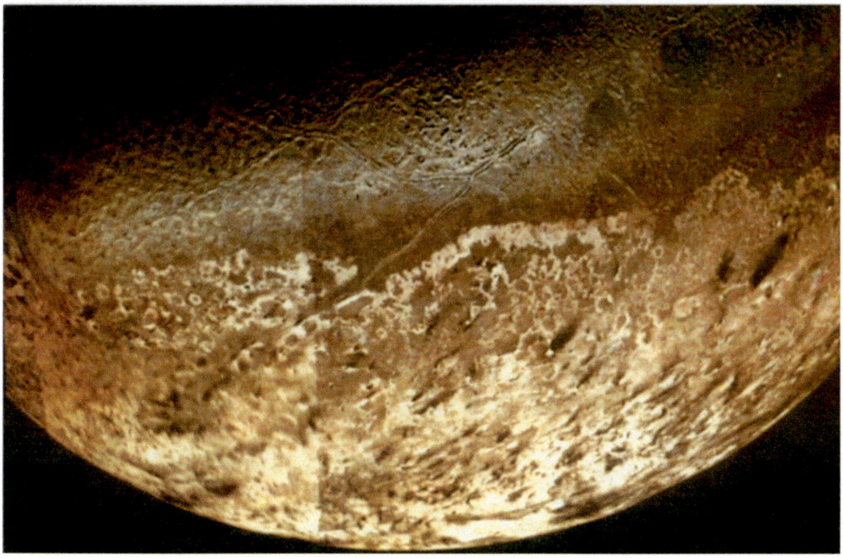

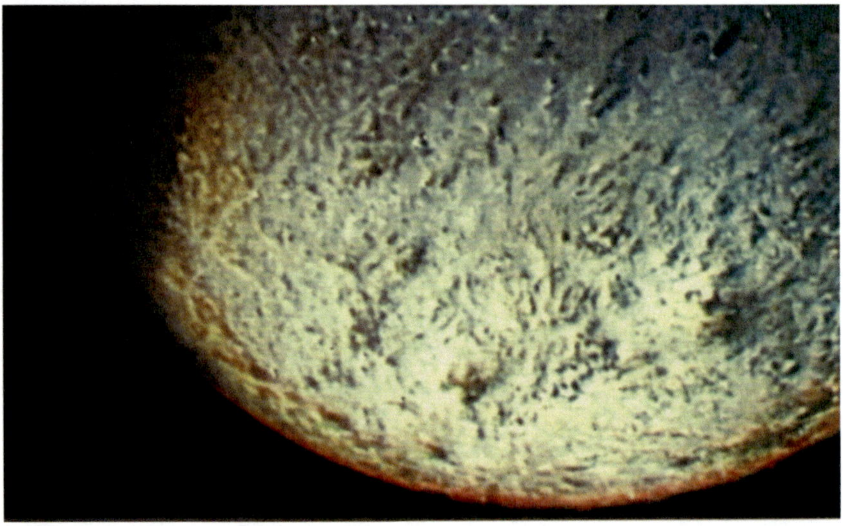

Top: **Bright southern hemisphere on Neptune's Triton.** ***Bottom:*** **About 480 km across Triton's surface; both photographs Voyager 2, August 1989.**

Part III

The Other Moons of the Solar System

Pronunciation Guide

The mark ' comes after the syllable to be stressed.

a=a as in apple
ā=a as in gate
ä=a as in father
â=a as in dare
b=b as in bay
d=d as in dog
e=e as in end
ē=e as in emu
ə=e as in piker
f=f as in fat
g=g as in give
h=h as in hope
ī=i as in write
i=i as in ink
j=j as in jam
k=k as in king
l=l as in long
m=m as in meet
n=n as in night
o=o as in top
ō=o as in pose
ô=o as in core
o͞o=oo as in moon
oo=ou as in should
p=p as in pack
r=r as in robe
s=s as in sink
t=t as in tank
u=u as in butter
ū=oo as in balloon
v=v as in van
w=w as in wait
y=y as in young
z=z as in zoo
sh=sh as in show
th=th as in thin

The Other Moons A–Z

Adrastea

see also ***Ananke; Himalia***

Other names: Jupiter XIV, Jupiter 14, J14 (sometimes seen as J17), 1979 J1. Not to be confused with ***Ananke*** (whose original, unofficial, name was Adrastea, or Andrastea), and ***Himalia***

Named for: Adrastea, the nymph who suckled the infant Zeus in Greek mythology

Pronunciation: ad ras tē' ə, ad ras tā' ə

Distance from Jupiter: Its mean distance from the center of Jupiter is 128,980 km

Location: The second innermost satellite of Jupiter, it lies just outside the edge of the Jovian ring. It is thought to be the physical barrier containing the ring dimensions, or at least it may help stabilize Jupiter's ring

Synodic period: 7 hours 9 mins

Sidereal period: 0.29826 days

Orbital eccentricity: 0

Orbital inclination: 0 degrees

Escape velocity: About 0.01 km/sec

Visible magnitude: 19.1, but it appears as a 5th magnitude star in the Jovian ring

Albedo: Low, about 0.05, similar to that of Amalthea

Absolute magnitude: +12.4

Orbital velocity: 30 km/sec (nearly 70,000 mph)

Mean angular distance from Jupiter, at mean opposition distance: 42"

Diameter: 24×20×16 km

Shape: Irregular

Subsolar temperature: 120° K

Surface: Dark. It may well be rocky, with no ice. It has no atmosphere

Origin: Probably broke away from Jupiter, and could be a source for the Jovian ring

Discovery: Discovered in October 1979 by David Jewitt, Stephen Synnott and Ed Danielson of Caltech, on Frame FDS 20630.53 of the Voyager 2 pictures taken on July 8 of that year. At first it was thought to be an image of a star trailed by the time exposure, but Jewitt and Danielson found that it did not correspond with any star position

Amalthea

Other names: Jupiter V, Jupiter Five, J5, Amaltea (in Spanish), Barnard's Satellite

Named for: Named by the French astronomer Flammarion for the goat whose milk nourished the infant Zeus in Greek mythology. The name became official in 1975

Pronunciation: am əl thē' ə

Distance from Jupiter: Its mean distance from the center of Jupiter is 181,300 km

Location: Deep within the gravity field of Jupiter, as well as being in a very intense part of Jupiter's magnetosphere. For 87 years it was thought to be the innermost moon of Jupiter

Synodic period: 11 hours 57 mins 27.619 secs

Sidereal period: 0.49817905 days

Orbit: Its rotation period is probably synchronous with its orbital period. The long axis of Amalthea points constantly toward Jupiter. Observations by Barnard and others just after its discovery established the orbit to be roughly circular

Orbital eccentricity: 0.0028

Orbital inclination: 0.455 degrees

Escape velocity: About 0.16 km/sec

Visible magnitude: 14.1. Amalthea is so small that it will not normally be seen from Earth, even with the largest telescopes

Albedo: Generally low, averaging about 0.056. The leading hemisphere averages 0.059, and the trailing hemisphere about 0.054. The bright, greenish patches on the satellite's surface have a reflectivity up to 20 percent and may be due to recently exposed material which contains a lesser quantity of sulfur-rich glass. Amalthea reflects only about 10 percent of the sunlight incident upon it. It is darker than the larger satellites of Jupiter

Absolute magnitude: +7.4

Mean angular distance from Jupiter, at mean opposition distance: 0'59".4

Diameter: 270×166×153 km., similar to the Trojan asteroid Hektor

Apparent diameter, as seen from the surface of Jupiter: 7'24". Viewed from the planet, Amalthea would eclipse the Sun

Volume: About $24 \times 10^6 km^3$

Temperature: The typical Amalthean temperature is 126° K. In the daytime the surface temperature ranges from 140 to 170° K

Subsolar temperature: 120° K

Surface: 60 percent of the surface of Amalthea has been usefully imaged for surface features. There is no atmosphere, and the moon looks like a dark red potato, complete with eyes. It is the reddest object in the solar system, although less red than some areas on Io. The red color is believed to have been caused by the coating of sulfur particles ejected from nearby Io. From a distance Amalthea looks like Phobos, but on closer inspection it is unlike any other satellite in the solar system. Its dark surface is heavily scarred by impact craters, and has probably been greatly changed by its environment, and by contamination from Io (especially by the sulfur particles). The intense bombardment of Amalthea by objects from space has led to a great cratering rate on the rocky surface of the satellite. The green spots (see above, under *Albedo*) are an enigma

Shape: The gravitational pull of the planet Jupiter has made Amalthea elongated and wildly irregular in shape. It is similar in shape to the Trojan asteroid Hektor (see also above, under *Diameter*)

Features: All the features named on Amalthea are for personages associated with Amalthea in mythology. All the craters on Amalthea should be bowl-shaped; there are two main ones, Pan and Gaea, both bowl-shaped, and five other possible ones, not named. Both Pan and Gaea have irregular rim crests, and the floors of both are visible in some Voyager photos.

Pan is 90 km in diameter, and well over 8 km deep, maybe 16 km. It lies between 10° and 80°N and 0° and 85°W, and bright areas occur on its eastern rim. It would be difficult to imagine a larger bowl-shaped crater on Amalthea, given the size of the satellite itself.

Gaea, like Pan, was named by the I.A.U. (International Astronomical Union), and is 75 km across. It is at least 10–20 km deep, and is probably the younger crater of the two. Gaea centers on 90°S, 180°W, and bright areas occur on each interior side of it. Between the two craters, from longitudes 0° to 60°W, is a complex region of troughs and ridges, tens of kilometers long and sometimes as wide as 20 km.

The two bright patches, or "green spots," described above (under *Albedo*), may well be mountains, and are called Ida and Lyctos. Both are about 15 km in diameter. Ida is at 10°N, 175°W, and Lyctos is at 10°S, 170°W

Origin: Because of its greatly irregular shape, it is possible that Amalthea is all that is left of a larger body, possibly a reasonably spherical object, some 270 km across, and that continued bombardment over the eons fashioned it into its present shape, with lost fragments perhaps having gone to Saturn or out of the solar system

Discovery: Discovered by E. E. Barnard just after midnight on September 9, 1892, using the great 0.9-meter refractor at the Lick Observatory. Barnard said that it was "much more difficult to see than the satellites of Mars." He observed it for 2½ hours, making his last measurement at 2:33 a.m. His discovery was confirmed at 11:30 that night. Soon there were people claiming to have preempted Barnard. Barnard considered the name Columbia for his new moon, because it was found on the 400th anniversary of Columbus's discovery of America. He also considered Eureka, that being the state motto of California. The French astronomer Flammarion suggested Amalthea, but Barnard did not like that. However, popular usage finally brought that name official recognition in 1975. Amalthea was the last satellite in the solar system to be discovered by visual means. The more recent satellite discoveries have been photographed or have been made by spacecraft. Not much was known of Amalthea until Voyager 1 flew by to within 420,000 km on March 4, 1979. Later in the year Voyager 2 got to within 558,270 km. Both craft imaged the satellite in detail

Bibliography: "View from Amalthea," by Isaac Asimov, *The Solar System and Back,* 1970. First printed in *The Magazine of Fantasy and Science Fiction,* December 1968

"Barnard's Satellite of Jupiter," by Dale P. Cruikshank, *Sky and Telescope,* September 1982

Photograph: see page 144

Ananke

Other names: Jupiter XII, Jupiter Twelve, J12, Adrastea, Andrastea (these last two were the original, unofficial names—*see also* ***Adrastea***), Hephaestus, Semele (for these last two, see below, under *Discovery*)

Named for: Fate personified, in Greek mythology

Pronunciation: ə nan' kā, a nan' kā, ənan' kē, a nan' kē

Distance from Jupiter: Its mean distance from the center of Jupiter is 21,200,000 km

Synodic period: 551 days

Sidereal period: 631 days retrograde

Orbital eccentricity: 0.16870

Orbital inclination: 147 degrees

Escape velocity: A mean of about 0.01 km/sec

Visible magnitude: 18.9

Albedo: About 0.02 to 0.03

Absolute magnitude: +12.2

Mean angular distance from Jupiter, at mean opposition distance: 1°55'52"

Diameter: Between 6 and 30 km across, probably closer to 28 km

Shape: Irregular

Surface: Probably rocky, with carbonaceous dirt and water ice. There is no atmosphere

Apparent diameter, as seen from the surface of Jupiter: 0'0".2

Origin: Probably a captured Trojan asteroid

Discovery: Seth Nicholson found it on September 29, 1951, using the 100-inch Mount Wilson reflector. For a while its identity was questioned, and some said it was actually Lysithea. A month later it was found to be a separate satellite. At first it was called Adrastea (or Andrastea), but this name finally went to another satellite (*see* ***Adrastea***). In 1962 USSR astronomer E. I. Nesterovich proposed the name Hephaestus, and in 1976 USSR astronomer Yuriy I. Karpenko proposed Semele. It was later named Ananke by German philologist Johann Blunck

Bibliography: Dictionary of Astronomical Names, by Adrian Room. Routledge, 1988.

"Jupiter XII," by Seth Nicholson, *Sky and Telescope,* February 1952

Atlas of the Solar System, by Patrick Moore and Garry Hunt. Rand McNally, 1985

Andrastea *see* ***Ananke***

Ariel

Other names: Uranus I, Uranus One

Named for: Named by Sir John Herschel in 1852 for Shakespeare's character in *The Tempest*

Features on Earth named for it: Mount Ariel, on Alexander Island, Antarctica

Pronunciation: âr' ē l

Distance from Uranus: 191,020 km from the center of Uranus. In 1860 it was thought to be 206,499 km

Location: It is the second nearest of the Big Five satellites (Miranda, Ariel, Umbriel, Titania, and Oberon) to the planet

Synodic period: 2 days 12 hours 29 mins 39 secs

Sidereal period: 2.52037935 days retrograde

Orbital eccentricity: 0.0034

Orbital inclination: 0.3 degrees

Escape velocity: A mean of 1.25 km/sec

Density: A mean of 1.6 gm/cm^3

Mass: 6.7×10^{20} kg. The mass of the Big Five is so low that it would be hard to get any melting in the core of each. Yet there is clear evidence of some kind of internal activity on Ariel (and indeed, on all the Big Five except Umbriel)

Visible magnitude: 14.16

Albedo: The third brightest of Uranus's moons, it shows strong ice absorption in its spectrum, and due to its icy surface, has a high albedo, of 0.34

Absolute magnitude: +1.45

Mean angular distance from Uranus, at mean opposition distance: 14".5

Diameter: 1167 km across

Apparent diameter, as seen from the surface of Uranus: 30'54". Viewed from the surface of Uranus, Ariel would appear to be by far the largest of the satellites

Shape: Roughly spherical

Surface: The lightest in color of the major Uranian moons, Ariel is almost completely covered with ice or frost, and has a landscape which looks "devastated." This now inert moon has a younger surface than Titania, Oberon and Umbriel, and has a sinuous network of smooth-floored valleys similar to rift valleys on Earth. Some of these rift valleys are 10–20 miles deep. These were almost certainly formed by a stretching and cracking of Ariel's crust billions of years ago, followed by the upwelling of warm material through splits in the valley floors. There are also many cliffs and other scars on the surface of Ariel

Features: Abans 16°S, 251°E. Agape (a literary fairy) 47°S, 236°E. Ataksak 53°S, 225°E. Befanak (Befana; Italian fairy) 17°S, 32°E. Berylune 23°S, 328°E. Brownie Chasma (type of fairy) 5–21°S, 325–357°E. Deive 23°S, 23°E. Djadek 12°S, 251°E. Domovoy (Slavic hearth-god) 72°S, 339°E. Finvara 16°S, 19°E. Gwyn (Welsh fairy king) 78°S, 23°E. Huon (French fairy story) 39°S, 33°E. Kachina Chasma (American Indian spirit) 24–40°S,

210–280°E. Kewpie Chasma (type of fairy) 15–42°S, 307–335°E. Korrigan Chasma (Breton fairy) 25–46°S, 328–353°E. Kra Chasma 32–36°S, 355–2°E. Laica 22°S, 44°E. Leprachaun Vallis (Irish fairy) 5–15°S, 350–25°E. Mab (British fairy queen) 39°S, 353°E. Melusine (French water fairy) 53°S, 9°E. Onagh 22°S, 244°E. Pixie Chasma (type of fairy) 18–25°S, 350–20°E. Rima (literary sprite) 18°S, 260°E. Sprite Falls (type of fairy) 12–17°S, 332–355°E. Sylph Chasma (type of fairy) 45–50°S, 328–15°E. Yangoor 68° S, 260°E

Origin: The moons of Uranus may be the result of a coalescing of gas produced by the planet after a mammoth collision with an Earth-sized object

Discovery: On October 24, 1851 by British astronomer William Lassell, with his 24-inch reflector telescope on the island of Malta. On January 24, 1986 Voyager 2 got to within 126,500 km of Ariel, and imaged the satellite from 130,000 km. (*See also* ***Oberon****—Discovery*)

Bibliography: "Voyager Among the Ice Worlds," by Andrew Chaikin, *Sky and Telescope,* April 1986

Photograph: see page 127

A-ring Shepherd see *Atlas*

Atlas

see also ***Himalia***

Other names: Saturn 17, 1980 S28, The A-ring Shepherd

Named for: The Titan in Greek mythology

Pronunciation: at' ləs

Distance from Saturn: Its mean distance from the center of Saturn is 137,670 km

Location: It orbits only 800 km beyond the outer edge of Saturn's A-ring, and is the outer shepherd moon for that ring, acting as a gravitational barrier that defines the outer edge of the ring (for a more detailed description of the function of shepherd moons, *see* ***Pandora****—Location*). Atlas is one of the three shepherd moons so far known in the Saturnian system (*see also* ***Prometheus*** and ***Pandora,*** but *see also* ***1981 S13***)

Synodic period: 14 hours 25 mins 46.2 secs

Sidereal period: 0.609166 days (tropical period)

Orbital eccentricity: 0.000

Orbital inclination: 0.3 degrees

Escape velocity: 15 m/sec

Visible magnitude: 18.1

Albedo: 0.9

Absolute magnitude: +8.4

Subsolar temperature: About 119° K.

Mean angular distance from Saturn, at mean opposition distance: 22"

Diameter: 38×30×26 km

Shape: Irregular and elongated

Surface: Relatively bright, and probably composed of dirty water ice

Origin: Possibly the icy fragment of a larger body

Discovery: Discovered on November 12, 1980 by Rich Terrile, from photos taken by Voyager 1 on November 7, 1980. Voyager 1 came within 219,000 km of Atlas's surface, and Voyager 2 within 287,170 km

Barnard's Satellite see *Amalthea*

Belinda

Other names: Uranus XIV, Uranus 14, Uranus Fourteen, 1986 U5

Named for: Named by the I.A.U. in 1988 for Pope's character in *The Rape of the Lock*

Pronunciation: bə lin' də

Distance from Uranus: Its mean distance from the center of Uranus is 75,258 km

Location: Between Miranda and the rings of Uranus
Synodic period: 14 hours 56 mins
Sidereal period: 0.623525 days
Orbit: Its rotational period is synchronous with its orbital period (i.e., the same face of Belinda is always shown to Uranus)
Orbital eccentricity: Low, probably 0
Orbital inclination: Low, probably 0 degrees
Escape velocity: Very low
Albedo: Low, about 0.1
Mean angular distance from Uranus, at mean opposition distance: 6"
Diameter: Approximately 50 km
Density: Almost certainly low
Shape: Unknown exactly, but probably roughly spherical
Surface: Dark and methane-coated
Origin: Probably formed from the accretion of comets
Discovery: On January 13, 1986, by Voyager 2
Bibliography: *Science* 233 (July 4, 1986), 39–109

Bianca

Other names: Uranus VIII, Uranus Eight, Uranus 8, 1986 U9
Named for: Named in 1988 by the I.A.U. for Shakespeare's character in *Othello*
Pronunciation: bē an' kə
Distance from Uranus: Its mean distance from the center of Uranus is about 59,173 km
Location: Between Miranda and the rings of Uranus
Synodic period: 10 hours 23 mins
Sidereal period: 0.434577 days
Orbit: Its rotational period is synchronous with its orbital period (i.e., the same face of Bianca is always shown to Uranus)
Orbital eccentricity: Low, probably 0
Orbital inclination: Low, probably 0 degrees
Escape velocity: Very low
Albedo: Low, about 0.1
Mean angular distance from Uranus, at mean opposition distance: 4"
Diameter: Approximately 50 km
Density: Almost certainly low
Shape: Unknown exactly, but probably roughly spherical
Surface: Dark and methane-coated
Origin: Probably formed from the accretion of comets
Discovery: January 24, 1986, by Voyager 2
Bibliography: *Science* 233 (July 4, 1986), 39–109

Calixto *see* Callisto

Callisto

Other names: Jupiter IV, Jupiter 4, Calixto (in Spanish), Kallisto (in German)
Named for: One of Zeus's lovers in Greek mythology
Pronunciation: kə lis' tō
Features on Earth named for it: Callisto Cliffs on Alexander Island, Antarctica
Distance from Jupiter: Its mean distance from the center of Jupiter is 1,880,000 km
Location: It orbits in the plane of Jupiter's equator, so it always seems to be stretched out close to a line drawn through Jupiter. When it moves in front of Jupiter we see its shadow fall on the planet. It is the outermost of the 4 Galilean satellites (*see **Io***). As Callisto lies outside the main radiation zone of Jupiter, it may well become the first Jovian world to be visited by humans
Synodic period: 16 days 18 hours 05 mins 6.916 secs
Sidereal period: 16.6890184 days
Orbit: Its rotational period is synchronous with its orbital period (i.e., Callisto always keeps the same face toward Jupiter)

Orbital eccentricity: 0.0075

Orbital inclination: 0.2 degrees

Escape velocity: A mean of 2.43 km/sec

Density: It has the lowest density of the Galileans, with a mean of 1.81 gm/cm^3, a near twin to Ganymede

Mass: Determined by de Sitter and Sampson in the 1920s to be 10.64×10^{23} kg

Obliquity: Average is 3°.08

Temperature: Temperatures range from the surface equatorial noon-time highs of about 140–150° K (153° K maximum) to subsurface averages of 100° K or less. Typical temperature is 122° K. Night-time temperature is a minimum of 79° K

Subsolar temperature: About 168° K

Surface gravity: 122.1 cm/sec^2

Visible magnitude: 5.65. It can be seen even with a small telescope

Albedo: 0.17

Absolute magnitude: −1.05

Mean angular distance from Jupiter, at mean opposition distance: 10'17".6

Diameter: 4820 km. It is planet-sized, 2 percent larger than Mercury, and a near twin to Ganymede in size. Stower first measured its diameter in 1822

Apparent diameter, as seen from the surface of Jupiter: 9'30"

Shape: Roughly spherical

Surface: Smooth, with no significant mountains or valleys, Callisto is nevertheless the most densely cratered object in the solar system (as revealed by Voyager 1). The satellite itself is probably a large rocky core surrounded by a thick mantle of water and ice. The surface is almost certainly a mixture of water ice and rocky material. The evolution of Callisto came to a standstill billions of years ago. The surface is very old, and very individualistic. There is no other object like Callisto. The satellite has no "plains" between the craters. Beneath Callisto's ice and rock crust is a subterranean ocean. The surface of this moon is probably airless, but Callisto may have an oxygen atmosphere

Features: On March 2, 1979, large circular features were first discovered on Callisto, by Voyager 1. On March 6 Valhalla was discovered. Valhalla is the largest of several enormous, bright, target-like pattern-forms of concentric ridges. These are called multi-ring systems. At their centers are palimpsests (faint, discolored patches) which probably mark the sites of former impact basins. Valhalla is so outstanding and unusual in its effect that it is called "the bullseye of Callisto," even "the bullseye of the solar system." Its bright central area is about 300 km across, therefore it seems logical to assume that the original impact crater was this size. There is no crater there now, only the palimpsest (or "ghost-crater"), this flat central region of generally higher reflectivity than average. The object that cratered Valhalla was a relatively small impact, and that object almost certainly went right through the icy crust of Callisto into the ocean beneath its surface. Radiating outward from the palimpsest of Valhalla is a larger central area (which includes the palimpsest of about 300 km in diameter) of about 600 km. Discontinuous concentric ridges radiate out to about 1500 km from the center, making the overall diameter of Valhalla about 3000 km. It is similar in many respects to the large circular impact basins that dominate the surface of Earth's Moon, and that of Mercury.

Impact craters are the only features that have been discovered on Callisto. There are no smooth "plains" regions, and no basins. There is a wide variety of craters, however, including bowl-shaped, flat-floor, central-peaked, and central-pit, as well as the giant multi-ring systems of ridges and furrows (such as Valhalla). Fifteen palimpsests have been identified. Asgard (400 km in diameter) is the second largest multi-ring system on Callisto. The number of craters found, by diameter size: 11.3 to 16.0 km, 1311; 16.0 to 22.6 km, 696; 22.6 to 32.0 km, 346; 32.0 to 45.3 km, 211; 45.3 to 64.0 km, 92; 64.0 to 90.5 km, 22; 90.5 to 128 km, 7; 128 to 256 km, 2; 256 to 724 km, 3.

Myth-related names were given to some craters and to the catenae (chains of craters) on Callisto. The craters and large-ringed features were mostly named in association with Far Northern myths (on Earth).

CATENA: Gipul (Norse river) 65–73° N, 68°36°W. LARGE-RINGED FEATURES: Adlinda (a place in the depths of the ocean where Eskimo souls go after death) 54°S, 21°W. Asgard (home of the Norse gods) 28°N, 142°W. Valhalla (Odin's hall) 17°N, 57°W. CRATERS: Adal (Norse: son of Karl and Erna) 76°N, 82°W. Ägröi (Finno-Ugric god of twins) 44°N, 11°W. Akycha (Alaskan name of the Sun) 73°N, 317°W. Alfr (Norse dwarf) 10°S, 224°W. Ali (Norse: strongest ancient man) 60°N, 56°W. Anarr (Norse dwarf) 44°N, 0°W. Aningan (Greenland Eskimo moon god) 53°N, 352° W. Askr (first man) 52°N, 324°W. Balkr (Norse: Ottar's ancestor) 30° N, 12°W. Bavorr (Norse dwarf) 50° N, 20°W. Beli (Norse giant) 63°N, 82°W. Bragi (Norse skald-god) 77°N, 78°W. Brami (Norse: Ottar's ancestor) 29°N, 19°W. Bran (omnipotent Celtic god) 25°S, 208°W. Buga (Tunga [USSR] heaven god) 22°N, 324°W. Buri (Norse dwarf) 36°S, 43°W. Burr (giant: his sons held up the sky) 42°N, 135°W. Dag (Norse: Ottar's ancestor) 59°N, 77°W. Danr (Norse: son of Karl and Erna) 63°N, 78°W. Dia (Greek: Callisto's sister) 72°N, 64°W. Dryops (Greek: son of Dia by Apollo) 78°N, 20°W. Durinn (Norse dwarf) 68°N, 91°W. Egdir (Norse: shepherd for the giants) 35°N, 36°W. Erlik (Russian first man: became a devil) 65°N, 349°W. Fadir (Norse farmer) 57°N, 12°W. Fili (Norse dwarf) 64°N, 341° W. Finnr (Norse dwarf) 16°N, 4°W. Freki (Norse: wolf's name meaning "insatiable") 80°N, 348°W. Frodi (Norse: Hledi's father) 68°N, 137°W. Fulla (Norse: Figg's maid) 74°N, 111° W. Fulnir (Norse: son of Thrael and Thyr) 61°N, 35°W. Geri (Norse: wolf's name meaning "greedy") 65°N, 344° W. Gisl (Norse: horse ridden by Aesir) 58°N, 33°W. Gloi (Norse dwarf) 50°N, 243°W. Goll (Norse servant to the gods) 57°N, 319°W. Gondul (Valkyrjur maiden) 60°N, 116°W. Grimr (Norse: another name for Odin) 41°N, 214°W. Gunnr (Valkyrjur maiden) 65°N, 106°W. Gymir (another name for Aegir, the Norse god) 64°N, 53°W. Habrok (Norse hawk) 76°N, 136°W. Haki (Norse giant) 25°N, 315°W. Har (Norse dwarf) 3°S, 358°W. Hepti (Norse dwarf) 65°N, 23°W. Hodr (Norse god: Baldr's blind brother) 70°N, 91°W. Hoenir (Norse god: gave blood to first humans) 33°S, 263°W. Hogni (Norse: Ottar's ancestor) 12°S, 5°W. Igaluk (Alaskan name for the Moon) 7°N, 315°W. Ivarr (Norse: Ottar's ancestor) 6°S, 322°W. Jumo (Finno-Ugric heaven god) 61°N, 9°W. Kari (Norse: Ottar's ancestor) 47°N, 103°W. Karl (Norse: son of Rigr and Amma) 55°N, 329°W. Lodurr (Norse god: gave color to first humans) 49°S, 274°W. Loni (Norse dwarf) 4°S, 215°W. Losy (evil Mongolian snake) 65°N, 322°W. Mera (Greek nymph seduced by Zeus) 65°N, 76°W. Mimir (Norse giant) 33°N, 54°W. Mitsina (old Alaskan man who died while hunting) 59°N, 102°W. Modi (Norse: son of Thor and Sif) 67°N, 122°W. Nama (Russian hero) 57°N, 330°W. Nar (Norse dwarf) 1°S, 46°W. Nerivik (Alaskan heroine) 16°S, 56°W. Nidi (Norse dwarf) 67°N, 97°W. Nori (Norse dwarf) 45°N, 343°W. Nuada (Irish chieftain god) 64°N, 270°W. Oski (Norse: another name for Odin) 59°N, 267°W. Ottar (Freyja's favorite) 62°N, 105°W. Pekko (Finno-Ugric god of barley) 19°N, 6°W. Reginn (Norse dwarf) 40°N, 91°W. Rigr

(Heimdallr in disguise) 72°N, 238°W. Saga (another name for Frigg) 1°N, 326°W. Sarakha (Finno-Ugric goddess of childbed) 3°S, 54°W. Seginek (Seqinek) (Eskimo Sun) 56°N, 25°W. Sholmo (Finno-Ugric heaven god) 54° N, 16°W. Sigyn (Norse: Loki's wife) 36°N, 29°W. Skoll (Norse wolf) 56°N, 315°W. Skuld (Norse maiden who governed fate of humans) 11°N, 38°W. Sudri (Norse dwarf) 56°N, 138°W. Sumbur (Bariat [USSR] world mountain) 67°N, 324°W. Tindr (Norse: Ottar's ancestor) 2°S, 356°W. Tornarsuk (legendary Greenland hero) 29°N, 129°W. Tyn (great god of Germanic peoples) 72°N, 226°W. Valfodr (Norse: another name for Odin) 1°S, 248°W. Vali (Norse: Ottar's ancestor) 10°N, 325°W. Vestri (Norse dwarf) 50°N, 53°W. Vitr (Norse dwarf) 22°S, 350° W. Ymir (Norse: giant from whom the Earth was created) 52°N, 102°W

Origin: Possibly the oldest object in the solar system. There seems to be no history of geologic activity

Discovery: Discovered simultaneously by Galileo and Simon Mayr in 1610 (*see **Io**—Discovery*). Dollfus was the first to map it, albeit very roughly, in 1961, but it was effectively merely a point of light in the sky until Pioneer 11 photographed it from a distance of 490,000 miles on December 4, 1974. Then came the Voyager trips of 1979, both craft photographing Callisto in detail. Voyager 1 got to within 123,950 km of the surface, and Voyager 2 to within 212,510 km. Voyager 2 photographed the hemisphere not seen by Voyager 1

Bibliography: Moons and Planets, 2d ed., by William K. Hartmann. Wadsworth, 1983

Photographs: see pages 118, 145

Calypso

Other names: Saturn XIV, Saturn 14, Saturn Fourteen, 1980 S13

Named for: The nymph in Greek mythology

Pronunciation: kə lip' sō̄

Distance from Saturn: Its mean distance from the center of Saturn is 294,660 km

Location: One of the Tethys Lagrangians, it leads Tethys (by 60 degrees) in that larger satellite's orbit around Saturn (*see also **Telesto***)

Synodic period: 1 day 22 hours 15 mins

Sidereal period: 1.8878 days (tropical period)

Orbital eccentricity: Probably 0

Orbital inclination: About 2 degrees

Escape velocity: 13 m/sec

Visible magnitude: Between 18.8 and 18.4

Albedo: Between 0.53 and 0.75

Absolute magnitude: +9.1

Mean angular distance from Saturn, at mean opposition distance: 0'47".6

Diameter: 30×24×16 km

Shape: Irregular

Surface: Icy

Origin: Possibly the fragment of a larger body

Discovery: In March 1980 Pascu, Seidelmann, Baum and Currie of the "Space Telescope" Wide Field/Planetary Camera Instrument Definition team, the same team that discovered Telesto, discovered Calypso from Earth. Later in the year, Voyager 1 got to within 432,295 km of the satellite, and in 1981 Voyager 2 got to within 153,518 km

Carme

Other names: Jupiter XI, Jupiter 11, Jupiter Eleven, J11, Daedalus (see below, under *Discovery*), Leda (see below, under *Discovery*), Karme (alternate spelling), Pan (this was its original, unofficial name)

Named for: the lover of Zeus in Greek mythology

Pronunciation: kär' mā̄, kär' mē̄

Distance from Jupiter: Its mean distance from the center of Jupiter is 22,600,000 km

Synodic period: 597 days

Sidereal period: 692 days retrograde

Orbital eccentricity: 0.20678

Orbital inclination: Between 163 and 164 degrees

Escape velocity: A mean of about 0.02 km/sec

Visible magnitude: 18.0

Albedo: Probably 0.02 to 0.03

Absolute magnitude: +11.3

Diameter: Between 8 and 40 km, probably closer to 40

Apparent diameter, as seen from the surface of Jupiter: 0'0".2

Mean angular distance from Jupiter, at mean opposition distance: 2°03'31"

Shape: Irregular

Surface: Probably rocky, with carbonaceous dirt and water ice. There is no atmosphere

Origin: Probably a captured Trojan asteroid

Discovery: By Seth Nicholson, on July 30, 1938, accidentally, while he was checking on the position of Lysithea, with the 100-inch telescope at the Mount Wilson Observatory in Washington, D.C. Originally, and unofficially, this moon was called Pan, and in 1962 USSR amateur astronomer E. I. Nesterovich proposed the name Daedalus. In 1976 USSR astronomer Yuriy A. Karpenko proposed the name Leda, but this name was officially given to another satellite (*see* ***Leda***). It was later officially called Carme, by German philologist Johann Blunck

Bibliography: Dictionary of Astronomical Names, by Adrian Room. Routledge, 1988

Cerberus see Sinope

Charon

Other names: Pluto I, Pl, Pluto One, 1978 Pl

Named for: Named very shortly after its discovery in 1978, by its discoverer James W. Christy, for Charon, the Greek mythological ferryman of the dead

Pronunciation: kar' on (the correct pronunciation, strictly speaking, when saying the name of the mythological character), shar' on, shar' ən, kâr' on, shâr' on

Distance from Pluto: Its mean distance from the center of Pluto looks to be about 19,130 km

Synodic period: 6 days 9 hours 17 mins

Sidereal period: 6.3872 days retrograde

Orbit: Charon makes a retrograde orbit north-south of Pluto, and around the planet, in 6 days 9 hours 17 mins. Pluto and Charon each make one rotation in the time it takes Charon to revolve around Pluto. Thus each body always presents the same face to the other. This is due to the fact that the two bodies are about the same size, and each exerts a tidal pull on the other. This is the only example of mutual tidal coupling in the solar system. It contrasts with the Earth-Moon system, where the Moon always presents the same face to Earth, while the Earth periodically presents its entire circumference to the Moon. So, the Pluto-Charon system is the only planet-satellite pair that both rotate and revolve synchronously. Viewed from Pluto, Charon might never be visible or might always be seen in the same place, depending on where on Pluto an observer stood. Charon's orbit is not normally seen edge-on from Earth

Orbital eccentricity: Probably 0

Orbital inclination: 94.3 degrees

Mean angular distance from Pluto, at mean opposition distance: Less than 01"

Visible magnitude: 16.8. Charon can be viewed from Earth only under excellent conditions, as an elongation of the image of Pluto. It was easiest to study the Pluto-Charon system between

1985 and October 1990, during which time Charon's orbit was nearly edge-on to Earth. It will not be that easy again until 2109. On Pluto a solar eclipse (when the Sun disappears behind Charon) would last 1 hour 37 mins (compared to the Sun going behind Earth's Moon, which takes a maximum of 7 mins)

Albedo: 0.34. Charon reflects about 34 percent of the sunlight incident upon it

Absolute magnitude: +0.9

Apparent diameter, as seen from the surface of Pluto: About 4'. Charon is actually 18,800 km above the surface of Pluto's equator, and it appears larger than any other moon appears from the surface of its planet. Charon is 20 times closer to Pluto than Earth's Moon is to the Earth. It covers almost 4 degrees in Pluto's sky—eight times as wide as Earth's Moon appears

Diameter: The latest calculation (December 1990) is 1186 km plus or minus 2 percent. Estimates have ranged from between 800 km and 2290 km, but it is almost certainly between 1000 and 1500 km. Charon is the largest satellite relative to its primary body in the solar system. This honor had been thought to belong to Earth's Moon. Charon is close to Pluto in size

Density: 0.8 gm/cm^3, suggesting a planet-like rocky core

Mass: 1.3×10^{21}kg plus or minus 10 percent

Temperature: Charon is thought to be the coldest satellite in the solar system (however, this may well be successfully challenged by Triton. See that entry, under *Surface*). Its mean distance from the Sun is 5,913,514,000 km. Its period of revolution around the Sun is 248.54 years. Charon has a surface temperature of −220° centigrade (or 53° centigrade above absolute zero)

Shape: Almost certainly roughly spherical, Charon has a maximum elongation from the planet of only 0.8 arc seconds

Surface: Charon is covered with ice, but devoid of methane in any form. The methane that may have been on the surface of Charon (as it is on Pluto) would have evaporated due to Charon's smaller mass and weaker gravity. It must be an uneven, cratered surface on Charon, but at any rate the surface is a light, neutral gray, somewhat darker and more even in color than Pluto's surface

Origin: There are several theories: (1) Charon may have once been a part of Pluto; (2) it may have been formed through the accretion of comets; (3) it may be a primordial object left over from the Big Bang, or whatever caused the Universe to come into being; (4) Pluto and Charon may both be escaped moons from Neptune, which may mean that Pluto-Charon is a double planet system, rather than a planet-satellite system

Discovery: Ever since Clyde Tombaugh discovered Pluto in 1930, the hunt had been on for a satellite. Fifty photographic plates of Pluto were taken from the U.S. Naval Observatory at Flagstaff, Arizona, in 1965, 1970 and 1971, and from 1965 onwards observers saw that the image of Pluto was "smudged," or elongated. On April 13 and 20 and on May 12, 1978, Anthony V. Hewitt photographed Pluto using the 61-inch Astrometric reflector at Flagstaff. There were two plates for each date, and three images of Pluto on each plate. They were marked "poor" because of the "smudge," or elongation. On June 22, 1978, James W. Christy obtained and examined these most recent plates, and noticed that, although Pluto seemed to be "smudged," the stars on the plate were not. He then studied the bulge on Pluto. On the April dates the bulge was to the south of Pluto, and on the May date it was to the north. Christy thought this bulge, or "smudge" might be a moon. On June 23 he studied the 50 earlier plates taken in 1965, 1970 and 1971.

Two plates from 1965 showed the bulge, and five plates taken during one week in 1970 showed the bulge progressing clockwise around Pluto in a 6-day period. Christy then told his colleague Robert S. Harrington that Pluto has a moon, and Harrington worked out its orbit. On July 2, 1978, Christy made the announcement to the world. On July 6, 1978, J. Graham confirmed it, using the 401-cm reflector at Cerro Tololo Observatory. Subsequently the existence of Charon was confirmed by D. Bonneau and R. Foy, using the 3.6-meter Canada-France-Hawaii telescope at Mauna Kea. Using the technique of speckle interferometry they recorded Pluto and its moon separately. The discovery of the motion of Charon showed that Pluto was smaller than was once thought.

Bibliography: Planets Beyond, by Mark Littmann. Wiley, 1988.

Chiron

Other names: 1977 UB (its asteroidal designation), 2060 (its asteroidal number)

Named for: The son of Kronos, in Greek mythology

Pronunciation: kī' ron, kī' rən

Location: Chiron is a mysterious object. It orbits between Saturn and Uranus, and takes 50.68 years to go around the Sun. At perihelion it comes to within 1,278,000 km of the Sun, and at aphelion to 2,827,000 km. The last two perihelia occurred in 1895 and 1945. The next is in 1996. At perihelion about one-sixth of its orbit lies within that of Saturn, leading some scientists to speculate that Chiron may be an escaped satellite of Saturn. It looks as if Chiron passes through Saturn's satellite system at intervals of approximately 100,000 years. In 1664 B.C. Chiron approached Saturn to within about 16 million km. This is only a little way farther, comparatively, than Phoebe. Chiron's orbit may not be stable, and in the future this object, whatever it is, may leave the solar system.

Orbital eccentricity: 0.3786

Orbital inclination: 6.923 degrees

Escape velocity: About 160 m/sec

Visible magnitude: At discovery it was 18.0. At perihelion it will rise to about 15.0

Albedo: Probably low

Diameter: May be as large as 650 km. Its size will be better determined when it occults a star (which will not happen in the near future). If Chiron is icy it may be only about 100 km in diameter. Recently, however, scientists have estimated it to be more rocky than icy, therefore the albedo will be low, so the diameter could be as much as 650 km. It is probably about 300 km.

Origin: At one time Chiron was thought to be a great comet. This is not so. There are several theories as to what Chiron is: (1) an escaped Saturnian satellite; (2) an unusual asteroid (it has been given an asteroidal number—see above, under *Other names*); (3) a planetesimal; (4) the brightest member of a trans-Saturn asteroid group.

Surface: Probably rocky or dusty, with ice. There is no atmosphere.

Discovery: On November 1, 1977, Charles Kowal discovered it from plates exposed on October 18 and 19, 1977, using the Schmidt Telescope at Palomar. It has since been traced on photographs taken as far back as 1895. In 1978 Kowal was asked, "What is Chiron?" He replied, "For now Chiron is just—Chiron"

Cordelia

Other names: Uranus VI, Uranus 6, U6, Uranus Six, 1986 U7, The Inner Epsilon Ring Shepherd

Named for: Named in 1988 by the I.A.U. for Shakespeare's character in King Lear

Pronunciation: kôr dē' lē ə

Distance from Uranus: Its mean distance from the center of Uranus is about 49,771 km

Location: Along with Ophelia, it is to be found on one of the sides of the epsilon ring of Uranus (*see* ***Ophelia***)

Orbit: Its rotational period is synchronous with its orbital period (i.e., the same face of Cordelia is always shown to Uranus)

Orbital eccentricity: Low, probably 0

Orbital inclination: Low, probably 0 degrees

Synodic period: 7 hours 55 mins

Sidereal period: 0.335033 days

Escape velocity: Very low

Density: Almost certainly low

Albedo: Low, about 0.1

Mean angular distance from Uranus, at mean opposition distance: 4"

Diameter: Approximately 50 km

Shape: Unknown exactly, but probably roughly spherical

Surface: Dark and methane-coated

Origin: Possibly formed through the accretion of comets

Discovery: January 20, 1986, by Voyager 2 (*see* ***Ophelia***)

Bibliography: *Science* 233 (July 4, 1986), 39–109

The Astronomical Almanac 1990, by the U.S. and U.K. governments

Photographs: see pages 128, 132

Cressida

Other names: Uranus IX, Uranus 9, U9, Uranus Nine, 1986 U3

Named for: Named by the I.A.U. in 1988 for Shakespeare's character in *Troilus and Cressida*

Pronunciation: kre' si də

Distance from Uranus: Its mean distance from the center of Uranus is about 61,777 km

Location: Between Miranda and the rings of Uranus

Synodic period: 11 hours 6 mins

Sidereal period: 0.463570 days

Orbital eccentricity: Low, probably 0

Orbital inclination: Low, probably 0 degrees

Escape velocity: Very low

Density: Almost certainly low

Orbit: Its rotational period is synchronous with its orbital period (i.e., the same face of Cressida is always shown to Uranus)

Mean angular distance from Uranus, at mean opposition distance: 5"

Albedo: Low, about 0.1

Diameter: Approximately 60 km

Shape: Unknown exactly, but probably roughly spherical

Surface: Dark and methane-coated

Origin: Possibly formed through the accretion of comets

Discovery: January 9, 1986, by Voyager 2 (*see* ***Puck***)

Bibliography: *Science* 233 (July 4, 1986), 39–109

Photograph: see page 128

Daedalus *see* ***Carme***

Danaë *see* ***Elara***

Deimos

Other names: M2, Mars 2, Mars Two, Mars II

Named for: Named on February 7, 1878, by its discoverer (*see also* ***Phobos***), Asaph Hall, at the suggestion of Mr. Madan of Eton, after one of the two chariot-horses (Phobos was the other) of the Roman god Mars (Deimos means "terror")

Pronunciation: dē' mos, dī' mos

Distance from Mars: Its mean distance from the center of Mars is 23,458.9 km. In 1726, 151 years before the discovery of the Martian satellites by Asaph Hall, Jonathan Swift described this moon (Deimos) as being 5 diameters from the center of Mars. Hall worked it out at 3.46 diameters

Features on Earth named for it: Deimos Ridge, on Alexander Island, Antarctica

Location: It is the outer of Mars's two satellites and orbits at approximately 12,000 miles from the surface of Mars. Tidal forces cause a recession of the satellite from Mars, and it may eventually leave Mars's orbit (*see also* ***Phobos*** under *Location*)

Synodic period: 1 day 6 hours 17 mins 54.87 secs, the same as its rotational period

Sidereal period: 1.2624407 days

Orbit: Swift (see above) in 1726 gave his outer Martian moon a 21½-hour period of revolution. In 1877 Asaph Hall gave it 30 hours 18 mins

Orbital eccentricity: 0.00082

Orbital inclination: 0.9–2.7 (variable) degrees

Orbital velocity: A mean of 1.4 km/sec

Escape velocity: A mean of 4.7 m/sec

Density: A mean of 2.1 gm/cm³ (for speculation on this, see ***Phobos***)

Mass: 2×10^{15} kg

Visible magnitude: 12.40. When viewed through a telescope from Earth, Deimos appears as a spot of light to the right of Mars, its home planet

Albedo: Very low, 0.06, making it difficult to see from Earth. Because of low albedo its surface is as dark as the darkest regions of Earth's moon

Absolute magnitude: +12.89

Mean angular distance from Mars, at mean opposition distance: 1'01".8

Maximum apparent magnitude, as seen from Mars: –0.1. Deimos is too near to Mars to be visible from all Martian latitudes. It does not appear at latitudes higher than 82.5 degrees North and South

Apparent diameter, as seen from the surface of Mars: Maximum 2', minimum 1'.7

Diameter: 15×12.2×11 km. Its longest axis is 7.5 km, its intermediate axis is 6.1 km, and its shortest axis is 5.5 km. This tiny moon is about half the size of Phobos

Area: 400 sq. km

Volume: 1000 km³

Surface gravity: 0.5 cm/sec³

Subsolar temperature: 314.4 degrees K

Shape: Mariner and Viking photographs showed Deimos to be irregularly shaped, roughly a triaxial ellipsoid. The long axis of the satellite constantly points toward Mars

Surface: 80 percent of the surface of Deimos has been usefully imaged for surface features. In 1930 E. M. Antoniadi falsely claimed that Deimos was bluish in color (*see* ***Phobos***—*Surface*). The Mariner 9 photographs of 1971 showed Deimos to be pitted with numerous craters. Viking 2 was navigated to within 30 km of Deimos. The satellite looks like many asteroids, smooth-textured and with the many craters almost buried in large quantities of fine debris. It is this debris which gives the satellite its smooth appearance. Early in its history Deimos probably underwent intense bombardment by meteor-like bodies. The debris that resulted flew up into the satellite's orbit and came back down, captured by the gravity of the satellite, as a kind of rain that blanketed the surface, covering the craters and fractures of the satellite

Features: Deimos has dark craters up to 1.3 km in diameter. The two named craters on Deimos were named for the literary figures who described the Martian moons a century or more before their discovery (*see* ***Phobos***—*Discovery*): Swift Crater (1.3 km diameter) 10°N, 358°W. Voltaire Crater (1 km in diameter) 23°N, 2°W

Origin: Deimos is probably of very old age. It may well have been captured by Mars's gravitational pull (*see* ***Phobos***—*Origin*)

Discovery: August 12, 1877, by Asaph Hall (*see* ***Phobos***—*Discovery*). The first detailed views of any natural satellite other than Earth's Moon, came on November 16, 1971, when Mariner 9

photographed Deimos. Mariner 9 proved Deimos to be about one degree behind its expected orbital position. Since then spacecraft searches have revealed no other Martian moons (at least, none bigger in diameter than 1.6 km)

Bibliography: Satellites, ed. by Joseph A. Burns and Mildred S. Matthews. University of Arizona Press, Tucson, 1986

Moons and Planets, 2d ed., by W. K. Hartmann. Wadsworth, Belmont, Calif., 1983

"The Moons of Mars," by Edmund Hamilton, *Captain Future* 4, 3(1942); and *see* ***Phobos****—Bibliography*

"Phobos and Deimos," by James Oberg, *Astronomy,* March 1977

"The Puzzling Moons of Mars," by Joseph Veverka, Peter Thomas, and Thomas Duxbury, *Sky and Telescope,* September 1978

"Swift's Forecast of Mars' Satellites," by Henry C. Briton, *Sky and Telescope,* September 1956

"Asaph Hall and the Moons of Mars," by John T. Kane, *Sky and Telescope,* September 1956

Intelligent Life in the Universe, by Iosef Shmuelovich. Shklovskii and Carl Sagan. Holden-Day, San Francisco, 1966. Chapter 26 of this pioneering work is called "Are the Moons of Mars Artificial Satellites?" This theory has been disproved

"The Moons of Mars," by Joseph Veverka and Joseph A. Burns, *Annual Review of Earth and Planetary Sciences* 8 (1980), 527–558. This is a detailed account of factual knowledge about the Martian moons up to that time

Photograph: see page 112

Demeter see *Lysithea*

Desdemona

Other names: Uranus X, Uranus Ten, Uranus 10, U10, 1986 U6

Named for: Named by the I.A.U. in 1988 for Shakespeare's character in *Othello*

Pronunciation: dez də mō' nə

Distance from Uranus: Its mean distance from the center of Uranus is about 62,676 km

Location: Between Miranda and the rings of Uranus

Synodic period: 11 hours 24 mins

Sidereal period: 0.473651 days

Orbit: Its rotational period is synchronous with its orbital period (i.e. the same face of Desdemona is always shown to Uranus)

Orbital eccentricity: Low, probably 0

Orbital inclination: Low, probably 0 degrees

Escape velocity: Very low

Albedo: Low, about 0.1

Mean angular distance from Uranus, at mean opposition distance: 5"

Diameter: Approximately 60 km

Density: Almost certainly low

Shape: Unknown exactly, but probably roughly spherical

Surface: Dark and methane-coated

Origin: Possibly formed through the accretion of comets

Discovery: January 13, 1986, by Voyager 2 (*see* ***Puck***)

Bibliography: Science 233 (July 4, 1986), 39–109

Despina

Other names: 1989 N3, Neptune 6, Neptune VI, Neptune Six, N6

Named for: Named in 1990 by the I.A.U. for the character associated with the sea in Greek mythology

Pronunciation: des pē' nə

Distance from Neptune: Its mean distance from the center of Neptune is 52,500 km

Location: This is one of the two shepherd moons (*see also* ***1989 N4***), orbiting 2000 km inside Neptunian ring 1989 N1 B

Orbital eccentricity: Probably 0

Orbital inclination: Less than 1 degree, probably 0

Sidereal period: About 0.33 days

Albedo: About 0.06

Shape: Irregular

Surface: Extremely dark, almost black like soot

Diameter: Approximately 150 km

Origin: Possibly formed through the accretion of comets

Discovery: July 7, 1989, by Voyager 2 (*see* ***Proteus***)

Photographs: see pages 136, 138

Dione

Other names: Saturn IV, Saturn 4, Saturn Four, Dioné (in French)

Named for: Named by Sir John Herschel in 1847 for the Titan woman in Greek mythology

Pronunciation: dī ō' nē, dē' ō' nē, dī o' nē

Features on Earth named for it: Dione Nunataks on Alexander Island, Antarctica

Distance from Saturn: Its mean distance from the center of Saturn is 377,420 km, the fourth closest of the original 9 Saturnian satellites to its home planet (hence the alternate name Saturn 4)

Orbit: Sluggish

Synodic period: 2 days 17 hours 42 mins 9.7 secs

Sidereal period: 2.736914742 days (tropical period)

Orbital eccentricity: 0.002230

Orbital inclination: 0.023 degrees

Escape velocity: 0.87 km/sec

Orbital velocity: 10.0 km/sec

Visible magnitude: 10.4

Albedo: Between 0.6 (its brightest) and 0.3 (its darkest). Its albedo contrast is second only to Iapetus in the solar system

Absolute magnitude: +0.88

Mean angular distance from Saturn, at mean opposition distance: 1'0".1

Diameter: 1118 km. It is an intermediate-sized satellite

Apparent diameter, as seen from the surface of Saturn: 12'24"

Density: A mean of approximately 1.43 gm/cm³. It is probably the most dense of all the Saturnian satellites except Titan. It may have an effect on Saturn's radio emission, since there seems to be a Saturn cycle of 2.7 days, the revolutionary period of Dione

Mass: 1.05×10^{21} kg

Surface gravity: 22.39 cm/sec²

Subsolar temperature: About 130° K

Shape: Roughly spherical

Surface: An icy moon, overlain with what seems to be wisps of frozen water, most of them between 5 and 20 km across. Not always a dead world, Dione was once geologically active. It has large, craterless regions and long, branching valleys tens of kilometers wide and hundreds of kilometers long

Features: Most of the features on Dione were named from Mandelbaum's 1972 translation of Virgil's *Aeneid.* The most prominent feature on Dione is Amata, which is 240 km in width. It is either a crater or a basin. Aeneas Crater is large and well-marked. Latium is a craterlet chain.

CRATERS: Adrastus (King of Argos) 64°S, 40°W. Aeneas (the Hero) 26°N, 47°W. Amata (mother of Lavinia) 7°N, 287°W. Anchises (father of Aeneas) 35°S, 63°W. Antenor (nephew of Priam) 6°S, 8°W. Butes (a boxer) 68°N, 50°W. Caieta (a nurse of Aeneas) 25°S, 80°W. Cassandra (prophetess: daughter of Priam) 42°S, 242°W. Catillus (one of the founders of Tibur) 1°S, 275°W. Coras (brother of Catillus) 3°N, 268°W. Creusa (first wife of Aeneas) 48°N, 78°W. Dido (Tyrian princess who founded Carthage) 22°S, 15°W. Halys (a Trojan ally) 60°S, 45°W. Ilia (or Rhea Silva: mother of Romulus and Remus) 3°N, 344°W. Italus (ancient hero) 20°S, 76°W. Latagus (soldier of Aeneas) 16°N, 26°W. Lausus (son of Mezentius)

38°N, 23°W. Magus (King of the Rutulians) 20°N, 24°W. Massicus (an Etruscan ally) 36°N, 52°W. Palinurus (pilot of Aeneas's fleet) 5°S, 62°W. Remus (co-founder of Rome) 10°S, 30°W. Ripheus (a Trojan ally) 56°S, 29°W. Romulus (co-founder of Rome) 8°S, 24°W. Sabinus (ancestor of the Sabines) 44°S, 190°W. Turnus (Rutulian king) 21°N, 342°W. LINEA: Carthage (ancient Etruscan city) 20–10°N, 337–310°W. Padua (city in Italy founded by Antenor) 5°N–40°S, 245–190°W. Palatine (one of the 7 Hills of Rome) 10°N–55°S, 285–320°W. CHASMA: Larissa (a town in Thessaly) 20–48°N, 15–65°W. Latium (the promised land in Italy) 3–45°N, 64–75°W. Palatine (one of the 7 Hills of Rome) 55–73°S, 75–320°W. Tibur (ancient town of Italy) 48–80°N, 60–80°W

Origin: Formed from the early Saturn gas and dust

Discovery: By G. D. Cassini on March 21, 1684, using an aerial telescope with a focal length of more than 40 meters. It was extremely difficult to see with the long refractors of the 17th century. Dione was the fifth Saturnian satellite to be found. In 1980 Voyager 1 approached to within 161,520 km, and Voyager 2 in 1981 got to within 502,520 km

Photographs: see pages 119, 147

Dione B see *Helene*

Dione Co-orbital see *1981 S7*

Elara

Other names: Jupiter VII, Jupiter 7, J7, Hera (this was its original, unofficial name), Heracles (see below, under *Discovery*), Danaë (see below, under *Discovery*)

Named for: One of the lovers of Zeus

Pronunciation: ə lä' rə, ē' l rə, e lä' rə

Distance from Jupiter: Its mean distance from the center of Jupiter is 11,737,000 km

Synodic period: 276.67 days

Sidereal period: 259.6528 days

Rotation period: 12 hours

Orbital eccentricity: 0.20719

Orbital inclination: 24.8 degrees

Escape velocity: A mean of about 0.05 km/sec

Visible magnitude: 16.77

Albedo: About 0.02 to 0.03

Absolute magnitude: +10.07

Mean angular distance from Jupiter, at mean opposition distance: 1°04'10"

Diameter: 76 km

Apparent diameter, as seen from the surface of Jupiter: 0'1".4

Shape: Irregular

Surface: Remarkably dark and neutral in color. It is probably rocky, and probably made of carbonaceous chondritic material and water ice. There is no atmosphere

Origin: Probably a captured Trojan asteroid

Discovery: Discovered by C. D. Perrine on a plate taken by the Crossley Telescope at the Lick Observatory on January 2, 1905. The plate was not studied until February 1905. The satellite's first, unofficial name was Hera. In 1962 USSR amateur astronomer E. I. Nesterovich proposed the name Heracles, and in 1976 USSR astronomer Yuriy A. Karpenko proposed Danaë. It was later named Elara by German philologist Johann Blunck

Bibliography: Dictionary of Astronomical Names, by Adrian Room. Routledge, 1988

Enceladus

Other names: Saturn 2, Saturn Two, Saturn II, Encélado (in Spanish)

Named for: Sir John Herschel named

it in 1847 for the Titan in Greek mythology

Pronunciation: en sel' ə dəs

Features on Earth named for it: Enceladus Nunataks on Alexander Island, Antarctica

Synodic period: 1 day 8 hours 53 mins 21.9 secs

Sidereal period: 1.370217855 days (tropical)

Distance from Saturn: Its mean distance from the center of Saturn is 238,020 km

Orbital eccentricity: 0.00452. It is in an eccentric orbit forced by Dione

Orbital inclination: 0.0 degrees

Escape velocity: 0.2 km/sec

Visible magnitude: 11.7. From Earth it is best seen by using at least an 8-inch telescope, at eastern or western elongation

Albedo: 1.0. It is the solar system's most reflective body. It is like a mirror, that is why its albedo (or reflectivity) is so high. This quality is probably caused by water ejected from the planet in the form of geysers, then falling back onto the surface, and freezing. This ejected water would come from inside the satellite's heated interior. This internal activity may be caused by "flexing" by the tidal forces of Saturn and Dione

Absolute magnitude: +2.1

Orbital velocity: 12.6 km/sec

Mean angular distance from Saturn, at mean opposition distance: 0'38".4

Density: A mean of approximately 1.16 gm/cm^3

Mass: 7.40×10^{19} kg

Diameter: 502 km. It is an intermediate-sized satellite

Apparent diameter, as seen from the surface of Saturn: 10'36"

Surface gravity: 7.69 cm/sec^2

Subsolar temperature: Up to 70° K

Temperature: The average daytime temperature of −200° centigrade is exceptionally cold, even in the Saturnian system

Shape: Roughly spherical

Surface: It was known before the Voyager 1 trip of 1980 that Enceladus was covered with unusually pure water ice. This ice seems to have been melted and reformed on a continuing basis, possibly by heat generated internally by tidal forces (see above, under *Albedo*). When Voyager 1 photographed it in 1980 its surface showed no topography at all. Voyager 2 showed 5 different terrains and a light-cratered, fresh surface with almost 100 percent reflectivity. The youngest plains regions contain grooves, but something is covering up its craters (it must have had a lot more craters than are now evident). This must be some "re-surfacing" process. The North polar region is heavily cratered

Features: Most of the features on Enceladus were named from Sir Richard Burton's "The Thousand Nights and a Night."

CRATERS: Ahmad (youngest son) 58°N, 304°W. Aladdin (hero of the lamp) 63°N, 17°W. Ali Baba (hero against the 40 thieves) 55°N, 11°W. Dalilah (cunning old woman) 53°N, 244°W. Duban (wise man) 58°N, 276°W. Dunyazad (sister of Shahrazad) 43°N, 200°W. Gharib (hero of many tales) 81°N, 245°W. Julnar (mermaid heroine) 54°N, 340°W. Musa (character in "The City of Brass") 73°N, 3°W. Peri-Banu (female genie) 63°N, 315°W. Salih (brother of Julnar) 0°, 60°W. Samad (a sheikh) 61°N, 353°W. Shahrazad [sic] (teller of the 1001 night tales) 49°N, 200°W. Shahryar (King to whom Shahrazad told the tales) 58°N, 222°W. Sindbad (voyager hero) 66°N, 210°W. FOSSAE: Bassorah (town from which Sindbad embarked on his third voyage) 40–50° N, 23–345°W. Daryabar (an "ocean region" land) 5–10°N, 20–335°W. Isbanir (Fakir Taj's home) 20°N–10°S, 0–350°W. PLANITIAE: Diyar (country in "Khudadad and his Brothers") 0°, 250°W. Sarandib (Island visited by Sindbad on his 6th voyage) 5°N, 300°W. SULCI: Harran (city where

Khudadad's father ruled) 35°N–5°S, 270–210°W. Samarkand (country ruled by Zaman, Shahryar's brother) 75°N–5°S, 300–340°W

Origin: Formed from the early Saturn gas and dust. Enceladus may be the source of Ring-E material. It is much smoother than other satellites of Saturn, so it may well have lost some of its surface to form the ring

Discovery: On August 19, 1787, William Herschel suspected that he had found a sixth Saturnian satellite, with his 20-foot 18.5-inch aperture reflector telescope. He did not pursue it until 1789 when, with his new 40-foot reflector with its 48-inch aperture, he verified its existence on August 29, 1789. It was difficult to see, even with the largest telescopes, until the middle of the 19th century. Voyager 1 approached to within 202,040 km in 1980, but saw it poorly. On August 15, 1981, Voyager 2 came to within 87,140 km

Photographs: see pages 121, 147

E-1, Earth-1 *see* ***Moon***

Epimetheus

Other names: Saturn 11, Saturn Eleven, Saturn XI, 1980 S3

Named for: The Titan in Greek mythology

Pronunciation: ep i mē' thē əs

Distance from Saturn: Its mean distance from the center of Saturn is 151,422 km

Synodic period: 16 hours 39 mins 49.5 secs

Sidereal period: 0.694333 days (tropical period)

Location: Epimetheus is co-orbital with Janus, both moons being located between Mimas and the F-ring. These two moons periodically exchange energy in order to avoid collision. Their mutual gravitational interaction is responsible for this phenomenon. Their orbital radii differ by less than their diameters. In 1991 Epimetheus is slightly closer to Saturn, and is moving faster than Janus, and will eventually catch it. They will exchange orbits, as they do about once every four years. They may come within a few kilometers of each other

Orbital eccentricity: 0.009

Orbital inclination: 0.34 degrees

Escape velocity: 45 m/sec

Visible magnitude: Between 15.5 and 15.1

Albedo: Between 0.42 and 0.60

Absolute magnitude: +5.4

Mean angular distance from Saturn, at mean opposition distance: 24"

Density: Almost certainly less than 1.0 gm/cm^{-3}, which is low

Diameter: 140×114×100 km

Shape: Irregular, like a tooth

Surface: 40 percent of Epimetheus's surface has been usefully imaged for surface features. The surface is icy, and heavily cratered

Subsolar temperature: About 112° K

Features: Up to 1984 there were 16 craters discovered on Epimetheus. Two of them are named—Hilairea and Pollux

Origin: Possibly the fragment of a larger body

Discovery: In 1978, by John Fountain and Stephen Larson. This was confirmed in March 1980 (*see* ***Janus***). This was the 11th Saturnian satellite to be discovered. In 1979 Pioneer 11 imaged Epimetheus, and one satellite orbit later Pioneer 11 passed within a few thousand kilometers, intersecting Epimetheus's magnetic wake. However, the full interpretation of the Janus-Epimetheus co-orbital system was not realized until Voyager 1 passed by in November 1980. Voyager 1 passed within 121,000 km, and in 1981 Voyager 2 passed within 147,010 km. The Voyager 1 photographs of Epimetheus were taken 13 mins apart, and show a narrow shadow moving across the satellite. This was probably the shadow of the F-ring, a few thousand kilometers away

E2, Earth-2 see Toro

Europa

Other names: Jupiter II, Jupiter Two, Jupiter 2, J2

Named for: One of Jupiter's lovers in mythology

Pronunciation: yo͞o rō' pə

Features on Earth named for it: Europa Cliffs on Alexander Island, Antarctica

Distance from Jupiter: Its mean distance from the center of Jupiter is 670,900 km

Synodic period: 3 days 13 hours 17 mins 53.736 secs

Sidereal period: 3.551181041 days

Orbital eccentricity: 0.009

Orbital inclination: 0.468 degrees

Orbit: It always keeps the same face toward Jupiter. It orbits in the plane of Jupiter's equator, so it always seems stretched out close to a line drawn through Jupiter. When Europa moves in front of Jupiter we see its shadow fall on the planet

Escape velocity: A mean of 2.10 km/sec (*see also* ***Io***)

Mean angular distance from Jupiter, at mean opposition distance: 3'40".1

Visible magnitude: 5.29. It can be seen even with a small telescope

Albedo: 0.64, the highest of the 4 Galilean moons

Absolute magnitude: −1.41

Density: The mean density of Europa is a relatively high 3.04 gm/cm^3, slightly less dense than Earth's Moon

Mass: 4.873×10^{23} kg, a figure determined by de Sitter and Sampson in the 1920s

Diameter: 3138 km. It is planet-sized, is the smallest of the 4 Galileans, and is 12 percent smaller than Earth's Moon. Stower first measured its diameter in 1822

Apparent diameter, as seen from the surface of Jupiter: 17'30"

Temperature: Typical temperature is 103° K, and the maximum daytime temperature is 125° K. The nighttime temperature is 85° K

Subsolar temperature: About 145° K

Surface gravity: 130.9 cm/sec^2

Shape: Roughly spherical. From a distance it looks like a giant snowball

Surface: Essentially Europa is a white, rocky, silicate-rich body with an ice and water crust of between 75 and 100 km thick and a rocky interior. Beneath its icy crust may be a vast liquid water ocean. Europa's surface has no volcanoes and is mostly covered with ice. At first this moon was thought to be smooth as a billiard ball. Although it is the smoothest satellite in the solar system, it does have some vertical relief, although not much—perhaps only a few hundred meters. Like all the Galilean moons of Jupiter, it has a unique surface, with an age of about one billion years (which is young, but not nearly as young as Io's).

Europa's surface does not seem to consist of one layer deposited geologically over another, rather it seems to have been formed through disruption of a rather thick, icy crust with subsequent intrusion of underlying material along nearly vertical fractures. The surface is almost free of impact craters, only 5 having been discovered in the 10–30 km range, and only one of these (Cilix) has been named. The best Voyager 1 photographs (November 1980) show a bright, low-contrast surface with darker mottlings and a tantalizing network of lines that crisscross much of Europa's globe. In fact the surface does consist of plains and mottled terrain. The plains are generally bright, smooth, and of uniform color. The dark mottled terrain is densely packed with spots and patches of dark material.

From Voyager 1 photographs it was thought that the third, very striking feature was a maze of canals across Europa's surface. Voyager 2 took better photos in 1981, and showed this to be a crisscross of dark and light bands, or linea—very complex. The individual dark bands are usually between 20 and 40 km in width, and stretch for thousands of kilometers across Europa's surface. These bands might be cracks in the surface which were filled with water that froze. From Voyager 2 photos this feature now looks like pack-ice in Earth's polar regions. They look like the old drawings of Mars, and are remarkable. In 1957 Kuiper suggested that Europa has a water ice surface, and in 1961 Moroz came to the same conclusion. In 1973 Fink and his colleagues demonstrated that water ice is the main material on the surface of Europa. The satellite may have an oxygen atmosphere

Features: The largest craters are no more than 20 km across. All the features on Europa were named for personages associated with Europa in Greek mythology.

CRATER: Cilix (brother of Europa) 1°N, 182°W. LINEA: Adonis (nephew of Europa) 38–60°S, 122–113°W. Agenor (Europa's father) 44–35°S, 221–175°W. Argiope (Europa's mother) 20–1°S, 204–171°W. Asterius (Europa's husband after Zeus) 29°S–29°N, 314–251° W. Belus (Agenor's twin brother) 14–26°N, 226–170°W. Cadmus (Europa's brother) 29–26°N, 251–170°W. Libya (Agenor's mother) 66–41°S, 263–153° W. Minos (son of Europa and Zeus) 45–31°N, 119–150°W. Pelorus (founder of Thebes) 26°S–90°N, 195–110°W. Phineus (brother of Europa) 26–29°S, 340–314°W. Sarpedon (son of Europa and Zeus) 23–51°S, 94–80°W. Thasus (brother of Europa) 58–76°S, 176–217°W. FLEXI: Cilicia (named for Cilix, who sought Europa) 70–58°S, 200–153°W. Gortyna (place where Zeus brought Europa) 62–50°S, 182–146°W. Sidon (where Europa was born) 70–64°S, 215–150°W. MACULAE: Thera (where Cadmus stopped while seeking Europa) 48°S, 181°W. Thrace (where Cadmus stopped while seeking Europa) 47°S, 172°W. Tyre (where Zeus carried Europa away) 32°N, 147°W

Origin: Formed as part of the Jovian system. Scientists speculate that it may have life (microorganisms)

Discovery: By Galileo and Simon Mayr, coincidentally and at about the same time, in 1610 (*see* ***Io***). The least observed of the 4 Galileans (again, *see* ***Io***), even today, Europa was considered the least interesting of these 4 inner moons, until the Voyager trips in 1979. In 1961 Dollfus mapped it, very roughly, and on December 4, 1973, Pioneer 10 photographed it from 200,000 miles. Voyager 1 saw it distantly as a bright globe crisscrossed by dark curvilinear markings, and got to within 732,230 km of it. Voyager 2 got to within 204,000 km on July 9, 1979, and got a much better look. Both spacecraft photographed Europa in great detail

Photographs: see pages 143, 144

Febe see *Phoebe*

Fobos see *Phobos*

Ganimedes see *Ganymede*

Ganymede

Other names: Jupiter III, Jupiter 3, Jupiter Three, J3, Ganymed (in German), Ganimedes (in Spanish)

Named for: One of the lovers of Jupiter in mythology

Pronunciation: ga' ni mēd

Features on Earth named for it: Ganymede Heights on Alexander Island, Antarctica

Distance from Jupiter: Its mean distance from the center of Jupiter is 1,070,000 km

Synodic period: 7 days 3 hours 59 mins 35.856 secs

Sidereal period: 7.15455296 days

Orbital eccentricity: Between 0.001 and 0.002

Orbital inclination: 0.21 degrees

Location: Ganymede orbits in the plane of Jupiter's equator, so it always seems to be stretched out close to a line drawn through Jupiter. When it moves in front of Jupiter we see its shadow fall on the planet. It always keeps the same face toward Jupiter (*see also **Io***)

Escape velocity: 2.78 km/sec

Obliquity: Average is 3°.8

Visible magnitude: 4.61. Ganymede can be seen even with a small telescope (and perhaps even with the naked eye—see below, under *Discovery*)

Albedo: 0.42. The dark regions, frequently angular or polygonal in shape, are somewhat higher in albedo than Callisto's, but considerably lower than Ganymede's global average. Their color also matches Callisto's closely

Absolute magnitude: −2.09

Density: A mean of 1.93 gm/cm³, a near twin to Callisto

Mass: Determined by de Sitter and Sampson in the 1920s to be 1.490×10^{23} kg

Escape velocity: 2.78 km/sec

Mean angular distance from Jupiter, at mean opposition distance: 5'51".2

Diameter: 5276 km. It is planet-sized, 8 percent larger than Mercury, and 75 percent of the size of Mars. It is a near twin to Callisto in size, but bigger. It is about half water by weight. Ganymede is the largest and heaviest satellite in the solar system, 2.02 times larger than Earth's Moon. Stower first measured its diameter in 1822. In 1972 Ganymede occulted the star SAO 186800 (8th Magnitude), giving an approximate diameter of 5270 km. This was extremely close. It is actually 5276 km

Apparent diameter, as seen from the surface of Jupiter: 18'06"

Surface gravity: 142.1 cm/sec²

Subsolar temperature: About 155° K

Temperature: The temperature on the surface of Ganymede is about −150° centigrade on the sunlit hemisphere, and less on the night side

Shape: Roughly spherical

Surface: Ganymede's surface, like that of the other Galilean satellites (*see **Io***), is very individualistic. Ganymede is probably a rocky core with an ice and water mantle. It probably has an ice and rock crust and may have an oxygen atmosphere, although no atmosphere has yet been detected. The crust is about 75 km thick, and the surface is composed largely of nonrock. The ice giant of the solar system, Ganymede is densely cratered (as revealed by Voyager 1). It has remnants of a multi-ring system (*see **Callisto*** for details of such a system). There are dark regions on Ganymede and regions of lighter, grooved terrain. The dark regions, very heavily cratered, have now been shown to be the oldest parts of Ganymede's surface. This dark-light makeup is similar to Earth's Moon. The dark regions are probably the remains of the original crust. Galileo Regio and Nicholson Regio are two of the largest of these dark areas (see below, under *Features*).

Ganymede's grooved terrain occupies about 60 percent of the satellite's surface. It is the most distinctive feature of Ganymede. The grooved terrain has been formed at the expense of the ancient cratered terrain. Nothing like it is to be found anywhere else in the solar system. The grooves dominate the lighter regions. They are parallel sets of ridges and troughs, kilometers to tens of kilometers wide, and with perhaps a few hundred meters of vertical relief.

They form sets, or "bands" of grooves which wander for thousands of kilometers across Ganymede's surface, forming intricate patterns, particularly when different sets intersect or interact with each other. These groove systems border the dark terrain everywhere, and in some cases seem to extend into the blocks of dark terrain. This whole pale area looks as if it has been raked with a giant comb. Smooth plains occur in a few large areas, where they resemble lunar plains.

Topographic relief on Ganymede is generally 300–400 meters, and reaches a maximum of about 700 meters. Slopes are gentle, averaging about 5 degrees. In 1957 Kuiper suggested Ganymede has a water ice surface, and in 1961 Moroz came to the same conclusion. In 1973 Fink and his colleagues demonstrated that water ice is the dominant material on Ganymede's surface

Features: The only feature on Ganymede able to be seen from Earth by telescope is Galileo Regio, the dusky crust marking a large part of the far side of Ganymede. This prominent dark, circular area is about 3200 km across, and contains light-colored, closely-spaced bands that resemble those seen on Callisto. Part of Galileo Regio may be covered with a bright frost. Galileo Regio is characterized by a relatively high crater density and broadly arcuate rimmed troughs. Galileo Regio and Nicholson Regio combined make up 4 percent of Ganymede's surface.

Aside from these dark regions, there is a wide variety of large craters, including bowl-shaped, flat-floor, central-peaked, central-pit, basins, and giant multi-ring systems of ridges and furrows (*see* ***Callisto****—Surface*). Twenty-two readily recognizable palimpsests (*see* ***Callisto*** for a description of such objects) have been found on Ganymede, and another 12 possibles.

Gilgamesh seems to be the youngest basin on Ganymede. It is a fresh, relatively unmodified basin, located in the grooved terrain (it centers on 59°S, 123°W). The floor of its conspicuous central depression is relatively smooth and flat, and is about 150 km in diameter. Several small peaks are arranged in an arc, in the center of the floor. The diameter of this arc is about 50 km. Faint radial lineations also appear to be present on the floor. A poorly-defined rim, about 175 km in diameter, bounds the central depression. A rugged, hilly-to-mountainous region surrounds the central depression, and extends for about 500 km. A great swarm of secondary craters and catenae (chains of craters) surrounds the Gilgamesh basin. These craters extend for a radial distance of about 400–1000 km from the center of the basin. The diameters of most secondary craters are less than 5 km, but some craters up to about 15 km are present in the swarm.

The number of craters found on Ganymede, by diameter size (CT=in the cratered terrain; G=in the grooved terrain): 4 to 5.7 km, CT 2231, G 0; 5.7 to 8.0 km, CT 1000, G 0; 8.0 to 11.3 km, CT 559, G 0; 11.3 to 16.0 km, CT 291, G 216; 16.0 to 22.6 km, CT 154, G 195; 22.6 to 32.0 km, CT 106, G 123; 32.0 to 45.3 km, CT 71; G 79; 45.3 to 64.0 km, CT 20; G 43; 64.0 to 90.5 km, CT 6, G 20; 90.5 to 128 km, CT 1, G 2; 128 to 256 km, CT 0, G 1; 256 to 724 km, CT 0; G 1.

The craters on Ganymede were named from the most ancient Middle Eastern civilizations on Earth. Myth-related names were given to the arrays of linear grooves and to a few craters. The astronomers who discovered the satellites of Jupiter are commemorated by the names of the ancient regions of low albedo on Ganymede, i.e. Galileo, Marius, Nicholson, etc.

CRATERS: Achelous (River god, father of Ganymede's mother) 61°N, 14°W. Adad (Assyrian god of thunder) 56°N, 0°W. Adapa (Babylonian hero) 72°N, 30°W. Ammura (Phoenician god of the West) 31°N, 344°W. Anat (goddess of dew) 3°S, 128°W. Anu (Babylonian-Sumerian-Akkadian heaven god) 64°N, 346°W. Asshur (Assyrian war god) 53°N, 335°W. Aya (Assyro-Babylonian: wife of Shamash) 66°N, 325°W. Ba'al (Canaanite god) 24°N, 332°W. Danel (Phoenician mythical hero: a diviner) 4°S, 25°W. Diment (Egyptian goddess of the home of the dead) 23°N, 353°W. Enkidu (Babylonian-Assyrian wild man of the desert) 17°S, 322°W. Enlil (Babylonian nature god) 53°N, 315°W. Eshmun (a divinity of Sidon [Phoenicia]) 18° S, 192°W. Etana (flew high on the eagle's back, then crashed) 73°N, 342°W. Gilgamesh (Babylonian hero) 62°S, 123°W. Gula (Assyro-Babylonian goddess of health) 63°N, 13°W. Hathor (Egyptian goddess of love) 70°S, 267°W. Isis (Egyptian goddess, wife of Osiris) 68°S, 197°W. Keret (legendary Phoenician hero) 16°N, 38°W. Khumbam (Elamite creator god) 25°S, 338°W. Kishar (Assyro-Babylonian progenitor goddess) 71°N, 351°W. Melkart (a divinity of Tyre [Phoenicia]) 10°S, 186°W. Mor (Phoenician spirit of harvest) 30°N, 329° W. Nabu (Assyro-Babylonian intellectual god) 47°S, 9°W. Namtar (Assyro-Babylonian plague demon) 62°S, 354°W. Nigirsu (Assyro-Babylonian war god) 63°S, 321°W. Nut (Egyptian sky goddess) 61°S, 268°W. Osiris (Egyptian god of the dead) 38°S, 165°W. Ruti (Byblos god) 10°N, 309° W. Sapas (torch of the gods) 57°N, 38°W. Sebek (Egyptian crocodile god) 60°N, 358°W. Sin (Assyrian moon god) 52°N, 359°W. Tanit (Carthaginian goddess) 57°N, 41°W. Teshub (Hurrian weather god) 7°S, 21°W. Tros (father of Ganymede) 12°N, 31° W. Zagar (Zaqar) (Sin's messsenger) 58°N, 42°W. SULCI: Anshar (Sumerian-Akkadian celestial world) 32–15° N, 211–192°W. Apsu (Sumerian-Akkadian primoridal ocean) 38–16°S, 242–218°W. Aquarius (Zeus set Ganymede among the stars as Aquarius) 38–53°N, 30–7°W. Dardanus (where Ganymede was abducted by the eagles) 50°S–4°N, 35–7°W. Harpagia (where Ganymede was abducted by the eagles) 0–2°N, 328–313°W. Kishar (Sumerian-Akkadian terrestrial world) 20°S–0°, 230–208°W. Mashu (mountain where the Sun rose and set) 25–44°N, 184–221°W. Mysia (where Ganymede was abducted by the eagles) 15°S–9°N, 19–331°W. Nun (Chaos: primordial ocean) 42–57°N, 340–321° W. Philus (where Ganymede and Hebe worshiped) 36–55°N, 218–200°W. Phrygia (where Ganymede was born) 4–18°N, 25–0°W. Sicyon (where Ganymede and Hebe worshiped) 30–43° N, 24–359°W. Tiamat (Sumerian-Akkadian tumultuous sea) 19°N–12°S, 223–197°W. Uruk (Babylonian city ruled by Gilgamesh) 28°N–10°S, 179–143°W. REGIONES: Barnard (Edward Barnard [1857–1923] U.S.) 5°S–27°N, 25–342°W. Galileo (Galileo Galilei [1564–1642] Italy) 1–65°N, 80–180°W. Marius (Simon Mayr [Marius] [1570–1642] Germany) 55°S–52°N, 240–180°W. Nicholson (Seth Nicholson [1891–1963] U.S.) 42–55°S, 61–310° W. Perrine (Charles Perrine [1867–1951] U.S.) 18–53°N, 75–340°W

Origin: Probably part of the Jovian system originally

Discovery: By Galileo and Simon Mayr, coincidentally and at the same time, in January 1610. These two astronomers both independently discovered the 4 Galilean satellites, as they became known (Io, Ganymede, Callisto and Europa—for more on this *see* ***Io***). However, Ganymede was quite possibly seen with the naked eye by Chinese astronomer Gan De in 364 B.C. It was merely a point of light in the sky until Pioneer 10 took low resolution photographs in 1974. On December 3, 1974, Pioneer 11 photographed it from a distance of 460,000 miles. It had been first mapped in 1961, albeit crudely, by Dollfus. In 1979 came the Voyagers which took greatly detailed photos. On

March 5, 1979 Voyager 1 took photos of impact craters and grooved terrain on Ganymede, and came within 114,700 km of its surface. Voyager 2 was aimed for a closer flyby of Ganymede, and came within 62,100 km, photographing the hemisphere not seen by Voyager 1

Bibliography: "Grooved Terrain on Ganymede," by Baerbel K. Lucchitta, *Icarus* 44 (1980) 481

Photographs: see pages 118, 145

Hades *see* ***Sinope***

Helena *see* ***Pasiphaë***

Helene

Other names: Saturn XII, Saturn 12, Saturn Twelve, S12, 1980 S6, Dione B

Named for: Helen (Helene) of Troy, in Greek myth

Pronunciation: he lēn', hə lēn', he len', hə len', hə lē'nē, he lē'nē

Distance from Saturn: Its mean distance from the center of Saturn is about 377,420 km

Synodic period: 2 days 17 hours 44 mins 18 secs

Sidereal period: 2.7369 days (tropical period)

Orbital eccentricity: 0.005

Orbital inclination: 0.0 degrees

Location: It is in the same orbit as the larger Dione, but leads it by 60 degrees, hence the original name of Dione B. It is also known as a Dione Trojan because of the hard work it does in pulling Dione along in its orbit

Escape velocity: 14 m/sec

Mean angular distance from Saturn, at mean opposition distance: 1'0".1

Visible magnitude: Between 18.2 and 17.8

Albedo: Between 0.46 and 0.66

Absolute magnitude: +8.4

Diameter: Approximately 36×34×28 km

Shape: Irregular

Surface: Nothing known for sure, but probably icy

Subsolar temperature: About 126.3° K

Origin: Possibly the fragment of a larger body

Discovery: In March 1980, by P. Laques and J. Lecacheux. It was the 12th Saturnian moon to be discovered, and the first Saturnian co-orbital (co-orbiting as it does with Dione—see above under *Location*). Originally called Dione B, it was the last Saturnian satellite to be discovered from Earth. In November of that year Voyager 1 got to within 230,000 km of Helene, and Voyager 2 to within 318,200 km. Helene was discovered from Earth when Saturn's ring system was edgewise as seen from Earth and the spotting of Helene was easier. It is easier to see small satellites close to Saturn when this occurs

Hephaestus *see* ***Ananke***

Hera *see* ***Elara***

Heracles *see* ***Elara***

Hestia *see* ***Himalia***

Himalia

Other names: Jupiter VI, Jupiter Six, Jupiter 6, J6, Hestia (this was its original, unofficial name), Atlas (a prior suggested name—see below, under *Discovery*), Adrastea (another prior name—also see below)

Named for: One of Zeus's lovers in Greek mythology

Pronunciation: hi mä' lē ə, hi'mə lē ə

Distance from Jupiter: Its mean

distance from the center of Jupiter is 11,470,000 km

Location: It is the best known of the prograde outer group (Himalia, Elara, Lysithea, Leda) of the Jovian system

Orbital eccentricity: 0.15798

Orbital inclination: 27.6 degrees

Escape velocity: A mean of 0.1 km/sec

Rotation period: 9.5 hours

Mean angular distance from Jupiter, at mean opposition distance: 1°02'46"

Visible magnitude: 14.84. The brightest of the outer satellites of Jupiter

Albedo: Probably 0.02 to 0.03

Synodic period: 266 days

Sidereal period: 250.5662 days

Absolute magnitude: +8.14

Diameter: 186 km

Apparent diameter, as seen from the surface of Jupiter: 0'8".2

Shape: Irregular

Surface: Remarkably dark, heavily cratered, and neutral in color. Probably rocky, and probably made of carbonaceous chondritic material and water ice. There is no atmosphere on Himalia

Origin: Possibly a captured Trojan asteroid

Discovery: By C. D. Perrine in 1904–1905, using the Crossley Reflector at the Lick Observatory, on a plate taken on November 3, 1904. Perrine was not certain that it was a new satellite; he thought it might be an asteroid. After several weeks, though, he was convinced. The first name (unofficial) to be given to Jupiter 6 was Hestia, but in 1962 USSR amateur astronomer E. I. Nesterovich proposed the name Atlas (a name that went subsequently to one of the Saturnian satellites). In 1976 USSR astronomer Yuriy A. Karpenko proposed Adrastea (a name that also went elsewhere—*see* ***Adrastea***). It was later named Himalia by German philologist Johann Blunck. Distant satellites of Jupiter, that have direct (prograde) orbits, have names ending in "a"

Bibliography: Dictionary of Astronomical Names, by Adrian Room. Routledge, 1988

Hiperion see Hyperion

Hyperion

Other names: Saturn VII, Saturn 7, Saturn Seven, Hiperión (in Spanish)

Named for: The Titan in Greek mythology

Features on Earth named for it: Hyperion Nunataks, on Alexander Island, Antarctica

Pronunciation: hī pēr' e ən

Distance from Saturn: Its mean distance from the center of Saturn is 1,481,100 km

Synodic period: 21 days 7 hours 39 mins 5.7 secs

Sidereal period: 21.2766088 days (tropical period)

Orbital eccentricity: 0.1042

Orbital inclination: 0.43 degrees

Escape velocity: 0.19 km/sec

Orbit: Hyperion orbits between Titan and Iapetus. Its major axis is tilted at 45 degrees to the plane of its orbit. Such a position is unstable. It has a chaotic rotation period which seems to be about 13 days, but which changes all the time as the satellite tumbles along in its orbit

Orbital velocity: 5.1 km/sec

Visible magnitude: 14.19

Albedo: 0.3. Bond (the U.S. astronomer) thought it was much less bright

Absolute magnitude: +4.63

Mass: 1.10×10^{20} kg

Mean angular distance from Saturn, at mean opposition distance: 3'59".4

Diameter: 410×260×220 km. It is the largest of the small Saturnian satellites

Apparent diameter, as seen from the surface of Saturn: 0'43"

Subsolar temperature: About 118° K

Shape: Highly irregular. The longest axis does not point directly at Saturn, as it should do dynamically

Surface: Forty percent of the surface of Hyperión has been usefully imaged for surface features. Its surface is mostly ice. There is dirty ice water on the surface. The color of the surface is uniformly reddish, similar to but brighter than the dark side of Iapetus. Although pockmarked, Hyperión is not heavily cratered

Features: One crater (Helios) is 120 km across. Others are 40–50 km. The Bond-Lassell Dorsum is 300 km long. The features on Hyperión were named for Sun and Moon gods:

CRATERS: Bahloo (the Moon: maker of girl babies) 36°N, 196°W. Helios (Greek Sun god) 71°N, 132°W. Jarilo ([USSR] god of the Sun and fertility) 61°N, 183°W. Meri (Bororo [southern Brazil] folk hero: the Sun) 3°N, 171°W. DORSUM (a scarp): Bond-Lassell (the two discoverers of Hyperión) 12–84°N, 171°W

Origin: It is probably a captured body. The capture may be relatively recent; or, it may be the subject of a recent major collision (see above, under *Orbit*)

Discovery: On September 16, 1848 William Cranch Bond, the American astronomer, discovered the 8th Saturnian moon as the Saturnian rings were approaching their edgewise aspect. Two nights later, in Stardfield, near Liverpool, England, William Lassell saw it. Lassell proposed the name Hyperión, and Bond agreed. By 1849 the name was universally accepted. In 1980 Voyager 1 got to within 880,440 km of Hyperión, and in 1981 Voyager 2 to within 470,840 km

Photographs: see pages 120, 147

Iapetus

Other names: Saturn VIII, Saturn 8, Saturn Eight, Japetus (original spelling), Japet (in French), Japeto (in Spanish)

Named for: Sir John Herschel named it in 1847 for the Titan in Greek mythology

Features on Earth named for it: Iapetus Nunatek on Alexander Island, Antarctica

Pronunciation: ī ap' i təs, yap' i təs

Distance from Saturn: Its mean distance from the center of Saturn is 3,561,300 km

Synodic period: 79 days 22 hours 4 mins 59 secs

Sidereal period: 79.3301825 days (tropical period). Cassini calculated its revolution period as a little less than 80 days (he was right)

Mean angular distance from Saturn, at mean opposition distance: 9'35"

Orbital eccentricity: 0.02828

Orbital inclination: 14.72 degrees. Future spacemen will see Saturn well from Iapetus because the rings will not be edgewise

Escape velocity: A mean of 0.67 km/sec

Orbital velocity: 3.3 km/sec

Orbit: Iapetus is the outermost of the larger Saturnian satellites and has the largest orbit of any of Saturn's bright satellites

Visible magnitude: Ranges from 10.1 to 11.9, with an average of 11.2. Cassini discovered that its brightness is variable; in fact during one orbit its brightness varies by a factor of 6. Its magnitude varies because one side of Iapetus reflects 50 percent of the sunlight striking it, as does freshly fallen snow. The other hemisphere is so dark that it reflects only 5 percent. When west of Saturn in the sky it can be seen with a small telescope from Earth. When east of Saturn it becomes much fainter

Albedo: On the bright side it is 0.5, and on the dark side it is 0.05. It has the largest albedo variance in the solar system

Absolute magnitude: +0.6 on the

bright side, and +2.3 on the dark side

Diameter: 1448 km. Iapetus is an intermediate-sized satellite. It is 40 percent of the size of Earth's Moon

Apparent diameter, as seen from the surface of Saturn: 1'48"

Density: A mean of approximately 1.16 gm/cm^3, only slightly greater than that of water

Mass: 1.93×10^{21} kg

Surface gravity: 35.65 cm/sec^2

Subsolar temperature: On the bright side it is 107.9° K, and on the dark side it is 124.3° K

Shape: Irregular

Surface: Iapetus is an icy moon. The leading hemisphere is about the color and brightness of coal, nearly black. Then comes a 200–300 km "transition zone" between this dark side and the light, bright, icy trailing hemisphere, which is the brightness and color of dirty snow. In fact, the entire surface of Iapetus has a red coloring to it. Because Iapetus is an icy satellite, the dark material on the leading hemisphere covers a bright surface. For some time it was not known whether this black is caused from within the satellite, or if it came from some external source, i.e., it may have been knocked off the surface of Phoebe by micrometeoritic impacts, then been pulled toward Saturn by the planet's gravitational pull, and been collected by Iapetus. Dale Cruikshank, however, discovered that Phoebe's constituent material is different to that on the dark side of Iapetus, thus favoring the internal theory. Besides, some of the craters on the bright side have dark floors. This may support the theory that the dark material came from within the satellite.

There is no evidence of craters on the dark side. If this dark material (which is actually dark red) erupted from the center of the satellite, then Iapetus may have a differentiated core. Iapetus has a large, mysterious equatorial dark ring, or ring of dark red material, close to the boundary of the bright and dark sides. This ring is 400 km in diameter. It has a dark spot in the center. The ring is probably an impact crater, outlined by dark material ejected from the point of impact. Iapetus is not as well known as the other large Saturnian satellites

Features: The smallest features that can be seen from Voyager 2 photographs are about 20 km across. The features are named from Sayers's 1967 translation of "The Song of Roland":

CRATERS: Almeric (one of the 12 peers) 53°N, 274°W. Baligant (emir of Babylon) 15°N, 225°W. Basan (Frankish baron) 30°N, 197°W. Berenger (one of the 12 peers) 59°N, 220°W. Besgun (chief cook for Charlemagne's army) 72°N, 296°W. Charlemagne (king of the Franks) 54°N, 266°W. Geboin (leader of Charlemagne's 2nd Column) 56°N, 175°W. Godefroy (bearer of Charlemagne's gonfalcon) 78°N, 253°W. Grandoyne (son of King Capuel of Cappadocia) 18°N, 215°W. Hamon (joint commander of Charlemagne's 8th Division) 10°N, 271°W. Lorant (division commander) 64°N, 165°W. Marsilion (Saracen king of Spain) 41°N, 177°W. Milon (guard of the Frankish dead) 75° N, 270°W. Ogier (Danish leader of Charlemagne's 3rd Column) 42°N, 274°W. Oliver (Roland's friend) 61°N, 203°W. Othon (one of the 12 peers) 24°N, 344°W. Roland (Charlemagne's nephew) 78°N, 30°W. Turpin (Archbishop of Rheims) 43°N, 0°. REGIO: Cassini (Italian discoverer of Iapetus) 55°N–48°S, 210–340°W. TERRA: Roncevaux (pass where Roland and his forces were ambushed by the Spanish) 90°N–30°S, 300–130°W

Origin: Probably a captured body

Discovery: By G. D. Cassini on October 25, 1671, using one of Campani's telescopes. In 1672 Cassini could not find it again, even though he knew where it was. To explain this he concluded that Iapetus has a dark side and a bright side, and that it always keeps the same face toward Saturn (as Earth's Moon does to Earth). The second Saturnian satellite to be discovered, Iapetus remains the most mysterious of Saturn's moons. Voyager 1 came within 2,470,000 km of it in 1980, and in 1981 Voyager 2 came within 909,070 km

Ida see *Sinope*

Inner Epsilon Ring Shepherd see *Cordelia*

Inner F-ring Shepherd see *Prometheus*

Io

Other names: Jupiter I, Jupiter One, J1, Jo (in German)

Named for: A lover of Jupiter in mythology

Pronunciation: ī' o, ē' o

Distance from Jupiter: Its mean distance from the center of Jupiter is 421,600 km

Synodic period: 1 day 18 hours 28 mins 35.946 secs

Sidereal period: 1.769137786 days

Location: Io orbits within the plane of Jupiter's equator, so it always seems stretched out close to a line drawn through Jupiter. We see its shadow fall on the planet when Io moves in front of Jupiter. The 4 Galilean moons, Io, Europa, Ganymede and Callisto, were the first moons discovered outside of Earth's Moon. These 4 satellites form a "mini solar system" and lie deep within the Jovian magnetosphere. Instead of being continually exposed to the solar wind, as Earth's Moon is, they are immersed in the Jovian plasma environment and are bombarded by high-energy trapped charge particles

Orbit: Io's mean orbit is almost exactly circular, and Jupiter's strong gravity keeps the same side of Io facing the planet at all times. The four Galilean satellites (Io, Ganymede, Europa and Callisto) perturb each other's orbits significantly, and an orbital resonance with nearby Europa forces Io into a slightly eccentric orbit. The magnetic field of Jupiter is constantly sweeping past Io at a relative speed of about 57 km per second. Galileo demonstrated that orbital motion can take place around a central body other than Earth when he found the Galileans. Stebbins and Jacobsen, in 1928, proved that the rotations of the Galileans were synchronous with their orbit around Jupiter. Beginning around 1950 the Galileans were studied closely with new techniques

Orbital eccentricity: 0.004 (see also above, under *Orbit*)

Orbital inclination: 0.04 degrees

Escape velocity: A mean of 2.56 km/sec

Mean angular distance from Jupiter, at mean opposition distance: 2'18".4

Visible magnitude: 5.02. It can be seen with even a small telescope. In a large telescope it can be seen as a tiny disk. On August 21, 1867, the four Galileans were invisible, a very rare occurrence

Albedo: By 1960 it was known to have the high albedo of 0.61

Absolute magnitude: −1.68

Diameter: 3632 km. Io is planet-sized, and is 2 percent larger than Earth's Moon. Stower was the first to measure its diameter in 1822. Later the four Galileans were measured by Barnard with the new refractors at the Yerkes and Lick Observatories. In 1928 Stebbins and Jacobsen obtained the first photoelectric measurements of the Galileans. Albert Michelsen measured the diameters of the four Galileans with his stellar interferometer. In 1971 Io occulted β Scorpii C (a magnitude 5 star). This was well observed from

Earth, and gave the first high precision diameter for a Jovian satellite—approximately 3660 km. It has since been refined even more

Apparent diameter, as seen from the surface of Jupiter: 35'40"

Density: Io's mean density is a relatively high 3.53 gm/cm^3, slightly more dense than Earth's Moon, and the densest of the Galileans

Mass: Determined by de Sitter and Sampson in the 1920s to be 8.916×10^{23} kg, similar to Earth's Moon

Temperature: Typical noontime highs on Io's equator are 120° K

Shape: Roughly spherical

Surface gravity: 179.4 cm/sec^2, about one-sixth that of Earth's

Surface: The surface of Io is totally individual, very unlike any other satellite in the solar system. It is also the most active body in the solar system, its most salient point being its volcanoes (see eruptive centers, under *Features,* below), and has an extremely youthful surface. Essentially Io is a rocky, silicate-rich body, with a molten silicate interior, and it has no appreciable atmosphere. Io has the greatest topographic relief of any of the Galilean satellites. About 95 percent of it is layered plains and vent flows. Mountain regions exist near both poles. The highest mountain rises 9 km from the surface. There are steep scarps up to 2 km high.

By 1960 it was known that the surface of Io is red and that it has no ice. However, there are wildly different colors on Io and the moon has a "diseased" appearance, with great splotchy regions of orange, yellow, white and black.

What look like craters are paterae (a patera is an albedo feature, an irregular depression). A total of 170 paterae had been mapped on 35 percent of Io's surface by 1982, together with 151 lineaments and grabens. No impact craters have been found. There are several "hot spots" on the surface of Io, and these hot spots have a temperature of 17° centigrade in a surrounding area of −146° centigrade.

Io is probably resurfaced at the rate of several centimeters a year, and this would be accomplished largely through the transport of liquids to the surface of the moon. The white patches on Io may be sulfur dioxide snow, and hydrogen sulfide has been found to exist in the form of frost. Nowhere else but on Earth has this substance been found. There is no water on Io or in its tenuous atmosphere. Sulfur dioxide gas has been found near Loki (*see* eruptive centers, under *Features,* below). Binder and Cruikshank first proposed the possibility of an Ionian atmosphere in 1964.

In 1973 the Pioneer 10 radio occultation firmly established the existence of an atmosphere—although not much of one. Sulfur dioxide is the major known constituent of Io's atmosphere; potassium is also present. Io's red-orange color is due primarily to the sulfur presence. In 1972 Brown discovered unexpectedly that sodium is emitted from Io, and several observers quickly demonstrated the existence of a large, nearby, banana-shaped cloud of sodium leading Io along its orbit. Pioneer 10 discovered that Io has a reasonably dense ionosphere, with electron densities of 10–1000 per cubic centimeter

Features: ERUPTIVE CENTERS: the main features of Io are the plumes. The surface of the moon is covered with volcanoes. The active ones have probably spewed out material into a doughnut-shaped ring, or "torus," enveloping Io's orbit. This is not to be confused with the thin, flat, disk-like ring close to Jupiter's surface. Now that such a torus has been seen by the Voyagers, older, uncertain observations made from Earth can be reinterpreted as early sightings of this structure. The low gravity and little atmosphere allow the volcanic gas and dust to rise unimpeded, geyserlike, to great heights, then fall back on the surface, frequently forming mushroom-shaped plumes. Io's fountainlike plumes are among the most impressive and beautiful sights in the solar system.

The first indication of Ionian volcanism was discovered on March 9, 1979, by Linda Morabito from Voyager 1 photographs, which showed that 8 volcanoes were in a state of eruption as Voyager 1 flew by that month. About 10 are probably erupting in 1991. Volcanic eruptions may last several years. The volcanoes are hot (about 440° F), and some are bigger than any ever seen on Earth. They seem to be caused by gravitational forces which in turn cause tidal stresses within Io, which intensely heats up the interior and leads to volcanoes. The volcanic vents are well over 500° centigrade in temperature, and very long lava flows stretch for hundreds of kilometers from some calderas.

As indicated before, the main Ionian features are these plumes (eruptions visible out of volcanoes, or calderas). There are perhaps 200 calderas with diameters greater than 20 km (Earth has only 15 or so, and its surface area is 3½ times that of Io). As for the naming of the features on Io, the original plan was to use names from Earth's equatorial-zone myths, but this idea was abandoned when prominent volcanic eruptions were discovered by the Voyagers in 1979. Instead, the features from which the eruptions (or plumes) emanated, and similar features thought to be dormant eruptive centers, were assigned names of fire, sun and smith gods associated with volcanoes on Earth. For example, the largest volcano on Io, Pele, was named for the Hawaiian goddess of volcanoes. Myth-related names were given to nonvolcanic features (see *Satellites of Jupiter* below, under *Bibliography*).

Plume 1: Pele. 19°S, 256°W. Named for the Hawaiian volcano goddess. Pele is the most active of the calderas on Io. When Voyager 1 went by in March 1979 the plume of Pele was 280 km high. Four months later, when Voyager 2 went by, it was quiet. Pele, which is dome-shaped, rises above the eastern limb of Io. *Plume 2:* Loki (West). 19–17°N, 306–301°W. Named for the Norse smith god. Originally called simply Loki, it was 100 km high when Voyager 1 went by. When Voyager 2 went by it was 225 km high and about 430 km wide. Loki (West) is rather asymmetrical, due to the shape of its vent. Later studies revealed that this was really Loki (West); Loki (East) was then added to the list of separate plumes. *Plume 3:* Prometheus. 2°S, 153° W. Named for the Greek fire god. It is one of the most distinctive surface markings on Io. It has a bright annulus about 330 km in diameter surrounding a darker region 230 km in diameter, with irregular black markings. It has a symmetrical umbrella shape and is about 270 km wide and 77 km high. Between the visits of Voyager 1 and Voyager 2 it had increased in size. *Plume 4:* Volund. 22°N, 177°W. Named for the supreme Germanic smith god. Very irregular in shape, like a mushroom with an elongated top slanted to one side, Volund's maximum height is about 120 km and the width is about 95 km. This is one of the few plumes whose height is greater than its width. *Plume 5:* Amirami. 28–21°N, 118°W. Named for the Georgian god of fire. Height between 70 and 95 km. *Plume 6:* Maui. 19°N, 122°W. Named for the Hawaiian demigod who sought fire for Mafuike. Between 70 and 95 km. Consists of two dark streaks that coincide with the two brightest components that make up its central core. *Plume 7:* Marduk. 27°S, 209°W. Sumero-Akkadian fire god. Consists of three dark markings, connected by an irregular black line. Height of Marduk is 120 km. *Plume 8:* Masubi. 39°S, 56°W. Named for the Japanese fire god. Height about 60 km, but its shape and width are uncertain due to faint photography. *Plume 9:* Loki (East). 17°N, 300°W. Named in association with Loki (West) (see Plume 2 above). Surt (see immediately below) *was* Plume 9, until the discovery that Loki was, in fact, two separate plumes, then Surt was relegated to Plume 10. Loki (East) is about 200 km high and about 400 km wide. *Plume 10:* Surt. 45°N, 338°W. Named for the Icelandic fire god. At first thought to be between 70 and 95 km in height, it is now believed to be as much as 300 km, and possibly 1200 km in width. It was not active during Voyager 1's flyby, but was possibly active during Voyager 2's flyby. *Plume 11:* Aten. 48°S, 312°W. Named for the Sun's disk in Egyptian mythology. About 300 km high, and possibly 1200 km wide. It was not active during either of the Voyager flybys.

CATENAE (a catena is a chain of craters, or crater-like features): Mazda (Babylonian sun god) 9°S, 313°W. Reshet (Reshef) (Syrian god) 1°N, 299°W. MONTES (Mountains): Boösaule Montes 2°S, 266°W. Crimea Mons (the country) 72°S, 244°W. Euboea Montes (Greek island) 47°S, 340°W. Haemus Mons (Io passed by here in her wanderings) 70°S, 50°W. Silpium Mons (Io died of grief here) 52°S, 274°W. PLANI (a planum is a high plateau): Argos (Io's homeland) 48°S, 321°W. Danube (river) 22°S, 256°W. Dodona (Io went here after the death of Argus) 50–60°S, 5–335°W. Ethiopia (the country) 44°S, 30°W. Hybristes 53°S, 18°W. Iopolis 35°S, 326°W. Lyrcea 40°S, 265°W. Nemea (where Io was turned into a cow by Zeus) 75–85°S, 210–320°W. FLUCTI (a fluctus is a wave-like feature): Euboea (the island) 45°S, 355°W. Tung Yo (Taoist god) 12°S, 352°W. Uta (Galla [Ethiopia] god) 30°S, 16°W. MENSAE (a mensa is a table-like feature): Echo (the nymph) 79°S, 358°W. Epaphus (son of Io and Zeus) 53°S, 240°W. Lynx 61°S, 303°W. Pan (the god) 52°S, 35°W. THOLI (a tholus is a circular, domed feature): Apis (another name for Epaphus, son of Io) 11°S, 349°W. Inachus (father of Io) 16°S, 349°W. REGIONES (a regio is a large, flat feature): Bactria (Io passed through here in her wanderings) 35–50°S, 120–130°W. Chalybes (Io passed through here in her wanderings) 45–70°N, 70–120°W. Colchis (the country) 10°N, 170°W. Joppa (Io passed through here in her wanderings) 0–50°N, 130–210° W. Media (Io passed through here in her wanderings) 20°S–30°N, 0–100° W. Lerna (meadows of Lyrcea) 55–70°S, 280–310°W. Mycenae (Io transformed here [in some legends]) 30–55°S, 130–180°W. Tarsus (ancient city) 30°S, 55°W. PATERAE (a patera is an irregular depression): Agni (Indian god) 42°S, 332°W. Amaterasu (Japanese Sun goddess) 38°N, 307°W. Angpetu 21°S, 12°W. Aramazd (Armenian creator of Heaven and Earth) 73° S, 337°W. Asha (Persian spirit of fire) 9°S, 226°W. Atar (Iranian personification of fire) 30°N, 279°W. Aten (Egyptian sun god) 48°S, 311°W. Babbar (Mongolian sun god) 40°S, 272°W. Bochica (Chibcha sky god) 61°S, 22°W. Carancho 2°N, 312°W. Cataquil 25°S, 19°W. Creidne (Celtic smith hero) 51°S, 344°W. Culann (Celtic smith hero) 18°S, 160°W. Daedalus (Greek smith hero) 19°N, 275°W. Dazhbog (Slavonic god of Sun) 55°N, 302°W. Dinjir (Sumerian word for "god") 5°S, 336°W. Emakong (Sulca [North Britain] man who brought fire) 3°S, 119°W. Fuchi (Ainu fire goddess) 28°N, 328°W. Galai (Mongolian fire god) 11°S, 288°W. Gibil (Assyrian fire god) 15°S, 295°W. Hatchawa 58°S, 36°W. Heiseb 30°N, 242°W. Heno (Iroquois thunder god) 57°S, 312°W. Hephaestus (Greek smith god) 2°N, 290°W. Hiruko (Japanese sun god) 65° S, 330°W. Horus (Egyptian falcon-headed sun god) 10°S, 340°W. Huo Shen 15°S, 329°W. Ilmarinen (Finnish smith god) 13°S, 15°W. Inti (Inca sun god) 68°S, 349°W. Kane (Hawaiian god of sunlight) 48°S, 14°W. Kava (Persian blacksmith in mythology) 18° S, 336°W. Khalla 6°N, 299°W. Kibero 12°S, 306°W. Loki (Norse smith god) 13°N, 310°W. Lu Huo 38°S, 350°W. Maasaw (Hopi god of fire and death) 40°S, 341°W. Mafuike (Hawaiian demigoddess whose fingers contained fire) 13°S, 260°W. Malik (Babylonian, Canaanite, Syrian Sun god) 34°S, 129° W. Mama (four mythological Inca sisters) 10°S, 352°W. Manua (Hawaiian sun god) 35°N, 322°W. Masaya (Nicaraguan sun god) 22°S, 349°W. Maui (Hawaiian demigod who sought fire for Mafuike) 16°N, 124°W. Mbali 32° S, 7°W. Menahka 31°S, 339°W. Mihr (Armenian fire god) 16°S, 306°W. Mithra (Persian god of light) 58°S, 267°W. Nina (Inca fire god) 38°S, 166°W. Ninurta (Babylonian god) 17°S, 310°W. Nusku (Assyrian fire god) 63°S, 7°W. Nyambe (Zambesi sun god) 4°S, 342°W. Päive 46°S, 1°W. Pautiwa (Zuñi lord of the dead) 33°S, 348°W. Podja 19°S, 299°W. Purgine (Finno-Ugric god of thunder) 2°S, 293°W. Pyerun 56°S, 252°W. Ra (Egyptian sun god) 8°S, 325°W. Reiden (Japanese thunder god) 13°S, 236°W. Ruwa (Wachaga [Africa] god associated with Kilimanjaro) 1°N, 4°W. Sed (Carthaginian sun god) 4°S, 299°W. Sengen (god of Fujiyama) 33° S, 304°W. Shakuru (Pawnee sun god of the east) 24°N, 266°W. Shamash (Assyro-Babylonian sun god) 34°S, 152°W. Shoshu 19°S, 324°W. Sium 50°S, 357°W. Sui Jen (Chinese fire god) 20°S, 2°W. Svarog (Russian smith god) 48°S, 267°W. Talos (Cretan brazen giant) 26°S, 356°W. Taranis (Gaulish thunder god) 72°S, 20°W. Taw 33°S, 1°W. Tohil (Central American god who gave fire to man) 25°S, 158°W. Tol-ava 1°N, 325°W. Tung Yo (Taoist god) 19°S, 358°W. Ülgen (Siberian progenitor god who struck first fire) 41°S, 289°W. Uta (Early Sumerian sun god) 35°S, 25°W. Vahagn (Armenian sun god) 26°S, 357°W. Viracocha (Quechua sun god) 62°S, 281°W

Origin: Formed as part of the original Jovian system, but its evolution is unknown

Discovery: Galileo first looked at Jupiter through a telescope one hour after sunset on the evening of January 7, 1610, in Padua, Italy. He saw three moons, the first moons to be discovered outside Earth's system. He also proved that orbital motion could exist around a body other than Earth. On January 10, 1610, he looked at Jupiter again and saw two moons. On January 12 he saw three again. On January 13 he saw four for the first time, four individual moons of Jupiter. Tradition has it that he saw Io, Europa and Ganymede first, on January 7, and finally Callisto on the 13th. However, many of his observations may have included two moons seen as one; so, in fact, he probably saw all four on the first night, but did not know it.

Galileo published his findings in *Siderius Nuncius* in March 1610, calling his four satellites the Medicean Stars, for his employers, the Medici. We now know them as the Galilean satellites, i.e. Io, Europa, Ganymede and Callisto (working outwards from Jupiter). Galileo did not name them individually, he simply numbered them, beginning with the moon closest to Jupiter (i.e., Io).

Around this time the German astronomer Simon Mayr (or Marius) claimed to have discovered the big four Jovians first (in 1609), but since Galileo published first, he gets the credit. In October 1613 Kepler suggested the four individual names to Marius who published them thus in 1614. Ole Roemer used the eclipses of the Galileans to determine the speed of light. Much later came the first attempt to map the Galileans, by French astronomer Audouin Dollfus and his colleagues at the Pic du Midi Observatory in 1961.

These maps were of course, hopeless guesswork. In 1964 observers found that Io is bright for about 15 minutes after some, but not all, eclipses.

The Galileans remained merely points of light in the sky until Pioneer 10 became the first spacecraft to enter the Jovian system, in December 1973. Pioneer 10, launched from Earth in 1972, and its successor, Pioneer 11, launched in 1973, were designed to prove the ability of humans to send spacecraft into outer space. Their scientific discoveries of the Jovian system were a bonus. Pioneer 11 entered Jupiter's system in December 1974, photographing Io on December 4, from a distance of 470,000 miles.

In 1979 came the Voyagers. Just before the Voyager 1 encounter with Io, in March, Peale and his associates predicted that volcanic activity was probable on Io. At this point there were 12 known moons of Jupiter (13 if you included 1975 J1, discovered by Kowal in 1975). Voyager 1 was aimed for a close flyby of Io, and in March 1979 came within 20,600 km of its surface. Voyager 1, on March 2, 1979, first distinguished large circular features, and on March 8 images of volcanic eruptions were beamed to Earth. On March 11 additional eruptions and localized hot spots were identified. Voyager 2 was not particularly geared for Io, but it was reprogrammed for a 10-hour "Io watch" from a range of 10 million kilometers, in order to study the active volcanoes. Voyager 2's closest approach to Io was 1,129,900 km, in July 1979.

Preliminary maps of the Galileans were produced soon after the arrival of the pictures from the Voyagers. Schaber mapped Io in 1981. The area photographed in detail by Voyager 1 and mapped by Schaber lies between 250° and 323°W and includes the volcanic plumes Pele and Loki (West)

Bibliography: Planetary Satellites, ed. by J. A. Burns. University of Arizona Press, Tucson, 1977. The result of an international meeting at Ithaca, N.Y., on August 18–21, 1974, to discuss the 34 known satellites at that time

Satellites of Jupiter, ed. by David Morrison. University of Arizona Press, Tucson, 1982

"The View from Io," by William K. Hartmann, *Astronomy,* May 1981

"Galileo's First Records of Jupiter's Satellites," by Jean Meeus, *Sky and Telescope,* September 1962

"Evolution of Io," by David Morrison, *Astronomy,* February 1976

"The Enigma Called Io," by David Morrison, *Sky and Telescope,* March 1985

Vertical Dimensions of the Galilean Satellites, by D. W. G. Arthur. NASA TM 81776, 1981

Photograph: see page 146

Janus

Other names: Saturn 10, Saturn X, S10, Saturn Ten, 1980 S1, 1966 S1 (see below under *Discovery*)

Named for: The Roman god of beginnings and endings

Pronunciation: jā' nəs, ja' nəs

Distance from Saturn: Its mean distance from the center of Saturn is 151,472 km

Synodic period: 16 hours 40 mins 18.96 secs

Sidereal period: 0.694667 days (tropical period)

Location: Between Mimas and the F-ring, it is co-orbital with Epimetheus (q.v.)

Orbital eccentricity: 0.007

Orbital inclination: 0.14 to 0.15 degrees

Visible magnitude: 14.1

Albedo: 0.63

Absolute magnitude: +4.4

Mean angular distance from Saturn, at mean opposition distance: 24"

Escape velocity: 75 m/sec

Density: Almost certainly less than 1.0 gm/cm^{-3}, which is low

Diameter: 220×180×160 km

Subsolar temperature: About 112° K

Shape: Irregular, and pear-shaped

Surface: Fifty percent of the surface of Janus has been usefully imaged for features. The surface itself is relatively bright, heavily cratered and icy

Features: As of 1984 there were 12 craters observed on Janus, and four are named (for characters in Greek mythology): Castor, Idas, Lynceus, Phoibe

Origin: Possibly the fragment of a larger body

Discovery: In December 1966 Audouin Dollfus, the French astronomer, set out to find the object that was perturbing the Saturnian ring system. He predicted it to be a moon and so, using the 43-inch reflector at the Meudon Observatory, he found something during the excellent viewing conditions of December 15, 1966. Its images were found by Dollfus on three plates—east of Saturn on December 15, and west of Saturn on December 16 and December 17. Dollfus called it a "probable satellite." Richard L. Walker of the U.S. Naval Observatory in Flagstaff, Arizona, took photographs with his 61-inch astrometric reflector on the night of December 17–18, 1966, when visibility was poor, and on January 3, 1967 studied his plates and was able to "confirm" the new satellite. He estimated its magnitude to be between 13.5 and 14. Dollfus had put it at 14. It was later found that images on four plates taken by Jean Texereau of the McDonald Observatory in Texas on October 29, 1966, also showed the object, which was now tentatively named, as 1966 S1. It was also shown on the plate taken at Pic du Midi Observatory in France on January 9, 1967. Dollfus had originally given it a distance from Saturn of 315,000 km, with a revolution period of 18 hours (0.815 days).

In early 1967 an almost circular path was proposed, in 17 hours 58 mins 30 secs, at a distance of 2.65 Saturn radii from the center of the planet. Dollfus named it Janus. It was the first of ten in closeness to Saturn, and the last of ten to be discovered, so Dollfus named it for the god of beginnings and endings. His discovery was widely accepted (far more so than it should have been), and even included in the *American Ephemeris and Nautical Almanac.*

Additional information was given for this very faint moon located just clear of the outer edge of the ring system of Saturn: *distance from Saturn's center:* 157,000 (later 159,000) km; *diameter:* about 350 km (later 300 km); *Albedo:* about 0.6; *magnitude:* 14; *orbital period:* 17.98 hours; *orbital velocity:* 15.5 km/sec; *orbital eccentricity:* 0.00; *orbital inclination:* 0.00 degrees; *apparent diameter, as seen from the surface of Saturn:* 6'.3.

By and by it became clear that there was no such satellite moving in the orbit described by Dollfus and colleagues, although most satellite listings between 1966 and 1980 (the year of the revelatory Voyager 1 flyby) include a "tenth satellite" of Saturn in an orbit not corresponding to either present-day Janus or its co-orbital Epimetheus. In 1978 John Fountain and Stephen Larson observed what looked like the real "Janus," and this was, indeed, confirmed on November 12, 1980, by Voyager 1, which came within 297,000 km of the satellite. It was called 1980 S1. Voyager 2 came within 222,760 km, and the name Janus was applied to this new satellite, in its new position. What Dollfus had seen in 1966 was probably the real Janus and Epimetheus combined

Photograph: see page 123

Japet, Japeto, Japetus see *Iapetus*

J8, Jupiter VIII see *Pasiphaë*

J11, Jupiter XI *see* ***Carme***

J15, Jupiter XV *see* ***Thebe***

J5, Jupiter V *see* ***Amalthea***

J4, Jupiter IV *see* ***Callisto***

J14, Jupiter XIV *see* ***Adrastea***

J14, Jupiter XIV *see* ***1975 J1***

Jo *see* ***Io***

J1, Jupiter I *see* ***Io***

J9, Jupiter IX *see* ***Sinope***

J7, Jupiter VII *see* ***Elara***

J17, Jupiter XVII *see* ***Adrastea***

J6, Jupiter VI *see* ***Himalia***

J16, Jupiter XVI *see* ***Metis***

J10, Jupiter X *see* ***Lysithea***

J13, Jupiter XIII *see* ***Leda***

J3, Jupiter III *see* ***Ganymede***

J12, Jupiter XII *see* ***Ananke***

J2, Jupiter II *see* ***Europa***

Juliet

Other names: Uranus XI, Uranus 11, Uranus Eleven, U11, 1986 U2

Named for: Named by the I.A.U. in 1988 for Shakespeare's character in *Romeo and Juliet*

Pronunciation: jo͞o' lē ət, jo͞o' lē et

Distance from Uranus: Its mean distance from the center of Uranus is about 64,352 km

Location: Between Miranda and the rings of Uranus

Synodic period: 11 hours 50 mins

Sidereal period: 0.493066 days

Orbital eccentricity: low, probably 0

Orbital inclination: low, probably 0 degrees

Escape velocity: Very low

Density: Almost certainly low

Orbit: Its rotational period is synchronous with its orbital period (i.e., the same face of Juliet is always shown to Uranus)

Mean angular distance from Uranus, at mean opposition distance: 5"

Diameter: Approximately 80 km

Albedo: Low, about 0.1

Shape: Unknown exactly, but probably roughly spherical

Surface: Dark and methane-coated

Origin: Probably formed from the accretion of comets

Discovery: On January 3, 1986, by Voyager 2 (*see* ***Puck***)

Bibliography: Science, 233 (July 4, 1986), 39–109

Kallisto *see* ***Callisto***

Karme *see* ***Carme***

Larissa *see* ***1989 N2***

Latona see *Lysithea*

Leda

see also ***Carme***

Other names: Jupiter XIII, Jupiter 13, Jupiter Thirteen, J13

Named for: Named by its discoverer Kowal for a lover of Jupiter in mythology

Pronunciation: lē' də

Distance from Jupiter: Its mean distance from the center of Jupiter is 11,110,000 km

Synodic period: 254 days

Sidereal period: 238.72 days

Orbital eccentricity: 0.14762

Orbital inclination: 26.07 degrees

Escape velocity: A mean of about 0.005 km/sec

Visible magnitude: 20.2

Albedo: Probably 0.02 to 0.03

Mean angular distance from Jupiter, at mean opposition distance: 1°00'39"

Diameter: Between 2 and 16 km, probably closer to 14 km. It is possibly the smallest satellite in the solar system (although *see* ***1981 S12***)

Apparent diameter, as seen from the surface of Jupiter: 0'0".15

Absolute magnitude: +13.5

Shape: Irregular

Surface: Probably carbonaceous dirt and water ice. There is no atmosphere

Origin: May be a captured Trojan asteroid

Discovery: On September 14, 1974, by Charles T. Kowal. On that day he was inspecting photographs he had taken on the nights of September 10, 11 and 12 of that year with the Palomar 48-inch Schmidt Telescope, as part of the search for Jovian satellites. He found one. On September 22, 1974, R. Weymann and R. Cromwell confirmed it from plates taken using the 90-inch Steward Observatory telescope on Kitt Peak, Arizona. From these plates Carolyn McCarthy found Leda within 2 mins of arc from the expected place. On October 16 and 17, 1974, Kowal refound Leda

Lysithea

Other names: Jupiter X, Jupiter 10, Jupiter Ten, J10, Demeter (this was its original, unofficial name), Prometheus (a prior suggested name; see below, under *Discovery*), Latona (another suggested name; see below, under *Discovery*)

Named for: Mother of Dionysius and mother of Zeus in Greek mythology

Pronunciation: lī si thē' ə, li si thē' ə

Distance from Jupiter: Its mean distance from the center of Jupiter is 11,720,000 km

Synodic period: 276 days

Sidereal period: 259.22 days

Orbital eccentricity: 0.1074

Orbital inclination: 29 degrees

Escape velocity: A mean of about 0.01 km/sec

Mean angular distance from Jupiter, at mean opposition distance: 1°04'04"

Visible magnitude: 18.4

Albedo: Probably 0.02 to 0.03

Absolute magnitude: +11.7

Diameter: Between 6 and 36 km, probably closer to 32 km

Apparent diameter, as seen from the surface of Jupiter: 0'0".03

Shape: Irregular

Origin: Possibly a captured Trojan asteroid

Surface: Probably carbonaceous dirt and water ice. There is no atmosphere

Discovery: By Seth Nicholson, on July 6, 1938, at the Mount Wilson Observatory, near Pasadena, Calif., on photographs taken by the 100-inch telescope at the observatory. Originally it was unofficially called Demeter, and in 1962 USSR amateur astronomer E. I. Nesterovich suggested the name Prometheus (a name that later went to another satellite—*see* ***Prometheus***). In 1976 USSR astronomer Yuriy A.

Karpenko proposed Latona, but it was later named Lysithea by German philologist Johann Blunck

Bibliography: Dictionary of Astronomical Names, by Adrian Room. Routledge, 1988

Metis

Other names: Jupiter XVI, Jupiter 16, J16, Jupiter Sixteen, 1979 J3

Named for: The goddess who caused the child-devouring Saturn to spit out Jupiter's siblings

Pronunciation: me' tis, mē' tis

Distance from Jupiter: Its mean distance from the center of Jupiter is 127,960 km. It is 56,200 km above Jupiter's cloud tops

Synodic period: 7 hours 6 mins

Sidereal period: 0.294780 days

Location: The innermost satellite of Jupiter. It may help stabilize Jupiter's ring

Orbital eccentricity: 0

Orbital inclination: 0 degrees

Escape velocity: A mean of about 0.02 km/sec

Orbital velocity: 113,600 km per hour (31.6 km/sec), which makes it the fastest moving moon yet discovered in the solar system

Visible magnitude: 17.5

Albedo: Low, probably 0.05

Absolute magnitude: +10.8

Mean angular distance from Jupiter, at mean opposition distance: 42"

Diameter: Approximately 40×40 km

Subsolar temperature: 120° K

Shape: Irregular

Surface: Dark. It may well be rocky, with no ice. There is no atmosphere

Origin: Possibly a source for the Jovian ring, it may have been formed by an accretion of dust from Jupiter

Discovery: By Stephen Synnott in 1980 from Voyager photographs. It has been seen only in transit across Jupiter's disk

Mimas

Other names: Saturn I, Saturn One

Named for: Named in 1847 by Sir John Herschel for the giant in Greek mythology

Pronunciation: mī' mas, mī' məs, mē' mas, mē' məs

Features on Earth named for it: Mimas Peak, on Alexander Island, Antarctica

Art: In 1981 Ron Miller painted "View from Mimas." This painting can be seen through the NASA Art Program. It was the first painting of a Saturnian satellite, and shows an imaginary view looking across Herschel crater at Saturn

Distance from Saturn: Its mean distance from the center of Saturn is 185,520 km

Synodic period: 22 hours 37 mins 12.4 secs

Sidereal period: 0.942421813 days (tropical period)

Location: It is the smallest and innermost of the "classical" spherical, regular, brighter satellites of Saturn, and is to be found between rings G and E

Orbital eccentricity: 0.0202

Orbital inclination: 1.53 degrees

Escape velocity: A mean of 0.1 km/sec

Mean angular distance from Saturn, at mean opposition distance: 0'30"

Density: A mean of 1.44 gm/cm^3 approximately

Mass: 3.76×10^{19} kg

Diameter: 394 km. It is an intermediate-sized satellite

Apparent diameter, as seen from the surface of Saturn: 10'54"

Visible magnitude: 12.9. Look for it with at least an 8-inch telescope, at eastern or western elongation. It is very hard to find

Albedo: 0.5 to 0.7

Absolute magnitude: +3.3

Orbital velocity: 14.4 km/sec

Shape: Roughly spherical

Surface gravity: 6.57 cm/sec^2

Subsolar temperature: About 103° K

Surface: Mimas has a high density of craters on its old surface, and it was known before 1980 that water ice is present. Mimas is icy inside and out, and became a rock-hard, icy surface long ago

Features: The main feature on Mimas is Herschel, an enormous crater 130 km across, almost one-third the diameter of Mimas itself. It is difficult to understand how the satellite could have received such an impact and survived. It must have nearly wrecked Mimas. The walls of Herschel have an average height of 5 km, and the crater may be more than 10 km. The crater has a massive central mountain, with a base measuring 30×20 km. It rises to 6 km above the floor of the crater. Originally to be called Arthur crater, Herschel is nearly centered on the leading hemisphere of Mimas. The next leading crater, after Herschel, is less than half its size. The features on this moon (except Herschel) were named from Baines's 1962 translation of Malory's "Morte d'Arthur":

CRATERS: Accolon (companion of Arthur) 68°S, 166°W. Arthur (the King) 35°S, 190°W. Balin (a knight) 22°N, 82°W. Ban (father of Sir Lancelot) 47°N, 149°W. Bedivere (a knight) 10°N, 145°W. Bors (King of Gaul) 45°N, 165°W. Dynas (a knight) 8°N, 75°W. Elaine (mother of Sir Galahad) 44°N, 102°W. Gaheris (son of King Lot) 46°N, 287°W. Galahad (a knight) 47°S, 135°W. Gareth (a knight) 44°S, 280°W. Gawain (a knight) 60°S, 254°W. Gwynevere (wife of King Arthur) 12°S, 312°W. Herschel (the astronomer, William Herschel) 0°, 104°W. Igraine (mother of Arthur) 40°S, 225°W. Iseult (lover of Tristram) 48°S, 35°W. Kay (a knight) 48°N, 116°W. Lamerok (son of Pellinore) 65°S, 283°W. Lancelot (a knight) 10°S, 317°W. Lot (father of Sir Gawain) 30°S, 227°W. Mark (King of Cornwall) 28°S, 297°W. Merlin (Arthur's magician) 38°S, 215°W. Modred (Arthur's son) 5°N, 213°W. Morgan (Arthur's half-sister) 25°N, 240°W. Palomides (Saracen enemy of Tristram) 4°N, 157°W. Pellinore (king in pursuit of the "Questing Beast") 35°N, 128°W. Percivale (a knight) 1°S, 171°W. Tristram (a knight) 58°S, 26°W. Uther (Arthur's father) 35°S, 244°W. CHASMA (grooves): Avalon (Arthurian paradise) 20–57°N, 160–120°W. Camelot (home of the Round Table) 25–60°S, 0–45°W. Oeta (a mountain in Greek myth) 10–35°N, 130–105°W. Ossa (a mountain in Greek myth) 10–30°S, 305–280°W. Pangea (a mountain in Greek myth) 25–55°S, 340–290°W. Pelion (a mountain in Greek myth) 20–25°S, 235–200°W. Tintagel (home of Arthur's mother) 43–60°S, 235–190°W

Origin: Formed from the early Saturn gas and dust

Discovery: By William Herschel on September 17, 1789. It was the 7th satellite of Saturn to be discovered, and Herschel spotted it with his smaller, 20-foot reflector telescope. It was difficult to see, even with the largest telescopes, until the middle of the 19th century. On November 12, 1980, Voyager 1 came to within 88,440 km of it, and in 1981 Voyager 2 came to within 309,990 km

Photographs: see pages 122, 147

Mimas Co-orbital *see* *1981 S12*

Miranda

Other names: Uranus Five, Uranus 5, Uranus V, U5

Named for: Named by its discoverer Gerard Kuiper in 1948 for Shakespeare's character in *The Tempest*

Pronunciation: mi ran' də

Features on Earth named for it: Miranda Peaks on Alexander Island, Antarctica

Distance from Uranus: Its mean distance from the center of Uranus is 129,390 km

Location: The nearest of the Big Five (i.e., Miranda, Titania, Umbriel, Ariel and Oberon) to Uranus

Synodic period: 1 day 9 hours 55 mins 31 secs

Sidereal period: 1.41347925 days

Orbital eccentricity: 0.0027

Orbital inclination: 4.2 degrees

Escape velocity: A mean of 0.46 km/sec

Mean angular distance from Uranus, at mean opposition distance: 9".9

Visible magnitude: 16.3

Albedo: 0.27

Absolute magnitude: +1.02

Diameter: 485 km. It is the smallest of the Big Five (i.e., Uranus's major moons)

Apparent diameter, as seen from the surface of Uranus: 17'54"

Density: A mean of 2.0 gm/cm^3

Mass: 3.4×10^{19} kg. This is very low (*see* ***Umbriel—****Mass*)

Shape: Roughly spherical

Surface: Miranda has a tortured and deeply scarred surface. For example, a precipice soars out of the satellite for 12 miles; there are two huge, almost rectangular, regions resembling enormous racetracks (scientists have nicknamed these features Circi Maximi). The moonscape bounding them is scored with ridges, as if furrowed by a giant plow. It has ridges, craters, canyons, cliffs, escarpments and other scars that are 100–300 km wide, and three large closed patterns of light and dark bands. Some of Miranda's cliffs are over 3 miles high. There is a gigantic chevron-shaped formation as well—one of the satellite's notable features. Within the three main features (i.e., the chevron and the two racetracks) is light and dark material arranged in grooves, ridges and scarps, all interwoven chaotically. There are fewer craters within these three features, indicating their relative newness, although large and small craters generally cover the visible surface of Miranda. Some of the canyons on Miranda are 6–12 miles deep. There are fault valleys with steep, terraced walls. All of this indicates a cataclysmic past. Miranda once had considerable internal heat, and the possible premature death of this internal heat may have resulted in an incomplete differentiation of the satellite. This may account for the strange features on Miranda. In 1985–86, when Voyager 2 flew by, only the southern hemisphere was available for study. The northern hemisphere was in darkness

Features: Alonso (character in *The Tempest*) 47°S, 345°E. Arden Corona (forest in *As You Like It*) 10–60°S, 30–120°E; this is a large, tropical region, some 200–300 km across. Argier Rupes (Shakespearean locale) 40–50°S, 310–340°E. Dunsinane Regio (forest in *Macbeth*) 20–75°S, 345–65°E. Elsinore Corona (location of *Hamlet*) 10–42°S, 215–305°E; like Arden Corona. Ferdinand (character in *The Tempest*) 36°S, 208°E. Francisco (character in *The Tempest*) 70°S, 246°E. Gonzalo (character in *The Tempest*) 13°S, 75°E. Inverness Corona (Shakespearean locale) 38–90°S, 0–360°E; like Arden Corona. Mantua Regio (Shakespearean locale) 10–90°S, 75–300°E. Prospero (character in *The Tempest*) 35°S, 323°E. Sicilia Regio (Shakespearean locale) 10–50°S, 295–340°E. Stephano (character in *The Tempest*) 36°S, 239°E. Trinculo (character in *The Tempest*) 67°S, 168°E. Verona Rupes (Shakespearean locale) 10–40°S, 340–350°E

Origin: Miranda possibly shattered billions of years ago in a collision with planetary debris. Attracted by their mutual gravity, the fragments would have later regrouped but were too cold to meld fully, leaving Miranda with its corrupted surface

Discovery: By Gerard P. Kuiper on a photograph taken by him on February

16, 1948, using the 82-inch reflector telescope at McDonald Observatory in Texas. On January 24, 1986, Voyager 2 got to within 29,000 km of Miranda, which was the closest that probe had gotten to any of the bodies it had encountered in its whole mission. It took photos that showed detail down to 2000 feet across. *See also* ***Oberon****—Discovery*

Bibliography: "The Pock-Marked Face of Miranda," by Ian Anderson, *New Scientist,* February 6, 1986

"Uranus—The Voyage Continues," by Richard Berry, *Astronomy,* April 1986

"Voyager: Discovery at Uranus," by Richard Berry, *Astronomy,* May 1986

Photographs: see pages 127, 131, 133, 148, 149

M1, Mars I see *Phobos*

M2, Mars II see *Deimos*

Naiad

Other names: 1989 N6, Neptune 8, N8, Neptune Eight, Neptune VIII

Named for: Named by the I.A.U. in 1990 for the water spirit in Greek mythology

Pronunciation: nī' ad, nā' ad

Distance from Neptune: Its mean distance from the center of Neptune is 48,200 km

Location: It is the nearest satellite to Neptune

Sidereal period: 0.30 days

Orbital eccentricity: Probably 0

Orbital inclination: Probably 0 degrees

Diameter: About 54 km

Albedo: About 0.06

Shape: Irregular

Surface: Extremely dark, almost black like soot

Origin: Probably formed through the accretion of comets

Discovery: July 1989, by Voyager 2. Discovered in close encounter search images of the Voyager photos

N8, Neptune VIII see *Naiad*

Nereid

Other names: N II, Neptune 2, Neptune Two, N2, Nerida or Nereo (both in Spanish)

Named for: The sea nymphs lured by Triton's conch-shell music in mythology

Pronunciation: nē' rē id, nə rē' id, nə rā' id

Distance from Neptune: Its mean distance from the center of Neptune is 5,511,000 km (see also below, under *Orbit*)

Synodic period: 362 days 11 hours

Sidereal period: 359.881 days

Orbit: Nereid is the most eccentric of any satellite in the solar system when it comes to orbit (with the possible exception of ***Chiron*** [q.v.], if that body is indeed a moon). Nereid follows a wild path, skewed out of plane, swinging to within 1,390,500 km of Neptune, and then back out some 9,733,500 km into space, in a long, looping orbit. It resembles Chiron in more than its movement

Orbital eccentricity: 0.74934

Orbital inclination: 27.6 degrees

Escape velocity: A mean of 0.3 km/sec

Mean angular distance from Neptune, at mean opposition distance: 4'23".9

Visible magnitude: 18.7 plus or minus 1.5

Albedo: Probably 1.0 for the bright side, and 0.24 for the dark side

Absolute magnitude: +4.0

Diameter: About 340 km. It is the

smaller of the two Neptunian satellites known before 1989. It is a smallish rock, similar in size to an asteroid. In 1988 M. E. Davies estimated its diameter at 690 km plus or minus 360 km

Apparent diameter, as seen from the surface of Neptune: Average of 19"

Shape: Seems to be roughly spherical

Surface: Probably ice and carbonaceous rock. It is a dark gray color

Origin: Possibly a captured asteroid

Discovery: In 1852 British astronomer William Lassell thought he saw a second Neptunian satellite (Triton had already been discovered), but it was probably a star or an optical fault. In *Outlines of Astronomy,* 1869, Sir John Herschel writes of there being no doubt that there are at least two Neptunian moons. On September 24, 1892, J. Schaeberle, using the Lick Observatory 36-inch refractor, suspected a new satellite—a faint object 24 seconds of arc from Neptune which seemed to change in position angle by two degrees over a period of 1 hour 40 mins. This was unconfirmed as well. On May 1, 1949, Gerard P. Kuiper found it on two plates exposed at the prime focus of the 82-inch McDonald telescope in Texas. Two pairs of photos taken during subsequent weeks confirmed it

Bibliography: *The Planet Neptune,* by Patrick Moore. Ellis Horwood, U.K., 1988

Photograph: see page 142

*1975..., 1980..., 1981..., 1989...: satellites bearing these names are strictly alphabetized, as follows: **1989 N4; 1989 N2; 1981 S8; 1981 S11; 1981 S9; 1981 S7; 1981 S10; 1981 S13; 1981 S12; 1980 S34; 1975 J1;** see also the cross references (strictly alphabetized)*

N5, Neptune V *see* ***1989 N4***

N4, Neptune IV *see* ***1989 N2***

1985 U1 *see* **Puck**

1989 N5 *see* **Thalassa**

1989 N4

Other names: Neptune V, Neptune Five, Neptune 5, N5

Distance from Neptune: Its mean distance from the center of Neptune is 62,000 km

Location: This is one of the two shepherd moons (*see also* ***Despina***) accompanying Neptunian ring 1989 N1 A with its bright "ring-arc" segments. It lies just inside that ring

Orbital eccentricity: Probably 0

Orbital inclination: Probably 0 degrees

Sidereal period: 0.43 days

Albedo: About 0.05

Shape: Irregular

Surface: Extremely dark, almost black like soot

Diameter: 160 km

Origin: Possibly formed through the accretion of comets

Discovery: July 7, 1989, by Voyager 2 (*see* ***Proteus***)

Photographs: see pages 136, 137

1989 N1 *see* **Proteus**
see also ***1989 N2***

1989 N6 *see* **Naiad**

1989 N3 *see* **Despina**

1989 N2

Other names: 1981 N1 (*see* ***Proteus****—Discovery*), Neptune IV, Neptune 4, N4, Neptune Four

Distance from Neptune: Its mean distance from the center of Neptune is 73,600 km

Location: The next in from the outside of the new moons discovered by Voyager 2 in 1989
Sidereal period: 13.3 hours
Orbital eccentricity: Probably 0
Orbital inclination: Less than 1 degree, probably 0
Diameter: Approximately 210×180 km. It is half the size of Proteus
Albedo: About 0.06. The surface of 1989 N2 reflects only 6 percent of the sunlight that falls on it
Shape: Irregular
Surface: Extremely dark, almost black like soot. It has numerous craters between 30 and 50 km wide
Origin: Probably formed through the accretion of comets
Discovery: On July 7, 1989, by Voyager 2. The origins of the discovery of 1989 N2 are to be found under the entry ***Proteus.*** The orbit of this new moon was pinned down by Rich Terrile of the Jet Propulsion Laboratory in Pasadena, California. Terrile was the first member of the Voyager imaging team to work out the orbit. Because Harold Reitsema observed it in 1981 (*see* ***Proteus***), but could not prove it until Terrile, 1989 N2 is officially listed as a joint discovery by Reitsema and company, and Terrile. It will probably be called Larissa (Reitsema's choice of name)
Photographs: see pages 135, 136

1981 S8

Distance from Saturn: Its mean distance from the center of Saturn is approximately 380,000 km
Mean angular distance from Saturn, at mean opposition distance: 1'0".30
Albedo: High
Diameter: Approximately 18 km
Shape: Almost certainly irregular
Surface: Icy, bright and cratered
Origin: Probably the fragment of a once-larger body
Discovery: In 1982 by Stephen Synnott of the Jet Propulsion Laboratory, from images taken by Voyager 2 in 1981. All of the above information must be treated with caution, as 1981 S8 and 1981 S7 may be the same object

1981 S11

Distance from Saturn: Its mean distance from the center of Saturn is about 330,000 km, although some sources say 350,000 km, which means it may not be the same object as 1981 S10 and 1980 S34, as skeptics say. However, all of the information in this entry must be treated with some degree of caution, as these three objects may, indeed, be one and the same, or two may be the same.
Mean angular distance from Saturn, at mean opposition distance: About 0'54".3
Location: Between Tethys and Dione
Orbital period: About 2.44 days
Diameter: Approximately 18 km
Shape: Almost certainly irregular
Surface: Icy, bright and cratered
Albedo: High
Origin: Probably the remnant of a once-larger body
Discovery: In 1982 Stephen Synnott of the Jet Propulsion Laboratory found it on photos taken by Voyager 2 in 1981. (But see above, under *Distance from Saturn*)

1981 S9

Distance from Saturn: Its mean distance from the center of Saturn is approximately 469,900 km
Location: Between Dione and Rhea (if it exists at all)
Mean angular distance from Saturn, at mean opposition distance: About 1'14".5
Orbital period: 3.8 days
Diameter: Approximately 18 km
Albedo: High
Shape: Almost certainly irregular
Surface: Icy, bright and cratered
Origin: Probably the remnant of a once-larger body

Discovery: In 1982 by Stephen Synnott of the Jet Propulsion Laboratory, from images taken by Voyager 2 in 1981. All of the above information must be treated with caution, as 1981 S9 may not exist at all. It has not been confirmed

1981 S7

Other names: Dione co-orbital

Distance from Saturn: Its mean distance from the center of Saturn is 377,420 km

Location: It trails Dione in its orbit, being one of the Dione Trojans, and lies about 60 degrees behind Dione

Synodic period: 2 days 17 hours 44 mins 18 secs

Sidereal period: 2.7369 days (tropical period)

Orbital eccentricity: About 0.001

Orbital inclination: About 0.3 degrees

Mean angular distance from Saturn, at mean opposition distance: 1'0".1

Diameter: Approximately 18 km

Albedo: High

Shape: Almost certainly irregular

Surface: Icy, bright and cratered

Origin: Possibly the fragment of a once-larger body

Discovery: In 1982 by Stephen Synnott of the Jet Propulsion Laboratory, from images taken by Voyager 2 in 1981. All of the above information must be treated with caution, as 1981 S7 and 1981 S8 may be the same object

1981 S10

Distance from Saturn: Its mean distance from the center of Saturn is approximately 330,000 km

Mean angular distance from Saturn, at mean opposition distance: About 0'54".3

Location: Between Tethys and Dione (if it exists at all)

Diameter: Approximately 18 km

Albedo: High

Shape: Almost certainly irregular

Orbital period: About 2 days 6 hours

Surface: Icy, bright and cratered

Origin: Probably the remnant of a once-larger body

Discovery: In 1982 Rich Terrile and Stephen Synnott of the Jet Propulsion Laboratory found it on photos taken by Voyager 2 in 1981. The above information must be treated with caution, as 1981 S10, 1981 S11 and 1980 S34 may all be the same object

1981 S13

Other names: Saturn 18, S18, Saturn Eighteen, Saturn XVIII

Location: Along the inner and outer edges of Encke's Gap in Saturn's A-ring. The moon apparently created this gap

Diameter: About 20 km

Albedo: High, about 0.5

Shape: Almost certainly irregular

Surface: Apparently water-ice, and bright

Discovery: In 1985 Jeffrey N. Cuzzi and Jeffrey D. Scargle of NASA's Ames Research Center in Mountain View, California, detected wavy ripples in the Voyager 2 photos of Saturn's Encke's Gap. In 1986 Cuzzi and Mark Showalter proposed an orbit for a moon which could cause these ripples, and which might be pushing material away from its orbit. They could not find it, even in the best photos, but they determined that it was there. On July 16, 1990, Showalter found it in 11 images while using a computer program he wrote to analyze 30,000 lesser quality Voyager 2 photos taken over a 48-hour period in 1981. It is the 18th confirmed Saturnian satellite, and the official discoverer is Showalter. He wants to call it Pan, for the Greek god of shepherds

Bibliography: Science News, August 4, 1990, p. 69

1981 S12

Other names: Mimas co-orbital

Distance from Saturn: Its mean distance from the center of Saturn is 185,520 km

Location: Located between Saturn rings G and E, it is either a co-orbital of Mimas, or close to that moon's orbit (see also below, under *Discovery*). Note: this satellite may not exist at all; it has not been confirmed

Mean angular distance from Saturn, at mean opposition distance: 0'30"

Synodic period: 22 hours 37 mins 12.4 secs

Sidereal period: 0.942421813 days (tropical period)

Diameter: About 10 km which, if it exists at all, may make it the smallest satellite yet known in the solar system (however, *see* ***Leda***)

Orbital eccentricity: About 0.2

Orbital inclination: About 1.5 degrees

Albedo: High

Shape: Almost certainly irregular

Surface: Icy, bright and cratered

Origin: Probably the remnant of a once-larger body

Discovery: In February 1982 Rich Terrile and Stephen Synnott of the Jet Propulsion Laboratory determined that an object apparently trailed Mimas in its orbit by almost 108 degrees. Terrile had noted a conspicuous streak in an image taken two weeks before Voyager 2 passed Saturn in 1981. This they determined to be 1981 S12, although no satellite has yet been found, and in fact may not exist at all

1986 U8 *see* ***Ophelia***

1986 U5 *see* ***Belinda***

1986 U4 *see* ***Rosalind***

1986 U9 *see* ***Bianca***

1986 U1 *see* ***Portia***

1986 U7 *see* ***Cordelia***

1986 U6 *see* ***Desdemona***

1986 U3 *see* ***Cressida***

1986 U2 *see* ***Juliet***

1980 S1 *see* ***Janus***

1980 S6 *see* ***Helene***

1980 S13 *see* ***Calypso***

1980 S34

Distance from Saturn: Approximate mean distance from the center of Saturn is 330,000 km

Mean angular distance from Saturn, at mean opposition distance: About 0'54".3

Location: If it exists at all, it is between Tethys and Dione

Orbital period: About 2 days 6 hours

Diameter: Approximately 18 km

Shape: Almost certainly irregular

Surface: Icy, bright and cratered

Albedo: High

Origin: Probably the remnant of a once larger body

Discovery: In 1982 Stephen Synnott found it on photos taken by Voyager 1 in 1980. At first he suspected that it was a third Tethys Lagrangian (i.e., a small moon pulling or pushing Tethys in its orbit, and sharing the orbit of that larger body), and put the distance from Saturn at about 294,700 km. Since then it is believed that its orbit is greater than was once thought. However, 1980 S34, 1981 S10 and 1981 S11 may all be the same object

1980 S3 see *Epimetheus*

1980 S28 see *Atlas*

1980 S25 see *Telesto*

1980 S27 see *Prometheus*

1980 S26 see *Pandora*

1978 P1 see *Charon*

1975 J1

Other names: J14

Location: One of the outer satellites of Jupiter, if it exists

Orbit: Observations were insufficient to determine whether it was prograde or retrograde

Visible magnitude: 21

Shape: Probably irregular

Origin: Could be a captured temporary comet. Over the course of the last century seven comets spent periods of a few months to a few years as captured satellites of Jupiter. These belong to Jupiter's comet family

Discovery: On September 30, October 1 and October 2, 1975, Charles T. Kowal photographed an extremely fast-moving object 48 minutes of arc NW of Jupiter. He was using the Palomar 48-inch Schmidt telescope. But he lost the object and could not find it again. On October 6, 1975, Elizabeth Roemer also photographed it, using the Steward Observatory 90-inch reflector at Kitt Peak, Arizona. It would be the 14th Jovian satellite, if it really is a moon. This explains the numbering of some of the later satellites (for example, Adrastea is sometimes referred to as J17)

1979 J1 see *Adrastea*

1979 J3 see *Metis*

1979 J2 see *Thebe*

1977 UB see *Chiron*

1966 S1 see *Janus*

N1, Neptune I see *Triton*

N7, Neptune VII see *Thalassa*

N6, Neptune VI see *Despina*

N3, Neptune III see *Proteus*

N2, Neptune II see *Nereid*

Oberon

Other names: Uranus 4, Uranus IV, U4, Uranus Four

Named for: Named in 1852 by Sir John Herschel for the Shakespeare character in *A Midsummer Night's Dream*

Pronunciation: ō' bə ron

Distance from Uranus: In 1860 it was thought to be 631,543 km from

Uranus, but it has since been proved to have a mean distance from the center of Uranus of 583,520 km

Location: It is the furthermost satellite from Uranus. The Big Five (as Oberon, Titania, Umbriel, Ariel and Miranda) have been called since the 1985–86 Voyager 2 discovery of the 10 smaller Uranians) all lie in the plane of the planet's equator

Features on Earth named for it: Oberon Peak on Alexander Island, Antarctica

Synodic period: 13 days 11 hours 15 mins 36.5 secs

Sidereal period: 13.4632389 days retrograde

Orbital eccentricity: 0.0008

Orbital inclination: Less than 0.1 degrees

Escape velocity: A mean of 1.34 km/sec

Mean angular distance from Uranus, at mean opposition distance: 44".5

Visible magnitude: 13.94. Before the Voyager 2 expedition, only 5 moons of Uranus were known, and then only as points of light in the Uranian sky. Due to the 1985–86 discovery of 10 smaller moons of Uranus, the original 5 became known collectively as the Big Five. Titania and Oberon are the brightest of the Big Five (a mnemonic for the Big Five is M-AUTO)

Albedo: 0.24

Absolute magnitude: +1.23

Diameter: 1554 km

Apparent diameter, as seen from the surface of Uranus: 9'48"

Density: A mean of 1.6 gm/cm^3

Mass: 8.2×10^{20} kg, which is very low (*see* ***Umbriel****—Mass*)

Shape: Roughly spherical

Surface: The surfaces of the Big Five are surprisingly variable in appearance. Oberon shows strong ice absorptions in its spectrum. The surface is almost completely covered with ice or frost, giving it its high reflectivity. It is a pock-marked surface and the floors of at least three of its craters (Falstaff, Hamlet and Othello) are flooded with a dark material. One of its mountains protrudes at least 20 km above Oberon's surface (which is a phenomenal height), and there is another, 6 km high, on the limb of the satellite, near the Macbeth crater

Features (all but one named for Shakespearean characters): Anthony 28°S, 65°E. Caesar 27°S, 61°E. Coriolanus 11°S, 345°E. Falstaff 22°S, 19° E. Hamlet 46°S, 45°E. Lear 5°S, 31°E. Macbeth 59°S, 112°E. Mommur Chasma 16–20°S, 240–343°E. Othello 65°S, 44°E. Romeo 28°S, 88°E

Origin: The moons of Uranus may be the result of a coalescing of gas produced by the planet after a mammoth collision with an Earth-sized object

Discovery: British astronomer William Herschel had been looking for Uranian moons ever since he discovered the planet in 1781, when, on January 11, 1787, he detected two faint objects close to the planet. They were not visible on the following night. On the night of February 7–8, 1787, he watched from 6 p.m. to 3 a.m., and followed the motion of one of the satellites (Oberon). The following evening he confirmed the nature of the second satellite (Titania). In 1790 Herschel claimed that he found two more Uranian moons, unnamed. The first was 1,263,141 km from the planet, and had an orbital period of 38.08 days. The second was 364,470 km from the planet and had an orbital period of 5.89 days. By February 28, 1794, he claimed another two. The first was at a distance of 2,526,004 km from Uranus with an orbital period of 107.69 days. The second was at a distance of 550,940 km from the planet with an orbital period of 10.98 days. None of these four exists. By 1889 they were no longer on the record books. In 1847 Otto Struve, the Russian astronomer, may have seen Umbriel, Ariel or Miranda (probably Umbriel, if any) from the Dorpat Observatory in Estonia, but there is no proof of this. What Herschel saw were probably faint stars, or tricks in his telescope. In 1894, 1897 and 1899 W. H. Pickering made unsuccessful searches for extra Uranian satellites, and Gerard Kuiper searched, also unsuccessfully, in the late 1940s and early 1950s, but it took Voyager 2 to discover more. Oberon was the first of the Big Five to be scrutinized by Voyager 2 in 1985–86, and the spacecraft imaged Oberon from 660,000 km. The closest it got to the surface was 468,800 km. It is highly unlikely that in the next few generations man or machine will get out to the Uranian satellites. So, any further investigations will have to be done from a long way away

Bibliography: "The Moons of Uranus, Neptune and Pluto," by Robert Hamilton Brown and Dale P. Cruikshank, *Scientific American,* July 1985

"The Moons of Uranus," by Torrence V. Johnson, Robert Hamilton Brown and Laurence A. Soderblom, *Scientific American,* April 1987

Atlas of Uranus, by Garry Hunt and Patrick Moore. Cambridge University Press, 1989

Photograph: see page 129

Ophelia

Other names: Uranus VII, Uranus 7, Uranus Seven, U7, 1986 U8, Outer Epsilon Ring Shepherd

Named for: Named by the I.A.U. in 1988 for Shakespeare's character in *Hamlet*

Pronunciation: ō fē' lē ə, ō fē' lyə, ə fē' lē ə, ə fē' ly ə, ō fēl yə

Distance from Uranus: Its mean distance from the center of Uranus is about 53,796 km

Location: Ophelia is one of the two tiny shepherd moons (*see also* ***Cordelia***) on either side of Uranus's epsilon ring

Synodic period: 8 hours 55 mins

Sidereal period: 0.376409 days

Mean angular distance from Uranus, at mean opposition distance: 4"

Density: Almost certainly low

Escape velocity: Very low

Orbit: Its rotational period is synchronous with its orbital period (i.e., the same face of Ophelia is always shown to Uranus)

Orbital eccentricity: 0.1

Orbital inclination: Probably 0 degrees

Diameter: Approximately 50 km

Albedo: About 0.1

Shape: Unknown exactly, but probably roughly spherical

Surface: Dark and methane-coated

Origin: Probably formed through the accretion of comets

Discovery: On January 20, 1986, by Voyager 2 (*see also* ***Puck***). Voyager 2 found only two tiny shepherd moons (later called Cordelia and Ophelia), fewer than had been anticipated. Without the gentle gravitational pull of such moons (which play a key role in containing the rings of Saturn) scientists can not work out how the Uranian rings can remain sharp-edged and narrow—most are less than 10 miles wide. Perhaps the rings were formed quite recently by the disintegration of a small inner moon

Bibliography: Science, 233 (July 4, 1986), 39–109

Photograph: see page 128

Outer Epsilon Ring Shepherd *see* Ophelia

Outer F-ring Shepherd *see* Pandora

Pan *see* Carme; 1981 S13

Pandora

Other names: Saturn 15, Saturn XV, S15, Saturn Fifteen, 1980 S26, Outer F-ring Shepherd, S13 (seen as this in some sources)

Named for: The first woman in Greek mythology

Pronunciation: pan dôr' ə

Distance from Saturn: Its mean distance from the center of Saturn is 141,700 km

Synodic period: 15 hours 05 mins 4.8 secs

Sidereal period: 0.628541 days (tropical period)

Location: Pandora is the outer F-ring shepherd moon (Prometheus is the inner F-ring shepherd moon). The famous rings of Saturn are composed of particles created by the ripping apart of a Saturnian moon that once strayed within the Roche limit (*see* ***Phobos*** for a description of the Roche limit). Shepherd moons "shepherd" these particles in their ever-revolving orbit around the planet, and help stabilize the ring against disrupting nongravitational forces. In the case of Pandora and Prometheus, thee two shepherds prevent the F-ring from spreading, in this manner: Pandora, on the outside of the ring, lags behind the ring fragments, while Prometheus, on the inside of the ring, overtakes them. Every 23 days the two shepherds align, the faster Prometheus having caught up with the slower Pandora. When fragments of the ring drift outwards, Pandora attracts them from behind with its gentle gravity, reducing the speed of the errant particles so that they fall inward again. On the other hand, Prometheus passes inward-straying fragments, and pulls them forward, speeding them up, and returning them to the F-ring's thin stream, as they all revolve in a never-ending procession around Saturn

Orbital eccentricity: 0.004

Orbital inclination: 0.0 degrees

Mean angular distance from Saturn, at mean opposition distance: 23"

Visible magnitude: 16.1

Albedo: 0.9

Diameter: 110×84×66 km

Absolute magnitude: +6.4

Shape: Irregular

Escape velocity: 35 m/sec

Surface: Icy

Origin: Possibly the fragment of a once larger body

Discovery: In November 1980, by Stewart Collins and Rich Terrile, from photos taken by Voyager 1 that month. The spacecraft came within 270,000 km of Pandora, and in 1981 Voyager 2 came within 107,000 km

Photographs: see pages 125, 126

Pasiphaë

Other names: Jupiter VIII, Jupiter 8, Jupiter Eight, J8, Poseidon (this was its original, unofficial name), Proserpine (a later, unofficial name), Helena (another later, unofficial name) (for these last two see below, under *Discovery*)

Named for: The mother of the Minotaur in Greek mythology

Pronunciation: pas i fī' ā, pas ə fī' ā, pə sif' ə ē, pə sif' ə ā

Distance from Jupiter: Its mean distance from the center of Jupiter is 23,330,000 km

Synodic period: 635 days

Sidereal period: 735 days (some sources say 744 days)

Mean angular distance from Jupiter, at mean opposition distance: 2°08'26"

Orbital eccentricity: 0.378

Orbital inclination: Between 145 and 147 degrees

Escape velocity: A mean of about 0.02 km/sec

Location: It is one of Jupiter's outer retrograde group (Pasiphaë, Sinope, Carme, Ananke)

Diameter: Between 8 and 50 km, probably closer to 46 km

Apparent diameter, as seen from the surface of Jupiter: 0'0".2

Visible magnitude: 17.03

Albedo: Probably 0.02 to 0.03

Absolute magnitude: +10.33

Shape: Irregular

Surface: Probably rocky, and probably made of carbonaceous chondritic material and water ice. It is near neutral in color and has no atmosphere

Origin: Probably a captured Trojan asteroid

Discovery: P. Melotte found it accidentally on January 27, 1908, at the Royal Greenwich Observatory while taking some check plates on Himalia and Elara. It was originally (and unofficially) called Poseidon. In 1962 USSR amateur astronomer E. I. Nesterovich suggested the name Proserpine, and in 1976 USSR astronomer Yuriy A. Karpenko proposed Helena. It was later officially named Pasiphaë by German philologist Johann Blunck. Distant satellites of Jupiter with retrograde orbits have names ending in "e"

Bibliography: Dictionary of Astronomical Names, by Adrian Room. Routledge, 1988

Phöbe *see* ***Phoebe***

Phobos

Other names: MI, Mars 1, Mars One, Fobos (in Spanish)

Named for: Named by its discoverer Asaph Hall on February 7, 1878 (*see also* ***Deimos***), at the suggestion of Mr Madan of Eton, after one of the two chariot-horses (Deimos was the other) of the Roman god Mars. The name Phobos means "fear"

Pronunciation: fō' bos

Features on Earth named for it: Phobos Ridge on Alexander Island, Antarctica

Distance from Mars: Its mean distance from the center of Mars is 9378.5 km

Mean angular distance from Mars, at mean opposition distance: 24".6

Location: The inner of the two Martian moons, its orbit is exceptionally close to the home planet, at a mean distance of 2.76 planetary radii from the center of Mars. In other words, it orbits less than 4000 miles from the surface of Mars. Its nearness to Mars may well spell its doom. It is within the Roche limit of 3 planetary radii. The Roche limit is the minimum distance at which a satellite, if it has no internal strength, can approach its primary body without being torn apart by gravitational forces. These gravitational, or tidal, forces speed Phobos's orbital motion and may ultimately cause the satellite to fall onto the surface of Mars, possibly in less than 100 million years (according to the *Encyclopaedia Britannica*), and latest estimates say in about 40 million years

Synodic period: 7 hours 39 mins 13.85 secs, the same as its rotational period. Phobos makes three trips around Mars each Martian day

Sidereal period: 0.31891023 days

Orbit: In 1964 Sharpless estimated the acceleration of Phobos as 19 degrees per century. In 1979 it was reconsidered at 3.3 degrees per century. In other words, Phobos is speeding up. This is caused by the drag of the Martian atmosphere (see above, under *Location*)

Orbital eccentricity: 0.0135

Orbital inclination: 1.074 degrees

Orbital velocity: 2.1 km/sec

Escape velocity: A mean of 7.8 m/sec

Visible magnitude: 11.3. From Earth, viewed through a telescope, Phobos appears as a bright spot to the left of Mars

Albedo: Very low, 0.05, which gives it a dark surface, making it difficult to see from Earth

Apparent magnitude, as seen from Mars: Maximum of −3.9. It is too near Mars to be visible from all Martian latitudes, and in fact does not appear at latitudes higher than 69.5 degrees North and South and, as seen from Mars, appears to rise in the west and set in the east

Absolute magnitude: +11.8

Diameter: 27×21.6×18.8 km. It is about 23 km at its equator and 18.8 km from Pole to Pole. The first accurate measurements were made by Mariner 9 in 1971–72. Phobos's longest axis is 13.5 km, its intermediate axis is 10.8 km, and its shortest axis is 9.4 km

Area: 1000 sq. km

Volume: 5000 km^3

Apparent diameter, as seen from the surface of Mars: Maximum: 12'.3 Minimum: 8'

Density: A mean of 1.9 gm/cm^3, so low that it resembles a hollow sphere, or balloon. This prompted I. S. Shklovskii in 1959 and 1966 to propose that Phobos (and Deimos) are artificial satellites created by Martians of long ago (see below, under *Bibliography*)

Mass: 9.8×10^{15} kg

Subsolar temperature: 314.4° K

Surface gravity: 1 cm/sec^2

Shape: Phobos was first photographed in some detail in 1969 by Mariner 7. These photos showed Phobos to be irregularly shaped, roughly a triaxial ellipsoid. Its long axis constantly points toward Mars. The 1969 photos of Phobos's shadow on Mars proved the satellite to be ellipsoid

Surface: Ninety-five percent of Phobos's surface has been usefully imaged for features. In 1930 E. M. Antoniadi falsely claimed that Phobos was white. He was using the 83-cm Meudon refractor. Phobos is, in fact, uniformly gray. The Mariner 7 photos of 1969 showed the surface of Phobos to be rugged and heavily cratered, caused by objects hitting it in its early history when it probably suffered from intense bombardment by meteor-like bodies. The debris caused by this bombardment either stayed in place on Phobos (where it now covers the surface of the satellite in a thin layer, or regolith), or it flew off the satellite and was lost to Mars. Phobos's surface also has a widespread system of linear grooves, or surface fractures, extending over most of the satellite (unknown until the Viking photos of 1977), each typically 100–200 meters wide, and 20–30 meters deep, and roughly parallel, many of them being geometrically related to the Stickney crater (see below, under *Features*) near where they are best developed. These grooves are mostly lined with small, contiguous pits. Other Mariner photos showed the extremely crater-pitted surface of Phobos, and in February 1977 Viking Orbiter 1 flew to within 100 km of the surface of Phobos, and made intensive photographic and infrared studies of the satellite from 300 miles. There is no atmosphere on Phobos. In 1989 Phobos 2 detected reddish material on the opposite side of Phobos from Stickney

Features: The actual craters on Phobos were first detected by Mariner 9 in 1971–72. The features (all craters except Kepler) named are: Wendell (Wendell, astronomer) 0°, 145°W. Todd (David Todd, astronomer) 5°S, 165°W. D'Arrest (Heinrich d'Arrest, astronomer) 43°S, 185°W. Sharpless (Isaac Sharpless, astronomer) 24°S, 170°W. Stickney (Angeline Stickney, Hall's wife) 0°, 50°W. Roche (Edouard Roche, astronomer) 56°N, 186°W. Kepler Dorsum (a ridge; Johann Kepler, astronomer). Hall (see below) (Asaph Hall, astronomer) 5°S, 265°W.

Stickney is about 6 miles across, and dominates the satellite. Long grooves radiate from Stickney and cover much of Phobos. There is a bluish area at the bottom of Stickney, found by Phobos 2 in 1989. The crater was named for C. Angelina Stickney, Asaph Hall's wife. Hall crater is about 6 km across, and was named for Asaph Hall. In 1989 Phobos 2 discovered 6 new craters, at least 1 km across, west of Stickney, and

11 new examples of the mysterious grooves that stretch across Phobos

Origin: Phobos, like Deimos, has a spectrum resembling those of certain C-type asteroids common to the outer asteroid belt, and to Jupiter's Trojan asteroids. Such material is believed to have a composition similar to carbonaceous chondrite meteorites. This suggests that Phobos and Deimos were at one time nearer to Jupiter, and that that planet perturbed them into an orbit that allowed their capture by Mars (*The New Solar System*). These tiny orbiting chunks of heavily cratered rock, comparable to some of the smaller asteroids, were not made round by gravity, like Earth's Moon (which is really a small planet) was, and indeed may have been captured by Mars's gravitational pull as they wandered through the solar system. Phobos and Deimos also seem to be extremely old. For a fanciful and untrue theory as to the origin of Phobos and Deimos, see below (*Bibliography—Intelligent Life in the Universe*)

Discovery: The discovery of the Martian satellites has a varied and long history. In 1610 Kepler suggested that because Venus has no moons, Earth has one, and Jupiter has 4 (at least, it did then, known ones), it was reasonable to assume that Mars had two. So great was Kepler's reputation that people accepted this as more fact than theory. In 1726 Jonathan Swift wrote the celebrated novel *Gulliver's Travels.* In Part III of the book, Laputa, Swift described the two satellites of Mars. He did not name them, but he described the inner one (later called Phobos) as being distant from the center of the primary planet (Mars) exactly 3 of the planetary diameters (Hall, its official discoverer, in 1877, put the figure at 1.38 planetary diameters, or 2.76 planetary radii). Swift said that it revolves in the space of 10 hours. Its actual period of revolution (as discovered by Hall) is 7 hours 39 mins. Swift also described Deimos (*see* ***Deimos****—Distance from Mars, Orbit*).

Since Phobos and Deimos, the Martian satellites, were not discovered until 1877, over 150 years later, this pretty accurate description seems at first sight to be rather uncanny. Von Däniken and some other modern writers have implied that Swift was tipped off by extraterrestrials. However, it was almost certainly a curious combination of lucky guesswork, an acceptance of the prevalent theory of geometric progression in the universe, and clever reasoning on Swift's part. He figured that if there were two moons, they would be both small and close to the home planet because no telescope had been able to spot them. This would also mean that their orbits would be more rapid around the planet than if the satellites were farther out.

In 1737 Lecompte's book *Empire of China* was published. He stated definitely that there were two satellites of Mars. In 1744 E. C. Kindermanns claimed to have seen a Martian satellite, that it had an atmosphere, and was four-tenths the size of Mars. In 1752, Voltaire wrote about the two Martian moons in his book *Micromégas.* In 1783 William Herschel made the first systematic search for the Martian satellites. He failed, as did Mädler in 1830 in Berlin with his 4-inch telescope. A good year to study Mars was 1862, as it was in opposition, i.e., unusually close to Earth. But H. d'Arrest in Copenhagen failed to find anything with his 10-inch telescope, as he did also in 1864.

Another opposition year was 1877. At the beginning of August that year Asaph Hall, inspired by his wife Angelina, so the story goes, started a deliberate search for Martian satellites, using the 26-inch refracting telescope at the U.S. Naval Observatory in Washington (the largest refracting telescope in the world at that time). At 2:40 a.m. on August 12 he detected a small bright dot moving with Mars and some 70 degrees to the east of it, against a background of fixed stars. A thick fog came up over the Potomac River near his observatory, and he lost it. On August 16 he saw this object again, and again on August 17. He followed it for 2 hours, and confirmed it as a satellite (this was Deimos). That last night, August 17, 1877, he also saw Phobos. Hall notified several astronomers who confirmed the discoveries. The news then went to the Smithsonian Institution who notified the world of Hall's discoveries on August 20.

The discovery of the Martian moons was very important because the period of their motion and other orbital characteristics provided an estimate of the mass and internal structure of Mars itself. In 1961, Kuiper, looking unsuccessfully for more Martian moons, ruled out the possibility of any other moons orbiting Mars with a diameter of more than three-quarters of a kilometer with an albedo of 0.05.

The first close up view of any natural satellite other than Earth's Moon, came on November 26, 1971, when Mariner 9 photographed Deimos. Phobos followed 3 days later. Mariner 9 proved Phobos to be about 2 degrees ahead of its expected orbital position. In 1973 it was first mapped by T. C. Duxbury. Humans have not yet landed on Phobos, but some day it will happen

Bibliography: "The Moons of Mars," by Joseph Veverka and Joseph A. Burns, *Annual Review of Earth and Planetary Sciences* 8 (1980), 527–558. This is a detailed account of factual knowledge about the Martian moons up to that time

Intelligent Life in the Universe, by Iosef Shmuelovich Shklovskii and Carl Sagan. Holden-Day, San Francisco, 1966. Chapter 26 of this pioneering work is called "Are the Moons of Mars Artificial Satellites ?" This speculation has been disproved

"Swift's Forecast of Mars' Satellites," by Henry C. Briton, *Sky and Telescope,* September 1956

"Asaph Hall and the Moons of Mars," by John T. Kane, *Sky and Telesope,* September 1956

"The Puzzling Moons of Mars," by Joseph Veverka, Peter Thomas and Thomas Duxbury, *Sky and Telescope,* September 1978

"Phobos and Deimos," by James Oberg, *Astronomy,* March 1977

Moons and Planets, 2d ed. by W. K. Hartmann. Wadsworth, Belmont, Calif., 1983

Satellites, ed. by Joseph A. Burns and Mildred S. Matthews. University of Arizona Press, Tucson, 1986

"The Moons of Mars," by Edmund Hamilton, *Captain Future* 4, 3 (1942). In this fictional work Phobos and Deimos are circular. On Phobos various features are named: Valley of Memory, Rocket Pits, Forest of Giant Grasses, Martian Observatory, Mountains of the Machine Kings, and the ruins of Pigmy City. On Deimos various features are also named: Entrance to Moonheart, Lake, Rocket Pits, Gardens

Small Worlds: Exploring the 60 Moons of Our Solar System, by Joseph W. Kelch. Messner, 1990

Photographs: see pages 114, 115, 116, 117

Phoebe

Other names: Saturn 9, Saturn Nine, Saturn IX, S9, Phöbe (in German), Febe (in Spanish)

Named for: Named by Pickering, its discoverer, in 1899, for the Titan woman in Greek mythology

Pronunciation: fē' bē

Features on Earth named for it: Mount Phoebe on Alexander Island, Antarctica

Distance from Saturn: Its mean distance from the center of Saturn is 12,952,000 km

Location: The outermost satellite of

the outskirts of the Saturnian system

Synodic period: 523 days 15 hours 36 mins, although this is subject to change

Sidereal period: 550.48 days retrograde (tropical period)

Orbit: Phoebe's orbit is retrograde, and discovery of this strange condition cast doubt on the nebular hypothesis of the creation of the world, which had held sway throughout the 19th century, basking in the comfort of the direct (prograde) motions of all the planets and satellites. This was the first retrograde body ever found in the solar system

Rotational period: About 9½ hours. It makes Phoebe the only Saturnian satellite whose rotational period is not synchronous with its orbital period

Orbital velocity: 1.7 km/sec

Orbital eccentricity: 0.16326

Orbital inclination: 177 degrees (relative to the ecliptic plane)

Escape velocity: A mean of 0.13 km/sec

Mean angular distance from Saturn, at mean opposition distance: 34'51"

Visible magnitude: 16.45

Albedo: 0.06

Absolute magnitude: +6.89

Density: Low

Mass: Low, but too great for Phoebe to be the remains of a comet

Diameter: Between 160 and 220 km. It is a small satellite.

Apparent diameter, as seen from the surface of Saturn: 0'3".2

Shape: Roughly spherical

Surface: Voyager 1 came within 13,537,000 km of Phoebe, and Voyager 2 to within 1,473,000 km; therefore the photos were not good. What was seen was a dark reddish surface. It is possibly a stony surface, and is essentially ice free

Subsolar temperature: About 126° K

Origin: It may be something spewed out of a primeval Jupiter. It has also been suggested that Phoebe is the encrusted nucleus of a giant comet (although see above, under *Mass*). It may also be a captured asteroid

Discovery: On August 16, 1898 W. H. Pickering exposed 4 plates for 2 hours each from the 24-inch Bruce astrograph, at Harvard University, Cambridge, Mass. In April 1899, he discovered Phoebe in one of them, but confirmation did not come until 1904 when Barnard saw it on other plates taken with the same telescope at Harvard. Phoebe was the first moon to be discovered using photography

Bibliography: *Stability of the Solar System and Its Minor Natural and Artificial Bodies,* ed. by V. Szebehely. Dordrecht-Reidel, 1985

Photograph: see page 123

P1, Pluto I see *Charon*

Portia

Other names: Uranus XII, Uranus 12, Uranus Twelve, U12, 1986 U1

Named for: Named by the I.A.U. in 1988 for the Shakespeare character in *The Merchant of Venice*

Pronunciation: pôr' shə

Distance from Uranus: Its mean distance from the center of Uranus is 66,085 km

Location: Between Miranda and the rings of Uranus

Synodic period: 12 hours 19 mins

Sidereal period: 0.513196 days

Escape velocity: Very low

Orbital eccentricity: Low, probably 0

Orbital inclination: Low, probably 0 degrees

Albedo: Low, about 0.1

Mean angular distance from Uranus, at mean opposition distance: 5"

Orbit: Its rotational period is synchronous with its orbital period (i.e., the same face of Portia is always shown to Uranus)

Density: Almost certainly low

Diameter: Approximately 80 km

Shape: Unknown exactly, but probably roughly spherical

Surface: Dark and methane-coated

Origin: Probably formed through the accretion of comets

Discovery: January 3, 1986, by Voyager 2 (*see* ***Puck***)

Bibliography: Science 233 (July 4, 1986), 39–109

Photograph: see page 128

Poseidon see *Pasiphae*

Prometheus

see also ***Lysithea***

Other names: Saturn XVI, Saturn 16, Saturn Sixteen, S16, 1980 S27, S14 (some sources list it as this), Inner F-ring Shepherd

Named for: The Titan in Greek mythology

Pronunciation: prə mē' thē əs, prō mē' thē əs

Distance from Saturn: Its mean distance from the center of Saturn is 139,353 km

Location: Prometheus is the inner shepherd moon for Saturn's F-ring (*see* ***Pandora*** for details)

Synodic period: 14 hours 42 mins 43.2 secs

Sidereal period: 0.613000 days (tropical period)

Mean angular distance from Saturn, at mean opposition distance: 23"

Orbital eccentricity: 0.003

Orbital inclination: 0 degrees

Escape velocity: 50 m/sec

Visible magnitude: Between 15.6 and 15.2

Albedo: Between 0.49 and 0.68

Absolute magnitude: +6.4

Subsolar temperature: About 125° K

Diameter: 140×100×80 km

Shape: Irregular

Surface: Icy

Origin: Possibly the fragment of a once-larger body

Discovery: In November 1980, by Stewart Collins and Rich Terrile, from photos taken by Voyager 1 that month. Voyager 1 flew within 300,000 km of Prometheus, and Voyager 2 got to within 246,590 km in 1981

Photographs: see pages 124, 125, 126

Proserpine see *Pasiphaë*

Proteus

Other names: 1989 N1, 1981 N1 (see below, under *Discovery*), Neptune III, Neptune 3, N3, Neptune Three

Named for: Named by the I.A.U. in 1990 for the sea god in mythology

Pronunciation: prō' tē əs

Distance from Neptune: Its mean distance from the center of Neptune is 117,600 km

Location: Proteus is the outermost of the new Neptunian satellites

Orbit: Circular

Sidereal period: 27 hours

Orbital eccentricity: Probably 0

Orbital inclination: Probably 0 degrees. Certainly less than 1 degree.

Albedo: About 0.06. Proteus's surface reflects only 6 percent of the sunlight that falls on it

Diameter: It varies from 400 to 435 km across, with an average diameter of 415 km

Shape: Slightly but distinctively out of round. An ellipsoid

Surface: Proteus is frozen hard, and has never melted or softened. Its surface is extremely dark, almost black like soot, and heavily cratered, as well as being icy

Origin: Possibly formed through the accretion of comets

Discovery: In May 1981, Harold Reitsema of Ball Aerospace in Boulder, Colorado, was heading a team of observers from the Lunar and Planetary Laboratory in Arizona when, on May 24, using the occultation method, he "discovered" a new Neptunian moon, the third yet found in that system. When Neptune made a close approach to a faint star in the background, two telescopes, 6 km apart, simultaneously recorded an 8-second "blink" of the star (or, to put it another way, the star flickered as it passed behind an object near Neptune). This could have been due to a Neptunian satellite about 180 km or more in diameter, orbiting at a distance of around 50,000 km from the center of Neptune, closer in than either Triton or (certainly) Nereid. There was doubt as to whether Reitsema's find was indeed a satellite, but Reitsema was convinced it was, and named it (temporarily) "1981 N1." If 1981 N1 was indeed a satellite, and the chances that it was are excellent, it could have been any one of the six new satellites discovered by Voyager 2 on July 7, 1989, and most probably the second one, 1989 N2 (this also is a temporary name; no real name has yet been given—see that entry). Discovery of 1989 N1 (later called Proteus) was announced that day, July 7, 1989

Photograph: see page 142

Puck

Other names: 1985 U1, Uranus XV, Uranus 15, U15, Uranus Fifteen

Named for: Named unofficially by the Voyager team in 1986 for Shakespeare's character in *A Midsummer Night's Dream.* The name was made official by the I.A.U. in 1988

Pronunciation: puk

Distance from Uranus: Its mean distance from the center of Uranus is about 85,892 km

Location: Between Miranda and the rings of Uranus. It is the largest and outermost of the 10 smaller satellites of Uranus

Synodic period: 18 hours 17 mins

Sideral period: 0.761832 days

Mean angular distance from Uranus, at mean opposition distance: 7"

Orbit: Its rotational period is synchronous with its orbital period (i.e., the same face of Puck is always shown to Uranus)

Orbital eccentricity: Low, probably 0

Orbital inclination: Low, probably 0 degrees

Escape velocity: Very low

Density: Almost certainly low

Albedo: Low, about 0.1

Diameter: Approximately 170×160 km

Shape: Slightly irregular

Surface: Dark as coal, and methane-coated. It has an uneven surface

Features: Three craters were recorded by Voyager 2. Their names are Bogle, Lob, and Butz

Origin: Possibly formed through the accretion of comets

Discovery: In 1985–86 Voyager 2 reached the Uranian system. It discovered 10 smaller moons of Uranus, the first being the outermost one, which was temporarily called 1989 U1 (later Puck), on December 30, 1985. Six more of these inner Uranians were discovered in early January 1986, and three more a little later on in January. On January 24, 1986, a single image was taken of Puck from a range of 515,000 km. One picture of Miranda had to be sacrificed for this shot. Earth received the photo on January 26, 1986, after an antenna problem on Voyager. By this date all the small moons had been found and numbered—1985 U1 (Puck, the only one to be found in 1985), and 1986 U1 through 1986 U9 (all later named with the individual entry names to be found in this book). The photo taken of Puck is JPL [Jet Propulsion Laboratory] P-29519, in black and white. Just before the Voyager 2 flyby, Dale Cruikshank searched from Earth for Uranian moons up to 23 Magnitude and found none orbiting outside Oberon's orbit. Astronomers had hoped for 18 new moons of Uranus, instead of the 10 they found. Scientists had discovered 9 Uranian rings from Earth (Voyager 2 discovered two more), so they expected two shepherd moons per ring. Only two are shepherds, Cordelia and Ophelia (*see* ***Ophelia*** for more details)

Bibliography: *Science* 233 (July 4, 1986), 39–109

Photograph: see page 129

Rhea

Other names: Saturn V, Saturn 5, S5

Named for: Named by Sir John Herschel in 1847 for one of the Titan women in Greek mythology

Pronunciation: rē' ə

Features on Earth named for it: Rhea Corner, a cliff on Alexander Island, Antarctica

Distance from Saturn: Its mean distance from the center of Saturn is 527,040 km

Synodic period: 4 days 12 hours 27 mins 56.2 secs

Sidereal period: 4.517500436 days (tropical period)

Orbit: Sluggish

Orbital eccenticity: 0.00098

Orbital inclination: 0.35 degrees

Escape velocity: A mean of 0.57 km/sec

Density: A mean of approximately 1.33 gm/cm^3

Mass: 2.28×10^{21} gm

Visible magnitude: 9.7

Albedo: 0.65

Absolute magnitude: +0.16

Orbital velocity: 8.7 km/sec

Diameter: 1528 km. It is an intermediate-sized satellite and is Saturn's second largest moon. It is nearly a twin to Iapetus in size, but lacks its dark material

Apparent diameter, as seen from the surface of Saturn: 10'42"

Mean angular distance from Saturn, at mean opposition distance: 1'25".1

Subsolar temperature: About 103° K

Surface gravity: 28.37 cm/sec^2

Shape: Roughly spherical

Surface: Rhea is composed of ice and rock in about equal quantities, but the interior of the satellite must be almost entirely of ice. The surface is water ice plus some other material. There is little internal activity on Rhea. The surface is totally saturated by craters, to the extent that new impacts on Rhea wipe out many old craters. Parts of the cratered surface bear a striking resemblance to the highlands of Earth's Moon. Rhea also has some large "craterless" regions, probably brought about by an era of "resurfacing" in its past. Wispy, white streaks, perhaps deposits of snow exuded from fractures in the satellite's crust, crisscross the surface on the trailing hemisphere. This is darker on average than the heavily cratered leading hemisphere which faces Saturn during its orbit. Light-colored rims on several craters may be fresh exposures of ice or condensed volatiles clinging to steep slopes

Features: The craters are irregular, and the largest ones are about 300 km across. Izanagi is the most prominent crater. Bumba and Ormazd are other huge ones. Torom is the most southerly and Uku the most northerly. Rhea's features were named for characters and places from creation myths around the world (Earth, that is). Asian names form the majority.

CRATERS: Aananin (Korean god of the heavens) 39°N, 330°W. Adjua (ancestress of the Ulci tribe [USSR]) 46°N, 126°W. Agunua (San Cristobal [Melanesia] god who made sea, land and people) 70°N, 65°W. Ameta (Ceram [Indonesia] ancestor whose blood made Hainuwele) 59°N, 14°W. Arunaka (Inca creator of all things) 14°S, 21°W. Atum (old creator god of Heliopolis) 45°S, 0°W. Bulagat (mythical ancestor of the Buriat tribe of Mongolia) 35°S, 14°W. Bumba (Bushongo [Africa] god) 70°N, 40°W. Burkhan (Buriat [Siberia] god who created the world) 69°N, 288°W. Con (South American creator god) 24°S, 10°W. Djuli (first man in Neghidahan [Ukraine] myth) 26°S, 46°W. Ellyay

(Yakutian [USSR] ancestor of people) 78°N, 95°W. Faro (Mande [Africa] mythical character) 52°N, 121°W. Haik (mythical ancestor of the Armenians) 34°S, 27°W. Haoso (Manchurian creator of all things) 9°N, 8°W. Heller (Araucanian [South America] creator) 9°N, 310°W. Iraca (Inca creator god who became the Moon) 45°N, 120°W. Izanagi (Japanese creator god: brother and husband of Izanami) 49°S, 298°W. Izanami (creator goddess of Japan) 46°S, 310° W. Jumo (Marijam [USSR] sky god) 56°N, 65°W. Karora (ancestor of the Arunda [Australia]) 7°N, 16°W. Khado (first shaman in Nanajan [USSR] myth; he built the world) 45°N, 349°W. Kiho (Tuamotu [Society Islands] ancestor) 10°S, 354°W. Kumpara (Jivaro [Ecuador] creator god) 11°N, 321°W. Leza (Thonga [Africa] god of heaven and nature) 19°S, 304°W. Lowa (Marshall Islands creator god) 45°N, 9°W. Malunga (Yao [Africa] first god) 74°N, 49°W. Manoid (Negrito [Malaysia] first goddess) 33°N, 2°W. Melo (original man of the Minyong [India]) 51°S, 6°W. Mubai (Tibetan god of heaven) 61°N, 11°W. Num (Samoyed god of Heaven) 23°N, 93°W. Ormazd (Persian god of light) 62°N, 52°W. Pan Ku (Miao [China] creator of all things) 72°N, 115°W. Pedn (Negrito [Malaysia] god who created man) 48°N, 340°W. Qat (New Hebrides god) 23°N, 347°W. Sholmo (Buriat [Siberia] devil) 13°N, 340°W. Taaroa (Tahitian creator god) 14°N, 99°W. Thunupa (Inca creator of all things) 51°N, 15°W. Tika (Abkhaz [USSR] supreme god) 25°N, 87°W. Tore (Pygmy creator of all things) 1°N, 355°W. Torom (Turm) (Ostya [USSR] sky god) 68°S, 345°W. Uku (Estonian super-god) 85°N, 115°W. Whanin (Korean creator of all things) 74°N, 121°W. Wuraka (Kakadu [Australia] giant ancestor of all people) 28°N, 357°W. Xamba (Bushman creator of all things) 4°N, 347°W. Xu (Huwe) (Bushman creator) 61°N, 70° W. Yu-ti (supreme primal Chinese god, the "August Personage of Jade") 55°N, 85°W. Chasma: Kun Lun (Chinese mountain dwelling place of the immortals) 37–50°N, 275–300°W. Pu Chou (mountain attacked by King Chung in Chinese mythology) 10–35° N, 85–115°W

Origin: Formed about 4 to 5 billion years ago

Discovery: On December 23, 1672, by G. D. Cassini. It was extremely difficult to see in those days. It was the third Saturnian satellite to be discovered. From 1684 onwards the five known Saturnians at that time were numbered Saturn 1, Saturn 2, Saturn 3, etc., working outwards from the planet. In 1789 Sir William Herschel announced his discovery of two more Saturnian moons, nearer to Saturn than the other five. So they were now numbered S7, S6, S1, S2, S3, S4, S5. In 1847, in order to end this confusion, and to avoid even greater confusion should more Saturnians be discovered, Sir John Herschel renamed them for mythological characters associated with the god Saturn. On April 8, 1921, Rhea vanished completely for over half an hour. It was eclipsed by the shadow of Titan. Six English observers saw this phenomenon independently: A. E. Levin, P. W. Hepburn, L. J. Comrie, E. A. L. Attkins, F. Burnerd, and C. J. Spencer. In 1980 Voyager 1 came within 73,980 km of Rhea, and in 1981 Voyager 2 came within 645,280 km

Photograph: see page 147

Rosalind

Other names: 1986 U4, Uranus XIII, Uranus 13, U13

Named for: Named in 1988 by the I.A.U. for the Shakespeare character in *As You Like It*

Pronunciation: ro' zə lind

Distance from Uranus: Its mean

distance from the center of Uranus is about 69,942 km

Location: Between Miranda and the rings of Uranus

Synodic period: 13 hours 24 mins

Sidereal period: 0.558459 days

Mean angular distance from Uranus, at mean opposition distance: 5"

Orbit: Its rotational period is synchronous with its orbital period (i.e., the same face of Rosalind is always shown to Uranus)

Orbital eccentricity: Low, probably 0

Orbital inclination: Low, probably 0 degrees

Albedo: Low, about 0.1

Density: Almost certainly low

Escape velocity: Very low

Diameter: Approximately 60 km

Shape: Unknown exactly, but probably roughly circular

Surface: Dark and methane-coated

Origin: Possibly formed through the accretion of comets

Discovery: On January 13, 1986, by Voyager 2 (*see* ***Puck***)

Bibliography: *Science* 233 (July 4, 1986), 39–109

Photograph: see page 128

S8, Saturn VIII *see* ***Iapetus***

S18, Saturn XVIII *see* ***1981 S13***

S11, Saturn XI *see* ***Epimetheus***

Semele *see* ***Ananke***

S15, Saturn XV *see* ***Pandora***

S5, Saturn V *see* ***Rhea***

S4, Saturn IV *see* ***Dione***

S14, Saturn XIV *see* ***Calypso***

Sinope

Other names: Jupiter IX, Jupiter 9, Jupiter Nine, J9, Hades (this was its original, unofficial name), Cerberus, Ida (these last two: see below, under *Discovery*)

Named for: The Greek mythological maiden

Pronunciation: si nō' pā, si nō' pē

Distance from Jupiter: Its mean distance from the center of Jupiter is 23,700,000 km

Synodic period: 645 days

Sidereal period: 758 days retrograde

Mean angular distance from Jupiter, at mean opposition distance: 2°09'31"

Orbital eccentricity: 0.275

Orbital inclination: Between 153 and 156 degrees

Escape velocity: A mean of about 0.01 km/sec

Location: The outermost of all the satellites of Jupiter

Visible magnitude: 18.3

Albedo: Probably 0.02 to 0.03

Absolute magnitude: +11.6

Diameter: Between 6 and 36 km, probably 35 km

Apparent diameter, as seen from the surface of Jupiter: 0'0".2

Shape: Irregular

Surface: Probably rocky, with carbonaceous dirt and water ice. There is no atmosphere

Origin: Probably a captured Trojan asteroid

Discovery: In July 1914 Seth B. Nicholson set out to photograph Pasiphaë, which had been discovered 6 years earlier. When he developed his plate, on July 21, he found Pasiphaë and Sinope. It was therefore discovered by accident. It was originally called Hades, but this name was unofficial. In 1962 USSR amateur astronomer E. I. Nesterovich proposed the name Cerberus, and in 1976 USSR astronomer Yuriy A. Karpenko suggested Ida, but the name which became official was Sinope, named by German philologist Johann Blunck

Bibliography: Dictionary of Astronomical Names, by Adrian Room. Routledge, 1988

S9, Saturn IX see *Phoebe*

S1, Saturn I see *Mimas*

S7, Saturn VII see *Hyperion*

S17, Saturn XVII see *Atlas*

S6, Saturn VI see *Titan*

S16, Saturn XVI see *Prometheus*

S10, Saturn X see *Janus*

S13, Saturn XIII see *Telesto*

S3, Saturn III see *Tethys*

S12, Saturn XII see *Helene*

S2, Saturn II see *Enceladus*

Telesto

Other names: 1980 S25, Saturn XIII, Saturn 13, S13, Saturn Thirteen

Named for: One of the daughters of Oceanus and Thetis in Greek mythology

Pronunciation: te les' tō̆, tə les' tō̆

Distance from Saturn: Its mean distance from the center of Saturn is 294,660 km

Location: One of the Tethys Lagrangians, it trails Tethys by 60 degrees in its orbit around Saturn. Calypso (q.v.) is the other Tethys Lagrangian, and that moon leads Tethys in its orbit

Synodic period: 1 day 22 hours 15 mins

Sidereal period: 1.8878 days (tropical period)

Orbital eccentricity: Probably 0

Orbital inclination: 2 degrees, or thereabouts

Visible magnitude: Between 18.5 and 18.1

Albedo: Between 0.81 and 1.15

Absolute magnitude: +8.9

Mean angular distance from Saturn, at mean opposition distance: 0'47".6

Escape velocity: 11 m/sec

Diameter: 34×28×26 km

Shape: Irregular

Surface: Icy, and relatively bright

Origin: Possibly the fragment of a larger body

Discovery: Discovered from Earth in March 1980 by the "Space Telescope" Wide Field/Planetary Camera Instrument Definition team of Brad Smith, John Fountain, Stephen Larson and Harold Reitsema, led by Smith. Voyager 1 got to within 237,332 km in November 1980, and Voyager 2 to within 284,396 km in August 1981

Bibliography: "All About Telesto," *Astronomy,* July 1984

Temis see *Themis*

Tethys

Other names: Saturn 3, Saturn III, Saturn Three, S3, Tetis (in Spanish)

Named for: Named by Sir John Herschel in 1847 for the sea goddess, Dione's mother, in Greek mythology

Pronunciation: te' this, tē' this

Features on Earth named for it: Tethys Nunataks, on Alexander Island, Antarctica

Distance from Saturn: Its mean distance from the center of Saturn is 294,660 km

Mean angular distance from Saturn, at mean opposition distance: 0'47".6

Orbit: Tethys is sluggish in its orbit, and shares the trip around Saturn with co-orbitals Calypso and Telesto

Synodic period: 1 day 21 hours 18 mins 54.8 secs

Sidereal period: 1.887802160 days (tropical period)

Orbital eccentricity: 0

Orbital inclination: 1.86 degrees

Escape velocity: A mean of 0.47 km/sec

Density: A mean of approximately 1.21 gm/cm^3

Mass: 6.26×10^{20} kg

Visible magnitude: 10.2

Albedo: 0.9

Absolute magnitude: +0.6

Orbital velocity: 11.3 km/sec

Diameter: 1048 km. It is an intermediate-sized satellite

Apparent diameter, as seen from the surface of Saturn: 17'36"

Subsolar temperature: About 86° K

Shape: Roughly spherical

Surface gravity: 15.06 cm/sec^2

Surface: It was known before 1980 that the surface of Tethys has water ice on it. In fact the whole satellite is made mostly of ice, inside and out. It is heavily cratered, and has long branching valleys tens of kilometers wide and hundreds of kilometers long, as well as regions of low crater-density, indicative of a "resurfacing" process in its history. It has not always been a dead world. Geological activity and evolution took place on this moon long ago. A large trough cuts through the Pole of Tethys

Features: The most distinctive feature is Ithaca Chasma, a very large valley 50–100 km wide and 4–5 km deep, that extends nearly two-thirds the way around the satellite, and which amounts to about 10 percent of the surface of Tethys. The rim of the chasma rises to half a kilometer above the outer terrain. Odysseus is the largest crater anywhere in the Saturnian system, and is almost as wide as the radius of the satellite itself. It is about 500 km in diameter and is the largest crater with a well-developed central peak anywhere in the solar system. Most features on Tethys were named from Bates's 1900 translation of Homer's *Odyssey*.

CRATERS: Ajax (a hero) 30°S, 285° W. Anticleia (mother of Odysseus) 55°N, 38°W. Antinoüs (chief wooer of Penelope) 62°S, 265°W. Arete (mother of Nausicaa) 4°S, 300°W. Circe (enchantress) 8°S, 49°W. Elpenor (follower of Odysseus) 54°N, 268°W. Eumaeus (swineherd faithful to Odysseus) 27°N, 47°W. Eurycleia (faithful old nurse of Odysseus) 56°N, 247°W. Laertes (father of Odysseus) 50°S, 60°W. Melanthius (disloyal goatherd) 62°S, 204°W. Mentor (friend of Odysseus) 3°N, 39°W. Nausicaa (advised Odysseus) 80°N, 352° W. Nestor (wise old king of Greece) 57°S, 58°W. Odysseus (the Hero) 30°N, 130°W. Penelope (wife of Odysseus) 10°S, 252°W. Phemius (minstrel to the wooers of Penelope) 12°N, 290°W. Polyphemus (the Cyclops) 5°S, 285°W. Teiresias (a prophet) 62°N, 5°W. Telemachus (son of Odysseus) 56°N, 338°W. CHASMA: Ithaca (home of Odysseus) 50°N–80°S, 30–340°W.

Origin: Formed from the early Saturn gas and dust

Discovery: By G. D. Cassini on March 21, 1684, using an aerial telescope with a focal length of more than 40 meters. It was the fourth Saturnian satellite to be found, and was extremely difficult to see with the long refractor telescopes of the period. In 1980 Voyager 1 came to within 415,670 km of Tethys, and in 1981 Voyager 2 came to within 93,000 km

Photographs: see pages 119, 147

Tetis see *Tethys*

Thalassa

Other names: 1989 N5, Neptune 7, Neptune Seven, Neptune VII, N7

Named for: Named in 1990 by the I.A.U. for the Greek mythological character associated with the sea

Pronunciation: thə la' sə, tha' lə sə, tha' lə sa, tha lə sa'

Distance from Neptune: Its mean distance from the center of Neptune is 50,000 km

Sidereal period: 0.31 days

Orbital eccentricity: Probably 0

Orbital inclination: Probably around 4.5 degrees

Diameter: Approximately 80 km

Shape: Irregular

Surface: Extremely dark, almost black like soot

Origin: Possibly formed through the accretion of comets

Discovery: Discovered on July 7, 1989, by Voyager 2, and by a ground crew using close encounter search images (*see* ***Proteus***)

Thebe

Other names: 1979 J2, Jupiter XV, Jupiter 15, Jupiter Fifteen, J15

Named for: Named by the I.A.U. in 1982 for the lover of Zeus in Greek mythology

Pronunciation: thē' bē

Distance from Jupiter: Its mean distance from the center of Jupiter is 221,900 km. It orbits 151,000 km above the cloud tops of Jupiter

Location: It moves between the orbits of Amalthea and Io

Synodic period: 16 hours 16 mins

Sidereal period: 0.6745 days

Mean angular distance from Jupiter, at mean opposition distance: 1'13"

Orbital eccentricity: 0.013

Orbital inclination: 0.9 degrees

Escape velocity: A mean of about 0.08 km/sec

Visible magnitude: 15.6

Albedo: 0.05

Absolute magnitude: +8.9

Diameter: 110×100×90 km

Shape: Oval-shaped

Surface: Seems to consist of carbonaceous chondritic material mixed with sulfur (possibly supplied by Io). There is no atmosphere

Subsolar temperature: 120° K

Discovery: The second Jovian satellite to be discovered by the Voyager mission, it was found by Stephen Synnott in the spring of 1980 from pictures taken by Voyager 1 on March 5, 1979, during an examination to confirm the existence of Adrastea (q.v.). It was imaged from Earth by Jewett and his colleagues in 1982. At a meeting of the I.A.U. (International Astronomical Union) in Greece in 1982 it was named Thebe

Themis

Other names: Temis (in Spanish)

Named for: Named by its discoverer Pickering in 1905 for the wife of Zeus in Greek mythology

Pronunciation: the' mis, thē' mis

Features on Earth named for it: Themis Nunatak on Alexander Island, Antarctica

Sidereal period: 20.85 days
Distance from Saturn: Its mean distance from the center of Saturn is 1,460,000 km
Location: Between Titan and Hyperion, if it exists at all, which is very doubtful, if not impossible
Orbital eccentricity: 0.23, which is high
Orbital inclination: 39 degrees
Mean angular distance from Saturn, at mean opposition distance: 3'55".9
Diameter: Uncalculated
Shape: Irregular
Surface: Icy, if it exists, which it almost certainly does not
Origin: It was possibly an asteroid that Pickering saw, or perhaps another Saturnian moon
Discovery: By W. H. Pickering on April 25, 1905, at Cambridge, Mass., from 13 photographic plates taken in 1899. Themis's orbital data were worked out from these plates. It was not confirmed, however, and eventually was dismissed by the astronomical world, although elements of its orbit continued to be published in some astronomical almanacs as late as 1960

Titan

Other names: Saturn 6, Saturn VI, Saturn Six, S6
Named for: Named by Sir John Herschel in 1847 for the giant in Greek mythology
Pronunciation: tīt' ən
Features on Earth named for it: Titan Nunatak on Alexander Island, Antarctica
Distance from Saturn: Its mean distance from the center of Saturn is 1,221,830 km
Mean angular distance from Saturn, at mean opposition distance: 3'17".3
Synodic period: 15 days 23 hours 15 mins 31.5 secs
Sidereal period: 15.94542068 days. A year on Titan is equal to 30 Earth years.
Orbit: Almost circular
Location: It lies almost precisely in the equatorial plane of Saturn
Orbital eccentricity: 0.29192
Orbital inclination: 0.33 degrees
Escape velocity: 2.47 km/sec
Density: A mean of 1.881 gm/cm^3
Mass: 1.346×10^{23} kg
Visible magnitude: Never brighter than 8.28. It can still be seen from Earth as a small, starlike point of light, even with a small telescope. In a telescope it may have a faint orange tinge
Albedo: 0.21. Titan absorbs about 80 percent of the sunlight falling on it
Absolute magnitude: −1.28
Obliquity: Titan has an assumed obliquity of 26°.7
Orbital velocity: 5.6 km/sec
Diameter: 5150 km (with its clouds). It is the largest of the Saturnian moons, slightly larger than the planet Mercury, and nearly half the size of Earth. It is the second largest satellite in the solar system (behind Ganymede)
Apparent diameter, as seen from the surface of Saturn: 17'10"
Shape: Would seem to be roughly spherical
Subsolar temperature: 126.3° K
Reference temperature: 85.1° K
Surface gravity: 135.9 cm/sec^2. Formerly reckoned at 144 cm/sec^2
Magnetic field: $<3\times10^{-4}$ gauss
Atmospheric pressure: 1.6 bars
Surface pressure: About 1.5 bars
Surface temperature: Must be about 92° K
Surface: Rocky material comprises probably 52 percent of Titan's mass, with the remainder ice. It probably has a silicate core, about half the volume of the visible globe, overlaid by a thick, acqueous crust. Titan may well have continents on it. The satellite's northern hemisphere is darker than its southern hemisphere, indicating that there may be seasons on Titan, and it has a dark polar cap. A liquid nitrogen

rain probably collects as vast seas at the poles. The first suggestion of an atmosphere around Titan was made in 1908 by Spanish astronomer José Comas Solá who, from Barcelona, noted that the satellite appeared brighter at its center than near the limb. In 1944 Kuiper detected the presence of methane gas on Titan, thus proving that it has an atmosphere, and leading to speculation that the satellite might foster life. In fact, until 1981 it was thought to be the extraterrestrial place where life might most likely exist.

Until the Voyager flybys of 1980 and 1981 it was thought that Titan's atmosphere was largely methane. Voyager 1 indicated that it was 90–99 percent nitrogen, with methane limited to the balance. Since then the estimate of the mix has been revised. Scientists now think that there is 85 percent nitrogen in Titan's atmosphere, with the remaining 15 percent being mostly argon, with about 1 percent of methane, and traces of ammonia, ethane, ethylene, acetylene, and hydrogen cyanide. Titan's atmosphere is thicker than Earth's, and the orange color when seen from Space is probably the result of complex hydrocarbons produced through photolysis of methane in the upper atmosphere.

Titan absorbs about 80 percent of the sunlight that falls on it, most of that sunlight being absorbed by the dense, 200 km–deep smog layer which is Titan's atmosphere. Titan is able to have an atmosphere, albeit a continually evolving one, because of its large mass, and because it has a temperature range that permits the retention of ammonia and methane in gas form. In fact, Titan is the only satellite in the solar system known to possess a substantial atmosphere (probably made up of opaque layers of gas and particles), and is the only other object besides Earth in the solar system to have molecular nitrogen as the principal constituent of its atmosphere. But, it is unlivable because of the other poisonous gases.

Oxygen is scarce because the water lies frozen to Titan's surface, unable to evaporate. The temperature gradually cools the higher one goes off the surface to about 70° K at 40 km high. Titan produces substantial plasma and magnetic effects in its wake, and apparently loses nitrogen gas from its upper atmosphere into the magnetosphere

Origin: Titan is a natural moon, formed within the Saturnian system (as opposed to being captured)

Discovery: In 1610 Galileo looked at the planet Saturn through his telescope, and announced that it was a triple planet, with "ears," i.e. with a companion on each side of the planet and nearly touching it. One of these "ears" was, in fact, Titan, and on March 25, 1655, Christiaan Huygens discovered Titan 3 minutes from the planet on the line of the very narrow ansae. He immediately guessed it to be a satellite, and confirmed this within a few days. He was using a 12-foot refractor telescope. Actually Hevelius in Poland and Wren in England had spotted Titan earlier than Huygens, but had perceived it to be a fixed star. Until 1966 only the "classical nine" satellites of Saturn were known within that system, Titan being the largest. (A memory aid for the 9 original moons of Saturn is MET DR. THIP, remembering that Titan is the second T).

In 1966 Janus was "discovered," and that made 10. In September 1979 Pioneer 11 flew by, and did not reveal any new moons of Saturn. Pioneer showed Titan to be featureless, but at least it was the only Saturnian moon seen up to that time as anything more than just a speck of light. However, the dense, smog-like atmosphere covering Titan obscured any views of its surface. In 1980 another two moons were discovered within Saturn's system, before the arrival there of Voyager 1. That spacecraft yielded another 11, bringing the total of Saturnian satellites to (a possible) 23.

Until that time Titan was thought to be the largest satellite in the solar system, but it was found to about 70 km less in diameter than Ganymede (Jupiter's largest moon). It was hoped that the Voyager 1 encounter with Titan, at around 0540:20 spacecraft event time on November 12, 1980, would give photos of this most interesting satellite, but Voyager 1, which passed as close as 6490 km to Titan, took disappointing photos. All it could see was the vast orange-brown atmosphere. Voyager 2 flew by on August 25, 1981, to within 665,960 km, with the same results.

Because its surface has not been seen, Titan remains one of the most interesting bodies in the solar system. It will remain an enigma until an unmanned probe can land on its surface, or at least penetrate the cloud-cover. The Cassini spacecraft, planned for the year 2002, will orbit Saturn and carry a probe to plumb the atmosphere of Titan

Bibliography: Saturn, ed. by Tom Gehrels and Mildred S. Matthews. University of Arizona Press, Tucson, 1984

"Voyager One at Saturn," by Richard Berry, *Astronomy,* January 1981

"Voyager: Science at Saturn," by Richard Berry, *Astronomy,* February 1981

"Voyager 2 at Saturn," by Richard Berry, *Astronomy,* November 1981

"The Saturnian Moons," by Robert Burnham, *Astronomy,* December 1981

The Planet Saturn, by A. F. O'D. Alexander. Macmillan, New York, 1962

"Titan," by Tobias Owen, *Scientific American,* February 1982

"Flight on Titan," by Stanley G. Weinbaum. 1935. This is a fictional short story

Trouble on Titan, by Alan E. Nourse. 1954. A juvenile novel about colonization on Titan

The Sirens of Titan, by Kurt Vonegut. 1959. A novel, the climax of which takes place on Titan

As on a Darkling Plain, by Ben Bova. 1972. In this novel, Titan is the location of huge alien machines

Imperial Earth, by Arthur C. Clarke. 1976. In this novel, Titan has an elegantly described colony.

If the Stars Are Gods, by Gregory Beuford and Gordon Eklund. 1977. In this novel, Titan is the home of the strange life-form which provides the climax

Photographs: see pages 147, 148

Titania

Other names: Uranus 3, Uranus III, Uranus Three, U3

Named for: Named by Sir John Herschel in 1852 for Shakespeare's character in *A Midsummer Night's Dream*

Pronunciation: ti tan' yə, ti tā'nē ə, tī tan' yə, tī tā' nē ə

Features on Earth named for it: Titania Peak on Alexander Island, Antarctica

Distance from Uranus: Its mean distance from the center of Uranus is 435,910 km. In 1860 it was reckoned at 472,116 km

Location: Titania is the second farthest of the Big Five away from the planet

Mean angular distance from Uranus, at mean opposition distance: 33".2

Synodic period: 8 days 17 hours 0 mins 1.2 secs

Sidereal period: 8.7058717 days retrograde

Orbital eccentricity: 0.0022

Orbital inclination: 0.14 degrees

Escape velocity: A mean of 1.65 km/sec

Visible magnitude: 13.73. Titania

and Oberon are the brightest of the Big Five

Albedo: 0.27. Titania shows strong ice absorptions in its spectrum, and this accounts for its high albedo

Absolute magnitude: +1.02

Density: A mean of 1.6 gm/cm^3

Mass: 1.2×10^{21} kg, which is very low (*see* ***Umbriel—Mass***)

Diameter: 1610 km

Apparent diameter, as seen from the surface of Uranus: 15'00"

Shape: Roughly spherical

Surface: Almost completely covered with ice or frost. There are great winding valleys, hundreds of miles long, which indent the surface. These may have formed when water inside Titania froze and expanded, cracking the moon's thin, stiff crust

Features: Adriana (character in *Comedy of Errors*) 20°S, 4°E. Belmont Chasma 4–25°S, 25–35°E. Bona (character in *Henry VI, Part III*) 55°S, 351°E. Calpurnia (character in *Julius Caesar*) 42°S, 292°E. Elinor (character in *King John*) 44°S, 334°E. Gertrude (character in *Hamlet;* this is the largest crater recorded—over 200 km in diameter) 15°S, 288°E. Imogen (character in *Cymbeline*) 25°S, 318°E. Iras (character in *Antony and Cleopatra*) 19°S, 339°E. Jessica (character in *The Merchant of Venice*) 55°S, 286°E. Katherine (character in *Love's Labor's Lost*) 51°S, 333°E. Lucetta (character in *Two Gentlemen of Verona*) 9°S, 277°E. Marina (character in *Pericles*) 15°S, 316°E. Messina Chasma (this is a fault valley, up to 1500 km in length) 8–28°S, 325–5°E. Mopsa (character in *The Winter's Tale*) 11°S, 302°E. Phrynia 24°S, 309°E. Roussillon Rupes (cliffs) 7–25°S, 17–38°E. Ursula (200 km crater cut by a younger fault valley over 100 km wide) 13°S, 44°E. Valeria (character in *Coriolanus*) 34°S, 4°E

Origin: The moons of Uranus may be the result of a coalescing of gas produced by the planet after a mammoth collision with an Earth-sized object

Discovery: By William Herschel on January 11, 1787 (*see* ***Oberon***). Voyager 2 got to within 231,000 miles on January 24, 1986

Photographs: see pages 130, 131

Toro

This seems to be the right place to discuss the possibility of a second Earth moon. The reason it is under Toro is arbitrary. Toro is one of the asteroids, Asteroid #1685, a pretty ordinary asteroid discovered in 1948 by Wirtanen at the Lick Observatory. It is very small and can not be seen with the naked eye. Its mean distance from the Sun is about the same as Earth's, but it is not moving in Earth's orbit or system, Toro's orbit being much more eccentric. Some thought it was a second Earth satellite, but it is not. It moves around the Sun in the usual way, and occasionally comes close to Earth, but not even within 2 million miles. On August 8, 1972, it came within 0.14 A.U.s of Earth (an Astronomical Unit is the mean distance of the Earth from the Sun, or about 93 million miles). That is nothing. On October 30, 1937, the asteroid Hermes came within 56,000 miles of Earth, and others have come much closer than Toro.

The idea of a second Earth moon seems to stem from the 19th century, although for centuries before that the individual voice had always proposed that theory. In the 19th century Petit, director of the Observatory at Toulouse, published a paper suggesting one, 4650 miles from the Earth's surface, with a period of 3 hours 20 mins. In 1957 Clyde Tombaugh made a thoroughly systematic search for secondary Earth satellites, and found none. He also looked carefully for a satellite of the Moon itself (the Moon, Earth's Moon, is to some scientists technically a planet), as W. H. Pickering had done in his time. Both astronomers had no luck in that area. Tombaugh says that there can be no natural lunar satellite with a diameter greater than about 15 feet. These investigations seem to disprove the old belief, current among some, that there was another moon behind ours, but one which we could not see.

In 1913 Hans Hörbiger wrote in *Glazial-Kosmogonie* that there have been at least 6 other Earth satellites, all of which have crashed into Earth, and all of which produced cataclysms in Earth's past.

On March 6 and April 6, 1961, K. Kordylewski, who had started looking for minor satellites in 1951 from Poland, claimed to have found on photos two faint "clouds" moving in the same orbit as Earth's Moon, one cloud ahead of the lunar body, and one behind it. These clouds, if they exist (no confirmation has ever been made) are probably made up of meteoritic material. These little pieces of debris would, in fact, then be secondary satellites of minute size (but such pieces of space debris do not fall within the scope of this book)

A safe statement: Earth has only one Moon, but may have had more than one in the past

Bibliography: "Intralunar Satellite," by Richard A. Proctor, *English Mechanic* 20 (1874), 94

"Has the Earth More Than One Satellite?" by S. R. King, *English Mechanic* 61 (1895), 350

"Earth's Natural Satellites," *Science Newsletter* 80 (1961), 82

"New Natural Satellites of the Earth," *Sky and Telescope* 22 (1961), 10

"More About the Earth's Cloud Satellites," *Sky and Telescope* 22 (1961), 63

"Terrestrial Satellites: Some Direct and Indirect Evidence," by John P. Bagby, *Icarus* 10 (1969), 1

"Bagby's Phantom Moonlets," by Jean Meeus, *Icarus* 19 (1973), 547

"Evidence of an Ephemeral Earth Satellite," by John P. Bagby, *Nature* 211 (1966), 285

"Natural Earth Satellites," by John P. Bagby, *British Interplanetary Society Journal* 34 (1981), 289

The Moon and the Planets, compiled by William R. Corliss. Sourcebook Project, 1985

Triton

Other names: Neptune I, N1, Neptune One

Named for: In 1905 French astronomer Fouché mentioned the name, and his fellow astronomer Camille Flammarion named it thus. In 1932 H. N. Russell said, "It might well achieve general recognition." It has. It was named for Neptune's son in mythology

Pronunciation: trī' ən

Features on Earth named for it: Triton Point on Alexander Island, Antarctica

Distance from Neptune: Its mean distance from the center of Neptune is 354,290 km, closer than the Earth's Moon is to Earth

Mean angular distance from Neptune, at mean opposition distance: 16".9

Synodic period: 5 days 21 hours 3 mins 29.8 secs

Sidereal period: 5.8768433 days retrograde

Orbit: This fast-moving moon was originally assumed to revolve around its primary body in the same direction as the planet's rotation (no retrograde satellites were known then; *see* ***Phoebe***). In 1928 careful spectroscopic work at the Lick Observatory in California showed Triton's orbit to be circular, and retrograde. It is the only retrograde orbit among the major moons of the solar system. The tidal forces it creates on Neptune because of this retrograde orbit means that Triton is slowly spiraling in toward Neptune; in fact its orbit is changing noticeably with time. It is getting nearer to Neptune, and in about 100 million years will be ripped apart by Neptune's gravity (in other words it will fall within the Roche limit of 3 planetary radii, and be doomed—*see* ***Phobos***) and probably will form rings around the planet

Orbital eccentricity: Probably 0

Orbital inclination: 159.945 degrees

Escape velocity: A mean of 4.9 m/sec

Density: A mean of 2.03 gm/cm^3, a little over twice the density of water

Mass: 21.3×10^{21} kg

Visible magnitude: 13.47. It is the brightest of Neptune's moons, and was seen edge-on from Earth in 1953

Albedo: Greater than 0.19, probably as much as 0.4. Lassell said that one half is brighter than the other, but this does not seem to be the case

Absolute magnitude: −1.24

Diameter: 2720 km. It is the largest of the Uranian satellites. It is almost planetary in size, and about 15 times wider than Nereid, the second largest of the Neptunians. Triton is similar in size to the planet Pluto, and until Voyager 2 flew by within 38,000 km of Triton on August 24–25, 1989, it was generally thought to be larger than Earth's Moon. In 1954 Kuiper measured it at 3800 km, using the Hall reflector at Palomar. Later estimates varied between 6000 km and 2500 km. In 1984 Dale Cruikshank and S. F. Dermott both individually put it at 3500 km, and the same year L. Trafton estimated its diameter at 4200 km. In 1986 D. Bonneau and F. Foy measured it at 2500 km, using speckle interferometry at the Canada-France-Hawaii telescope at Mauna Kea. In 1988 the I.A.U., chaired by M. E. Davies, put it at 3500 km, plus or minus 500 km. The general feeling before Voyager 2 was that the average estimate of Triton's diameter was about 3700 km

Apparent diameter, as seen from the surface of Neptune: 1°01'

Atmospheric pressure: At the surface of Triton it is only 10 microbars

Temperature: 38° K

Subsolar temperature: Greater than 68.2° K

Surface gravity: 187.5 cm/sec^2

Shape: Roughly spherical

Surface: It looks as if Triton is made from ice and rock, not pure ice as had been expected. Its interior is melted and differentiated, but its surface is cratered, dark, pinkish, and pearlescent, with large areas of rugged, broken terrain, flatter areas marked by long, straight, intersecting fault lines, and even smoother patches where liquids seem to have welled up like lava flows. The surface is generally similar to Pluto's, and is a rolling "canteloupe"-type terrain, and 200 mile per hour winds blow across it. It is the coldest place in the solar system, colder even than Pluto, with a temperature of −370° Fahrenheit (−220° centigrade).

There is a vast polar cap, pinkish-white in color and trending toward perfectly white, and this polar cap is covered with frozen nitrogen-methane frost. The cap extends from the South Pole three-quarters of the way to Triton's equator, and reflects back into space much of the sunlight that falls onto Triton. Clearly visible on the cap are dozens of dark, feathery streaks all trending roughly northeast. The surface of Triton also has freezing seas or lakes of dark liquid nitrogen, dotted with methane icebergs.

Much of Triton's equatorial zone is the pinkish, slightly reddish, "canteloupe" terrain, the color being caused by surface hydrocarbon sludge. This area has low relief, polygonal ridges and valleys. Crossing the canteloupe terrain in many places are long, thin ridges where, presumably, the crust of Triton split and a thick slush oozed out before freezing (similar oozing to Uranus's moon, Ariel). There are also the broad, smooth plains (as mentioned above), evidence of large-scale lava-flooding. The dark streaks on Triton's surface result from still-active volcanoes.

In 1944 Kuiper found possible evidence of methane in Triton's spectrum, and in 1978 Dale P. Cruikshank detected a light methane atmosphere. The atmosphere of Triton is cold, thin, and composed probably of nitrogen-methane and carbon dioxide. The satellite has a very complicated seasonal cycle that takes more than 600 years to complete. Weak sunlight now shines stronger on the South Pole than it has in centuries.

When Voyager 2 viewed Triton close-up for the first time, in 1989, a volcano was detected spewing nitrogen ice and gas, geyser-like, 8 km into the atmosphere. On December 6, 1989, scientists discovered from the Voyager photos four new volcanoes like that one, and they say that there may be a dozen or so altogether. This was the first sign of active volcanism to be found in the solar system other than Earth or Io. Voyager 2 gave indications that Triton has been violently active in the past as well (see the broad, smooth plains mentioned above)

Features: The two most obvious geysers identified to date are at 50°S, 3°E, and at 57°S, 41°E. Both of their plumes extend to the WNW

Origin: Possibly a captured asteroid

Discovery: Seventeen days after the discovery of Neptune, William Lassell discovered Triton, the largest satellite in the Neptunian system. This took place at Liverpool, England, on October 10, 1846, using a 24-inch reflector

Bibliography: "Triumph at Neptune," by Richard Berry, *Astronomy,* November 1989

"First Discoveries at Neptune," by Richard Berry, *Astronomy,* October 1989

"Neptune Revealed," by Richard Berry, *Astronomy,* December 1989

"Approaching Neptune," by Richard Berry, *Astronomy,* August 1989

"Getting to Know Neptune," by J. Kelly Beatty, *Sky and Telescope,* February 1990

"The Pillows," by Margaret St. Clair. 1950. A short story

Triton by Samuel Delany. 1976. A novel

Photographs: see pages 134, 139, 140, 141, 149, 150

2060 *see* ***Chiron***

U8, Uranus VIII *see* ***Bianca***

U11, Uranus XI *see* ***Juliet***

U15, Uranus XV *see* ***Puck***

U5, Uranus V *see* ***Miranda***

U4, Uranus IV *see* ***Oberon***

U14, Uranus XIV *see* ***Belinda***

Umbriel

Other names: Uranus II, Uranus 2, U2, Uranus Two

Named for: Named by Sir John Herschel in 1852 for the Alexander Pope character in *The Rape of the Lock*

Pronunciation: um' brē əl, oom' brē əl

Features on Earth named for it: Mount Umbriel on Alexander Island, Antarctica

Distance from Uranus: Its mean distance from the center of Uranus is 266,300 km. In 1860 it was thought to be 287,821 km

Location: It is the middle one of the Big Five satellites of Uranus

Synodic period: 4 days 3 hours 28 mins 25.8 secs

Sidereal period: 4.1441772 days retrograde

Orbit: Circular (the Big Five are nearly all in the same plane; the Uranian system resembles the Saturnian system in this respect)

Mean angular distance from Uranus, at mean opposition distance: 20".3

Orbital eccentricity: 0.0050

Orbital inclination: 0.36 degrees

Escape velocity: A mean of 0.75 km/sec

Density: A mean of 1.8 gm/cm³

Mass: 7.6×10^{20} kg. The mass of the Big Five is so low that it would be hard to get any melting in the core, yet there is very clear evidence of some kind of internal activity on all but Umbriel

Visible magnitude: 14.81

Albedo: 0.16 to 0.19. Umbriel reflects only 19 percent of the sunlight that hits it

Absolute magnitude: +2.10

Diameter: 1191 km

Apparent diameter, as seen from the surface of Uranus: 14'12"

Shape: Roughly spherical

Surface: Umbriel is much darker than the other major Uranian moons, suggesting the presence of rocky or soily material overlying the otherwise ice-rich satellite. It has a drab, intensely cratered surface, but no ray craters. The small amount of ice on the surface may account for why Umbriel is not as bright as Ariel, Titania and Oberon

Features: The most prominent crater on Umbriel is Skynd, 110 km in diameter, which has a single white ring inside it, possibly a bright central peak, later dubbed the "fluorescent cheerio" (after the breakfast cereal Cheerios). The cheerio seems to consist of ice kicked up from Umbriel's cold interior. The question is, why is there only one cheerio? Wunda, 140 km in diameter, is a possible crater near Umbriel's equator. This is the most reflective feature on the satellite

Alberich 31°S, 43°E. Fin 36°S, 41°E. Gob 9°S, 26°E. Kanaloa (named for the Hawaiian sea god) 11°S, 351°E. Malingee 22°S, 13°E. Peri 9°S, 6°E. Setibos (or Minerva) 31°S, 350°E. Skynd 1°N, 335°E. Vuver 2°S, 311°E. Wokolo 33°S, 7°E. Wunda 6°S, 274°E. Zlyden 24°S, 330°E

Origin: The moons of Uranus may be the result of a coalescing of gas produced by the planet after a mammoth collision with an Earth-sized object

Discovery: In actuality William Herschel recorded it in 1802 and was the actual discoverer. It just could not be confirmed by anyone else at the time (*see* ***Oberon****—Discovery*). On October 24, 1851, the British astronomer William Lassell was in Malta to escape the smoky atmosphere of England, and discovered Umbriel with his 24-inch reflector. He is listed as the official discoverer. On January 24, 1986, Voyager 2 came to within 202,000 miles of Umbriel

Photograph: see page 132

U9, Uranus IX see *Cressida*

U1, Uranus I see *Ariel*

U7, Uranus VII see *Ophelia*

U6, Uranus VI see *Cordelia*

U10, Uranus X *see* ***Desdemona***

U13, Uranus XIII *see* ***Rosalind***

U3, Uranus III *see* ***Titania***

U12, Uranus XII *see* ***Portia***

U2, Uranus II *see* ***Umbriel***

Part IV

Appendices

1. The Moons Planet by Planet

This appendix lists the planets (and the number of moons and supposed moons assigned to each); under each planet are three columns: the moons in order of discovery, the moons ordered by distance from the planet working outward, and the moons in order of size. A question mark means a conjectured satellite not ratified by the weight of scientific opinion. The existence of Toro (under Earth*) has very little scientific support.*

Earth (2)

Discovery	*Distance from Planet*	*Size*
Moon	Moon	Moon
Toro ?	Toro ?	Toro ? (unknown)

Jupiter (17)

Discovery	*Distance from Planet*	*Size*
Ganymede	Metis	Ganymede
Io	Adrastea	Callisto
Europa	Amalthea	Io
Callisto	Thebe	Europa
Amalthea	Io	Amalthea
Himalia	Europa	Himalia
Elara	Ganymede	Thebe
Pasiphaë	Callisto	Elara
Sinope	Leda	Pasiphaë
Lysithea	Himalia	Metis
Carme	Lysithea	Carme
Ananke	Elara	Sinope
Leda	Ananke	Lysithea
1975 J1 ?	Carme	Ananke

Discovery	*Distance from Planet*	*Size*
Adrastea	Pasiphaë	Adrastea
Metis	Sinope	Leda
Thebe	1975 J1 ?	1975 J1 ? (unknown)

Mars (2)

Deimos	Phobos	Phobos
Phobos	Deimos	Deimos

Neptune (8)

Triton	Naiad	Triton
Nereid	Thalassa	Proteus
Proteus	Despina	Nereid
1989 N2	1989 N4	1989 N2
1989 N4	1989 N2	1989 N4
Despina	Proteus	Despina
Thalassa	Triton	Thalassa
Naiad	Nereid	Naiad

Pluto (1)

Charon	Charon	Charon

Saturn (27)

Titan	1981 S13	Titan
Iapetus	Atlas	Rhea
Rhea	Prometheus	Iapetus
Dione	Pandora	Dione
Tethys	Epimetheus	Tethys
Enceladus	Janus	Enceladus
Mimas	Mimas	Hyperion
Hyperion	1981 S12 ?	Mimas
Phoebe	Enceladus	Chiron ?
Themis ?	Calypso	Janus
Janus	Tethys	Phoebe
Chiron ?	Telesto	Epimetheus
Epimetheus	1980 S34 ?	Prometheus
Helene	1981 S10 ?	Pandora
Telesto	1981 S11 ?	Atlas
Calypso	Helene	Helene
Atlas	Dione	Telesto
Pandora	1981 S7 ?	Calypso

Discovery	*Distance from Planet*	*Size*
Prometheus	1981 S8 ?	1981 S13
1980 S34 ?	1981 S9 ?	1980 S34 ?
1981 S7 ?	Rhea	1981 S7 ?
1981 S8 ?	Titan	1981 S8 ?
1981 S9 ?	Themis ?	1981 S9 ?
1981 S10 ?	Hyperion	1981 S10 ?
1981 S11 ?	Iapetus	1981 S11 ?
1981 S12 ?	Phoebe	1981 S12 ?
1981 S13	Chiron ?	Themis (unknown)

Uranus (15)

Oberon	Cordelia	Titania
Titania	Ophelia	Oberon
Ariel	Bianca	Umbriel
Umbriel	Cressida	Ariel
Miranda	Desdemona	Miranda
Puck	Juliet	Puck
Portia	Portia	Portia
Juliet	Rosalind	Juliet
Cressida	Belinda	Rosalind
Rosalind	Puck	Desdemona
Belinda	Miranda	Cressida
Desdemona	Ariel	Belinda
Cordelia	Umbriel	Bianca
Ophelia	Titania	Ophelia
Bianca	Oberon	Cordelia

2. Order of Discovery

1. The Moon ?
2. Ganymede Jan. 7, 1610
3. Io Jan. 7, 1610
4. Europa Jan. 7, 1610
5. Callisto Jan. 13, 1610
6. Titan March 25, 1655
7. Iapetus Oct. 25, 1671
8. Rhea Dec. 23, 1672
9. Dione March 21, 1684
10. Tethys March 21, 1684
11. Oberon Jan. 11, 1787
12. Titania Jan. 11, 1787
13. Enceladus Aug. 29, 1789
14. Mimas Sept. 17, 1789
15. Triton Oct. 10, 1846
16. Hyperion Sept. 16, 1848
17. Ariel Oct. 24, 1851
18. Umbriel Oct. 24, 1851
19. Deimos Aug. 12, 1877
20. Phobos Aug. 17, 1877
21. Amalthea Sept. 9, 1892
22. Phoebe April 1899
23. Himalia Nov. 3, 1904
24. Elara Jan. 2, 1905
25. Themis April 25, 1905
26. Pasiphaë Jan. 27, 1908
27. Sinope July 21, 1914
28. Lysithea July 6, 1938
29. Carme July 30, 1938
30. Miranda Feb. 16, 1948
31. Nereid May 1, 1949
32. Ananke Sept. 29, 1951
33. Janus Dec. 15, 1966
34. Leda Sept. 14, 1974
35. 1975 J1 Sept. 30, 1975
36. Chiron Nov. 1, 1977
37. Charon June 22, 1978
38. Epimetheus 1978
39. Adrastea Oct. 1979
40. Helene March 1980
41. Metis 1980
42. Thebe Spring 1980
43. Telesto March 1980
44. Calypso March 1980
45. Atlas Nov. 12, 1980
46. Pandora Nov. 1980
47. Prometheus Nov. 1980
48. 1980 S34 1982
49. 1981 S7 1982
50. 1981 S8 1982
51. 1981 S9 1982
52. 1981 S10 1982
53. 1981 S11 1982
54. 1981 S12 Feb. 1982
55. Puck Dec. 30, 1985
56. Portia Jan. 3, 1986

57. Juliet Jan. 3, 1986
58. Cressida Jan. 9, 1986
59. Rosalind Jan. 13, 1986
60. Belinda Jan. 13, 1986
61. Desdemona Jan. 13, 1986
62. Cordelia Jan. 20, 1986
63. Ophelia Jan. 20, 1986
64. Bianca Jan. 24, 1986
65. Proteus July 7, 1989
66. 1989 N2 July 7, 1989
67. 1989 N4 July 7, 1989
68. Despina July 7, 1989
69. Thalassa July 7, 1989
70. Naiad July 7, 1989
71. 1981 S13 July 16, 1990

3. Order of Size

Diameter in kilometers

1.	Ganymede	5276	**26.**	1989 N2	c.210×180
2.	Titan	5150	**27.**	Phoebe	between 160 and 220
3.	Callisto	4820	**28.**	Himalia	186
4.	Io	3632	**29.**	Puck	c.170×160
5.	Moon	3475.6	**30.**	1989 N4	160
6.	Europa	3138	**31.**	Despina	c.150
7.	Triton	2720	**32.**	Epimetheus	140×114×100
8.	Titania	1610	**33.**	Prometheus	140×100×80
9.	Oberon	1554	**34.**	Thebe	110×100×90
10.	Rhea	1528	**35.**	Pandora	110×84×66
11.	Iapetus	1448	**36.**	Thalassa	c.80
12.	Umbriel	1191	**37.**	Portia	c.80
13.	Charon	c.1186	**38.**	Juliet	c.80
14.	Ariel	1167	**39.**	Elara	76
15.	Dione	1118	**40.**	Rosalind	c.60
16.	Tethys	1048	**41.**	Desdemona	c.60
17.	Enceladus	502	**42.**	Cressida	c.60
18.	Miranda	485	**43.**	Naiad	c.54
19.	Proteus	415	**44.**	Belinda	c.50
20.	Hyperion	410×260×220	**45.**	Bianca	c.50
21.	Mimas	394	**46.**	Ophelia	c.50
22.	Nereid	c.340	**47.**	Cordelia	c.50
23.	Chiron	c.300	**48.**	Pasiphaë	c.46
24.	Amalthea	270×166×153	**49.**	Metis	c.40×40
25.	Janus	220×180×160	**50.**	Carme	c.40

51. Atlas	38×30×26
52. Helene	c.36×34×28
53. Sinope	c.35
54. Telesto	34×28×26
55. Lysithea	c.32
56. Calypso	30×24×16
57. Ananke	c.28
58. Phobos	27×21.6×18.8
59. Adrastea	24×20×16
60. 1981 S13	c.20
61. 1980 S34	c.18
62. 1981 S7	c.18
63. 1981 S8	c.18
64. 1981 S9	c.18
65. 1981 S10	c.18
66. 1981 S11	c.18
67. Deimos	15×12.2×11
68. Leda	c.14
69. 1981 S12	c.10

Themis and 1975 J1 are unknown.

4. Order of Visible Magnitudes

1.	Moon (full)	−11
2.	Ganymede	4.6
3.	Io	5.0
4.	Europa	5.3
5.	Callisto	5.6
6.	Titan	8.3
7.	Rhea	9.7
8.	Tethys	10.2
9.	Dione	10.4
10.	Iapetus	average 11.2
11.	Phobos	11.3
12.	Enceladus	11.7
13.	Deimos	12.4
14.	Mimas	12.9
15.	Triton	13.5
16.	Titania	13.7
17.	Oberon	13.9
18.	Amalthea	14.1
19.	Janus	14.1
20.	Hyperion	14.2
21.	Ariel	14.2
22.	Himalia	14.7
23.	Umbriel	14.8
24.	Epimetheus	15.1–15.5
25.	Prometheus	15.2–15.6
26.	Thebe	15.5
27.	Pandora	16.1
28.	Phoebe	16.3
29.	Miranda	16.5
30.	Chiron	average 16.5
31.	Charon	16–17
32.	Elara	16.8
33.	Pasiphaë	17.1
34.	Metis	17.4
35.	Helene	17.8–18.2
36.	Carme	18.0
37.	Atlas	18.1
38.	Telesto	18.1–18.5
39.	Sinope	18.3
40.	Lysithea	18.4
41.	Calypso	18.4–18.8
42.	Nereid	18.7
43.	Adrastea	18.9
44.	Ananke	18.9
45.	Leda	20.2
46.	1975 J1	21

Themis, and the newly-discovered satellites of Saturn, Uranus and Neptune, are unknown.

5. Moons with an Atmosphere

Callisto: May have an oxygen atmosphere.

Europa: May have an oxygen atmosphere.

Ganymede: May have an oxygen atmosphere.

Io: Not much of an atmosphere, but it is composed of sulfur dioxide and potassium.

Titan: The only satellite in the solar system known to have a substantial atmosphere. Nitrogen, argon, methane, ammonia, ethane, ethylene, acetylene, hydrogen cyanide, oxygen.

Triton: A light, thin, cold atmosphere, composed of nitrogen, nitrogen-methane, and carbon dioxide.

6. The Early Discoverers

Galileo Galilei. *Io, Europa, Ganymede, Callisto.* Italian astronomer; b. February 15, 1564, Pisa; d. January 8, 1642, Arcetri, near Florence. Great pioneer of astronomy, and developer of the telescope. Supporter of the Copernican theory.

Christiaan Huygens. *Titan.* Dutch astronomer; b. April 14, 1629, The Hague; d. July 8, 1695, The Hague. Son of Constantijn Huygens. Founded the wave theory of light, and discovered the true shape of the Saturnian rings.

Giovanni Domenico Cassini. *Iapetus, Rhea, Dione, Tethys.* Italian astronomer; b. June 8, 1625, Perinaldo; d. September 14, 1712, Paris. Discovered Cassini's Division, the dark gap between the A and B rings of Saturn. Correctly determined the nature of Saturn's rings. Became a French citizen in 1673. Father of Jacques Cassini.

William Herschel. *Oberon, Titania, Enceladus, Mimas.* German-British astronomer; b. November 15, 1738, Hanover; d. August 25, 1822, Slough, Bucks, England. Originally a German musician named Friedrich Wilhelm Herschel, he came to England in 1757 and became more British than the British. Brother of Caroline Herschel, and father of Sir John Herschel. Knighted in 1816. Telescope developer, and one of the major figures of his age. Discovered Uranus in 1781.

William Lassell. *Ariel, Umbriel, Triton.* British astronomer; b. June 18, 1799, Bolton, Lancs; d. October 5, 1880, Maidenhead, Berks. A brewer, he was also president of the Royal Astronomical Society from 1870 to 1872. He came within two days of being the discoverer of a fourth moon—Hyperion, which he did get to name.

William Cranch Bond. *Hyperion.* American astronomer; b. September 9, 1789, Falmouth (now Portland), Maine; d. January 29, 1859, Cambridge, Mass. Father of George P. Bond. Discovered Saturn's innermost ring, the crepe ring. He took the first recognizable photo of Earth's Moon, in 1857. Became the first director of the Harvard Observatory, in 1847. The first

American to be elected associate of the Royal Astronomical Society. Despite conflicting reports, W. C. Bond was the sole discoverer of Hyperion.

Asaph Hall. *Phobos, Deimos.* American astronomer; b. October 15, 1829, Goshen, Conn.; d. November 22, 1907, Annapolis, Md. Father of Asaph Hall, Jr. Professor of mathematics at the U.S. Naval Observatory in Washington from 1863 to 1891, and professor of astronomy at Harvard from 1896 to 1901.

Edward Emerson Barnard. *Amalthea.* American astronomer; b. December 16, 1857, Nashville, Tenn.; d. February 6, 1923, Williams Bay, Wisc. The leading astronomer of his time, he discovered 16 comets, and in 1916 Barnard's Star. From 1895 to 1923 he was at Yerkes Observatory. He had phenomenal eyesight, and was a pioneer in celestial photography.

William Henry Pickering. *Phoebe, Themis.* American astronomer; b. February 15, 1858, Boston; d. January 17, 1938, Mandeville, Jamaica. Brother of Edward Pickering. Built the observatory and telescope at Flagstaff, Ariz., for Percival Lowell. In 1919 he predicted and gave a position for Planet X (Pluto).

Charles Dillon Perrine. *Himalia, Elara.* American astronomer; b. July 28, 1867, Steubenville, Ohio; d. June 21, 1951, Villa General Mitre, Argentina. Discovered 13 comets. From 1909 to 1936 was director of the Cordoba Astronomical Observatory in Argentina.

Philibert Jacques Melotte. *Pasiphaë.* French astronomer; b. 1880; d. 1961. On the staff of the Royal Observatory at Greenwich from 1895 to 1948. He was president of the British Astronomical Society from 1944 to 1946.

Seth Nicholson. *Sinope, Lysithea, Carme, Ananke.* American astronomer; b. November 12, 1891, Springfield, Ill.; d. July 2, 1963, Los Angeles. Worked at Mount Wilson Observatory from 1915 to 1957. Investigator of sunspots.

Gerard Peter Kuiper. *Miranda, Nereid.* Dutch-American astronomer; b. December 7, 1905, Harenkarspel, Netherlands; d. December 23, 1973, Mexico City. Originally Gerrit Pieter Kuiper. U.S. citizen from 1937. Director of the Yerkes and McDonald Observatories, 1947–49 and 1957–60. Discovered carbon dioxide in Mars's atmosphere, and measured the visual diameter of Pluto.

Audouin-Charles Dollfus. *Janus.* French astronomer; b. November 12, 1924, Paris. Principal French authority on the solar system. Made the first stratospheric balloon ascent in France.

7. Relevant Space Missions

Mariner 4. Launched November 28, 1964. USA. Flew by Mars on July 14, 1965.

Mariner 6. Launched February 25, 1969. USA. Flew by Mars on July 31, 1969.

Mariner 7. Launched March 27, 1969. USA. Flew by Mars on August 5, 1969.

Mars 2. Launched May 28, 1971. USSR. The orbiter circled Mars on November 27, 1971. Capsule landed on Mars.

Mars 3. Launched May 28, 1971. USSR. Orbited Mars on December 2, 1971. Capsule landed on Mars.

Mariner 9. Launched May 30, 1971. USA. Reached Mars on November 13, 1971. Orbited the planet. Mission terminated October 27, 1972.

Pioneer 10. Launched March 3, 1972. USA. The first spaceship to cross the main asteroid belt. Flew by Jupiter on December 4, 1973. On June 13, 1983, it crossed the orbit of Neptune, and became the first man-made object to go out of the solar system.

Pioneer 11. Launched April 6, 1973. USA. Passed Jupiter on December 3, 1974. On September 1, 1979, it passed Saturn, then headed toward the edge of the solar system and beyond.

Mars 5. Launched July 25, 1973. USSR. Orbited Mars on February 2, 1974.

Mars 6. Launched August 5, 1973. USSR. Capsule landed on Mars on March 12, 1974.

Viking 1. Launched August 20, 1975. USA. Arrived at Mars on June 19, 1976. Orbited the planet. A lander landed on Mars on July 20, 1976.

Viking 2. Launched September 9, 1975. USA. Arrived at Mars on July 7, 1976. A lander landed on Mars on September 3, 1976.

Voyager 2. Launched by a Titan-Centaur rocket from Cape Canaveral on August 20, 1977. USA It was called Voyager 2 because eventually Voyager 1 would overtake it. Flew by Jupiter in July and August 1979, by Saturn in August 1981, by Uranus in December 1985–January 1986, by Neptune in July 1989, then headed out of the solar system.

Voyager 1. Launched September 5, 1977. USA. Overtook Voyager 2 just after entering the asteroid belt in mid–December 1977. Flew by Jupiter in March and April 1977, by Saturn in November 1980, and then headed out of the solar system.

Phobos 1 and Phobos 2. Launched July 1988. USSR. Their mission: to study Mars and to explore Phobos. On board one of these craft was a photographic transfer on aluminum of Asaph Hall's telescopic log book dated August 17, 1877, the night of his discovery of Phobos. Phobos 1 was lost, through human error, 6 weeks after launch, and Phobos 2 went out of control in Mars's orbit on March 27, 1989, after having seen Phobos from 270 miles and recording some new data (*see* ***Phobos****—Surface, Features*). Phobos 2 never got to make its intended flyby of 150 feet above the surface of Phobos.